Excel Charts

Excel Charts

John Walkenbach

Wiley Publishing, Inc.

Excel Charts

Published by
Wiley Publishing, Inc.
10475 Crosspoint Boulevard
Indianapolis, IN 46256
www.wiley.com

Copyright © 2003 by Wiley Publishing, Inc., Indianapolis, Indiana

Published simultaneously in Canada

Library of Congress Control Number: 2002110312

ISBN: 0-7645-1764-3

Manufactured in the United States of America

10 9 8 7 6 5 4 3 2 1

1O/QR/RR/QS/IN

For general information on our other products and services or to obtain technical support, please contact our Customer Care Department within the U.S. at (800) 762-2974, outside the U.S. at (317) 572-3993 or fax (317) 572-4002.

Wiley also publishes its books in a variety of electronic formats. Some content that appears in print may not be available in electronic books.

Ⓦ**Wiley Publishing, Inc.** is a trademark of Wiley Publishing, Inc.

About the Author

John Walkenbach is a leading authority on spreadsheet software and principal of JWalk and Associates Inc., a small San Diego–based consulting firm that specializes in spreadsheet application development. John is the author of about 30 spreadsheet books and has written more than 300 articles and reviews for a variety of publications, including *PC World, InfoWorld, PC Magazine, Windows,* and *PC/Computing.* He also maintains a popular Web site (*The Spreadsheet Page,* www.j-walk.com/ss) and is the developer of the Power Utility Pak, an award-winning add-in for Microsoft Excel. John graduated from the University of Missouri and earned a Masters and Ph.D. degree from the University of Montana.

Credits

ACQUISITIONS EDITOR
Greg Croy

PROJECT EDITOR
Susan Christophersen

TECHNICAL EDITOR
Jon Peltier

COPY EDITOR
Susan Christophersen

EDITORIAL MANAGER
Carol Sheehan

VICE PRESIDENT AND
EXECUTIVE GROUP PUBLISHER
Richard Swadley

VICE PRESIDENT AND
EXECUTIVE PUBLISHER
Bob Ipsen

EXECUTIVE EDITORIAL DIRECTOR
Mary Bednarek

PROJECT COORDINATOR
Nancee Reeves

GRAPHICS AND PRODUCTION
SPECIALISTS
Beth Brooks
Jeremey Unger

QUALITY CONTROL TECHNICIAN
Andy Hollandbeck

PERMISSIONS EDITORS
Laura Moss
Carmen Krikorian

MEDIA DEVELOPMENT SPECIALIST
Megan Decraene

PROOFREADING AND INDEXING
TECHBOOKS Production Services

For Pamn.

Acknowledgments

I've written many Excel books, but this one was probably the most challenging. I learned quite a bit during this project, and it furthered my belief that Excel is a never-ending source of surprises, even for us old-timers. Excel's charting feature is like an iceberg: There is much more to it than appears on the surface.

Special thanks are due to Jon Peltier, one of the planet's leading Excel chart experts and Microsoft MVP. I was able to convince Jon to be the technical editor for this book, and his contributions are sprinkled liberally throughout the pages. As in the past, it was a pleasure working with Susan Christophersen, my project editor. I'm also grateful to Greg Croy, acquisitions editor at Wiley, for giving me the go-ahead to write this book.

The Excel community tends to be very open with their ideas, and this is especially apparent in the area of charting. I owe a special debt to many people who provided the inspiration for several of the examples in this book. Thanks to Stephen Bullen, Debra Dalgleish, and Tushar Mehta, all of whom are Microsoft Excel MVPs and frequent contributors to the microsoft.public.excel.charting newsgroup. I'm also indebted to Andy Pope, who enlightened me in the area of 3D scatterplots and motivated me to devote an entire day to creating the Gradient Contour Chart add-in (included on the CD-ROM). I'm also grateful to Debbie Gewand, who amazed me with her Excel clip art. Thanks also to Nick Hodge, an Excel MVP who likes to see his name in my books.

Many folks throughout the world have sent me charting examples. Although there wasn't room for most of them, many of the general ideas were incorporated into my examples. I send a special thanks to the following: Fernando Cinquegrani, John Crane, Gilbert Dubourjale (GeeDee), Thierry Fahmy, Serge Garneau, Steve Kearley, Gary Klass, Bill Koran, Linda Mabree, Ken Mahrer, Joan Maslin, Sanjay S. Mundkur, Michael O'Callaghan, and Tony Sleigh.

Finally, I'd like to acknowledge the work of Edward R. Tufte. His books should be required reading for anyone who takes chart-making seriously.

Contents at a Glance

Contents

Introduction

Welcome to *Excel Charts*. This book is intended for spreadsheet users who want to get the most out of Excel's charting and graphics features. I approached this project with one goal in mind: to write the ultimate Excel charting book that would appeal to users of all levels.

As you probably know, most bookstores offer dozens of Excel books. The vast majority of these books are general-purpose user guides that explain how to use the features available in Excel (often by simply rewording the text in the help files). Most of these books include a chapter or two that cover charts and graphics. None, however, provide the level of detail that you'll find in this book.

I've used Excel for more than a decade, and I've been creating charts for more than 30 years. Back in the pre-computer days, I often spent hours creating a publication-quality chart by hand, using rulers, graph paper, and rub-off lettering. Today, creating such a chart with Excel would require only a few minutes – and would probably look much better.

I spend a lot of time participating in the Excel newsgroups on the Internet. I've come to the conclusion that many Excel users tend to overlook the powerful charting features available. For many, creating anything but the simplest chart often seems like a daunting task. This book starts with the basics and covers every aspect of charting, including macros. If I've done my job, working through this book will give you some new insights and perhaps a greater appreciation for Excel.

What You Should Know

This is *not* a book for beginning Excel users. If you have absolutely no experience with Excel, this may not be the best book for you. To get the most out of this book, you should have some background using Excel. Specifically, I assume that you know how to:

- Create workbooks, enter data, insert sheets, save files, and other basic tasks.
- Navigate through a workbook.
- Use Excel's menus, toolbars, and dialog boxes.
- Create basic formulas.
- Use common Windows features, such as file management and copy and paste techniques.

Later chapters cover VBA programming, and the main focus is on creating and controlling charts using VBA. Although I provide a basic introduction to VBA, this book is not intended to teach VBA programming to nonprogrammers. Those who have some experience with VBA or another programming language will benefit most from these programming chapters. They'll be able to customize the examples and make them even more powerful. Others, however, should be able to modify the examples to work with their own data.

What You Should Have

To make the best use of this book, you need a copy of Microsoft Excel. When I wrote the current edition of the book, I was using Excel 2002 (which is part of Microsoft Office XP). Most of the material in this book also applies to all earlier versions of Excel that are still in use. Fact is, Microsoft has made very few significant changes to Excel's charting features over the years. Where applicable, I point out differences in previous versions.

To use the examples on the companion CD-ROM, you'll need a CD-ROM drive. The examples on the CD-ROM are discussed further in the appendix.

 I use Excel for Windows exclusively, and do not own a Macintosh. Therefore, I can't guarantee that all the examples will work with Excel for Macintosh. Excel's cross-platform compatibility is pretty good, but it's definitely not perfect.

As far as hardware goes, the faster the better. And, of course, the more memory in your system, the happier you'll be. I strongly recommend using a high-resolution video mode: at least 1024 x 768, preferably higher. When working with charts, it's very convenient to be able to see lots of information without scrolling.

Conventions Used in This Book

Take a minute to skim this section and learn some of the typographic conventions used throughout this book.

Formula listings

Formulas usually appear on a separate line in monospace font. For example, I may list the following formula:

```
=VLOOKUP(StockNumber,PriceList,2,False)
```

VBA code listings

This book also contains examples of VBA code. Each listing appears in a `monospace font`; each line of code occupies a separate line. To make the code easier to read, I usually use one or more tabs to create indentations. Indentation is optional, but it does help to delineate statements that go together.

If a line of code doesn't fit on a single line in this book, I use the standard VBA line continuation sequence: a space followed by an underscore character. This indicates that the line of code extends to the next line. For example, the following two lines comprise a single VBA statement:

```
If ActiveChart Is Nothing Then _
    MsgBox "Please select a chart or activate a Chart sheet."
```

You can enter this code either exactly as shown on two lines, or on a single line without the trailing underscore character.

Key names

Names of keys on the keyboard appear in normal type, for example Alt, Home, PgDn, and Ctrl. When you should press two keys simultaneously, the keys are connected by a plus sign: "Press Ctrl+G to display the Go To dialog box."

Functions, procedures, and named ranges

Excel's worksheet functions appear in all uppercase, like so: "Use the SUM function to add the values in column A."

Macro and procedure names appear in normal type: "Execute the UpdateChart procedure." I often use mixed upper- and lowercase to make these names easier to read. Named ranges appear in italic: "Select the *WeeklySales* range."

Unless you're dealing with text inside quotation marks, Excel is not sensitive to case. In other words, both of the following formulas produce the same result:

```
=SUM(A1:A50)
=sum(a1:a50)
```

Excel will, however, convert the characters in the second formula to uppercase.

In Part III, the VBA chapters, terms such as names of objects, properties, and methods that appear in code listings show up in `monospace` type in regular paragraphs as well: "In this case, `Application.ActiveChart` is an object, and `HasTitle` is a property of the object."

Mouse conventions

The mouse terminology in this book is all standard fare: "pointing," "clicking," "right-clicking," "dragging," and so on. You know the drill.

What the icons mean

Throughout the book, icons appear next to some text to call your attention to points that are particularly important.

I use Note icons to tell you that something is important — perhaps a concept that may help you master the task at hand or something fundamental for understanding subsequent material.

Tip icons indicate a more efficient way of doing something, or a technique that may not be obvious. These will often impress your office mates.

These icons indicate that an example file is on the companion CD-ROM. (See the appendix for more details about the CD-ROM.)

I use the Cross-Reference icon to refer you to other chapters that have more to say on a particular topic.

How This Book Is Organized

There are many ways to organize this material, but I settled on a scheme that divides the book into three main parts.

Part 1: Chart Basics

This part is introductory in nature and consists of Chapters 1 through 6. Chapter 1 presents an overview of Excel's charting features. Chapter 2 presents some terminology and introduces the types of charts Excel supports. In Chapter 3, I discuss various ways to work with chart data series. Chart formatting and customizations are covered in Chapter 4. Chapter 5 discusses chart analytical features such as trendlines and error bars. The part concludes with Chapter 6, a discussion of other types of graphics supported by Excel.

Part II: Mastering Charts

Part II consists of six chapters that cover intermediate to advanced material. Chapter 7 covers interactive charts – charts that can be modified easily by an end-user. Chapter 8 contains a wide variety of common and not-so-common charts, including ways to generate quite a few "nonstandard" charts. Chapter 9 covers pivot charts (charts generated from a pivot table), and Chapter 10 discusses various ways to use Excel charts in other applications. Chapter 11 offers suggestions to help you avoid common mistakes and make your charts visually appealing. The final chapter in this part is Chapter 12, which is devoted to nonserious charting applications, yet contains lots of useful information.

Part III: Using VBA with Charts

The four chapters in Part III deal with VBA. Chapter 13 is a broad introduction to VBA, and Chapter 14 presents a quick overview of basic programming concepts. Chapter 15 deals with objects, properties, and methods appropriate to charting. Chapter 16 presents many examples of using VBA with charts.

Appendix and bonus material

The appendix describes all the files on the companion CD-ROM.

This book was supposed to have three additional appendixes, but I went a bit overboard on the main chapters and we ran out of pages! So, you'll find these missing appendixes on the CD-ROM instead. These files are in HTML format, so you can read them using your browser software. You'll find these documents in the "Bonus Material" folder on the CD-ROM:

◆ "Excel's Color System" contains lots of useful information about how Excel uses colors.

◆ "Excel Charting FAQ" presents answers to common questions about Excel charts.

◆ "Other Charting Resources" lists additional charting-related resources on the Internet.

See the "What's on the CD-ROM" appendix for more details about the CD-ROM that accompanies this book.

How to Use This Book

You can use this book any way you please. If you choose to read it cover to cover while lounging on a sunny beach in Maui, that's fine with me. More likely, you'll want to keep it within arm's reach while you toil away in your dimly lit cubicle.

Owing to the nature of the subject matter, the chapter order is often immaterial. Most readers will probably skip around, picking up useful tidbits here and there. If you're faced with a challenging task, you may want to check the index first to see whether the book specifically addresses your problem.

About the Power Utility Pak Offer

At the back of the book, you'll find a coupon that you can redeem for a discounted copy of my award-winning Power Utility Pak — a collection of useful Excel utilities plus many new worksheet functions. I developed this package using VBA exclusively.

You can also use this coupon to purchase the complete VBA source code for a nominal fee. Studying the code is an excellent way to pick up some useful programming techniques. You can take the product for a test drive by installing the trial version from the companion CD-ROM.

 Power Utility Pak requires Excel 2000 for Windows or later.

Reach Out

I'm always interested in getting feedback on my books. The best way to provide this feedback is via e-mail. Send your comments and suggestions to:

author@j-walk.com

Unfortunately, I'm not able to reply to specific questions. Posting your question to one of the Excel newsgroups is, by far, the best way to get such assistance. For more information about newsgroups, see "Other Charting Resources" in the Bonus Material folder on the CD-ROM.

Also, when you're out surfing the Web, don't overlook my Web site ("The Spreadsheet Page"):

http://www.j-walk.com/ss/

Now, without further ado, it's time to turn the page and expand your charting horizons.

Part I

Chart Basics

Chapter 1

Introducing Excel Charts

IN THIS CHAPTER

- ◆ What is a chart?
- ◆ How Excel handles charts
- ◆ Embedded charts versus Chart sheets
- ◆ The parts of a chart
- ◆ Using the Chart Wizard to create charts
- ◆ Printing charts

WHEN MOST PEOPLE THINK OF A spreadsheet product such as Excel, they think of crunching rows and columns of numbers. But, as you probably know already, Excel is no slouch when it comes to presenting data visually, in the form of a chart. This chapter presents an introductory overview of Excel's charting ability and is intended primarily for those who have little or no experience creating charts with Excel.

 If you already know how to create basic charts in Excel, you may ignore this chapter or just skim through it quickly.

What Is a Chart?

Let's start with the basics. A *chart* is a visual representation of numeric values. Charts (also known as graphs) have been an integral part of spreadsheets since the early days of Lotus 1-2-3. Charts generated by early spreadsheet products were quite crude but have improved significantly over the years. You'll find that Excel provides you with the tools to create a wide variety of highly customizable charts.

3

Although Excel can produce some great charts, it certainly doesn't generate the best-looking charts possible. And, you'll eventually encounter some limitations with Excel's charting features. Not surprisingly, other software products that are devoted exclusively to charting can generate higher-quality charts and provide a great deal more flexibility. Refer to other resources.htm, found in the Bonus Material folder on the CD-ROM, for a list of other charting software that's available.

Displaying data in a well-conceived chart can make your numbers more understandable. Because a chart presents a picture, charts are particularly useful for summarizing a series of numbers and their interrelationships. Making a chart can often help you spot trends and patterns that might otherwise go unnoticed.

Figure 1-1 shows a worksheet that contains a simple column chart that depicts a company's sales volume by month. Viewing the chart makes it very apparent that sales were off in the summer months (June through August), but they increased steadily during the final three months of the year. You could, of course, arrive at this same conclusion simply by studying the numbers. But viewing the chart makes the point much more quickly.

A column chart is just one of many different types of charts that you can create with Excel.

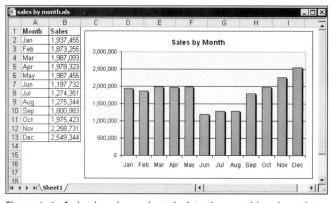

Figure 1-1: A simple column chart depicts the monthly sales volume.

How Excel Handles Charts

Before you can create a chart, you must have some numbers – sometimes known as data. The data, of course, is stored in the cells in a worksheet. Normally, the data that is used by a chart resides in a single worksheet, but that's not a strict requirement.

As you'll see, a chart can use data that's stored in any number of worksheets, and the worksheets can even be in different workbooks.

A chart is essentially an "object" that Excel creates upon request. This object consists of one or more *data series*, displayed graphically. The appearance of the data series depends on the selected *chart type*. For example, if you create a line chart that uses two data series, the chart contains two lines, each representing one data series. The data for each series is stored in a separate row or column. Each point on the line is determined by the value in a single cell, and is represented by a marker. You can distinguish each of the lines by its thickness, line style, color, or data markers.

Figure 1-2 shows a line chart that plots two data series across a 12-year period. The series are identified by using different data markers (squares vs. circles), shown in the *legend* at the bottom of the chart.

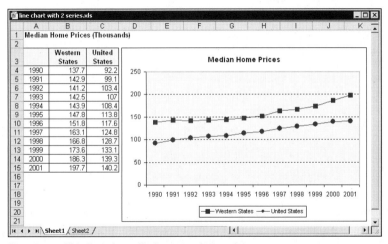

Figure 1-2: This line chart displays two data series.

A key point to keep in mind is that charts are dynamic. In other words, a chart series is linked to the data in your worksheet. If the data changes, the chart is updated automatically to reflect those changes.

After you've created a chart, you can always change its type, change the formatting, add new data series to it, or change an existing data series so that it uses data in a different range.

Before you create a chart, you need to determine whether you want it to be an embedded chart or one that resides on a Chart sheet.

Embedded charts

An embedded chart basically floats on top of a worksheet, on the worksheet's drawing layer. The charts shown previously in this chapter are both embedded charts.

As with other drawing objects (such as a text box or a shape), you can move an embedded chart, resize it, change its proportions, adjust its borders, and perform other operations. Using embedded charts enables you to print the chart next to the data that it uses.

To make any changes to the actual chart in an embedded chart object, you must click it to *activate* the chart. When a chart is activated, Excel's menu changes: The Chart menu replaces the Data menu.

Chart sheets

When you create a chart on a Chart sheet, the chart occupies the entire sheet. If you plan to print a chart on a page by itself, using a Chart sheet is often your better choice. If you have many charts to create, you may want to create each one on a separate Chart sheet to avoid cluttering your worksheet. This technique also makes locating a particular chart easier because you can change the names of the Chart sheets' tabs to provide a description of the chart that it contains.

Excel's menus change when a chart sheet is active, similar to the way that they change when you select an embedded chart. The Chart menu replaces the Data menu, and other menus include commands that are appropriate for working with charts.

Excel displays a chart in a chart sheet in WYSIWYG mode: The printed chart looks just like the image on the chart sheet. If the chart doesn't fit in the window, you can use the scrollbars to scroll it or adjust the zoom factor.

You can also size the chart in a Chart sheet according to the window size by using the View→Sized with Window command. When this setting is enabled, the chart adjusts itself when you resize the workbook window (it always fits perfectly in the window). In this mode, the chart that you're working on may or may not correspond to how it looks when printed. Figure 1-3 shows a Chart sheet with the Sized with Window setting enabled, and Figure 1-4 show the same chart without this setting enabled.

If you create a chart on a Chart sheet, you can easily convert it to an embedded chart. Choose Chart→Location and then select the worksheet that holds the embedded chart from the As Object In drop-down box. Excel deletes the chart sheet and moves the chart to the sheet that you specify. This operation also works in the opposite direction: You can select an embedded chart and relocate it to a new Chart sheet.

A Chart sheet can also contain one or more embedded charts. You can use the Chart→Location command to move embedded charts to an existing Chart sheet. The second drop-down box in the Chart Location dialog box includes Chart sheets as well as worksheets.

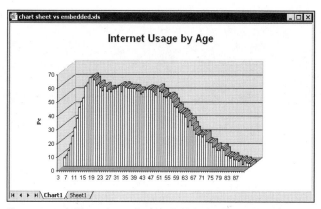

Figure 1-3: A Chart sheet displayed with the Size with Window setting enabled

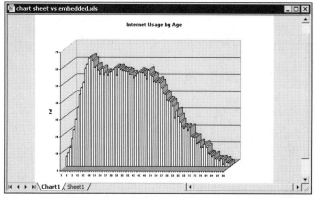

Figure 1-4: A Chart sheet displayed without the Size with Window setting enabled

Parts of a Chart

Refer to the chart in Figure 1-5 as you read the following description of the chart's elements.

This particular chart is a "combination" chart that displays two *data series*: Income and Profit Margin. Income is plotted as vertical columns, and the Profit Margin is plotted as a line with a square markers. Each bar (or marker on the line) represents a single *data point* (the value in a cell).

The chart has a horizontal axis, known as the *category axis*. This axis represents the category for each data point (January, February, and so on). The label at the bottom, *Months*, is the category axis label.

Chart Limitations

The following table lists the limitations of Excel charts. Most users never find these limitations to be a problem.

Item	Limitation
Charts on a worksheet	Limited by available memory
Worksheets referred to by a chart	255
Data series in a chart	255
Data points in a data series	32,000
Data points in a data series (3-D charts)	4,000
Total data points in a chart	256,000

Notice that this chart has two vertical axes. These are known as *value axes*, and each one has a different scale. The axis on the left is for the columns (Income) and the axis on the right is for the line (Profit Margin).

The value axes also display scale values. The axis on the left displays scale values from 0 to 250,000, in "major unit" increments of 50,000. The value axis on the right uses a different scale: 0 percent to 14 percent, in increments of 2 percent.

A chart with two value axes is appropriate because the two data series vary dramatically in scale. If the Profit Margin data were plotted using the left axis, the line would not even be visible.

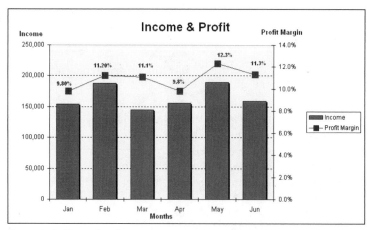

Figure 1-5: Parts of a chart

Most charts provide some method of identifying the data series or data points. A *legend*, for example, is often used to identify the various series in a chart. In this example, the legend appears on the right side of the chart. Some charts also display *data labels* to identify specific data points. The example chart displays data labels for the Profit Margin series, but not for the Income series. In addition, most charts (including the example chart) contain a *chart title* and additional labels to identify the axes or categories.

The example chart also contains horizontal *gridlines* (which correspond to the left value axis). Gridlines are basically extensions of the value axis scale, which makes it easier for the viewer to determine the magnitude of the data points.

In addition, all charts have a *chart area* (the entire background area of the chart) and a *plot area* (the part that shows the actual chart, including the plotted data, the axes, and the axis labels.).

Charts will have additional parts or fewer parts, depending on the chart type. For example, a pie chart (see Figure 1-6) has "slices" and no axes. A 3-D chart may have *walls* and a *floor* (see Figure 1-7).

Many other types of items can be added to a chart. For example, you can add a *trendline* or display *error bars*.

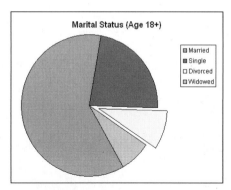

Figure 1-6: A pie chart

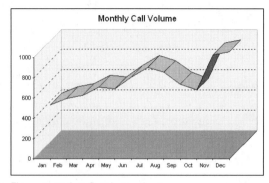

Figure 1-7: A 3-D column chart

Refer to Chapters 4 and 5 for additional information about the elements available for various chart types.

Creating Charts

This section discusses the various methods available to create a chart. For maximum flexibility, you'll probably want to use the Chart Wizard for creating most of your charts.

Creating a chart with one keystroke

For a quick demonstration of how easily you can create a chart, follow these instructions. This example creates a chart on a separate Chart sheet.

1. Enter data to be charted into a worksheet. Figure 1-8 shows an example of data that's appropriate for a chart.

2. Select the range of data that you entered in Step 1, including the row and column titles. For example, if you entered the data shown in Figure 1-8, select A1:C4.

3. Press F11. Excel inserts a new chart sheet (named Chart1) and displays the chart, based on the selected data. Figure 1-9 shows the result.

	A	B	C	D	E
1		Region 1	Region 2		
2	Jan	1,843	983		
3	Feb	2,283	1,092		
4	Mar	2,184	1,143		
5					
6					

Figure 1-8: This data would make a good chart.

In this simple example, Excel created its default chart type (which is a two-dimensional column chart), using the default settings. This chart, like all charts, can be further customized in many ways. For example, you would probably want to add a title to the chart, and you may prefer to change the colors used in the columns.

Creating a chart with a mouse click

To create an embedded chart with a single mouse click:

1. Make sure that the Chart toolbar is displayed. If the toolbar is not displayed, right-click any toolbar and choose Chart.

2. Select the data to be charted.

3. Click the Chart Type tool on the Chart toolbar and select a chart type from the displayed icons.

Excel adds the chart to the worksheet, using the default settings for the chart type you selected.

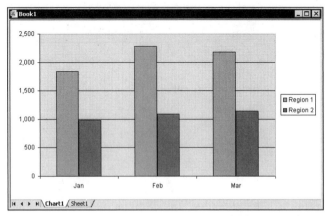

Figure 1-9: This chart was generated with one keystroke.

The Chart Type tool on the Chart toolbar displays an icon for the last selected chart. However, this tool works like a list box; you can expand it to display 18 chart types (refer to Figure 1-10). Just click the arrow to display the additional chart types. For more information about the Chart toolbar, refer to the sidebar, "The Chart Toolbar."

Using the Chart Wizard

The preceding sections describe two quick ways to generate a chart. The resulting chart may or may not be what you were expecting. If not, you can always modify the chart, or start over and use the Chart Wizard for more control.

The most common — and the most flexible — way to create a chart is to use the Chart Wizard. To use the Chart Wizard:

1. Select the data that you want to chart (optional).

2. Choose Insert→Chart (or click the Chart Wizard tool on the Standard toolbar).

3. Specify various options in Steps 1 through 4 of the Chart Wizard.

4. Click Finish to create the chart.

The next section provides additional information about using the Chart Wizard.

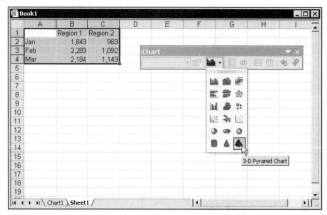

Figure 1–10: The Chart Type tool expands so that you can create the type of chart you want.

Hands On: Creating a Chart with the Chart Wizard

The Chart Wizard consists of four sequential dialog boxes that prompt you for various settings for your chart. By the time that you reach the last dialog box, the chart is usually fairly close to what you need. In case you've never created an Excel chart, this section introduces this feature with a hands-on example.

Selecting the data

Before you start the Chart Wizard, select the data that you want to include in the chart. Your selection should include items such as labels and series identifiers (row and column headings). Preselecting the chart data isn't necessary but makes creating the chart easier. If you don't select the data before invoking the Chart Wizard, you can select it in the second Chart Wizard dialog box.

Figure 1-11 shows a worksheet with a range of data set up for a chart. This data consists of the percentage of U.S. citizens who read a daily newspaper, categorized by year and by education level.

The Chart Toolbar

The Chart toolbar is a context-sensitive toolbar that appears when you click an embedded chart, activate a chart sheet, or choose View→Toolbars→Chart. This toolbar, shown in the accompanying figure, includes nine tools. You can use these tools to make some common chart changes:

◆ **Chart Objects:** When a chart is activated, the name of the selected chart element is displayed in this control. In addition, you can select a particular chart element by using the drop-down list.

◆ **Format Selected Object:** Displays the Format dialog box for the selected chart element.

◆ **Chart Type:** Expands to display 18 chart types when you click the arrow. After it's expanded, you can drag this tool to a new location — creating, in effect, a miniature floating toolbar.

◆ **Legend:** Toggles the legend display in the active chart.

◆ **Data Table:** Toggles the display of the data table in a chart.

◆ **By Row:** Plots the data by rows.

◆ **By Column:** Plots the data by columns.

◆ **Angle Clockwise:** Displays the selected text at a −45-degree angle.

◆ **Angle Counterclockwise:** Displays the selected text at a +45-degree angle.

If you press Ctrl while you click either of the Angle Text tools, Excel no longer angles the selected text.

In addition, several tools on the other toolbars work with charts, including the Fill Color, Font Color, Bold, Italic, and Font tools.

Excel includes several other chart-related tools that aren't on the Chart toolbar. You can customize the toolbar to include these additional tools. To customize your Chart toolbar:

1. Make sure the Chart toolbar is displayed.

2. Choose View→Toolbars→Customize to display the Customize dialog box.

3. Select the Commands tab.

4. Choose Charting from Categories list box.

5. Click an item in the Commands list and drag it to your Chart toolbar.

6. Repeat Step 5 for other commands that you'd like to add.

For this example, select the range A3:E9. This range includes the category labels but not the title (which is in A1).

hands-on example.xls				
	A	B	C	D	E
1	Newspaper Readership by Education Level				
2					
3	Years	No HS Degree	HS Degree	College Degree	Graduate Degree
4	1990	53%	55%	71%	70%
5	1992	47%	56%	59%	70%
6	1995	42%	46%	55%	60%
7	1997	41%	44%	53%	59%
8	1999	36%	40%	48%	57%
9	2001	23%	43%	48%	59%
10					

Figure 1-11: Data to be charted

The data that you use in a chart doesn't have to be contiguous. You can press Ctrl and make a multiple selection. The initial data, however, must be on a single worksheet. If you need to plot data that exists on more than one worksheet, you can add more series after the chart is created (or use the Series tab in Step 2 of the Chart Wizard). In all cases, however, data for a single chart series must reside on one sheet. In other words, the data for a chart series cannot extend across multiple worksheets. This issue is addressed in Chapter 3.

After you select the data, start the Chart Wizard, either by clicking the Chart Wizard button on the Standard toolbar or by selecting Insert→Chart. Excel displays the first of four Chart Wizard dialog boxes.

While using the Chart Wizard, you can go back to the preceding step by clicking the Back button. Or, you can click Finish to close the Chart Wizard. If you close the Chart Wizard early, Excel creates the chart using the information that you provided up to that point.

Don't be too concerned about creating the perfect chart. You can always change, at any time, any choice that you make in the Chart Wizard.

Chart Wizard – Step 1 of 4

Figure 1-12 shows the first Chart Wizard dialog box, in which you select the chart type. This dialog box has two tabs: Standard Types and Custom Types. The Standard Types tab displays the 14 basic chart types and the subtypes for each. The Custom Types tab displays some customized charts (including user-defined custom charts).

For this example, a Line chart with markers might be a good choice for this data. Select Line from the Chart type list box and then click the appropriate icon for the subtype.

TIP When you work in the Custom Types tab, the dialog box shows a preview of your data with the selected chart type. In the Standard Types tab, you get a preview by clicking the button labeled Press and Hold to View Sample. When you click this button, keep the mouse button pressed.

When you decide on a chart type and subtype, click the Next button to move to the next step.

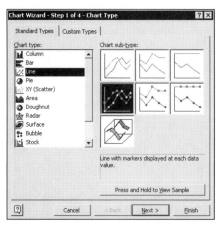

Figure 1-12: The first of four Chart Wizard dialog boxes

Chart Wizard – Step 2 of 4

In the second step of the Chart Wizard (shown in Figure 1-13):

◆ Verify the data ranges to be used in the chart – and change them if necessary.

◆ Specify the orientation of the data (whether the data series are arranged in rows or in columns).

◆ Verify that Excel correctly identified the category data and the series data.

VERIFYING THE DATA RANGE

This step of the Chart Wizard dialog box contains two tabs: Data Range and Series. Click the Data Range tab.

The Data range field displays the range address that was selected when you started the Chart Wizard. If you selected only a single cell, this field displays Excel's best guess regarding the range to be plotted.

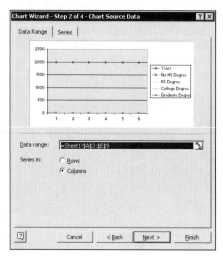

Figure 1-13: Step 2 of the Chart Wizard dialog box

If the data range is not correct, you can change it by clicking in the Data range field and then selecting the correct range by dragging in the worksheet. Or, you can edit the range address manually.

 TIP When you activate the Data Range field, you'll discover that this field is in "point mode." Using the arrow keys on your keyboard selects data in the worksheet. If you would like to edit the actual range address listed in the Data Range, press F2 to get into "edit mode."

For this example, the data range that was selected originally is correct.

CHANGING THE DATA ORIENTATION

The orientation of the data has a drastic effect on the look of your chart. Excel has its own rules that it uses to determine the data orientation. If Excel guesses incorrectly, you can change it by selecting the Rows or Columns option button. This step of the Chart Wizard displays a small preview of your chart so that you can immediately see the effect of changing the chart's orientation.

For this example, Excel guessed correctly: The data is arranged in columns.

SPECIFYING THE CATEGORY DATA AND SERIES DATA

Look carefully at the preview and you'll see that the chart is not correct. Excel (incorrectly) identified the years in Column A as a data series. In fact, the years are categories names and should be treated as text, not plotted as numeric values.

Because the Chart Wizard did not identify the categories, a change is required. This change is made using the Series tab in Step 2 of the Chart Wizard (see Figure 1-14).

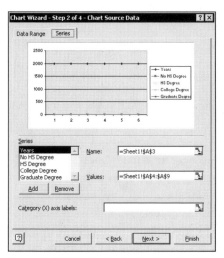

Figure 1-14: The Series tab in Step 2 of the Chart Wizard

The Series list box shows the names of all the data series for the chart. Select a series in the list box, and the range address for its name and data are shown in the fields to the right. In this example, the Years series has its Name in range A3 and its Values in range A4:A9.

Because the series labeled *Years* is not really a series (it contains the category (X) axis labels), you need to delete it from the Series list box. To do so, select it and click Remove. After removing the incorrect series, the preview will update. Now the chart is looking better – but the years are not displayed along the category (horizontal) axis.

The field for the Category (X) axis labels is empty, so you need to specify the range for the category labels. To do so, click in the field and select A4:A9. Now the preview chart looks correct (see Figure 1-15). The years appear as categories on the horizontal axis, and the chart displays the four data series.

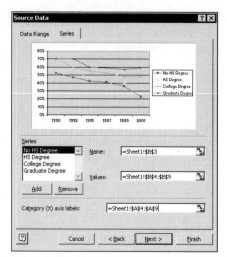

Figure 1-15: The incorrect series has been removed and the Category axis labels have been specified.

Excel uses the data type to identify category data. In this example, the years in Column A are numeric values, so Excel treats them as data. Also, note that when category data is not specified, Excel uses consecutive integers on the Category axis: 1, 2, 3, and so on. In this example, you might think that formatting the years as Text would cause Excel to treat them as categories — but it doesn't work. You can, however, precede each year value with an apostrophe. In such a case, the years are interpreted as text and assigned as the categories. Yet another option is to remove the column heading (Years) from cell A3. After you do so, Excel will correctly identify the data as category labels.

Click the Next button to advance to the next dialog box.

Chart Wizard — Step 3 of 4

In the third Chart Wizard dialog box, shown in Figure 1-16, you specify most of the options for the chart. This dialog box has six tabs:

◆ **Titles:** Add titles to the chart. Note that these fields are not range selector fields. You must enter text, not a cell address.

◆ Axes: Turn on or off axes display and specify the type of axes.

- ◆ **Gridlines:** Specify gridlines, if any.

- ◆ **Legend:** Specify whether to include a legend and where to place it.

- ◆ **Data Labels:** Specify whether to show data labels and what type of labels.

- ◆ **Data Table:** Specify whether to display a table of the data.

 The options available in Step 3 of the Chart Wizard depend on the type of chart that you selected in Step 1.

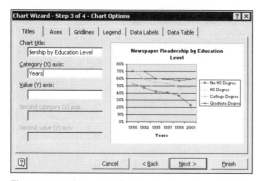

Figure 1-16: You specify the chart options in the third Chart Wizard dialog box.

When you make changes, the changes are reflected in the preview chart.

For this example, just accept the default setting, except for the Titles tab. Specify the following titles:

Chart title: Newspaper Readership by Education Level

Category (X) axis: Years

After you select the chart options, click Next to move to the final dialog box.

Chart Wizard – Step 4 of 4

Step 4 of the Chart Wizard, shown in Figure 1-17, is used to specify the location for the chart. Select As New Sheet to create the chart on a Chart sheet, or select As Object In to create an embedded chart. Make your choice and click Finish.

Excel creates and displays the chart.

Changing the Default Chart Type

I mention the default chart type several times in this chapter. The *default chart type* is the chart that is created if you don't specify the type. Excel's default chart type is a 2D clustered column chart with a light-gray plot area, a legend on the right, and horizontal gridlines.

If you don't like the looks of this chart or if you typically use a different type of chart, you can easily change the default chart in the following manner:

1. Select the Chart→Chart Type command.

2. Choose the chart type that you want to use as the default chart. This can be a chart from either the Standard Types tab or the Custom Types tab.

3. Click the button labeled Set As Default Chart Type. You are asked to verify your choice.

If you have many charts of the same type to create, changing the default chart format to the chart type with which you're working is much more efficient than separately formatting each chart. Then, you can create all your charts without having to select the chart type

If you create an embedded chart, Excel centers the chart in the workbook window and activates the chart. The proportions of the chart correspond to the proportions of the workbook window.

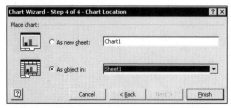

Figure 1-17: Step 4 of the Chart Wizard asks you where to put the chart.

Figure 1-18 shows the complete chart. You may or may not be satisfied with the chart. If not, it's a simple matter to modify the chart to your liking.

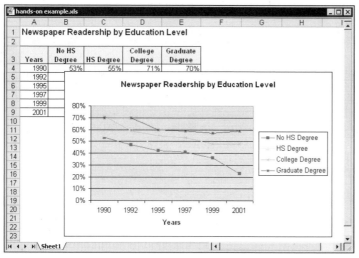

Figure 1-18: The end result of using the Chart Wizard

Basic Chart Modifications

After you've created a chart, you can modify it in many ways. The modifications you can make to a chart are extensive. This section covers some of the more common chart modifications:

◆ Moving and resizing the chart

◆ Changing the chart type

◆ Moving chart elements

◆ Deleting chart elements

◆ Formatting the chart elements

 Before you can modify a chart, the chart must be activated. To activate an embedded chart, click it. Doing so activates the chart and also selects the element that you click. To activate a chart on a Chart sheet, just click its sheet tab.

Moving and resizing a chart

If your chart is an embedded chart, you can freely move and resize it. Click the chart's border and then drag the border to move the chart. Drag any of the eight "handles" to resize the chart. The handles are the black squares that appear on the chart's corners and edges when you click the chart's border.

Changing the chart type

To change the chart type of the active chart, use either of the following methods:

- ◆ Choose the Chart Type button on the Chart toolbar. Click the drop-down arrow, and this button expands to show 18 basic chart types.

- ◆ Choose the Chart→Chart Type command.

- ◆ Right-click and choose Chart Type from the shortcut menu

The Chart→Chart Type command displays a dialog box much like the first step of the ChartWizard. Click the Standard Types tab to select one of the standard chart types (and a subtype), or click the Custom Types tab to select a customized chart. After selecting a chart type, click OK. The selected chart will be changed to the type you selected.

If you've customized some aspects of your chart, choosing a new chart type from the Custom Types tab may override some or all of the changes you've made. For example, if you've added gridlines to the chart and then select a custom chart type that doesn't use gridlines, your gridlines disappear. Therefore, it's a good idea to make sure that you're satisfied with the chart before you make too many custom changes to it. However, you can always use Edit→Undo to reverse your actions.

In the Custom Types tab, if you click the User-defined option, the list box displays the name of any user-defined custom formats.

Copying a chart

To make an exact copy of an embedded chart, press and hold down the Ctrl key. Click the chart and then drag the mouse pointer to a new location. To make a copy of a Chart sheet, use the same procedure but drag the Chart sheet's tab.

Deleting a chart

To delete an embedded chart, press Ctrl and click the chart (this selects the chart as an object). Then press Del. To delete a chart sheet, right-click its sheet tab and choose Delete from the shortcut menu.

Moving and deleting chart elements

Some of the elements within a chart can be moved. The movable chart elements include the titles, the legend, and data labels. To move a chart element, simply click it to select it; then drag it to the desired location in the chart. To delete a chart element, select it and then press Delete.

Other modifications

When a chart is activated, you can select various parts of the chart to work with. Modifying a chart is similar to everything else you do in Excel. First, you make a selection (in this case, select a chart element). Then you issue a command to do something with the selection. Right-clicking an element in a chart displays a shortcut menu. This menu often (but not always) contains the command you need.

You can use the Fill Color tool on the Formatting toolbar to change colors. For example, if you want to change the color of a series, select the series and choose the color you want from the Fill Color tool. You'll find that many other toolbar tools work with charts. For example, you can select the chart's legend and then click the Bold button to make the legend text bold.

When you double-click a chart element (or press Ctrl+1 after selecting it), its Formatting dialog box appears. The dialog box that appears varies, depending on the item selected. In most cases, the dialog box is of the tabbed variety. Many modifications are self-evident – for example, changing the font used in a title. Others, however, are a bit more tricky.

Chapter 4 discusses these chart modifications in detail.

In addition, you can right-click a chart element and get a shortcut menu that contains commands related to that element.

Printing Charts

Printing embedded charts is nothing special; you print them the same way that you print a worksheet. As long as you include the embedded chart in the range that you want to print, Excel prints the chart as it appears on-screen. When printing a sheet that contains embedded charts, it's a good idea to preview first to ensure that your charts do not span multiple pages.

If you select an embedded chart and then choose File→Print (or click the Print button), Excel prints the chart on a page by itself and does *not* print the worksheet.

If you don't want a particular embedded chart to appear on your printout, right-click the chart and choose Format Chart Area from the shortcut menu. Click the Properties tab in the Format Chart Area dialog box and remove the check mark from the Print Object check box.

If you created the chart on a Chart sheet, Excel prints the chart on a page by itself. If you open Excel's Page Setup dialog box when the chart sheet is active, the Sheet tab is replaced with a tab named Chart. Figure 1-19 shows the Chart tab of the Page Setup dialog box, which has several options.

◆ **Use full page:** Excel prints the chart to the full width and height of the page margins. This usually isn't a good choice because the chart's relative proportions change and you lose the WYSIWYG advantage.

◆ **Scale to fit page:** Expands the chart proportionally in both dimensions until one dimension fills the space between the margins. In other words, the aspect ratio of the chart is maintained. This option usually results in the best printout.

◆ **Custom:** Prints the chart as it appears on your screen. Select View→Sized with Window to make the chart correspond to the window size and proportions. The chart prints at the current window size and proportions.

The Printing quality options work just like those for worksheet pages. If you choose the Draft quality option for a chart sheet, Excel prints the chart, but its quality may not be high (the actual effect depends on your printer). Choosing the Print in Black and White option prints the data series with black-and-white patterns rather than colors. Most noncolor printers handle this fine, even if this option is not set. But you might want to experiment to determine the best output quality for your printer.

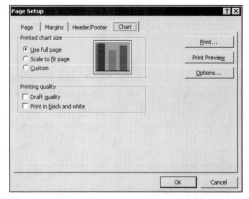

Figure 1-19: The Chart tab of the Page Setup dialog box

Chapter 2

Understanding Chart Types

YOU'RE PROBABLY FAMILIAR WITH many types of charts: bar charts, line charts, pie charts, and so on. Excel supports all the basic chart types and even some esoteric chart types, such as radar charts and doughnut charts. This chapter presents examples of each of these chart types, along with information that may help you determine which type of chart to use to present your data.

Conveying a Message with a Chart

People who create charts usually do so in order to make a point or to communicate a specific message. Often, the message is explicitly stated in the chart's title or in a text box within the chart. The chart itself provides visual support.

Choosing the correct chart type is often a key factor in making the message compelling. Therefore, it's often well worth your time to experiment with various chart types to determine which one is most effective.

In almost every case, the underlying message in a chart is some type of *comparison*. Examples of some general types of comparisons include:

◆ **Compare item to other items:** For example, a chart may compare sales in each of a company's sales regions.

◆ **Compare data over time:** For example, a chart may display sales by month and indicate trends over time.

◆ **Make relative comparisons:** An example is a common pie chart that depicts relative values in terms of pie "slices."

◆ **Compare data relationships:** An XY chart is ideal for this. For example, you might show the relationship between marketing expenditures and sales.

◆ **Frequency comparison:** A common histogram, for example, can be used to display the number (or percentage) of students who scored within a particular range.

◆ **Identify "outliers" or unusual situations:** If you have thousands of data points, creating a chart may help identify data that is not representative.

Choosing a Chart Type

A common question among Excel users is, "How do I know which chart type to use for my data?" Unfortunately, there is no cut-and-dried answer to this question. Perhaps the best answer is a vague one: *Use the chart type that gets your message across in the simplest way.*

Figure 2-1 shows the same set of data plotted using six different chart types. Although all six charts represent the same information (monthly Web site visitors), they look quite different from one another.

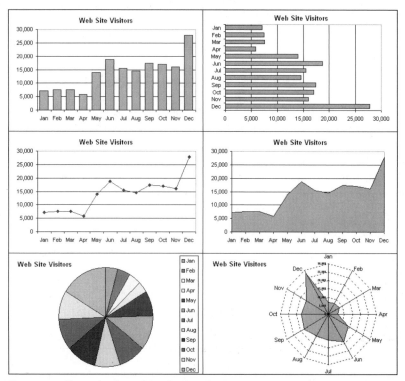

Figure 2-1: The same data, plotted using six chart types

The column chart (upper left) is probably the best choice for this particular set of data because it clearly shows the information for each month in discrete units. The bar chart (upper right) is similar to a column chart, but the axes are swapped. Most people are more accustomed to seeing time-based information extend from left to right rather than from top to bottom.

The line chart (middle left) may not be the best choice because it seems to imply that the data is continuous – that points exist in between the 12 actual data points. This same argument could be made against using an area chart (middle right).

The pie chart (lower left) is simply too confusing and does nothing to convey the time-based nature of the data. Pie charts are most appropriate for a data series in which you want to emphasize proportions among a relatively small number of data points. If you have too many data points, a pie chart can be impossible to interpret.

The radar chart (lower right) is clearly inappropriate for this data. People are not accustomed to viewing time-based information in a circular direction!

Fortunately, changing a chart's type is a very easy procedure, so you can experiment with various chart types until you find the one that represents your data accurately and clearly – and as simply as possible.

The remainder of this chapter contains lots of information about Excel's various chart types. The examples and discussion may give you a better handle on determining the most appropriate chart type for your data.

Standard Chart Types

When you use the Chart Wizard to create a chart, the first step is to select the type of chart. The first step of the Chart Wizard dialog box contains two tabs: Standard Types and Custom Types. Selecting an item in the Chart type list box displays a number of subtypes for the chart type. For example, a Column chart has seven subtypes. Table 2-1 lists the standard chart types along with the number of subtypes associated with each.

TABLE 2-1 EXCEL'S STANDARD CHART TYPES

Chart Type	Subtypes
Area	6
Bar	6
Column	7
Line	7

Continued

TABLE 2-1 **EXCEL'S STANDARD CHART TYPES** *(Continued)*

Chart Type	Subtypes
Pie	6
Doughnut	2
Radar	3
XY (Scatter)	5
Surface	4
Bubble	2
Stock	4
Cylinder	7
Cone	7
Pyramid	7

The remainder of this section discusses each of Excel's standard chart types and shows examples of each.

All the subsequent examples are available on this book's companion CD-ROM.

Column charts

Column charts are one of the most common chart types. A column chart displays each data point as a vertical column, the height of which corresponds to the value. The value scale is displayed on the vertical axis, which is usually on the left side of the chart. You can specify any number of data series, and the corresponding data points from each series can be stacked on top of each other. Typically, each data series is depicted in a different color or pattern.

Column charts are often used to compare discrete items, and they can depict the differences between items in a series or items across multiple series.

Table 2-2 lists Excel's seven column chart subtypes.

TABLE 2-2 COLUMN CHART SUBTYPES

Chart Type	Description
Clustered column	Standard Column chart.
Stacked column	Column chart with data series stacked.
100% stacked column	Column chart with data series stacked and expressed as percentages.
3-D clustered column	Standard Column chart with a perspective look.
3-D stacked column	Column chart with a perspective look. Data series are stacked and expressed as percentages.
3-D 100% stacked column	Column chart with a perspective look. Data series are stacked and expressed as percentages.
3-D column	A column chart with multiple series arranged along a third axis.

Figure 2-2 shows an example of a column chart that depicts annual sales for two products. From this chart, it is clear that Sprocket sales have always exceeded Widget sales. In addition, Widget sales have been declining over the years, whereas Sprocket sales are increasing.

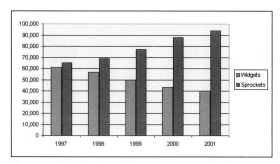

Figure 2-2: This column chart compares sales for two products.

The same data, in the form of a stacked-column chart, is shown in Figure 2-3. This chart has the added advantage of depicting the combined sales over time. It shows that total sales have remained relatively steady over the years, but the relative proportions of the two products have changed.

Figure 2-4 shows the same sales data plotted as a 100% stacked-column chart. This chart type shows the relative contribution of each product by year. Notice that the value axis displays percentage values, not sales amounts. This chart provides no information about the actual sales volumes. This type of chart is often a good alternative to using several pie charts. Instead of using a pie to show the relative sales volume in each year, the chart uses a column for each year.

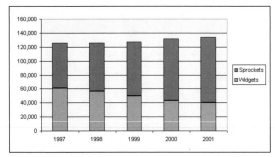

Figure 2-3: This stacked-column chart displays sales by product and depicts the total sales.

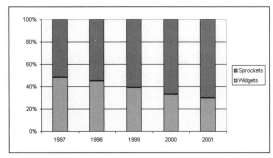

Figure 2-4: This 100% stacked-column chart displays annual sales as a percentage.

The data is plotted with a 3-D column chart in Figure 2-5. Many people use this type of chart because it has more visual pizzazz. Although it may be more appealing visually, this type of chart often makes it difficult to make precise comparisons because of the distorted perspective view. Generally speaking, a 3-D column chart is best used when the goal is to show general trends rather than precise comparisons.

Bar charts

A *bar chart* is essentially a column chart that has been rotated 90 degrees clockwise. One distinct advantage to using a bar chart is that the category labels may be easier to read. Figure 2-6 shows a bar chart that displays a value for each of ten survey items. The category labels are lengthy, and it would be difficult to display them legibly using a column chart.

Table 2-3 lists Excel's six bar chart subtypes.

3-D or Not 3-D? That Is the Question

Some of Excel's charts are referred to as *3-D charts*. This terminology can be a bit confusing, because some of these so-called 3-D charts aren't technically 3-D charts. Rather, they are 2-D charts with a perspective look to them; that is, they appear to have some depth. The accompanying figure shows two "3-D" charts.

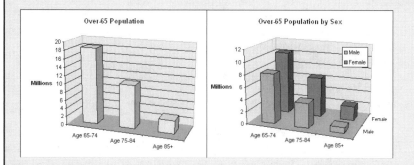

The chart on the left isn't a true 3-D chart. It's simply a 2-D chart that uses perspective to add depth to the columns. The chart on the right is a true 3-D chart because the data series extend into the third (depth) dimension.

A true 3-D chart has three axes: a value axis (the height dimension); a category axis (the width dimension); and a series axis (the depth dimension). The series axis is always a category axis — it cannot depict scaled numerical values.

When a 3-D chart is active, you can select Chart→3-D View to change the chart's perspective using the 3-D View dialog box. You'll find that you have a great deal of control. You can distort the chart so much that it becomes virtually unrecognizable.

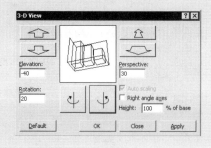

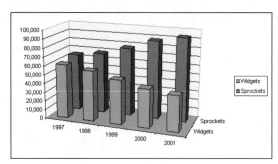

Figure 2-5: A 3-D column chart

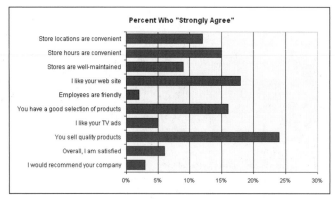

Figure 2-6: If you have lengthy category labels, a bar chart may be a good choice.

TABLE 2-3 BAR CHART SUBTYPES

Chart Type	Description
Clustered bar	Standard bar chart.
Stacked bar	Bar chart with data series stacked.
100% stacked bar	Bar chart with data series stacked and expressed as percentages.
3-D clustered bar	Standard bar chart with a perspective look.
3-D stacked bar	Bar chart with a perspective look. Excel stacks data series and expresses them as percentages.
3-D 100% stacked bar	Bar chart with a perspective look. Excel stacks data series and expresses them as percentages.

Unlike a column chart, there is no subtype that displays multiple series along a third axis (that is, there is no 3-D Bar Chart subtype type).

As with a column chart, you can include any number of data series in a bar chart. In addition, the bars can be "stacked" from left to right. Figure 2-7 shows a 100% stacked-bar chart. This chart summarizes the percentage of survey respondents who replied to each option.

Line charts

Line charts are often used to plot continuous data and are useful for identifying trends. For example, plotting daily sales as a line chart may enable you to identify sales fluctuations over time. Normally, the category axis for a line chart displays equal intervals.

Table 2-4 lists Excel's seven line chart subtypes.

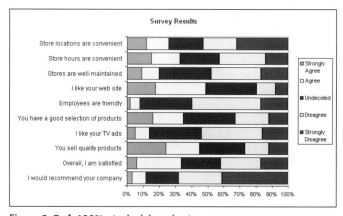

Figure 2-7: A 100% stacked-bar chart

TABLE 2-4 LINE CHART SUBTYPES

Chart Type	Description
Line	Standard line chart
Stacked line	Line chart with stacked data series

Continued

TABLE **2-4 LINE CHART SUBTYPES** *(Continued)*

Chart Type	Description
100% stacked line	Line chart with stacked data series expressed as percentages
Line with data markers	Line chart with data markers
Stacked line with data markers	Line chart with stacked data series and data markers
100% stacked line with data markers	Line chart with stacked data series and line markers, expressed as percentages
3-D line	Chart that displays "ribbon-like" lines, using a third axis

See Figure 2-8 for an example of a line chart that depicts daily sales (200 data points). Although the data varies quite a bit on a daily basis, the chart clearly depicts an upward trend.

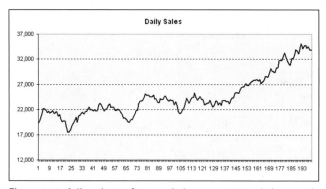

Figure 2-8: A line chart often can help you spot trends in your data.

A line chart can use any number of data series, and you distinguish the lines by using different colors, line styles, or markers. Figure 2-9 shows a line chart that uses three series, each with 48 data points. Each line is displayed in a different color and with a different marker. The series are identified by the legend.

Figure 2-10 shows a 3-D line chart that depicts population growth for three states. Most would agree that a 3-D line chart is definitely *not* a good chart type for this data. For example, the 3-D perspective makes it virtually impossible to determine the relative growths of Washington and Oregon. In fact, the chart may present an optical illusion that makes it impossible to discern the order of the line series across the depth axis.

Pie charts

A *pie chart* is useful when you want to show relative proportions or contributions to a whole. A pie chart can use only one data series. Pie charts are most effective with a small number of data points. Generally, a pie chart should use no more than five or six data points (or slices). A pie chart with too many data points can be very difficult to interpret.

The values used in a pie chart must all be positive numbers. If you create a pie chart that uses one or more negative values, the negative values will be converted to positive values — which is probably not what you intended!

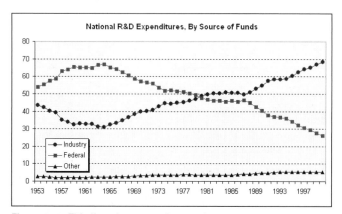

Figure 2-9: This line chart uses three series.

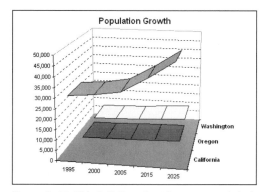

Figure 2-10: This 3-D line chart is not a good choice for this data.

You can "explode" one or more slices of a pie chart for emphasis (see Figure 2-11). Activate the chart and click any pie slice to select the entire pie. Then click the slice that you want to explode and drag it away from the center.

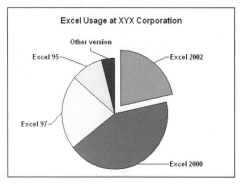

Figure 2-11: A pie chart with one slice exploded

Table 2-5 lists Excel's six pie chart subtypes.

TABLE 2-5 PIE CHART SUBTYPES

Chart Type	Description
Pie	Standard pie chart
3-D pie	Pie chart with perspective look
Pie of pie	Pie chart with one slice broken into another pie
Exploded pie	Pie chart with one or more slices exploded
Exploded 3-D pie	Pie chart with perspective look, with one or more slices exploded
Bar of pie	Pie chart with one slice broken into a column

The pie of pie and bar of pie chart types enable you to display a secondary chart that provides more detail for one of the pie slices. Refer to Figure 2-12 for an example. The pie chart shows the breakdown of four expense categories: Rent, Supplies, Miscellaneous, and Salary. The secondary bar chart provides an additional regional breakdown of the Salary category.

The data used in the chart resides in A2:B8. When the chart was created, the Chart Wizard used its built-in defaults to make a guess at which categories belong to the secondary chart. In this case, the guess was to use the last three data points for the secondary chart – and the guess was incorrect.

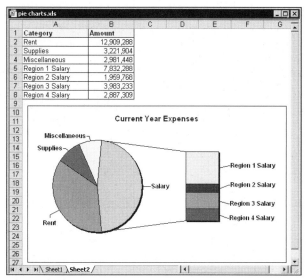

Figure 2-12: A bar of pie chart that shows detail for one of the pie slices

To correct the chart, double-click any of the pie slices to display the Format Data Series dialog box. Click the Options tab (see Figure 2-13) and make the changes. In this example, the series is split by Position, and the secondary chart contains the last four values in the series.

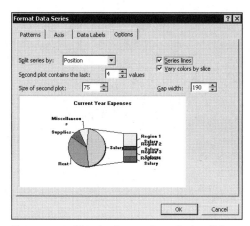

Figure 2-13: Use the Format Data Series dialog box to fine-tune a bar of pie chart.

XY (scatter) charts

Another common chart type is *XY charts* (also known as *scattergrams* or *scatter plots*). An XY chart differs from most other chart types in that both axes display values (there is no category axis in an XY chart).

This type of chart often is used to show the relationship between two variables. Figure 2-14 shows an example of an XY chart that plots the relationship between sales calls (horizontal axis) and actual sales (vertical axis). The chart shows that these two variables are positively related: Months in which more calls were made typically had higher sales volumes.

Although these data points correspond to time, it's important to understand that the chart does not convey any time-related information. In other words, the data points are plotted based only on their two values.

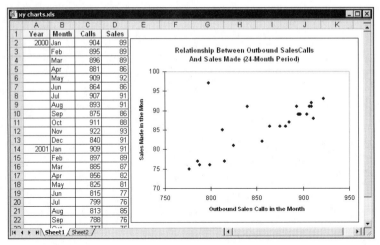

Figure 2-14: An XY chart shows the relationship between two variables.

Adding a trend line to this chart would assist in conveying the fact that the variables are positively correlated. See Chapter 5 for details on trend lines.

Table 2-6 lists Excel's five XY (Scatter) chart subtypes.

TABLE 2-6 XY (SCATTER) CHART SUBTYPES

Chart Type	Description
Scatter	XY chart with markers and no lines
Scatter with smoothed lines	XY chart with markers and smoothed lines
Scatter with smoothed lines and no data markers	XY chart with smoothed lines and no markers
Scatter with lines	XY chart with lines and markers
Scatter with lines and no data markers	XY chart with lines and no markers

Figure 2-15 shows another example of an XY chart, this one using the lines with markers subtype. As you can see, the data points, when connected, draw a right triangle.

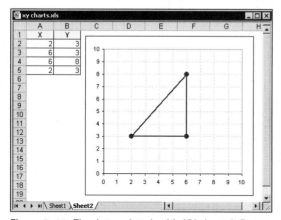

Figure 2-15: The data points in this XY chart define a right triangle.

Area charts

Think of an *area chart* as a line chart in which the area below the line has been colored in. Table 2-7 lists Excel's six area chart subtypes.

Figure 2-16 shows an example of a stacked area chart. Stacking the data series enables you to see clearly the total, plus the contribution by each series.

TABLE 2-7 AREA CHART SUBTYPES

Chart Type	Description
Area	Standard area chart
Stacked area	Area chart; data series stacked
100% stacked area	Area chart; expressed as percentages
3-D area	A true 3-D area chart with a third axis
3-D Stacked Area	Area chart with a perspective look; data series stacked
3-D 100% stacked area	Area chart with a perspective look; expressed as percentages

Figure 2-17 shows the same data, plotted as a 3-D area chart. Although this chart has lots of visual appeal, it has a serious weakness: The data toward the back is often obscured. In this example, the first three quarters for Product C are not even visible.

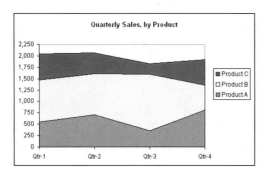

Figure 2-16: A stacked area chart

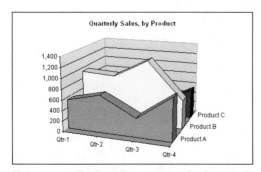

Figure 2-17: The first three quarters for Product C are not visible in this 3-D area chart.

This type of problem can sometimes be solved by rotating or changing the elevation of the 3-D chart to provide a different view. In some cases, plotting the series in reverse order will reveal the obscured data. For the most control, you can manually change the plot order of the series. These procedures are described in Chapter 4.

Doughnut charts

A *doughnut chart* is similar to a pie chart, with two exceptions: It has a hole in the middle and it can display more than one series of data. Figure 2-18 shows an example of a doughnut chart with two series (1st Half Sales and 2nd Half Sales). The legend identifies the data points. The arrows and series descriptions were added manually. A doughnut chart does not provide a direct way to identify the series!

Notice that Excel displays the data series as concentric rings. As you can see, a doughnut chart with more than one series can be very difficult to interpret. For example, the relatively larger sizes of the slices toward the outer part of the doughnut can be deceiving. Consequently, doughnut charts should be used sparingly. In many cases, a stacked-column chart for such comparisons expresses your meaning better than does a doughnut chart.

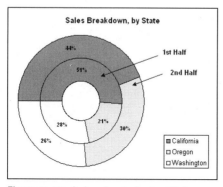

Figure 2-18: A doughnut chart with two data series

Perhaps the best use for a doughnut chart is to plot a single series as a visual alternative to a pie chart.

Table 2-8 lists Excel's two doughnut chart subtypes.

TABLE 2-8 DOUGHNUT CHART SUBTYPES

Chart Type	Subtype
Doughnut	Standard doughnut chart
Exploded doughnut	Doughnut chart with all slices exploded

Radar charts

You may not be familiar with radar charts. A *radar chart* has a separate axis for each category, and the axes extend outward from the center of the chart. The value of each data point is plotted on the corresponding axis.

Figure 2-19 shows four radar charts, each with three categories. These charts depict the red, green, and blue components for various colors using the RGB color system. In the RGB color system, each color is represented by a value (between 0 and 255) for red, green, and blue. Although this fact is not apparent in the figure, each chart also uses the color that it depicts.

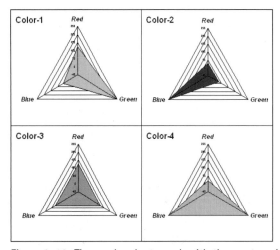

Figure 2-19: Three radar charts, each with three categories

Figure 2-20 shows another example of a radar chart. This chart plots two data series across 12 categories (months) and shows the seasonal demand for snow skis versus water skis. Note that the water ski series partially obscures the snow ski series.

Table 2-9 lists Excel's three radar chart subtypes.

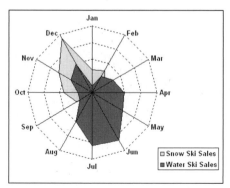

Figure 2-20: A radar chart with 12 categories and two series

TABLE 2-9 RADAR CHART SUBTYPES

Chart Type	Subtype
Radar	Standard radar chart (lines only)
Radar with data markers	Radar chart with lines and data markers
Filled radar	Radar chart with lines colored in

Surface charts

Surface charts display two or more data series on a surface. As Figure 2-21 shows, these charts can be quite interesting. Unlike other charts, Excel uses color to distinguish values, not to distinguish the data series. The number of colors used is determined by the major unit scale setting for the value axis. Each color corresponds to one major unit.

Table 2-10 lists Excel's four 3-D surface chart subtypes.

TABLE 2-10 SURFACE CHART SUBTYPES

Chart Type	Description
3-D surface	Standard 3-D surface chart
3-D surface (wireframe)	3-D surface chart with no colors

Continued

TABLE **2-10 SURFACE CHART SUBTYPES** *(Continued)*

Chart Type	Description
Surface (top view)	3-D surface chart as viewed from above
Surface (top view wireframe)	3-D surface chart as viewed from above; no color

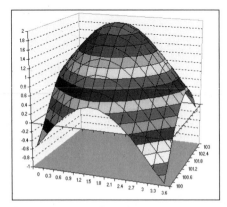

Figure 2-21: A surface chart

 It's important to understand that a surface chart does not plot 3-D data points. The series axis for a surface chart, as with all other 3-D charts, is a category axis — not a value axis. In other words, if you have data that is represented by x, y, and z coordinates, it cannot be plotted accurately on a surface chart unless the x and y values are equally spaced.

Bubble charts

Think of a bubble chart as an XY chart that can display an additional data series, which is represented by the size of the bubbles. As with an XY chart, both axes are value axes – there is no category axis.

Figure 2-22 shows an example of a bubble chart that depicts the results of a weight-loss program. The horizontal value axis represents the original weight, the vertical value axis shows the length of time in the program, and the size of the bubbles represents the amount of weight lost.

Table 2-11 lists Excel's two bubble chart subtypes.

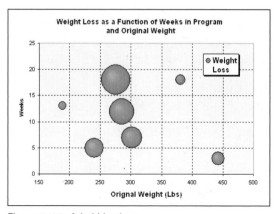

Figure 2-22: A bubble chart

TABLE 2-11 BUBBLE CHART SUBTYPES

Chart Type	Subtype
Bubble chart	Standard bubble chart
Bubble with 3-D effect	Bubble chart with 3-D bubbles

Stock charts

Stock charts are most useful for displaying stock market information. These charts require three to five data series, depending on the subtype.

Table 2-12 lists Excel's four stock chart subtypes.

TABLE 2-12 STOCK CHART SUBTYPES

Chart Type	Subtype
High-low-close	Displays the stock's high, low, and closing prices. Requires three data series.
Open-high-low-close	Displays the stock's opening, high, low, and closing prices. Requires four data series.

Continued

TABLE **2-12** STOCK CHART SUBTYPES *(Continued)*

Chart Type	Subtype
Volume-high-low-close	Displays the stock's volume and high, low, and closing prices. Requires four data series.
Volume-open-high-low-close	Displays the stock's volume and open, high, low, and closing prices. Requires five data series.

Figure 2-23 shows an example of each of the four stock chart types. The two charts on the bottom display the trade volume and use two value axes. The daily volume, represented by columns, uses the axis on the left. The "up-bars," sometimes referred to as candlesticks, depict the difference between the opening and closing price. A black up-bar indicates that the closing price was lower than the opening price.

A stock market chart can display any number of data points. Figure 2-24, for example, shows three years of data for a company. This chart plots all five variables: volume, open, high, low, and close. With this many data points, individual days are not discernible, but trends are easy to identify.

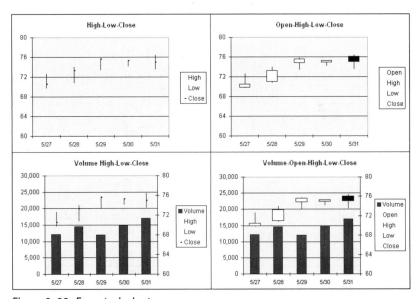

Figure 2-23: Four stock charts

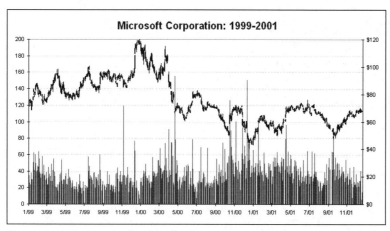

Figure 2-24: Three years (747 days) of stock market data

Keep in mind that stock charts are not limited to financial data, and this chart type can be used for a variety of other purposes. Figure 2-25 shows an example of daily temperature data displayed in a stock chart.

Cylinder, cone, and pyramid charts

These three chart types are essentially the same — except for the shapes that are used. You can use these charts in place of a 3-D bar or column chart.

Figure 2-26 shows an example of a simple pyramid chart and a cylinder chart.

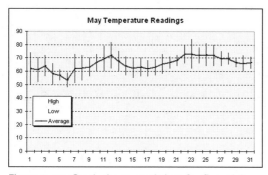

Figure 2-25: Stock charts aren't just for financial information.

Each of these chart types has seven subtypes, which are described in Table 2-13.

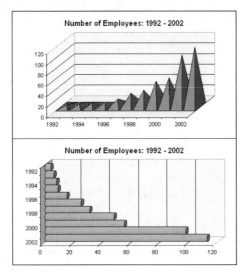

Figure 2-26: A pyramid chart and a cylinder chart

TABLE **2-13** CYLINDER, CONE, AND PYRAMID CHART SUBTYPES

Chart Type	Subtype
Clustered column	Standard column chart
Stacked column	Column chart with data series stacked
100% stacked column	Column chart with data series stacked and expressed as percentages
Clustered bar	Standard bar chart
Stacked bar	Bar chart with data series stacked
100% stacked bar	Bar chart with data series stacked and expressed as percentages
3-D column	A true 3-D column chart with a third axis

Custom Chart Types

The preceding sections cover Excel's standard chart types. This section discusses Excel's custom chart types, sometimes known as user-defined chart types.

About custom chart types

It's important to understand that the custom chart types are actually standard charts that have been customized in various ways. They are provided as a quick way to generate a customized chart.

Table 2-14 lists the custom chart types, including a brief description of how each type has been customized.

TABLE 2-14 EXCEL'S CUSTOM CHART TYPES

Chart Type	How it Has Been Customized
Area blocks	A rotated 3-D area chart, with two of the axes removed
B&W area	An area chart that uses black and white patterns rather than color
B&W column	A 3-D clustered column chart (with a data table) that uses black and white patterns
B&W line — timescale	An area chart that uses black and white gradient fill
B&W pie	A pie chart that uses black and white patterns rather than color
Blue pie	A pie chart with all slices exploded, data labels, and a gradient background
Colored lines	A line chart with brightly colored lines and gridlines on a black background
Column — area	A combination chart that combines a column chart and an area chart
Columns with depth	A 3-D column chart with added depth to the columns
Cones	A cone chart, rotated so that it is viewed from above
Floating bars	A bar chart in which one series has been made invisible
Line — column	A combination chart that combines a line chart and a column chart
Line — column on two axes	A combination chart that combines a line chart and a column chart and uses two value axes
Lines on two axes	A line chart that uses two value axes

Continued

TABLE 2-14 EXCEL'S CUSTOM CHART TYPES *(Continued)*

Chart Type	How it Has Been Customized
Logarithmic	A line chart that uses a logarithmic scale on the value axis
Outdoor bars	A bar chart with fill patterns that resemble wood, with a green background
Pie explosion	A 3-D pie chart with all slices exploded, on a dark background
Smooth lines	A line chart with smoothed lines
Stack of colors	A stacked-column chart, with a line connecting the top of each column
Tubes	A stacked-bar chart with gradient fill to simulate cylindrical bars

Several of the custom chart types are combination charts. A combination chart combines two different chart types, such as a column chart and a line chart. In such a case, each series is assigned its own chart type. A combination chart requires that the chart types use the same category axis, but they may use different value axes. Also, 3-D charts cannot be combined with another chart type.

Creating your own custom chart types

This section presents a hand-on example that demonstrates how to create your own custom chart type. After it's created, you can select it using the Chart Wizard, and your custom formatting will be applied instantly.

You can create as many custom chart types as you like. And you can share them with your co-workers simply by making a copy of your xlusrgal.xls file (see the sidebar, "Custom Chart Types: Behind the Scenes").

Figure 2-27 shows a worksheet with the results of a customer-satisfaction survey. The goal of this exercise is to create a custom chart type that will be used to plot the results of each survey item.

STEP 1: CREATE A CHART

The first step is to create a chart. Every chart must have some data, so I use the first survey item for the initial chart.

1. Select Range A1:F2.

2. Click the Chart Wizard button.

3. Choose Bar as the Chart type and Clustered Bar as the subtype.

4. Click Next.

5. The data series is satisfactory, so click Next.

6. Select the Titles tab. Because the chart has only one series, the Chart title defaults to the series name. Replace the chart title with *Annual Customer Survey Results*. You'll see the reason for this later.

7. Click the Legend tab and choose Top for the Placement position.

8. Click the Data Labels tab and choose the Show Value option.

9. Click Finish to create the embedded chart.

At this point, the chart resembles Figure 2-28.

	A	B	C	D	E	F
	Item	Strongly Agree	Agree	Neutral	Disagree	Strongly Disagree
2	Store locations are convenient	46%	24%	16%	13%	1%
3	Store hours are convenient	15%	13%	35%	30%	7%
4	Stores are well-maintained	14%	7%	24%	37%	18%
5	You are easy to reach by phone	9%	25%	24%	17%	25%
6	I like your web site	19%	21%	5%	12%	43%
7	Employees are friendly	25%	19%	18%	12%	26%
8	Employees are helpful	5%	13%	28%	35%	19%
9	Employee are knowledgeable	40%	20%	22%	12%	6%
10	Pricing is competitive	27%	27%	15%	20%	11%
11	You have a good selection of products	15%	27%	17%	29%	12%
12	I like your TV ads	3%	25%	29%	21%	22%
13	You sell quality products	29%	36%	12%	17%	6%
14	Overall, I am satisfied	20%	22%	13%	33%	12%
15	I would recommend your company	24%	33%	16%	17%	10%

Figure 2-27: This example creates a custom chart type for the data pictured here.

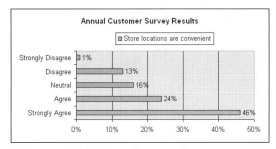

Figure 2-28: This chart will eventually serve as the basis for a custom chart type.

STEP 2: FORMAT THE CHART

The next step is to provide some formatting and customizations. I start with the chart title, which will be displayed in the bottom right corner of the chart (the legend will effectively serve as the title).

1. Double-click the chart's title to display the Format Chart Title dialog box.

2. Choose the Font tab and turn off the Auto scale option. Set the font to 10-point Arial, Italic.

3. Drag the title to the lower-right corner of the chart.

Notice that the font Auto scale option is turned off for all items in this chart. This ensures that charts created in this format will all use the same font size, regardless of the size of the chart.

Next, format the legend.

1. Double-click the chart's legend to display the Format Legend dialog box.

2. Choose the Patterns tab and set the Border to None and the Area to None.

3. Select the Font tab and turn off the Auto scale option. Set the font to 14-point Arial, Bold.

4. Select the Placement tab and choose the Top option.

The following steps make some adjustments to the Plot Area.

1. Select the Plot Area and resize it so that it fills the gap left by the legend. You may also need to adjust the height so that the chart title (in the bottom right corner) does not interfere with the axis labels.

2. Double-click the chart's plot area to display the Format Plot Area dialog box.

3. In the Patterns tab, set the color to light yellow.

At this point, the chart should resemble Figure 2-29.

More formatting is required. Let's do the axes next.

1. Double-click the horizontal value axis to display the Format Axis dialog box.

2. Select the Scale tab and set the Maximum to 0.6. Doing so overrides automatic scaling and ensures that all charts created from the custom chart type use the same scale.

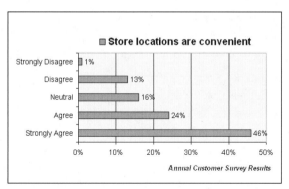

Figure 2-29: The chart, after some formatting

3. Select the Font tab and uncheck the Auto scale option. Set the font to 9-point Arial, Bold.

4. Click OK.

5. Double-click the vertical category axis to display the Format Axis dialog box.

6. Select the Patterns tab and set the Major tick mark type to None.

7. Click the Scale tab and add a checkmark to these two check boxes: Categories in Reverse Order and Value (Y) Axis Crosses at Maximum Category. These modifications cause *Strongly Agree* to appear at the top of the category list and *Strongly Disagree* to appear at the bottom of the category list.

8. Click the Font tab and uncheck the Auto scale option. Set the font to 10-point Arial, Bold.

9. Close the dialog box.

Next, you can work on the bars and data labels.

1. Double-click any bar to display the Format Data Series dialog box.

2. In the Patterns tab, click the Fill Effects button. In the Fill Effects dialog box, choose the Gradient tab. Select a two-color gradient going from red to black, with a Horizontal shading style. Click OK to return to the Format Data Series dialog box.

3. Click the Options tab and change the Gap width to 30. This creates wider bars.

4. Close the Format Data Series dialog box.

5. Double-click on any of the data labels. In the Font tab of the Format Data Labels dialog box, turn off the Auto scale option and set the font to 9-point Arial, Bold.

All that remains is the Chart Area.

1. Double-click the background area of the chart to display the Format Chart Area dialog box.

2. Select the Patterns tab and click Fill Effects. In the Fill Effects dialog box, click the Texture tab and choose the first Texture choice. Close the Fill Effects dialog box to return to the Format Chart Area dialog box.

3. In the Patterns tab, choose the Shadow and Round corners option.

4. Close the dialog box and take a look at your efforts, which should resemble Figure 2-30.

At this point, you may want to do some fine-tuning of the plot area size and position to ensure that all the elements are nicely balanced.

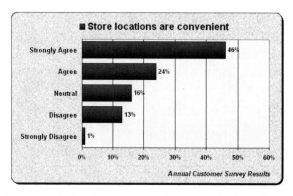

Figure 2-30: The chart, after the formatting is finished

STEP 3: ADD THE CHART TO THE CUSTOM CHART TYPE GALLERY

When you're satisfied with the look of the chart, add it to the custom chart type gallery.

1. Make sure that the chart is selected.

2. Choose Chart→Chart Type to display the Chart Type dialog box.

3. Select the Custom Types tab.

4. Choose the User-Defined option.

5. Click the Add button and you'll see the Add Custom Chart Type dialog box.

6. Enter a name and (optionally) a description for the custom chart type (see Figure 2-31).

7. Click OK and you'll see your new custom chart type listed in the Chart type list box.

8. Click OK again to close the Chart Type dialog box.

STEP 4: TEST AND REFINE

The final step is to test your creation. You should test the custom chart type with a different data series. For this example, you need to do a multiple selection.

1. Select the range A1:F1, press Ctrl, and then select A3:F3.

2. Click the Chart Wizard button.

3. Select the Custom Types tab in the Chart Wizard dialog box.

4. Choose the User-Defined option.

5. Select the Survey Results item in the Chart type list.

6. Click Finish.

Voilà! The data will be displayed in a highly customized chart that is perfect in every way. Or at least it *should* be. If the chart doesn't look right, you may need to make some additional changes to it. After doing so, you will need to go through the previous steps to add the chart to the custom gallery. If you use the same name, Excel will ask whether you want to replace the existing user-defined format. Answer in the affirmative.

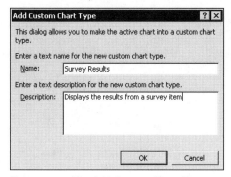

Figure 2-31: The Add Custom Chart Type
dialog box

Custom Chart Types: Behind the Scenes

You may be curious about how Excel keeps track of custom chart types. Custom chart information is stored in two files:

xl8galry.xls: Stores charts that are used for the built-in custom chart types

xlusrgal.xls: Stores user-defined custom chart types

Both of these files are standard workbooks, and you can open them to take a look. The exact location of these files will vary, but you can search your hard drive to locate them. The xlusrgal.xls does not exist until you create at least one user-defined custom chart type.

The accompanying figure shows one of the 20 Chart sheets in xl8galry.xls. Notice that the SERIES formula (displayed in the Formula bar) for the selected data series displays the data in arrays rather than as range references. This technique makes each chart self-sufficient so that it doesn't require any references to worksheets.

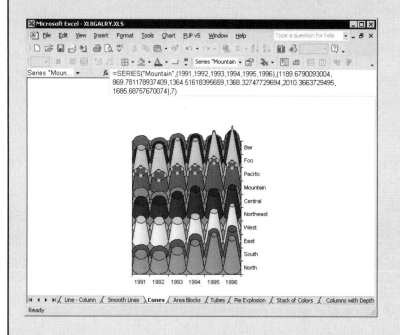

If you like, you can modify the charts in xl8galry.xls to further customize them. Before doing so, it's a good idea to make a backup copy of the file.

Chapter 3

Working with Chart Series

EVERY CHART CONSISTS OF AT least one series, and the data used in that series is (normally) stored in a worksheet. This chapter provides an in-depth discussion of data series for charts and presents lots of tips to help you modify the data used in your charts.

Specifying the Data for Your Chart

When you create a chart, you almost always start by selecting the worksheet data to be plotted. Normally, you select the numeric data as well as the category labels and series names, if they exist.

If you use the Chart Wizard to create your chart, you can then select a chart type and get a preview of how the selected data appears using the specified chart type. When creating a chart, a key consideration is the orientation of your data: by rows or by columns. In other words, is the data for each series in a single row or in a single column?

Excel attempts to guess the data orientation by applying a simple rule: If the data rows outnumber the data columns, then each series is assumed to occupy a column. If the data columns outnumber the data rows, then each series is assumed to occupy a row. In other words, Excel always defaults to a chart that has more categories than series.

Dealing with Numeric Category Labels

It's not uncommon to have category labels that consist of numbers. For example, you may create a chart that shows sales by year, and the years are numeric values. If your category labels include a heading, Excel will (incorrectly) interpret the category labels as a data series. The following figure shows an example.

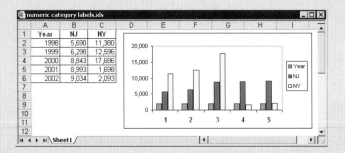

You can, of course, use the Source Data dialog box to fix the chart. But a more efficient solution is to make a simple change before you create the chart: Remove the header text above the category labels! The following figure shows the chart that was created when the heading was removed from the category label column.

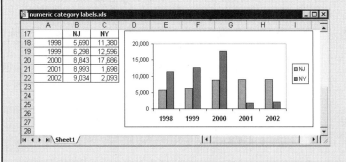

It's a simple matter to override Excel's orientation guess in Step 2 of the Chart Wizard. Or, you can change the orientation after the chart is created. To do so:

1. Activate the chart.

2. Choose Chart→Source Data.

3. In the Source Data dialog box, select the Data Range tab.

4. Choose the Rows or Columns option. You'll be able to get a preview of the chart for each orientation.

Or, if the Chart toolbar is displayed, you can simply click the By Row or By Value button to quickly change the chart's data orientation.

Your choice of orientation will determine how many series the chart has, and it will affect the appearance and (possibly) the legibility of your chart. Figure 3-1 shows two charts for the same data. The chart on the left uses three series, arranged in columns. The chart on the right uses four series, arranged in rows.

In the majority of cases, using the Chart Wizard to create a chart works perfectly well. In other situations, however, you may find it necessary to modify the ranges used by the chart. Specifically, you may want to

◆ Add a new series to the chart

◆ Delete a series from the chart

◆ Extend the range used by a series (show more data)

◆ Contract the range used by a series (show less data)

◆ Add or modify the series names

All these topics are covered in the following sections.

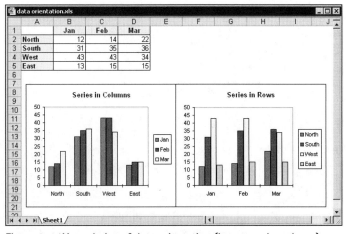

Figure 3–1: Your choice of data orientation (by row or by column) determines the number of series in the chart.

 Chart types vary in the number of series that they can use. All charts are limited to a maximum of 255 series. Other charts require a minimum number of series. For example, a high-low-close stock chart requires three series. A pie chart can use only one series.

Adding a New Series to a Chart

Excel provides several ways to add a new series to an existing chart:

♦ Select the data range for the new series and then drag it into the chart.

♦ Copy the range; then use Edit→Paste Special to paste the data into a chart.

♦ Use the Source Data dialog box.

♦ Use the Add Data dialog box.

Each of these methods is described in the sections that follow.

Actually, there is one other way to add a new series to a chart: Activate the chart, click in the Formula bar, and type a SERIES formula manually (SERIES formulas are described later in this chapter). This method offers no advantages and is very prone to errors.

Attempting to add a new series to a pie chart will have no apparent effect, because a pie chart can have only one series. The series, however, is added to the chart but will not be displayed. If you select a different chart type for the chart, the added series will then be visible.

Adding a new series using drag-and-drop

In some cases, the simplest way to add a new series to a chart is to drag it with the mouse. Start with an existing chart (it must be an embedded chart) and then:

1. Select the range that contains the data that will comprise the new series. Include the cell that contains the series name, if applicable.

2. Click a border of the selected range.

3. Drag the selected range into your chart.

This operation works much the same as moving a range of cells using drag-and-drop techniques. The difference, of course, is that the data remains in its original location.

If you find that you can't drag your data, choose Tools→Options and click the Edit tab of the Options dialog box. Make sure that the Allow Cell Drag-and-Drop option is enabled.

The drag-and-drop procedure described previously is actually equivalent to the following copy-and paste-procedure:

1. Select the range that contains the data.

2. Choose Edit→Copy.

3. Click the chart to activate it.

4. Choose Edit→Paste.

In fact, you can use these commands to add a new series to a Chart sheet.

Adding a new series using Paste Special

For more control when adding data to a chart, you can use the Paste Special command. Specifically:

1. Select the range that contains the data that will comprise the new series. Include the cell that contains the series name, if applicable.

2. Choose Edit→Copy.

3. Click the chart to activate it.

4. Choose Edit→Paste Special, which displays the Paste Special dialog box.

5. Specify your choices and click OK.

Figure 3-2 shows a new series (using data in column D) being added to a line chart.

Following are some pointers to keep in mind when you add a new series using the Paste Special dialog box:

◆ Make sure that the New Series option is selected.

◆ Excel will guess at the data orientation, but you should verify that the Rows or Columns option is guessed correctly.

◆ If the range you copied included a cell with the series name, ensure that the Series Names in First Row option is selected.

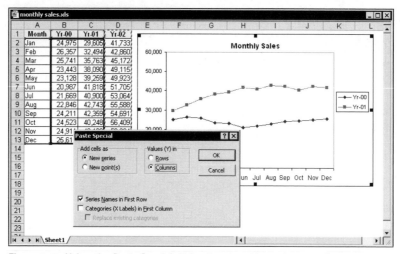

Figure 3-2: Using the Paste Special dialog box to add a series to a chart

♦ If the first column of your range selection included category labels, make sure that the Categories (X Labels) in First Column check box is selected.

♦ If you want to replace the existing category labels, place a checkmark in the Replace existing categories check box.

Adding a new series using the Source Data dialog box

The Source Data dialog box provides another way to add a new series to a chart, as follows:

1. Click the chart to activate it.

2. Choose Chart→Source Data to display the Source Data dialog box.

3. Select the Series tab.

4. Click the Add button and then use the range selector controls to specify the cell for the Name (optional), Values, and Category axis labels (optional). See Figure 3-3.

5. Click OK to close the dialog box, or click Add to add another series to the chart.

Adding a new series using the Add Data dialog box

Excel provides yet another way to add a new series: the Add Data dialog box.

1. Click the chart to activate it.

2. Choose Chart→Add Data to display the Add Data dialog box (see Figure 3-4).

3. Use the range selector box to specify the range for the new data series.

4. Click OK.

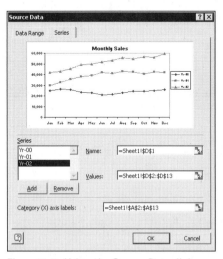

Figure 3-3: Using the Source Data dialog box to add a series to a chart

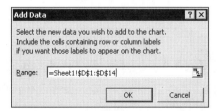

Figure 3-4: The Add Data dialog box

Deleting a Chart Series

The easiest way to delete a series from a chart is to use the keyboard: Select the series and press Del.

Deleting the only series in a chart does not delete the chart. Rather, it gives you an empty chart. If you'd like to delete this empty chart, just press Del a second time.

You can also use the series tab of the Source Data dialog box to delete a series. Just select the series name in the Series list box and click the Remove button. You can also delete a series via the chart's legend. Select the legend, click the legend key for the series (the marker next to the legend caption), and press Delete.

Modifying the Data Range for a Chart Series

After you've created a chart, you may want to modify the data ranges used by the chart. For example, you may need to expand the range to include new data. Or, you may wish to substitute an entirely different range. Excel offers a number of ways to perform these operations:

◆ Drag the range highlights

◆ Use the Source Data dialog box

◆ Edit the SERIES formula

Each of these techniques is described in the sections that follow.

Chapter 7 discusses a number of techniques that enable you to set up a "dynamic" range such that the chart adjusts automatically when you add new data.

Using range highlighting to change series data

When you click a chart series, Excel highlights the worksheet ranges used in that series. This range highlighting consists of one or more colored outlines around a range of cells. Figure 3-5 shows an example in which the chart series (Region 1) is selected. Excel highlights the following ranges: C2 (the series name), B3:B8 (the category labels), and C3:C8 (the values).

Each of the highlighted ranges contains a small "handle" at each corner. You can perform two operations with the highlighted data:

◆ **Expand or contract the data range:** Click one of the handles and drag it to expand the outlined range (specify more data) or contract the data range (specify less data). When you click a handle, the mouse pointer changes to a double arrow.

◆ **Specify an entirely different data range.** Click one of the borders of the highlight and then drag it to highlight a different range.

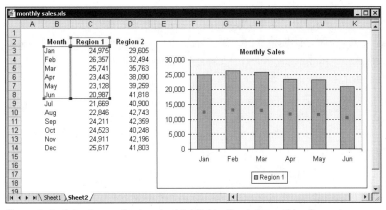

Figure 3-5: Selecting a chart series highlights the data used by the series.

Figure 3-6 shows the chart after the data range has been changed. In this case, the highlight around cell C2 was dragged to cell D2, and the highlight around C3:C8 was dragged to D3:D8 and then expanded to include D3:D14. Notice that the range for the category labels (A3:A8) has not been modified. To finish the job, that range needs to be expanded to A3:A14.

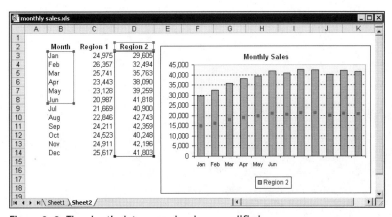

Figure 3-6: The chart's data range has been modified.

A surface chart is a special case. It is not possible to select an individual series in a surface chart. But when you select the plot area of a surface chart, Excel highlights all the data used in the chart. You can then use the range highlighting to change the ranges used in the chart.

Modifying chart source data by using the range highlights is probably the simplest method. Note, however, that this technique works only with embedded charts (not with Chart sheets). In addition, it does not work when the chart's data is on a worksheet other than the sheet that contains the embedded chart.

Using the Source Data dialog box to change series data

Another method of modifying a series data range is to use the Source Data dialog box. Click the chart series to select it; then choose Chart→Source Data. The Source Data dialog box has two tabs: Data Range and Series. Figure 3-7 shows the Series tab.

The dialog box displays the name of each chart series in the Series list box. As noted earlier in this chapter, you can use the Add button to add a new series to your chart, or use the Remove button to delete the series that is selected in the Series list box.

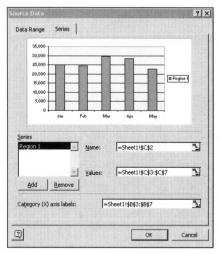

Figure 3-7: The Series tab of the Source Data dialog box

The range selector boxes display the range addresses associated with the series that is selected in the list box. You can use these controls to modify the ranges used for the series name, the values, and the category labels. You can change the range either by dragging in the worksheet or by editing the range reference directly. In either case, the dialog box displays a live preview of the chart.

The Source Data dialog box will vary somewhat, depending on the chart type. The Source Data dialog box for a bubble chart, for example, has four range selector controls: Name, X Values, Y Values, and Sizes (for the range that contains the size data for the bubbles).

Editing the SERIES formula to change series data

Every chart series has its own SERIES formula. When you select a data series in a chart, its SERIES formula appears in the formula bar. The formula bar, in Figure 3-8, shows one of two SERIES formulas for a chart that displays two data series.

Although a SERIES formula is displayed in the formula bar, it is not a "real" formula. In other words, you can't put this formula into a cell, and you can't use worksheet functions within the SERIES formula. You can, however, edit the arguments in the SERIES formula to change the ranges used by the series. To edit the SERIES formula, just click in the formula bar and use standard editing techniques. Refer to the sidebar "SERIES Formula Syntax" to learn about the various arguments for a SERIES formula.

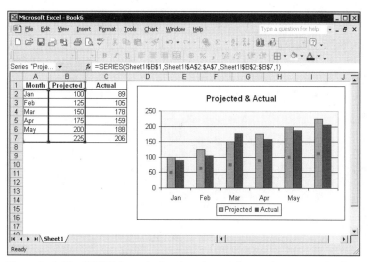

Figure 3-8: The SERIES formula for the selected data series appears in the formula bar.

When you modify a series data range using either of the techniques discussed previously in this section, the SERIES formula is also modified. In fact, those techniques are simply easy ways of editing the SERIES formula.

SERIES Formula Syntax

A SERIES formula has the following syntax:

```
=SERIES(series_name, category_labels, values, order, sizes)
```

The arguments you can use in the SERIES formula include:

◆ *series_name*: (Optional) A reference to the cell that contains the series name used in the legend. If the chart has only one series, the name argument is used as the title. This argument can also consist of text, in quotation marks. If omitted, Excel creates a default series name (for example, Series 1).

◆ *category_labels*: (Optional) A reference to the range that contains the labels for the category axis. If omitted, Excel uses consecutive integers beginning with 1. For XY charts, this argument specifies the X values. A noncontiguous range reference is also valid (the ranges addresses are separated by a comma and enclosed in parentheses. The argument may also consist of an array of comma-separated values (or text in quotation marks) enclosed in curly brackets.

◆ *values*: (Required) A reference to the range that contains the values for the series. For XY charts, this argument specifies the Y values. A noncontiguous range reference is also valid (the ranges addresses are separated by a comma and enclosed in parentheses. The argument may also consist of an array of comma-separated values enclosed in curly brackets.

◆ *order*: (Required) An integer that specifies the plotting order of the series. This argument is relevant only if the chart has more than one series. Using a reference to a cell is not allowed.

◆ *sizes*: (Only for bubble charts) A reference to the range that contains the values for the size of the bubbles in a bubble chart. A noncontiguous range reference is also valid (the ranges addresses are separated by a comma and enclosed in parentheses. The argument may also consist of an array of values enclosed in brackets.

Following is an example of a SERIES formula.

```
=SERIES(Sheet1!$B$1,Sheet1!$A$2:$A$7,Sheet1!$B$2:$B$7,1)
```

This SERIES formula:

◆ Specifies that cell B1 (on Sheet1) contains the series name

◆ Specifies that the category labels are in A2:A7 on Sheet1

◆ Specifies that the data values are in B2:B7, also on Sheet1

◆ Specifies that the series will be plotted first on the chart (the final
argument is 1)

Notice that range references in a SERIES formula always include the worksheet
name, and the range references are always absolute references. An absolute reference, as you may know, uses a dollar sign before the row and column part of the
reference. If you edit a SERIES formula and remove the sheet name or make the cell
references relative, Excel will override these changes.

Understanding Series Names

Every chart series has a name, which is displayed in the chart's legend. If you don't
explicitly provide a name for a series, it will have a default name such as *Series1*,
Series2, and so on.

The easiest way to name a series is to do so when you create the chart. Typically,
a series name is contained in a cell adjacent to the series data. For example, if your
data is arranged in columns, the column headers usually contain the series names.
If you select the series names along with the chart data, those names will be applied
automatically.

Figure 3-9 shows a chart with three series. The series names, which are stored
in B3:D3, are *Main, N. Cnty*, and *Westside*. The SERIES formula for the first data
series is

```
=SERIES(Sheet1!$B$3,Sheet1!$A$4:$A$8,Sheet1!$B$4:$B$8,1)
```

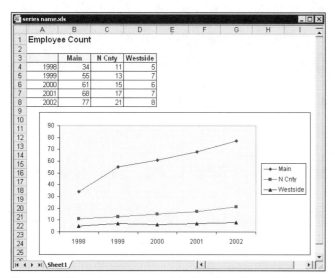

Figure 3-9: The series names are picked up from the worksheet.

Note that the first argument for this SERIES formula is a reference to the cell that contains the series name.

Changing a series name

The series name is the text that appears in a chart's legend. In some cases, you may prefer the chart to display a name other than the text that's in the worksheet. It's a simple matter to change the name of a series:

1. Activate the chart.

2. Choose Chart→Source Data.

3. In the Source Data dialog box, select the Series tab.

4. In the Series list box, select the series that you want to modify.

5. Type the new name in the Name box.

Normally, the Name box contains a cell reference. But you can override this and enter any text.

 After you enter text into the Name box, you can select another series to rename. If you go back to a series that you've already renamed, you'll find that Excel has converted your text into a formula — an equal sign, followed by the text you entered, in quotation marks.

Figure 3-10 shows the previous chart, after changing the series names. The first argument in each of the SERIES formulas no longer displays a cell reference. It now contains the literal text. For example, the SERIES formula for the first series is

```
=SERIES("Branch-1",Sheet1!$A$4:$A$8,Sheet1!$B$4:$B$8,1)
```

If you need to change the name of a series, you may find it easier to edit the SERIES formula directly.

Deleting a series name

To delete a series name, use the Source Data dialog box as described previously. Select the series name to delete; then, highlight the range reference (or text) in the Name box and press Del.

Alternatively, you can edit the SERIES formula and remove the first argument. Here's an example of a SERIES formula for a series with no specified name (it will use the default name):

```
=SERIES(,Sheet2!$A$2:$A$6,Sheet2!$B$2:$B$6,1)
```

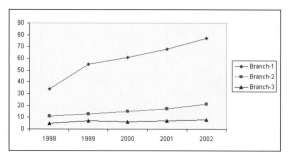

Figure 3-10: The series names have been changed; the new names are shown in the legend.

 When you remove the first argument in a SERIES formula, make sure that you do not delete the comma that follows the first argument. The comma is required as a placeholder to indicate the missing argument.

To create a series with no name, use a set of empty quotation marks for the first argument in the SERIES formula.

Adjusting the Series Plot Order

Every chart series has a plot order parameter. When you access the Series tab in the Source Data dialog box, the Series list box displays the chart series in the order in which they are plotted. In addition, a chart's legend displays the series names in the order in which they are plotted.

To change the plot order, access the Format Data Series dialog box for any series in the chart and then select the Series order tab. Select a series in the list box; then use the Move Up and Move Down buttons to adjust its position.

Alternatively, you can edit the SERIES formulas—specifically, the fourth parameter in the SERIES formulas. See the "SERIES Formula Syntax" sidebar for more information about SERIES formulas.

For some charts, the plot order is not important. For others, however, you may want to change the order in which the series are plotted. Figure 3-11 shows a stacked-column chart generated from the data in A1:E1. Notice that the columns are stacked, beginning with the first data series (Region 1) on the bottom. You may prefer to stack the columns in the order in which the data appears. To do so, you need to change the plot order.

After changing the plot order for the other SERIES formula, the chart now appears as in Figure 3-12.

Figure 3-13 shows another example. This area chart displays three data series in a 3-D Column Chart. The columns for the Laptops and PDA series are obscured by the columns for the Desktops series. One solution is to edit the plot order parameter of the SERIES formulas, as described previously. But in this case, there's a more direct solution:

1. Double-click the series axis (the "depth" axis, which contains the series names) to display the Format Axis dialog box.

2. Select the Scale tab in the Format Axis dialog box.

3. Place a checkmark next to Series in reverse order.

4. Click OK.

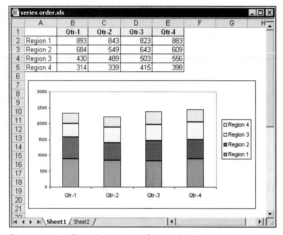

Figure 3-11: The plot order of this chart does not correspond to the order of the data.

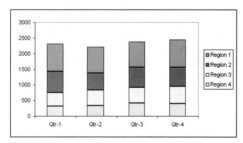

Figure 3-12: After changing the plot order, the stacked columns correspond to the order of the data.

The result, shown in Figure 3-14, is a much more legible chart. Note that the option to plot the series in reverse order does not actually change the plot order for the SERIES formula. The SERIES formulas remain the same, but Excel displays them in reverse order on the series axis. Consequently, the order of the entries in the legend remains the same.

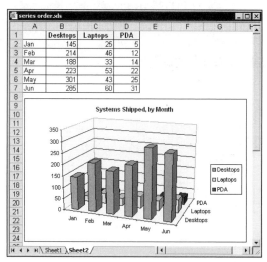

Figure 3-13: Some of the data points are obscured.

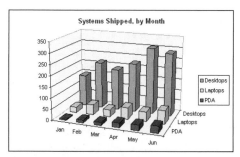

Figure 3-14: After I've reversed the series axis,
the chart is more legible.

Charting a Noncontiguous Range

Most of the time, a chart series consists of a contiguous range of cells. But Excel does allow you to plot data that is not in a contiguous range. Figure 3-15 shows an example of a noncontiguous series. This chart displays monthly data for the first and fourth quarter. The data in this single series is contained in rows 2:4 and 11:13.

The SERIES formula for this series is

```
=SERIES(,(Sheet1!$A$2:$A$4,Sheet1!$A$11:$A$13),(Sheet1!$B$2:$B$4,Sheet1!$B$11:$B
$13),1)
```

The first argument is omitted, so Excel uses the default series name. The second argument specifies six cells in column A as the category labels. The third argument specifies six corresponding cells in column B as the data values. Note that the range arguments for the noncontiguous ranges are displayed in parentheses, and each subrange is separated by a comma.

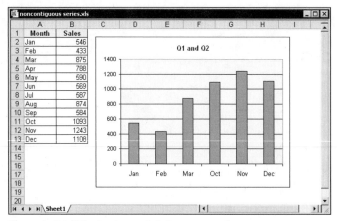

Figure 3-15: This chart uses data in a noncontiguous range.

Using Series on Different Sheets

Typically, data to be used in a chart resides on a single sheet. Excel, however, does allow a chart to use series from any number of worksheets, and the worksheets need not even be in the same workbook.

Although a chart series can refer to data in other worksheets, the data for each series must reside on a single sheet.

Normally, you select all the data for a chart and then use the Chart Wizard to create the chart. But if your chart uses data on different worksheets, you need to use several steps because the Chart Wizard cannot be activated when a multisheet selection is made. You need to create the chart using data from a single sheet and then add new series after the chart is made (see "Adding a New Series to a Chart," earlier in the chapter). Alternatively, you can select ranges from another worksheet in Step 2 of the Chart Wizard dialog box (Series tab).

Figure 3-16 shows a chart that uses data from two other worksheets.

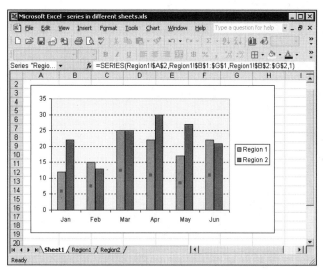

Figure 3-16: This chart uses data from two worksheets.

The SERIES formulas for this chart are

```
=SERIES(Region1!$A$2,Region1!$B$1:$G$1,Region1!$B$2:$G$2,1)
=SERIES(Region2!$A$2,,Region2!$B$2:$G$2,2)
```

TIP Another way to handle data on different worksheets is to create a summary range on a single worksheet. This summary range consists of simple formulas that refer to the data on other sheets. Then, you can create a chart from the summary range.

Handling Missing Data

Sometimes, data that you use in a chart may lack one or more data points. Excel offers several ways to handle the missing data. You can

- ◆ Ignore the missing data. Plotted data series will have a gap.

- ◆ Treat the missing data as zero values.

- ◆ Interpolate the missing data (for line and XY charts only).

For some reason, Excel makes these options rather difficult to locate. You don't specify these options in the Format Data Series dialog box or even in the Chart Options dialog box. In fact, you don't use the Chart menu at all. Rather, you must:

1. Select your chart.

2. Choose Tools→Options to display the Options dialog box.

3. Click the Chart tab (see Figure 3-17).

4. Choose the appropriate option.

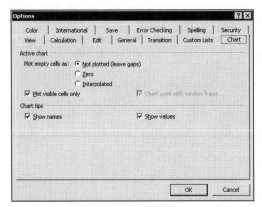

Figure 3-17: Use the Chart tab of the Options dialog box to specify how to handle missing data.

The setting that you choose applies only to the active chart and applies to all series in the chart. In other words, you can't specify a different missing data option for different series in the same chart. If a chart is not active when you open the Options dialog box, the missing data options are not available.

It's important to understand that these settings are applicable only for line charts, XY charts, and radar charts. For all other chart types, missing data is simply not plotted.

Figure 3-18 shows three charts that depict the three missing data options. The chart shows temperature readings at one-hour intervals, and three data points are missing. The "correct" missing data option depends on the message that you want to convey. In the top chart, the missing data is obvious because of the gaps in the line. In the middle chart, the missing data is shown as zero – which is clearly misleading. In the bottom chart, the missing data is interpolated. Because of the time-based and relatively "smooth" nature of the data, interpolating the missing data may be an appropriate choice.

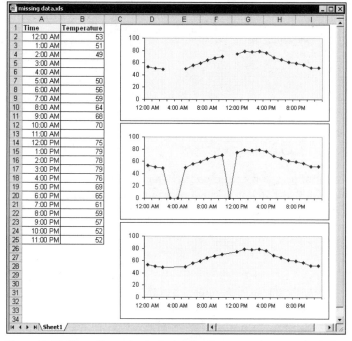

Figure 3-18: These three charts depict the three ways to present missing data in a chart.

 You can force Excel to interpolate values by placing =NA() in the appropriate cells. Those cell values will be interpolated, regardless of the missing data option that is in effect for the chart.

Controlling a Data Series by Hiding Data

Usually, Excel doesn't plot data that is in a hidden row or column. You can sometimes use this to your advantage, because it's an easy way to control what data appears in the chart.

In some cases, when you're working with outlines or Autofiltering (both of which use hidden rows), you may not like the idea that hidden data is removed from your chart. To override this, activate the chart and select the Tools→Options command. In the Options dialog box, click the Chart tab and remove the checkmark from the option labeled Plot Visible Cells Only.

The Plot Visible Cells Only setting applies only to the active chart. It is not a global setting that would be applied to all charts.

Using Range Names in a SERIES Formula

As you may know, Excel allows you to provide a name to a cell or range. After defining the name, you can use it in your formulas in place of the range reference. For example, if range A1:A12 is named *Sales*, you can use the following formula to calculate the sum of those cells:

```
=SUM(Sales)
```

When you create a formula that uses a named range, Excel will automatically substitute the name. But when you create a chart that uses a named range, Excel does *not* automatically substitute the name in the SERIES formulas. You can, however, edit the range references in a SERIES formula and replace the range references with the appropriate range name.

Using named ranges in a SERIES formula offers two advantages:

♦ The SERIES formulas are easier to read.

♦ When you change the range name definition, the chart will update automatically.

Figure 3-19 shows a simple chart with a SERIES formula that does not use named ranges. The SERIES formula for this chart is

```
=SERIES(Sheet1!$B$1,Sheet1!$A$2:$A$11,Sheet1!$B$2:$B$11,1)
```

When you edit the SERIES formula and replace the range references with names, make sure that you replace only the range address and keep the sheet reference and the exclamation point that precedes the range reference. When you press Enter after making the modification, you'll find that Excel changes the reference in the SERIES formula to include the workbook name. If you don't want to edit the SERIES formula, you can use the Series tab of the Source Data dialog box to substitute the name for the range address.

Naming Cells and Ranges

Excel provides a number of ways to name cells and ranges. The two most useful methods are the following:

◆ **Name one cell or range at a time:** Start by selecting the cell or range to be named. Choose Insert→Name→Define to display the Define Name dialog box. Enter a name in the Names in workbook field, verify that the range address in the Refers To field is correct, and click OK

◆ **Name several cells or ranges at a time:** This technique requires that the names be entered into a worksheet, adjacent to the cells or ranges to be named. Start by selecting the data (including the cells that contain the names). Choose Insert→Name→Create and specify the location that contains the names. In the following figure, the names are contained in the top row of the selection.

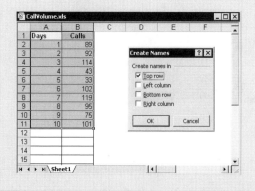

Following is the SERIES formula after it has been edited. The range A2:A11 is named *Days*, and range B2:B11 is named *Calls*. Notice that the SERIES formula now includes the workbook name, and the sheet name is no longer included:

```
=SERIES(Sheet1!$B$1,CallVolume.xls!Days,CallVolume.xls!Calls,1)
```

After inserting the names into the SERIES formula, you can then use the Insert→ Name→Define command to redefine *Days* and *Calls* to include additional rows. The chart then displays the data in the newly defined ranges (see Figure 3-20); no chart editing is necessary.

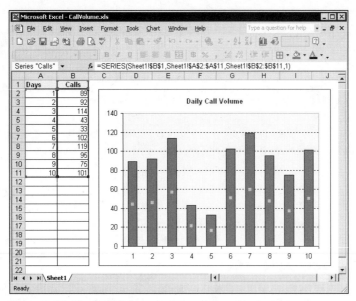

Figure 3-19: The SERIES formula does not use named ranges.

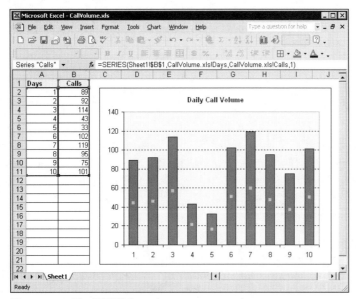

Figure 3-20: The SERIES formula uses two named ranges.

If you delete a name that is used in a chart SERIES formula, the chart will *not* revert back to the range address. The (now) invalid names will remain in the SERIES formula and the chart will not display properly. You'll need to reestablish the ranges used by the chart or recreate the chart.

As I noted previously, a SERIES formula cannot use worksheet functions. You *can*, however, create named formulas (which use functions) and use these named formulas in your SERIES formula. As you see in Chapter 7, this technique enables you to create "dynamic" chart series that update automatically when new data is entered.

Unlinking a Chart Series from Its Data Range

Normally, an Excel chart uses data stored in a range. Change the data in the range, and the chart updates automatically. In some cases, you may want to "unlink" the chart from its data ranges and produce a *static chart* — a chart that never changes. For example, if you plot data generated by various what-if scenarios, you may want to save a chart that represents some baseline so that you can compare it with other scenarios. There are two ways to create such a chart:

◆ Convert the chart to a picture.

◆ Convert the range references to arrays.

Converting a chart to a picture

To convert a chart to a static picture:

1. Create the chart as usual and make any necessary modifications.

2. Click the chart to activate it.

3. Press the Shift key and choose Edit→Copy Picture. The Copy Picture dialog box offers several options. For best results, choose As Shown When Printed for the Appearance option, and As Shown On Screen for the Size option.

4. Click any cell to unselect the chart.

5. Choose Edit→Paste.

The result is a picture of the original chart. This picture can be edited as a picture, but not as a chart. In other words, you cannot longer modify properties such as chart type, data labels, and so on.

EDITING PICTURES

Although a chart converted to a picture cannot be edited as a chart, it can be edited as a picture. After creating a picture of your chart, you can right-click the picture and choose Grouping→Ungroup. You'll get a message asking whether you want to convert the picture to a Microsoft Office drawing object. If you reply Yes, you can then format individual elements within the picture.

For even more control, right-click and choose Grouping→Ungroup a *second* time. This will break the picture into its component parts. You can then move and format each picture element, and even create some "impossible" charts. Figure 3-21 shows an example of a picture that has been ungrouped and modified (the columns have been tilted). Be aware that the second ungrouping can create a *lot* of objects! The picture in the figure, for example, contains 48 component objects.

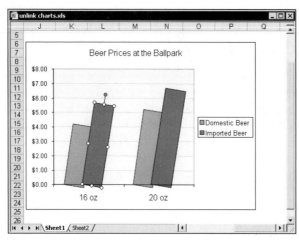

Figure 3-21: This chart has been converted to a picture.

 TIP After the picture is broken up into its parts, you can always put the parts back together into a single object. Right-click any element and choose Grouping→Regroup.

PROS AND CONS

Converting a chart to a picture is useful if you want to save a "snapshot" of a particular chart. The primary disadvantage is that it no longer functions as a chart. It will no longer update itself when the original source data is changed. And, as mentioned previously, you can no longer edit any of the normal chart elements — although they can be edited as picture objects.

Converting range reference to arrays

The other way to unlink a chart from its data is to convert the SERIES formula range references to arrays. Figure 3-22 shows an example of a pie chart that does not use data stored in a worksheet. Notice that the chart's data appears in the SERIES formula, which is

```
=SERIES(,{"Work","Sleep","Drive","Eat","Other"},{9,7,2,1,5},1)
```

The first argument, the series name, is omitted. The second argument consists of an array of five text strings. Notice that each array element appears in quotation marks and is separated by a comma. The array is enclosed in brackets. The chart's data is stored as another array (the third argument).

This chart was originally created by using data stored in a range. Then, the SERIES formula was "de-linked" from the range and the original data was deleted. The result is a chart that does not rely on data stored in a range.

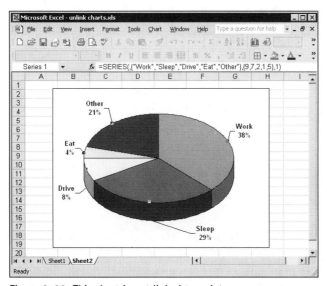

Figure 3-22: This chart is not linked to a data range.

To convert the range references in a SERIES formula to arrays:

1. Create the chart as usual.

2. Click the chart series (the SERIES formula will appear in the formula bar).

3. Click the formula bar.

4. Press F9.

5. Press Enter, and the range references will be converted to arrays.

Repeat this procedure for each series in the chart. This technique (as opposed to creating a picture) enables you to continue to edit the chart. Note that you can also convert just a single argument to an array. Highlight the argument in the SERIES formula and press F9.

 Excel imposes a 1,024-character limit to the length of a SERIES formula, so this technique will not work if a chart series contains a large number of values or category labels.

Using Combination Charts

A combination chart is a chart that combines two or more different chart types — for example, a column chart and a line chart.

Creating combination charts

Perhaps the most common way (but not the best way) to create a combination chart is to use the Chart Wizard and select one of the custom chart types. Excel offers a choice of only three combination charts:

- ◆ Column – area
- ◆ Line – column
- ◆ Line – column on two axes

Many users don't realize that Excel can create many other types of combination charts. The trick is to create a standard chart first and then modify the chart type setting for one or more of the series: Click the series, choose Chart→Chart Type, and then select the chart type for that series. When you need to create a combination chart, there is really no reason to start with one of Excel's custom chart types — unless it happens to be exactly what you're looking for.

 It's important to understand that the Chart→Chart Type command works differently, depending on what is selected when you issue the command. If a chart series is selected, this command changes the chart type for *that series only*. If any other chart element is selected, this command changes the chart type for the *entire chart*.

When you start experimenting with combination charts, you'll quickly discover that all 3-D charts are off limits for combination charts. You'll also find that some combinations are of limited value. For example, it's unlikely that anyone would need to create a chart that combines a radar chart and a line chart.

The combination chart shown in Figure 3-23 is an extreme example. It combines five chart types: area, column, line, pie, and XY. I resisted the urge to toss in a series formatted as a radar chart. This is for demonstration purposes only and is certainly *not* an example of an effective chart!

 A combination chart uses a single Plot Area. Therefore, it's not possible to create, say, a combination chart that displays three pie charts.

Working with multiple axes

A chart can use zero, two, three, or four axes, and any or all of them can be hidden if desired.

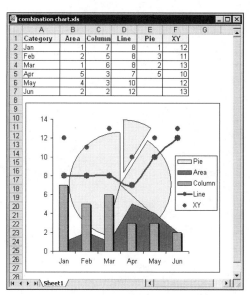

Figure 3-23: This combination chart is comprised of five chart types.

Pie charts and doughnut charts have no axes. Common chart types, such as a standard column or line chart, use a single category axis and a single value axis. If your chart has at least two series — and it's not a 3-D chart — you can create a secondary value axis. Each series is associated with either the primary or the secondary value axis. Why use two value axes? Two value axes are most often used when the data being plotted varies drastically in scale.

CREATING A SECONDARY VALUE AXIS

Figure 3-24 shows a line chart with two data series: Income and Profit Margin. Compared to the Income value, the Profit Margin numbers are so small that they barely show up in the chart. This is a good candidate for a secondary value axis.

To add a secondary value axis:

1. Select the Profit Margin series in the chart.

2. Select Format→Selected Data Series and click the Axis tab in the Format Data Series dialog box.

3. Choose the Secondary axis option.

A new value axis is added to the right side of the chart, and the Profit Margin series uses that value axis (see Figure 3-25).

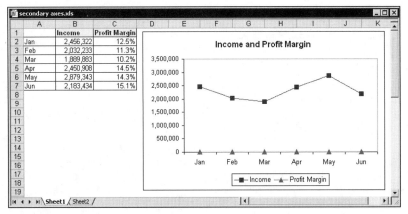

Figure 3-24: The values in the Profit Margin series are so small that they aren't visible in the chart.

CREATING A CHART WITH FOUR AXES

Very few situations warrant a chart with four axes. The problem, of course, is that using four axes almost always causes the chart to be difficult to understand. An exception is XY charts. Figure 3-26 shows an XY chart that has two series, and the series vary quite a bit in magnitude on both dimensions. If the objective is to compare the shape of the lines, this chart does not do a very good job because most of the chart consists of white space. Using four axes might solve the problem.

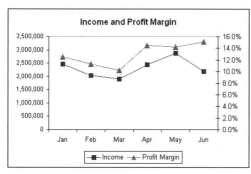

Figure 3-25: Using a secondary value axis for the
Profit Margin series

Creating a chart with four axes is a bit tricky. To add two new value axes for this
XY chart:

1. Select the 2002 series.

2. Select Format→Selected Data Series and click the Axis tab in the Format
   Data Series dialog box.

3. Choose the Secondary axis option. At this point, each of the series has its
   own Y value axis (one on the left, one on the right) but they share a common X value axis.

4. Access the Chart Options dialog box and select the Axes tab. This is where
   you have the option to add a secondary value axis. This option is available only if you've specified a secondary value axis for a series.

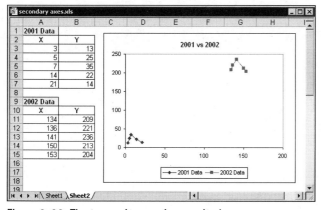

Figure 3-26: The two series vary in magnitude.

Figure 3-27 shows the result. The 2001 series uses the left and bottom axes, and the 2002 series uses the right and top axes. The scales for each axis can be adjusted separately.

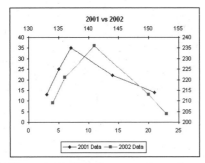

Figure 3-27: This chart uses four value axes.

Chapter 4

Formatting and Customizing Charts

IN THIS CHAPTER

- ◆ An overview of chart formatting
- ◆ Formatting patterns and borders
- ◆ Formatting chart background elements
- ◆ Working with chart titles
- ◆ Working with legends, data labels, gridlines, and data tables
- ◆ Understanding chart axes
- ◆ Formatting 3-D charts

THE CHART WIZARD DOES A DECENT job of transforming a range of numbers into a chart. Often, the basic chart that Excel creates is good enough. If you create a chart for your own use, spending a lot of time on formatting and customizing the chart may not be worth the effort. But if you want to create the most effective chart possible, or if you need to create a chart for presentation purposes, you'll probably want to take advantage of the additional customization techniques available in Excel.

This chapter discusses the ins and outs of formatting and customizing your charts. It's easy to become overwhelmed with all the chart customization options. However, the more you work with charts, the easier it becomes. Even advanced users tend to experiment a great deal with chart customization, and they rely heavily on trial and error — a technique that I strongly recommend.

Chart Formatting Overview

Customizing a chart involves changing the appearance of its elements, as well as possibly adding new elements to it. These changes can be purely cosmetic (such as changing colors or modifying line widths) or quite substantial (such as changing the axis scales or rotating a 3-D chart).

Increasing the Size of the Chart Objects Control

The Chart Objects control, located on the Chart toolbar, is useful for selecting chart elements and displaying the name of the selected chart element. If you find that the Chart Objects control is too narrow, you can increase its size:

1. Make sure that the Chart toolbar is displayed.

2. Select View→Toolbars→Customize to display the Customize dialog box.

3. With the Customize dialog box displayed, click the Chart Object control in the Chart toolbar.

4. Drag the left border or the right border to make the control wider.

5. Click Close to close the Customize dialog box.

Before you can customize a chart, you must activate it. To activate a chart on a chart sheet, click its sheet tab. To activate an embedded chart, click anywhere within the chart. To deactivate an embedded chart, just click anywhere in the worksheet.

In some cases, you may prefer to work with an embedded chart in a separate window. For example, if the embedded chart is larger than the workbook window, it's much easier to work with if it's in its own window. To display an embedded chart in a window, right-click the chart's Chart Area (the area near the border) and select Chart Window from the shortcut menu. This action creates a temporary floating window, which can be moved and resized. To close this temporary window, click the "X" in the chart window's title bar (or just click anywhere in the worksheet). Figure 4-1 shows an embedded chart displayed in a temporary window.

Selecting chart elements

Modifying a chart is similar to everything else you do in Excel: First you make a selection (in this case, select a chart element); then you issue a command to do something with the selection.

You can select only one chart element at a time. For example, if you want to change the font for two axis labels, you must work on each label separately. The exceptions to the single-selection rule are elements that consist of multiple parts, such as gridlines. Selecting one gridline selects them all.

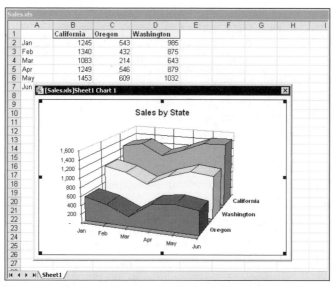

Figure 4-1: This embedded chart is displayed in a temporary floating window.

Excel provides three ways to select a particular chart element:

◆ Use the mouse

◆ Use the keyboard

◆ Use the Chart toolbar

These selection methods are described in the following sections.

SELECTING WITH THE MOUSE

To select a chart element with your mouse, just click it. To ensure that you've selected the chart element that you intended to select, check the Name box (to the left of the Formula bar). The Name box displays the name of the selected element. When a chart is activated, you can't actually access the Name box; it's simply a convenient place for Excel to display the selected chart element's name.

Unfortunately, the Name box is often too narrow to display the selected element's name completely. For a better view, display the Chart toolbar. The Chart Objects control in this toolbar also displays the selected element's name, and this control is a bit wider, so you can see more of the name.

TIP When you move the mouse over a chart, a small "chart tip" displays the name of the chart element under the mouse pointer. When the mouse pointer is over a data point, the chart tip also displays the value of the data point. If you find these chart tips annoying, you can turn them off. Select Tools→Options and click the Chart tab in the Options dialog box. Remove the checkmark from one or both items in the Chart tips section.

Some chart elements (such as a chart series, a legend, and data labels) consist of multiple items. For example, a chart series is made up of individual data points. To select a particular data point, you need to click twice: First click the series to select it; then click the specific element within the series (for example, a column or a line chart marker). Selecting the element enables you to apply formatting only to a particular data point in a series.

You may find that some chart elements are difficult to select with the mouse. If you rely on the mouse for selecting a chart element, it may take several clicks before the desired element is actually selected. Fortunately, Excel provides other ways to select a chart element, and it's worth your while to be familiar with them.

SELECTING WITH THE KEYBOARD
When a chart is active, you can use the Up and Down arrow keys on your keyboard to cycle among the chart's elements. Again, keep your eye on the Name box (or on the Chart Objects control) to determine which element is selected.

When a chart series is selected, use the Left and Right arrow keys to select an individual data point within the series. Similarly, when a set of data labels is selected, you can select a specific data label by using the Left or Right arrow key. And when a legend is selected, you can select individual elements within the legend by using the Left or Right arrow keys.

SELECTING WITH THE CHART TOOLBAR
The Chart Objects control on the Chart toolbar is a drop-down list that lets you select a particular chart element from the active chart (see Figure 4-2). This control lists only the "top level" elements in the chart. To select an individual data point within a series, for example, you need to select the series and then use one of the other techniques to select the desired data point.

NOTE When a single data point is selected, the Chart Object control *will* display the name of the selected element, even though it's not actually available for selection in the drop-down list.

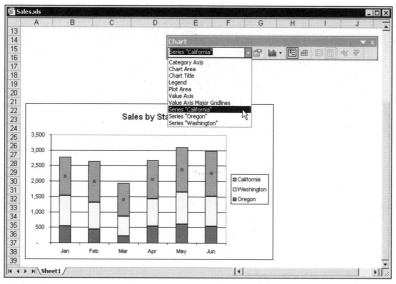

Figure 4-2: Use the Chart Objects control on the Chart toolbar to select an element in a chart.

Common chart elements

Table 4-1 contains a list of the various chart elements that you may encounter. Note that the actual chart elements that are present in a particular chart depend on the chart type and on the customizations that you've performed on the chart.

TABLE 4-1 CHART ELEMENTS

Part	Description
Category Axis	The axis that represents the chart's categories.
Category Axis Title	The title for the category axis.
Chart Area	The chart's background.
Chart Title	The chart's title.
Corners	The corners of 3-D charts (except 3-D pie charts). Select the corners if you want to rotate a 3-D chart using a mouse.

Continued

Table **4-1** **CHART ELEMENTS** (Continued)

Part	Description
Data Label	A data label for a point in a series. The name is preceded by the series and the point. Example: Series 1 Point 1 Data Label.
Data Labels	Data labels for a series. The name is preceded by the series. Example: Series 1 Data Labels.
Data Table	The chart's data table.
Display Units Label	The units label for an axis.
Down-Bars	Down-bars in a stock market chart.
Drop Lines	Lines that extend from each data point downward to the axis (line and area charts only).
Error Bars	Error bars for a series. The name is preceded by the series. Example: Series 1 Error Bars.
Floor	The floor of a 3-D chart.
Gridlines	A chart can have major and minor gridlines for each axis. The element is named using the axis and the type of gridlines. Example: Value Axis Major Gridlines.
High-Low Lines	High-low lines in a stock market chart.
Legend	The chart's legend.
Legend Entry	One of the text entries inside a legend.
Legend Key	One of the keys inside a legend.
Plot Area	The chart's plot area — the actual chart, without the legend.
Point	A point in a data series. The name is preceded by the series name. Example: Series 1 Point 2.
Secondary Category Axis	The second axis that represents the chart's categories.
Secondary Category Axis Title	The title for the secondary category axis.
Secondary Value Axis	The second axis that represents the chart's values.
Secondary Value Axis Title	The title for the secondary value axis.

Part	Description
Series	A data series.
Series Axis	The axis that represents the chart's series (3-D charts only).
Series Lines	A line that connects a series in a stacked column or stacked bar chart.
Trendline	A trendline for a data series.
Trendline Equation	The equation for a trendline.
Up-Bars	Up-bars in a stock market chart.
Value Axis Title	The title for the value axis.
Value Axis	The axis that represents the chart's values. There also may be a Secondary Value Axis.
Walls	The walls of a 3-D chart only (except 3-D pie charts).

Using the Format dialog boxes

When a chart element is selected, you can access the element's Format dialog box to format or set options for that element. Each chart element has a unique Format dialog box, and the dialog box usually has several tabs.

You can access the Format dialog box by using any of the following methods:

◆ Select the Format→ *Selected Element Name* command. The Format menu displays the actual name of the selected part. If the value axis is selected, the command is Format→Selected Axis.

◆ Double-click a chart element.

◆ Select the chart element and press Ctrl+1.

◆ Right-click the chart element and choose Format from the shortcut menu.

Any of these methods displays the appropriate Format dialog box that lets you make many changes to the selected chart element. Figure 4-3, for example, shows the Format Legend dialog box.

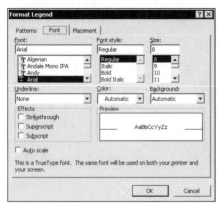

Figure 4-3: Each chart element has its own Format dialog box. This dialog box controls formatting for the chart's legend.

When a chart element is selected, you'll find that many of the toolbar buttons that you normally use for worksheet formatting also work with the selected chart element. For example, if you select the chart's Plot Area, you can change its color by using the Fill Color tool on the Formatting toolbar. If you select an element that contains text, you can use the Font Color tool to change the color of the text. Simple formatting using the toolbar buttons is usually more efficient than bringing up the dialog box.

Adjusting Borders and Areas: General Procedures

Many of the Format dialog boxes for chart elements include a tab named Patterns. This tab lets you adjust the border of the selected element, as well as the interior area.

About the Patterns tab

Figure 4-4 shows the Patterns tab in the Format Data Series dialog box. This tab has two sections: Border and Area.

Although the Patterns tab of the various Format dialog boxes are similar, they are not identical. Depending on the chart element, the dialog box may have additional options. For example, the Patterns tab of the Format Chart Area dialog box includes a check box that adds rounded corners to the object. The Patterns tab of the Format Axis dialog box looks completely different because an axis does not have an interior area.

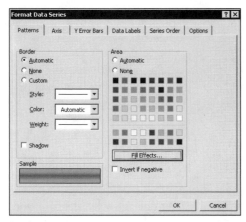

Figure 4-4: The Patterns tab of the Format Data Series dialog box

Formatting borders

A *border* is the line around an object. Excel offers three general choices for formatting a border: Automatic, None, and Custom. By default, borders are set to Automatic, which means that Excel chooses the border style, color, and weight. To hide the border around the selected element, choose None. If you modify the Style, Color, or Weight setting, the border is considered to be a Custom border.

The Border settings are fairly straightforward, so I don't go into any more detail. As always, the best advice is to experiment until you get the effect you're looking for.

Figure 4-5 shows a chart in which the chart title has been formatted. The title has a thick border and a shadow applied. By default, titles do not have a border.

Formatting areas

The *area* is the interior of a chart element. Not all chart elements have an area. Again, the Patterns tab of the Format dialog box offers three general choices for formatting an area: Automatic, None, and Custom.

Notice that the Patterns tab of the Format dialog box does not actually provide an option labeled Custom. It is assumed that if Automatic and None are not selected, then the area uses custom formatting.

For standard single-color formatting, just click a color from the palette displayed. The area labeled Sample displays the selected color.

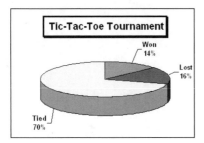

Figure 4–5: The chart title has a border
and a shadow.

For more interesting formatting options, don't overlook the Fill Effects button. This button displays the Fill Effects dialog box, shown in Figure 4-6. This dialog box contains four tabs:

◆ **Gradient:** Enables you to specify colors that are blended together in various ways. There are literally hundreds of possibilities here.

◆ **Texture:** Enables you to select from 24 built-in textures. Or, use the Other Texture button to use a graphic file as a texture.

◆ **Pattern:** Enables you to choose from 48 two-color patterns. You can choose the colors. These patterns are sometimes useful for charts that will be printed using a black-and-white printer, and grayscale doesn't work well. If you plan to print your charts, make sure that you do some test prints to ensure that the patterns print correctly on your printer.

◆ **Picture:** Enables you to specify a graphics file. You can control how the picture is displayed: stretched, stacked, or stacked and scaled. This feature can be put to good use in applying special effects to data series. See "Formatting Series," later in this chapter.

In the Gradient tab of the Fill Effects dialog box, the Transparency section is always disabled. Apparently, Excel is recycling this dialog box, which also is used to format shapes (the Transparency settings are enabled when a shape is selected). It is possible, however, to paste transparent shapes into a chart series. See Chapter 6 for an example.

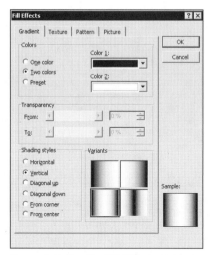

Figure 4-6: Use the Fill Effects dialog box to get a wide variety of formatting effects.

Formatting Chart Background Elements

Every chart has two key components that play a role in the chart's overall appearance:

◆ **The Chart Area:** The background area of the chart object. By default, the Chart Area is colored white.

◆ **The Plot Area:** The area (within the Chart Area) that contains the actual chart. The default color of the Plot Area is either gray or None (transparent), depending on the chart type.

Working with the Chart Area

The Chart Area is an object that contains all other elements in the chart. You can think of it as a chart's master background. For an embedded chart, the Chart Area is always the same size as the embedded chart object (the chart's container).

TIP For a chart sheet, the Chart Area is usually the entire sheet, but you can adjust it by using the Page Setup dialog box: Select File→Page Setup, select the Chart tab, and specify Custom for the Printed Chart Size. After you perform these steps, the Chart Areas borders will be revealed, and you can move or resize the chart area by dragging.

The Format Chart Area dialog box contains the following tabs:

◆ **Patterns:** Controls the Chart Area's border, color, and patterns (including fill effects).

◆ **Font:** Controls the default font attributes for the chart. Changing the font for the Chart Area affects the font attributes for all text elements in the chart.

◆ **Properties:** Available for embedded charts only. Controls how the chart is moved and sized with respect to the underlying cells. You also can set the Locked property and specify whether the chart will be printed.

NOTE If you delete the Chart Area, you delete the entire chart.

Figure 4-7 shows a chart in which the Chart Area was customized. In the Patterns tab, I selected the Shadow and Round Corners options. In the Font tab, I selected Times New Roman as the font.

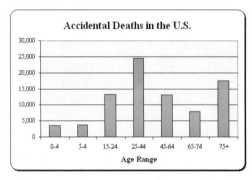

Figure 4-7: The Chart Area for this chart has been customized.

Working with the Plot Area

The Plot Area is the part of the chart that contains the actual chart. The Plot Area includes all chart elements except the chart title and the legend.

The Format Plot Area dialog box has only one tab: Patterns. This lets you change the color and pattern of the plot area and adjust its borders. Although the Plot Area consists of elements such as axes and axis labels, when you change the color of the Plot Area, these "outside" elements are not affected – except for a 3-D chart. Figure 4-8 shows a 2-D column chart and a 3-D column chart. Both charts have their Plot Area shaded and enclosed in a heavy dashed border. Notice that the Plot Area for the 3-D chart includes the axis labels. Typically, a 3-D has a transparent Plot Area, and color fills are used for the walls and floor.

 TIP If you set the Area option to None, the Plot Area will be transparent. Therefore, the color and patterns applied to the Chart Area will show through.

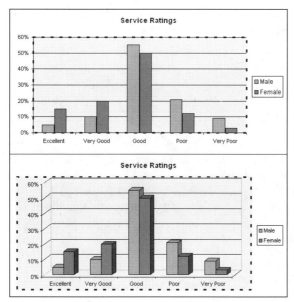

Figure 4-8: Formatting the Plot Area for a 3-D chart includes the axes and axes labels.

You can insert a picture or clip art for the Plot Area. To do so, click the Fill Effects button to display the Fill Effects dialog box. Then click the Picture tab and specify an image file. Figure 4-9 shows a column chart that uses a graphic in the Plot Area.

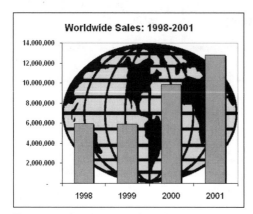

Figure 4-9: The Plot Area for this chart uses a
graphic image.

To reposition the Plot Area, select the Plot Area and then drag a border to move
it. To change the size of the Plot Area, drag on one of the corner "handles." If you
like, you can expand the Plot Area so that it fills the entire Chart Area. The Plot
Area of the chart in Figure 4-10 occupies the entire Chart Area. The title and legend
have been moved from their default locations and placed over the Plot Area.

Copying Chart Formatting

You created a killer chart and spent hours customizing it. Now you need to create
another one just like it. What are your options? You have several choices:

◆ **Copy the formatting.** Create a standard chart with the default formatting.
Then select your original chart and choose Edit→Copy. Click your new chart
and choose Edit→Paste Special. In the Paste Special dialog box, select
Formats. This procedure has an odd side effect: It overwrites the chart title
with the title from the copied chart. This is almost never what you want!

◆ **Copy the chart; change the data sources.** Press Ctrl while you click the original chart and drag. This will create an exact copy of your chart. Then use the
Chart→Source Data dialog box to specify the data for the new chart.

◆ **Create a user-defined chart type.** Select your chart and then choose
Chart→Chart Type. Click the Custom Types tab and select the User-defined
option. Click the Add button and then provide a name and description. When
you create your next chart, use this custom chart type.

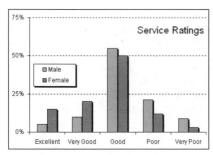

Figure 4-10: The Plot Area for this chart occupies the entire Chart Area.

 TIP   To remove all formatting from the Plot Area, select the Plot Area and press Del. The Plot Area remains, but the Border and Area settings are set to None.

You'll find that different chart types vary in how they respond to changes in the Plot Area dimensions. For example, you cannot change the relative dimensions of the Plot Area of a pie chart or a radar chart (it's always square). But with other chart types, you can change the aspect ratio of the Plot Area by changing either the height or the width.

Also, be aware that the size of the Plot Area can be changed automatically when you adjust other elements of your chart. For example, if you add a legend to a chart, the size of the Plot Area may be reduced to accommodate the legend.

 TIP   Changing the size and position of the Plot Area can have a dramatic effect on the overall look of your chart. When you're fine-tuning a chart, you'll probably want to experiment with various sizes and positions for the Plot Area.

Formatting Series

You'll often find that making a few simple formatting changes to a chart series can make a huge difference in the readability of your chart. When you create a chart, Excel uses its default colors and marker styles for the series. In many cases, you'll want to modify these colors or marker styles for clarity (basic formatting). In other cases, you may want to make some drastic changes for impact.

You can apply formatting to the entire series or to a single data point within the series — for example, make one column a different color to draw attention to it.

Basic series formatting

Basic series formatting is very straightforward: Just select the data series in your chart, access the Format Data Series dialog, select the Patterns tab, and make your changes.

Figure 4-11 shows a "chart makeover." The top chart is a simple combination chart, with default formatting for the two data series. Although the chart serves its purpose, most would agree that the bottom chart — which is the result of about two minutes of formatting work — is a significant improvement.

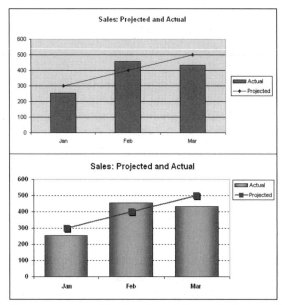

Figure 4–11: A combination chart, before and after applying some simple formatting

Following is a list of the simple changes made to this chart, using the Format Data Series dialog box:

◆ For the Projected series, the line color was changed to red, the line weight was increased, the Marker style was changed, and the marker foreground and background colors were set to match the line color. In addition, the marker size was increased and a shadow was added.

◆ For the Actual series, a gradient was added (using the Fill Effects dialog box) and the gap width was decreased (using the Options tab of the Format Data Series dialog box).

In addition, the Plot Area was made white, providing more contrast between the series and the background. The pattern for the gridlines was changed to a dashed line, and fonts were made bold.

Using pictures and graphics for series formatting

You can add a picture to several chart elements, including data markers in line charts, and series fills for column, bar, area, bubble, and filled radar charts. Figure 4-12 shows a column chart that uses a clip art image of a car. The picture was added using the Fill Effects dialog box. To display the Fill Effects dialog box, access the Format Data series dialog, select the Patterns tab, and click Fill Effects.

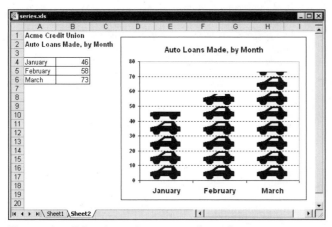

Figure 4-12: This column chart uses a clip art image.

 Data series elements are not the only type of chart element that can have a picture or graphic displayed. You can also apply a picture to the chart area, the plot area, or the legend. For 3-D charts, you can apply a picture to the walls or floor. Refer to Chapter 6 for more information about combining graphics with charts.

Additional series options

Chart series offer a number of additional options, listed in Table 4-2. The options vary, depending on the chart type of the series. These options are located in the Options tab of the Format Data Series dialog box. Figure 4-13 shows the options available for a doughnut chart.

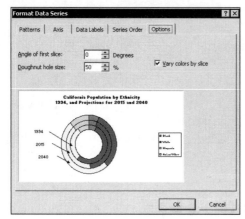

Figure 4-13: The Options tab of the Format Data Series dialog box lists additional options.

TABLE 4-2 CHART SERIES OPTIONS

Chart Type	Options
3-D area	Gap depth, Chart depth, Drop lines
3-D bar	Gap depth, Gap width, Chart depth, Vary color by point
3-D column	Gap depth, Gap width, Chart depth, Vary color by point
3-D line	Gap depth, Chart depth, Drop lines, Vary colors by point
3-D pie	Angle of the first slice, Vary colors by slice
3-D surface*	Chart depth, 3-D shading
Area	Drop lines
Bar	Overlap, Gap width, Series lines, Vary color by point
Bubble	Size represents (area or width), Scale bubble size, Show negative bubbles, Vary colors by point
Column	Overlap, Gap width, Series line, Vary colors by point
Doughnut	Angle of first slice, Doughnut hole size, Vary colors by slice
Line	Gap width, Drop lines, High-low lines, Up/down bars
Pie	Angle of first slice, Vary colors by slice
Radar	Category labels, Vary colors by point

Chart Type	Options
XY	Vary colors by point
Stock	Gap width, Drop lines, High-low lines, Up/down bars

Series in a 3-D surface chart are not selectable. Therefore, these options are available via the Format Legend Key dialog box.

Working with Chart Titles

A chart can have as many as five different titles:

- ◆ Chart title
- ◆ Category axis title
- ◆ Value axis title
- ◆ Secondary category axis title
- ◆ Secondary value axis title

The number of titles depends on the chart type. For example, a pie chart supports only a chart title because it has no axes. Figure 4-14 shows a chart that contains four titles: the chart title, the category axis title, the value axis title, and the secondary axis title.

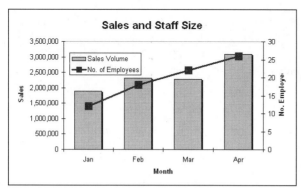

Figure 4-14: This chart has four titles.

If you examine the chart in this figure carefully, you'll see that the titles for the two value axes are not displayed correctly. The text has been cut off for both of these titles. This is a common problem with vertically oriented chart titles.

Excel's implementation of chart titles leaves a bit to be desired. In some cases, you may prefer to avoid using the built-in chart titles and create your own titles by using Text Boxes. For more information, refer to the sidebar, "Adding Free-Floating Text to a Chart."

Adding titles to a chart

To add titles to a chart, activate the chart and use the Chart→Options command to display the Chart Options dialog box. Click the Titles tab and enter text for the title or titles. The titles that Excel adds are placed in the appropriate position on the chart, but you can click a title's border and drag it anywhere you like. Titles for vertical axes are rotated 90 degrees counterclockwise.

Contrary to what you might expect, it is not possible to resize a chart title. When you select a title, it displays the characteristic border and handles — but the handles cannot be dragged to change the size of the object. The only way to change the size is to change the size of the font used in the title.

Changing title text

To edit the text used in a chart title, click the title once to select it; then click a second time inside of the text area. If the title has a vertical orientation, it will be temporarily displayed in a horizontal orientation while you edit it. To force a line break in the title, just press Enter.

Alternatively, you can edit the titles in the Chart Options dialog box. Choose the Chart→Chart Options command and then select the Title tab in the Chart Options dialog. If you use this method, you cannot force a line break. For lengthy titles, Excel handles the line breaks automatically.

Formatting title text

To modify the formatting for any of a chart's titles, access its Format dialog box. This dialog box, which is identical for the chart title and the axes titles, has tabs for the following:

- ◆ **Patterns:** Allows changes to the background color and borders of the title

- ◆ **Font:** Allows changes to the font, size, color, and attributes

- ◆ **Alignment:** Allows changes to the vertical and horizontal alignment and orientation

You can easily modify the formatting for individual characters within a title. Select the title and then highlight the characters that you want to modify. Choose Format→Selected Chart Title. The formatting changes you make will affect only the selected characters. Alternatively, you can use the buttons and controls on the Formatting toolbar. Figure 4-15 shows an example of a two-line chart title that uses different sizes and styles of text.

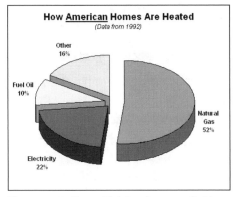

Figure 4-15: Formatting has been applied to individual characters in the chart's title.

Linking title text to a cell

When you add a title to a chart using the Chart Wizard, you must type the text. It's not possible to specify a reference to a cell that contains the text. But after the title has been created, you can then create a link to a cell. To do so:

1. Make sure that your chart has the particular title that you'd like to add a link to. The title can be the chart title or any of the axis titles.

2. Click the title to select it.

3. Click in the Formula bar.

4. Type an equal sign (=).

5. Click the cell that contains the text.

6. Press Enter.

Figure 4-16 shows an example of a chart title that is linked to cell A1 (the Formula bar displays the link formula, =Sheet3!$A$1). If cell A1 is changed, the changes will be reflected in the chart's title.

Adding Free-Floating Text to a Chart

Text in a chart is not limited to titles. In fact, you can add free-floating text anywhere you want. To do so, select any part of the chart except a title or data label. Then type the text in the Formula bar and press Enter. Excel adds a Text Box that contains the text you entered. The Text Box will appear in the center of the chart, but you can move it wherever you want it by dragging a border. Double-click the Text Box to display the Format Text Box dialog box, in which you can apply any formatting you desire.

Many people prefer to use a Text Box in place of a chart's "official" title elements. As noted in the text, Excel's chart titles have some problems. Perhaps the most annoying problem is that text is often cut off in vertical titles. Also, resizing a title is not possible (except by changing its font size). Using a Text Box overcomes both of these problems.

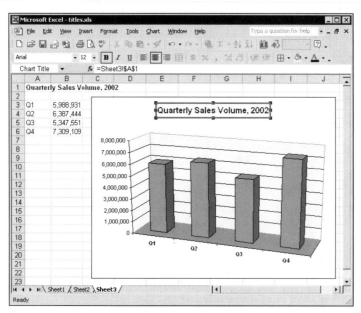

Figure 4-16: The chart title is linked to cell A1.

Working with a Chart's Legend

A chart legend identifies the series in the chart and consists of text and keys. A *key* is a small graphic image that corresponds to the appearance of the corresponding chart series. The order of the items within a legend varies, depending on the chart type.

If you've added a trendline to your chart, the trendline also appears in the legend. For more information about trendlines, refer to Chapter 5.

Legends are appropriate for charts that have at least two series. But even then, all charts do not require a legend. You may prefer to identify relevant data using other methods, such as data labels or AutoShapes. Figure 4-17 shows a chart in which the data series are identified by using AutoShapes, which were added to the chart using the Drawing toolbar.

Refer to Chapter 6 for more information about using AutoShapes with charts.

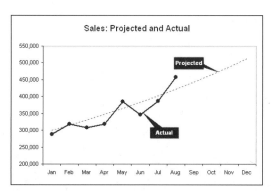

Figure 4-17: This chart uses AutoShapes as an alternative to a legend.

Adding or removing a legend

If you created your chart with the ChartWizard, you had an option (in Step 3) to include a legend. If you change your mind, you can easily delete the legend or add one if it doesn't exist.

To add a legend to your chart, use the Chart→Options command and then click the Legend tab in the Chart Options dialog box. Place a checkmark in the Show legend check box. You also can specify where to place the legend using the Placement option buttons.

The quickest way to remove a legend is to select the legend and press Del. Alternatively, you can use the Chart toolbar. The Legend tool in the Chart toolbar acts as a toggle. Use this button to add a legend if one doesn't exist and to remove the legend if one exists.

Moving or resizing a legend

To move a legend, click it and drag it to the desired location. Or you can use the legend's Format dialog box to position the legend (using the Placement tab).

Be aware that changing the position of a legend using the Placement tab may also change the size and position of the chart's Plot Area. After you move a legend from its default position, you may want to change the size of the Plot Area to fill in the gap left by the legend. Just select the plot area and drag a border to make it the desired size.

To change the size of a legend, select it and drag any of its corners. Excel will adjust the legend automatically and may display it in multiple columns.

Formatting a legend

The Format Legend dialog box contains three tabs:

- ◆ **Patterns:** Controls the legend's border, color, and patterns
- ◆ **Font:** Controls the default font for the text displayed in the legend
- ◆ **Placement:** Controls the location of the legend within the chart

You can select individual items within a legend and format them separately. To change the appearance of the text, access the Format Legend Entry dialog box (which has only a single tab: Font). For example, you may want to make the text bold to draw attention to a particular data series. It is not possible to change the formatting of individual characters in a legend entry.

The Format Legend Key dialog box also contains a single tab: Patterns. If you change the patterns in the dialog box, the patterns for the chart series are also changed. In other words, the legend key will *always* correspond to the data series.

 You can't use the Chart toolbar's Chart Objects drop-down list to select a legend entry or legend key. You must either click the item or select the legend itself, and then press the right arrow until the desired element is selected.

Changing the legend text

The legend text corresponds to the names of the series in the chart. If you didn't include series names when you originally selected the cells to create the chart,

Excel displays default series name (*Series 1, Series 2*, and so on) in the legend. To add series names, choose the Chart→Source Data command and then select the Series tab in the Source Data dialog box. Select a series from the Series list box, activate the Name box, and either specify a cell reference that contains the label or directly enter the series name. Alternatively, you can edit the SERIES formula, as described in Chapter 3.

Deleting a legend entry

For some charts, you may prefer that one or more of the data series not appear in the legend. To delete a legend entry, just select it and press Del. The legend entry will be deleted but the data series will remain intact.

If you press Del when a legend *key* is selected, the entire series will be deleted. The legend key is the graphic part of the legend entry.

If you've deleted one or more legend entries, you can restore the legend to its original state by deleting the entire legend and then adding it back. You can use the Show Legend check box in the Legend tab of the Chart Options dialog box to perform these actions.

Working with Chart Axes

As you know, charts vary in the number of axes that they use. Pie and doughnut charts have no axes. All 2-D charts have at least two axes, and they can have three (if you use a secondary-value or category axis) or four (if you use a secondary-category axis and a secondary-value axis). 3-D charts have three axes — the "depth" axis is known as the series axis.

Refer to Chapter 8 for a variety of chart examples that use additional axes.

Excel provides you with a great deal of control over the look of chart axes. To modify any aspect of an axis, access its Format Axis dialog box, which has five tabs:

◆ **Patterns:** Allows changes to the axis line width, tick marks, and placement of tick mark labels.

◆ **Scale:** Allows changes to the minimum and maximum axis values, units for major and minor gridlines, and several other properties.

◆ **Font:** Allows changes to the font and font style used for the axis labels. Because it's not possible to select a single axis label, the font formatting applies to all labels on the axis. In addition, it's not possible to apply special formatting to individual characters (for example, superscript formatting).

◆ **Number:** Allows changes to the number format used to display numerical axis labels.

◆ **Alignment:** Allows changes to the orientation for the axis labels.

All aspects of axis formatting are covered in the sections that follow.

Value Axis versus Category Axis

Before getting into the details of formatting, it's important to understand the difference between a category axis and a value axis. A category axis displays arbitrary text, whereas a value axis displays numerical intervals. Figure 4-18 shows a simple column chart with two series. The horizontal category axis displays labels that represent the categories. The vertical value axis, on the other hand, represents a numerical scale.

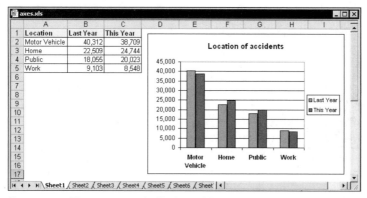

Figure 4-18: The category axis displays arbitrary labels, whereas the value axis displays a numerical scale.

In this example, the category labels happen to be text. Alternatively, the categories *could* be numbers. Figure 4-19 shows the same chart after replacing the category labels with numbers. Even though the chart becomes fairly meaningless, it should be clear that the category axis does not display a true numeric scale. The numbers displayed are completely arbitrary, and the chart itself was not affected by changing these labels.

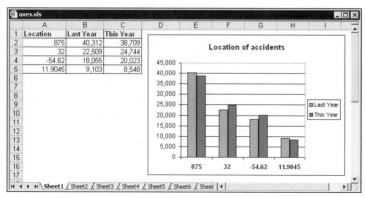

Figure 4-19: The category labels have been replaced with numbers — but the numbers do not function as numbers.

Two of Excel's chart types are different from the other chart types in one important respect. XY charts and bubble charts use *two* value axes. For these chart types, both axes represent numeric scales.

Figure 4-20 shows two charts (an XY chart and a line chart) that use the same data. The data shows world population estimates for various years. Note that the interval between the years is not consistent.

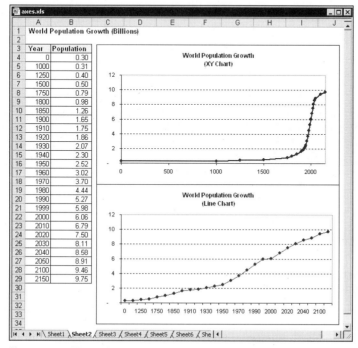

Figure 4-20: These charts plot the same data but present very different pictures.

The XY chart, which uses two value axes, plots the years as numeric values. The line chart, on the other hand, uses a (non-numeric) category axis and it assumes that the categories (the years) are equally spaced. This, of course, is not a valid assumption, and the line chart presents a very inaccurate picture of the population growth: It appears to be linear, but it's definitely not!

For more information about time-based axes, refer to "Using Time-Scale Axes," later in this chapter.

Value axis scales

The numerical range of a value axis represents the axis's scale. By default, Excel automatically scales each value axis. It determines the minimum and maximum scale values for the axis, based on the data. Excel also automatically calculates a major unit and a minor unit for each axis scale. These settings determine how many intervals (or tick marks) are displayed on the axis, and determine how many gridlines are displayed. In addition, the value at which the axis crosses the category axis is also calculated automatically.

You can, of course, override this automatic behavior and specify your own minimum, maximum, major unit, minor unit, and cross-over for any value axis. You set these specifications in the Scale tab of the Format Axis dialog box (see Figure 4-21).

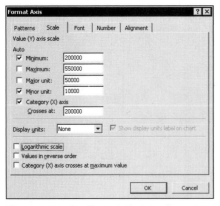

Figure 4-21: The Scale tab of the Format Axis dialog box

How Excel Calculates Automatic Axis Scales

Most people use automatic axis scaling for their charts. Did you ever wonder how Excel calculates the minimum and maximum scale values? The answer can be found at Microsoft's Product Support Services Web site.

It turns out that Excel uses a relatively complex algorithm. The calculation varies, depending on the sign of the minimum and maximum values (both positive, both negative or zero, or one is negative and the other is positive). The calculations depend on: (1) the "major unit" specified in the Scale tab of the Format Axis dialog box; (2) the minimum value (MIN); and (3) the maximum value (MAX).

When the values to be plotted are all positive numbers, the automatic maximum scale value for the value axis is the first major unit that is greater than or equal to the value returned by this expression:

```
MAX + 0.05 * (MAX - MIN)
```

Otherwise, the automatic maximum for the value axis is the first major unit greater than or equal to the maximum value. But if the difference between the maximum and minimum values is greater than 16.667% of the value of the maximum value, the automatic minimum for the value axis is zero.

If the difference between the maximum and minimum values is less than 16.667% of the maximum value, the automatic minimum for the value axis is the first major unit that is less than or equal to the value returned by this expression:

```
MIN - ((MAX - MIN) / 2)
```

But wait! If the chart is an XY chart or a bubble chart, the automatic minimum for the value axis is the first major unit that is less than or equal to the minimum value.

Got all that?

A category axis does not have a scale because it simply displays arbitrary category names. For a category axis, the Scale tab of the Format Axis dialog box displays a number of other options that determine the appearance and layout of the axis.

The checkmarks below the Auto label indicate whether Excel calculates these values automatically. If a setting does not have a checkmark, Excel uses the value specified in the text box. In the example shown in Figure 4-21, all scale values are determined automatically, except the Maximum and Major unit.

Adjusting the scale of a value axis can dramatically affect the chart's appearance. Reducing the range can emphasize differences among values, and increasing the range can minimize differences.

The actual scale that you use for an axis depends on the situation. No hard-and-fast rules exist about axis scaling, except that you shouldn't misrepresent data by manipulating the chart to prove a point that doesn't exist.

If you're preparing several charts that use similarly scaled data, keeping the scales constant across all charts facilitates comparisons across charts. The charts in Figure 4-22 show the distribution of responses for two survey questions. For the top chart, the value axis scale ranges from 0% to 50%. For the bottom chart, the value axis scale extends from 0% to 35%. Because the same scale was not used on the value axes, however, comparing the responses across survey items is difficult.

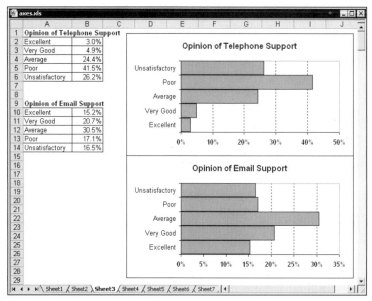

Figure 4-22: These charts use different scales on the value axis, making a comparison between the two difficult.

USING A LOGARITHMIC SCALE

If the values to be plotted cover a very large range, you may want to use a logarithmic scale for the axis. A log scale is most often used for scientific applications. This option is found in the Scale tab of the Format Axis dialog box.

A log scale works only for positive values, and the default minimum scale value is 1. You'll receive an error message if the scale includes 0 or negative values. Also, the axis labels will always be a power of 10, regardless of what you specify for the major unit.

Figure 4-23 shows two charts that plot data with a very large numeric range. The top chart uses a standard scale; the bottom chart uses a logarithmic scale. Note that the major unit value is 10, so each scale value in the chart is 10 times greater than the one below it. Increasing the major unit to 100 would result in a scale in which each tick mark value is 100 times greater than the one below.

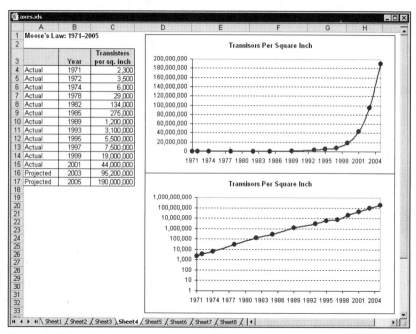

Figure 4-23: The bottom chart uses a logarithmic scale.

OTHER AXIS OPTIONS

The Scale tab of the Format Axis dialog box includes a few other options, which I briefly discuss in this section. The options available depend on the type of axis that is selected.

- ◆ **Display Units:** If your values consist of large numbers, you may wish to display the axis values in terms of a unit. For example, you might want to display values in millions, so a scale value of 5,000,000 would be displayed as 5. If you would like the unit name to appear on the chart, select the check box labeled Show Display Units Label on Chart. This option is not available in versions prior to Excel 2000.

- ◆ **Values in Reverse Order:** When this option is selected, the scale values extend in the opposite direction. For a value axis, for example, selecting this option displays the smallest scale value at the top and the largest at the bottom (the opposite of how it normally appears).

- ◆ **Type Axis Crosses at Maximum Value:** When this option is selected, the axis is positioned at the maximum value of the perpendicular axis (normally, the axis is positioned at the minimum value of the perpendicular axis). The exact wording of this option (*Axis Type*) varies, depending on which axis is selected.

Using time-scale axes

When you create a chart, Excel is smart enough to know whether your category axis contains date or time values. If so, it creates a time-series chart. Figure 4-24 shows a simple example. Column A contains dates, and column B contains the values plotted in the column chart. The data consists of values for only 10 dates, yet Excel created the chart with 31 intervals on the category axis. It recognized that the category axis values were dates, and created an equal-interval scale.

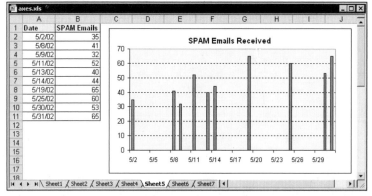

Figure 4-24: Excel recognizes the dates and creates a time-based category axis.

OVERRIDING A TIME-SCALE AXIS

If you would like to override Excel's decision to use a time-based category axis, you need to access the Axes tab of the Chart Options dialog box. There, you'll discover that the category axis option is Automatic. Change this option to Category, and the chart will resemble Figure 4-25.

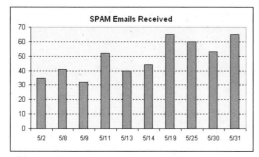

Figure 4-25: The previous chart, using a standard category axis

 A time-scale axis option is available only for the category axis (not the value axis).

USING TIME VALUES

For a time-scale axis, the minimum unit is a day. If you need a time-scale axis for smaller units (such as hours), you need to use a standard XY chart. Figure 4-26 shows an XY chart that plots scheduled versus actual arrival times for flights. Note that both of the value axes display times, in one-hour increments.

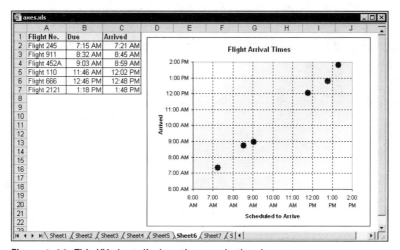

Figure 4-26: This XY chart displays times on both value axes.

Fortunately, Excel allows you to specify time values in the Scale tab of the Format Axis dialog box. These time values are then converted to serial number times. For this chart, I entered the following scale values:

Minimum axis scale value: 6:00 am

Maximum axis scale value: 2:00 pm

Major unit: 1:00:00

Excel converts these times to numerical values. Time values are expressed as a percentage of a 24-hour day. For example, "6:00 am" was converted to 0.25 because 6:00 a.m. is 25 percent of a 24-hour day. The Major unit value (1:00:00) was converted to 0.0416666666666667 – the value that represents ¹/₂₄ of a day.

Creating a multiline category axis

Most of the time, the labels in a category axis consist of data from a single column or row. You can, however, create multiline category labels, as shown in Figure 4-27. This chart uses the text in columns A:C for the category axis labels.

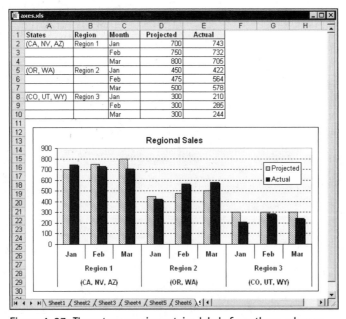

Figure 4-27: The category axis contains labels from three columns.

When this chart was created, range A1:E10 was selected. Excel determined automatically that the first three columns would be used for the category axis labels. Alternatively, you can use the Series tab of the Source Data dialog box to change the range used for the category axis labels.

This type of data layout is common when you work with pivot tables, and pivot charts often use multiline category axes. Refer to Chapter 9 for more information about pivot tables and pivot charts.

Formatting axis patterns and tick marks

An axis is a line, and Excel offers the standard line formatting option (style, color and weight). You adjust these formatting options in the Patterns tab of the Format Axis dialog box.

An axis also has tick marks — the short lines that depict the scale units and are perpendicular to the axis. You can select the type of tick mark for the major units and the minor units. The options are as follows:

- ◆ **None:** No tick marks
- ◆ **Inside:** Tick marks on the inside of the axis only
- ◆ **Outside:** Tick marks on the outside of the axis only
- ◆ **Cross:** Tick marks on both sides of the axis

You can also control the position of the tick mark labels. The options are as follows:

- ◆ **None:** No labels
- ◆ **Low:** For a horizontal axis, labels appear at the bottom of the plot area; for a vertical axis, labels appear to the left of the plot area
- ◆ **High:** For a horizontal axis, labels appear at the top of the plot area; for a vertical axis, labels appear to the right of the plot area
- ◆ **Next to axis:** Labels appear next to the axis (the default setting)

Major tick marks are the axis tick marks that normally have labels next to them. Minor tick marks are between the major tick marks.

Figure 4-28 demonstrates why you might want to change the position of the tick mark labels. In this XY chart, the axes cross in the center of the chart. In the top chart, the tick mark labels for both axes are in the default position (Next to axis). In the chart on the bottom, the tick mark labels have been moved to the Low position for both axes, making the chart much easier to read.

In some cases you may want to hide an axis. To do so, access the Format Axis dialog box, select the Patterns tab, and set all options to None.

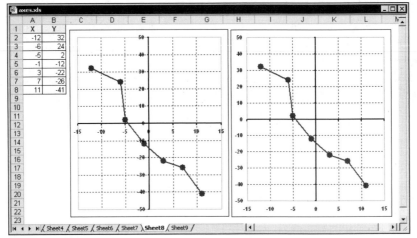

Figure 4–28: In the chart on the right, the axis labels were moved from their default location.

Removing axes

To remove an axis from the chart, use the Axes tab of the Chart Options dialog box (see Figure 4-29). The contents of this tab will vary, depending on the chart type and the number of axes used in the chart.

To remove an axis, just remove the checkmark from the appropriate check box. Removing an axis also hides the axis labels (but not the axis titles). This dialog box provides a preview, so you can get an idea of how the chart will look with or without a particular axis.

A more direct way to remove an axis is to select it and then press Del.

Axis number formats

A value axis, by default, displays its values using the same number format used by the chart's data. You can provide a different number format, if you like, by using the Number tab of the Format Axis dialog box. Changing the number format for a category axis that displays text will have no effect.

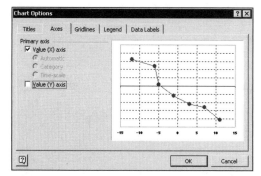

Figure 4-29: The Axes tab of the Chart Options dialog box

Don't forget about custom number formats. Figure 4-30 shows a chart that uses the following custom number format for the value axis: *General " mph"*. This number format causes the text *mph* to be appended to each value.

Don't Be Afraid to Experiment — on a Copy

I'll let you in a secret: The key to mastering charts in Excel is experimentation, otherwise known as trial and error. Excel's charting options can be overwhelming, even to experienced users. This book, despite being almost comprehensive, doesn't even pretend to cover all the charting features. Your job, as a potential charting guru, is to dig deep and try new options with your charts.

After you've created a basic chart, you might want to make a copy of the chart for your experimentation. That way, if you mess it up you can always revert to the original. To make a copy of an embedded chart, press the Ctrl key while you click the chart and drag the mouse pointer to a new location. To make a copy of a Chart sheet, press Ctrl while you click the sheet tab and drag it to a new location among the other tabs.

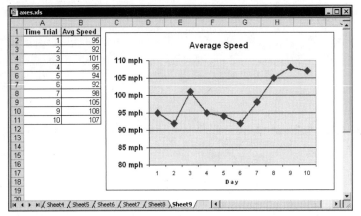

Figure 4-30: The value axis uses a custom number format to provide units for the values.

Working with Gridlines

Gridlines can help the viewer determine the values represented by the series in the chart. Gridlines are optional, and you have quite a bit of control over the appearance of gridlines. Gridlines simply extend the tick marks on the axes. The tick marks are determined by the major unit and minor unit specified for the axis.

Gridlines are applicable to all chart types except pie charts and doughnut charts.

Some charts look better with gridlines; others appear more cluttered. It's up to you to decide whether gridlines can enhance your chart. Sometimes, horizontal gridlines alone are enough, although XY charts often benefit from both horizontal and vertical gridlines.

Adding or removing gridlines

To add or remove gridlines, use the Chart→Options command and select the Gridlines tab. Each axis has two sets of gridlines: major and minor. Major units are the ones displaying a label. Minor units are those between the labels. You can choose which to add or remove by checking or unchecking the appropriate check boxes. If you're working with a chart that has a secondary category axis, a secondary value axis, or a series axis (for a 3-D chart), the dialog box has additional options for three sets of gridlines.

A more direct way to remove a set of gridlines is to select the gridlines and press Del.

 If a chart uses a secondary axis, the gridlines will always be associated with the primary axis. It is not possible to display gridlines for a secondary axis.

Formatting gridlines

To modify the properties of a set of gridlines, select one gridline in the set (which selects all in the set) and access the Format Gridlines dialog box. This dialog box has two tabs:

◆ **Patterns:** Contains controls for changing the line style, width, and color of the gridlines.

◆ **Scale:** Adjusts the scale used on the axis. The options here are identical to those found in the Scale panel of the Format Axis dialog box.

Figure 4-31 shows an XY chart with gridlines displayed for both axes (major units only). These gridlines have been formatted to display as dashed lines.

The gridline feature has some known problems. For example, if you format gridlines as white, you'll find that they always appear solid, regardless of the Style setting.

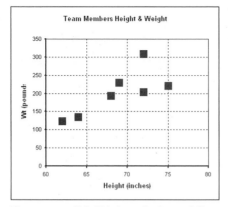

Figure 4–31: This XY chart displays gridlines for both axes.

It is not possible to apply different formatting to individual gridlines within a set of gridlines. All gridlines in a set are always formatted identically.

Working with Data Labels

For some charts, you may wish to identify the individual data points in a series. Excel's data label feature provides you with several options. The types of information that can be displayed in data labels are as follows:

◆ The series name

◆ The category name

◆ The numeric value

◆ The value as a percentage of the sum of the values in the series

◆ The bubble size (for bubble charts only)

Not all these options are available for all chart types, and earlier versions of Excel do not offer the category name option. If you select the check box labeled Show Legend Key Next to Label, each label displays its legend key next to it.

For versions prior to Excel 2002, a data label can consist of only one of the items in the preceding list. Excel 2002 enables you to display multiple items, separated by a user-defined separator. If you use Excel 2002, be aware that there are some known compatibility problems with data labels. If you plan to share your workbook with users of earlier versions of Excel, limit the data labels to display values only.

Adding or removing data labels

When you create a chart using the Chart Wizard, you can specify data labels in Step 3 (using the Data Labels tab). To add data labels to an existing chart, use the Data Labels tab of the Chart Options dialog box (see Figure 4-32). In both cases, data labels are added to all the series in the chart.

To add data labels to a specific series in the chart, select the series and access the Format Data Series dialog box. Select the Data Labels tab and specify the type of labels.

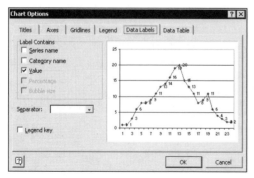

Figure 4–32: The Data Labels tab of the Chart Options
dialog box

    To remove all the data labels in a chart, use the Format Options dialog box and
uncheck all the options in the Data Labels tab. To remove the data labels from a
specific data series, click the data labels for the series and press Del.

Editing data labels

After adding data labels to a series, you can apply formatting to the labels by using
the Format Data Labels dialog box. This dialog box lets you specify the background
color, borders, font style, number format, and alignment. For some chart types, you
can specify the position of the data labels relative to the data point. This is done
using the Label Position drop-down control in the Alignment tab.

    Figure 4-33 shows an XY chart in which the data labels substitute for the series
markers. In this chart, the markers were set to none, and the data labels were positioned using the Center option.

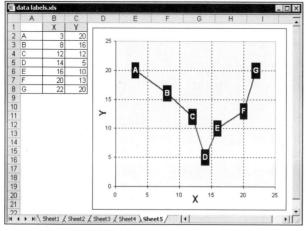

Figure 4–33: Using data labels in place of series markers

If you would like to override a particular data label with other text, select the label and enter the new text. To select an individual data label, click once to select all the data labels; then click the specific data label to select it.

To link a selected data label to a cell: Click in the Formula bar; type an equal sign (=); click the cell that contains the text; press Enter.

After adding data labels, you'll often find that the data labels aren't positioned optimally. For example, one or more of the labels may be obscured by another data point or a gridline. If you select an individual label, you can drag the label to a better location.

Figure 4-34 shows two 3-D column charts with data labels. The data labels in the top chart are in their default positions and are virtually illegible. The bottom chart has undergone some formatting modification to make the data labels more legible. Specifically:

- The color of the Plot Area was changed to a lighter color to provide more contrast.

- The value axis scale was increased to provide more space for the data labels.

- The value axis gridlines were removed.

- Bold formatting was applied to the data label font.

- The location of each data label was manually adjusted.

You may notice that the data labels display the values for each data point. For this particular chart, it would be preferable to display the value as a percentage of the total. Unfortunately, the Percent option is available only for a pie or doughnut chart. The alternative is to calculate the percentages using formulas, and then plot the percentage data rather than the actual value data.

Problems and limitations with data labels

As you work with data labels, you will probably discover that Excel's data labels feature leaves a bit to be desired. For example, it would be nice to be able to specify a range of text to be used for the data labels. This would be particularly useful in XY charts in which you want to identify each data point with a particular text item. Figure 4-35 shows an XY chart. If you would like to apply data labels to identify each data point, you're out of luck.

Despite what must amount to thousands of requests, Microsoft still has not added this feature to Excel! You need to add data labels and then manually edit each label.

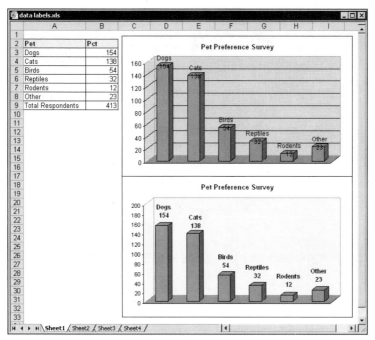

Figure 4-34: The bottom chart has been modified to make the data labels more legible.

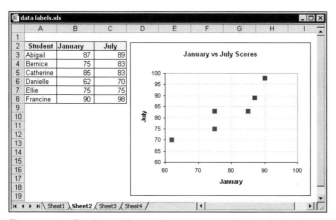

Figure 4-35: Excel provides no direct way to add descriptive data labels to the data points.

The JWalk Chart Tools add-in (available on the companion CD-ROM) includes a utility that makes it easy to add data labels to a chart (see Figure 4-36). You can specify the range that contains the labels.

A Data Label Trick

One way to get around Excel's data label limitation is to use a custom number format for each of your x values. The trick is to use a number format that consists only of text. The cell will still be treated as a number, but only the text will be displayed. Also, the formatted value is what appears in the chart data label!

The accompanying figure shows a chart that uses the data in columns C and D. Column C contains actual values, but the cells are formatted to display as text. Each value uses a (different) custom number format. For example, the value in cell C2 uses this custom number format: "Abigail." The x values are duplicated in column B but formatted as numbers. The data labels in the chart use the X Value option, and the custom formats (not the actual values) are displayed. These custom labels also display along the x axis, so you'll need to change the number formatting for the axis.

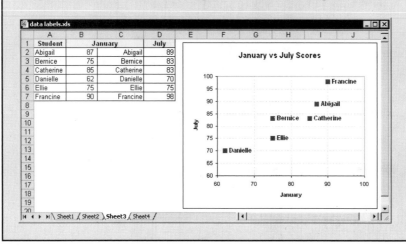

As you work with data labels, you'll find that this feature works best for series that contain a relatively small number of data points. The chart in Figure 4-37, for example, contains 24 data points. There is really no way to display data labels on this chart and keep the chart legible.

One option is to delete some of the individual data labels. For example, you might want to delete all the data labels except those at the high and low points of the series. Deleting only certain data labels is, however, a manual process. To delete an individual data label, select it and press Del. Yet another alternative is to use a data table, which is described in the next section.

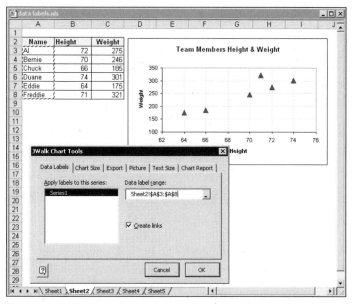

Figure 4-36: The Chart Data Labeler utility (part of the author's Power Utility Pak) overcomes a limitation in Excel.

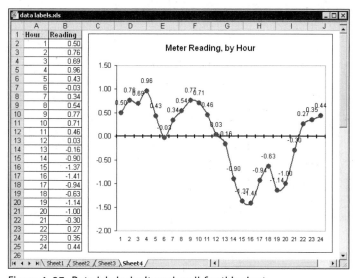

Figure 4-37: Data labels don't work well for this chart.

Working with a Chart Data Table

In some cases, you may want to display a data table for a chart. A data table displays the chart's data in tabular form, directly in the chart's Chart Area. Figure 4-38 shows a chart that has a data table.

Data tables can be used with only a few chart types. You cannot use a data table with XY charts, pie charts, doughnut charts, radar charts, bubble charts, and surface charts.

Adding and removing a data table

If you use the Chart Wizard, you can add a data table in the Data Table tab in Step 3. To add a data table to an existing chart, choose the Chart→Chart Options command and select the Data Table tab in the Chart Options dialog box. Place a checkmark next to the option labeled Show data table. You also can choose to display the legend keys in the data table. To remove a data table, select it and press Del.

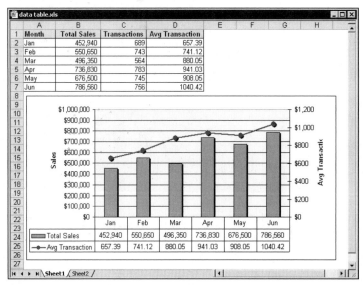

Figure 4-38: This chart includes a data table.

Problems and limitations with data tables

One problem with data tables, as I mentioned previously, is that this feature is available for only a few chart types. Formatting options for a data table are relatively limited. Data table formatting changes are made in the Format Data Table dialog box, which has two tabs: Patterns and Font. The Patterns tab is a bit misleading because it does not actually allow you to change the patterns in the data table. Rather, you are limited to formatting the borders for the data table. In addition, the dialog box has an option to display the legend keys or not.

Unfortunately, it is not possible to apply different font formatting to individual cells or rows within the data table. It is also not possible to change the number formatting. The numbers displayed in a data table always use the same number formatting as the source data.

When you add a data table to a chart, the data table essentially replaces the axis labels on the horizontal axis. The first row of the data table contains these labels, so losing them isn't a major problem. However, you will not be able to apply separate formatting to the axis labels — they will have the same formatting as the other parts of the data table.

Another potential problem with data tables occurs when they are used with embedded charts. If you resize the chart to make it smaller, the data table may not show all the data.

An exception to the behavior described in the preceding paragraph occurs with bar charts and charts with a time-scale category axis. For these types of charts, the data table is positioned below the chart and does not replace any axis labels.

Using a data table is probably best suited for charts on Chart sheets. If you need to show the data used in an embedded chart, you can do so using data in cells, which provides you with a lot more flexibility in terms of formatting.

Formatting 3-D Charts

One of the most interesting classes of Excel charts is 3-D charts. Certain situations benefit from the use of 3-D charts because these charts let you depict changes over two different dimensions. Even a simple column chart commands more attention if you present it as a 3-D chart. Be aware, however, that the perspective of a 3-D chart can often obscure differences among data points and make the chart more difficult to understand.

Not all charts that are labeled "3-D" are true 3-D charts. A true 3-D chart has three axes. Some of Excel's 3-D charts are simply 2-D charts with a perspective look to them.

Modifying 3-D charts

All 3-D charts have a few additional parts that you can customize. For example, most 3-D charts have a *floor* and *walls,* and the true 3-D charts also have an additional axis (the series axis). You can select these chart elements and format them to your liking. To change the depth of a 3-D chart, you need to go to the options tab of the Format Series dialog box (not the Format Floor dialog box, as you might expect).

Figure 4-39 shows a 3-D column chart that uses the default settings (left) and the same chart after making some formatting changes in the Options tab of the Format Series dialog box. In this case, the gap depth and gap width were decreased and the chart depth was increased. It's not possible to change these parameters for a particular series. Changing them for one series changes them for all the series.

Rotating 3-D charts

When you start flirting with the third dimension, you have a great deal of flexibility regarding the viewpoint for your charts. Figure 4-40 shows a 3-D column chart that has been rotated to show four different views. It should be obvious that Excel allows you to rotate a 3-D chart in such a way that it becomes virtually incomprehensible.

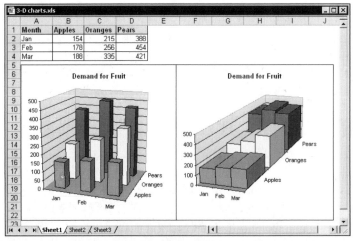

Figure 4-39: A few simple formatting changes make a dramatic difference in the look of this 3-D column chart.

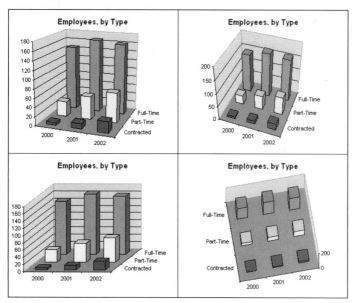

Figure 4-40: Four different views of the same chart

You can rotate a 3-D chart using either of these techniques:

◆ Activate the 3-D chart and choose the Chart→3-D View command. The dialog box shown in Figure 4-41 appears. You can make your rotations and perspective changes by clicking the appropriate controls. The sample that you see in the dialog box is *not* your actual chart. The displayed sample just gives you an idea of the types of changes that you're making. Click the Apply button to apply the settings to your chart without closing the dialog box. When you're satisfied with the result, click OK.

◆ Rotate the chart in real time by dragging corners with the mouse. Click one of the corners of the chart's walls. Black handles appear, and the word *Corners* appears in the Name box. You can drag one of these black handles and rotate the chart's 3-D box to your satisfaction. This method definitely takes some practice. If your chart gets totally messed up, click the Undo button to cancel your changes. Or, choose Chart→3-D View and click the Default button to return to the standard 3-D view.

When rotating a 3-D chart, hold down the Ctrl key while you drag to see an outline of the entire chart — not just the axes. This technique is helpful because when you drag only the chart's axes, you can easily lose your bearings and end up with a strange-looking chart.

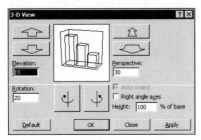

Figure 4-41: The 3-D View dialog box enables you to rotate and change the perspective of a 3-D chart. You also can drag the chart with the mouse.

Formatting a surface chart

A surface chart is different from the other chart types because you cannot select any of the series in the chart. Another difference is that the colors in the chart are based on the values.

The number of colored bands used in the chart depends on the major unit setting for the value axis. Figure 4-42 shows two surface charts. In the chart on the left, the value axis major unit is 0.05 (the default). In the chart on the right, the value axis major unit is 0.4, which covers the entire scale for the chart. Consequently, this chart displays a single color.

The procedure to adjust the colors used in a surface chart is rather counter-intuitive. First, you need to make sure that the chart displays a legend. Next, click the legend to select it and then double-click the color key that you want to change. This displays the Format Legend Key dialog box. Use the Patterns tab to change the color. The Options tab of this dialog box enables you to change the depth of the chart, as well as apply 3-D shading to the chart – an option that can make the chart look much better.

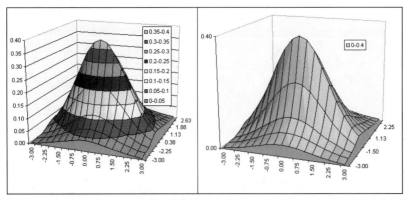

Figure 4-42: Changing the major unit for the value axis controls the number of colors used in a surface chart.

Chapter 5

Working with Trendlines and Error Bars

IN THIS CHAPTER

◆ Adding a trendline to a data series

◆ Forecasting and predicting with trendlines

◆ Using error bars

◆ Adding other types of series enhancements

THIS CHAPTER DISCUSSES CHARTING features that can make certain charts more meaningful: trendlines and error bars. A *trendline* is an additional line added to a chart that depicts general trends in your data. In some cases, you can forecast future data with a trendline. Error bars, used primarily in scientific applications, indicate "plus or minus" information that reflects uncertainty in the data. In addition, some chart series can display other enhancements such as series lines, drop lines, high-low lines, and up/down bars. These topics are all covered in this chapter.

Working with Trendlines

The best way to become acquainted with trendlines is to see one. Figure 5-1 shows an area chart that displays monthly income for 65 time periods. A trendline has been added to the chart. Although this data fluctuates quite a bit, the trendline indicates that income, in general, has been increasing — something that might not be readily apparent without the assistance of the trendline.

When a trendline is added to a chart, Excel draws the line such that it minimizes the differences between each data point and the corresponding value on the trendline. In other words, the trendline is the "best fit" line for the data series.

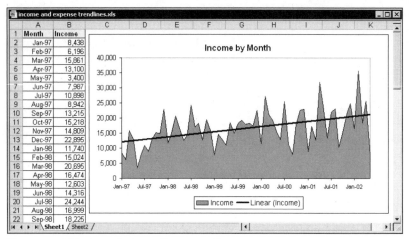

Figure 5-1: This chart displays a linear trendline.

Chart types that support trendlines

You can add a trendline to any of the following data series types:

- ◆ XY chart
- ◆ Area chart
- ◆ Bar chart
- ◆ Column chart
- ◆ Line chart
- ◆ Stock market chart
- ◆ Bubble charts

You *cannot* add a trendline to any type of 3-D chart, stacked chart, radar chart, pie chart, or doughnut chart. If you add a trendline and then change the chart type or data series to a nonsupported type, the trendline is deleted.

Data appropriate for a trendline

The type of data used in a chart determines whether the chart is appropriate for a trendline. Generally, charts that are suited for a trendline fall into two categories:

- ◆ Paired numeric data, as is typically plotted in an XY chart. Both axes are value axes.
- ◆ Time-based data, often plotted in XY charts, line charts, column charts, and area charts.

Trendlines assume that the category axis contains equal-interval values. This will always be the case with XY charts, bubble charts, and other chart types that use a time-based category axis. For example, a line chart that displays months or weeks along its category axis is a candidate for a trendline – as long as there are no gaps in the data.

Charts that use an arbitrary category axis are not appropriate for a trendline, although Excel won't object if you add one. If the chart uses an arbitrary category axis, the trendline interprets the categories as values beginning with 1 and incrementing by 1.

Figure 5-2 shows a column chart with a trendline. Because the category axis contains non-numeric text, Excel assigned the value of 1 to Ruth, 2 to Jerry, 3 to Pam, and so on. Consequently, the trendline is completely meaningless.

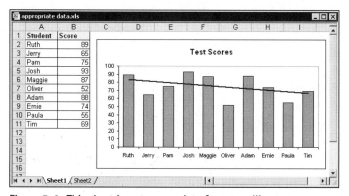

Figure 5-2: This chart is not appropriate for a trendline.

Figure 5-3 shows an example of a chart that *is* appropriate for a trendline. In this case, the chart compares individual performance on two tests using an XY chart. Because both axes are numeric, the trendline is valid. It indicates a positive linear relationship: Students who did well on Test 1 also tended to do well on Test 2.

Adding a trendline

A trendline is always associated with a particular data series. Although you might expect this option to appear in the Format Data Series dialog box, it doesn't. To add a trendline to a chart series, select the series and then choose Chart→Add Trendline to display the Add Trendline dialog box (see Figure 5-4). Or, you can right-click a data series and choose Add Trendline from the shortcut menu.

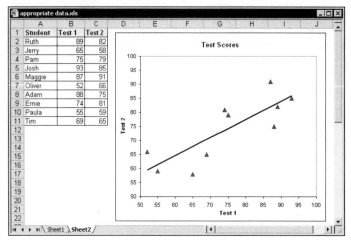

Figure 5-3: The trendline on this XY chart depicts a positive linear relationship between two variables.

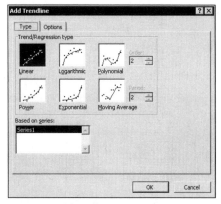

Figure 5-4: The Add Trendline dialog box offers several types of automatic trendlines.

To insert the trendline, choose the trendline type, verify that the correct series is selected in the list box, specify other options if necessary, and click OK. The Polynomial and Moving Average trendlines each have an additional parameter.

The Power and Exponential trendlines are not available if the data series contains any zero or negative values.

Figure 5-5 shows a chart with the monthly income data presented earlier in this chapter, along with an additional series for the corresponding monthly expenses (expressed as negative values). A trendline was added to each series. The trendlines indicate that income has been increasing, whereas expenses have remained relatively flat.

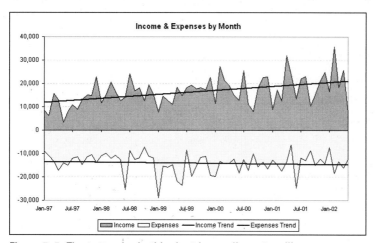

Figure 5-5: The two series in this chart have a linear trendline.

The type of trendline that you choose depends on your data. Linear trends are the most common type, but you can describe some data more effectively with other types of trendline.

When you click the Options tab in the Add Trendline dialog box, Excel displays the options shown in Figure 5-6. The Options tab contains additional options, and not all options are available for all trendline types. The options are briefly described in the list that follows and are discussed in more detail later in the chapter.

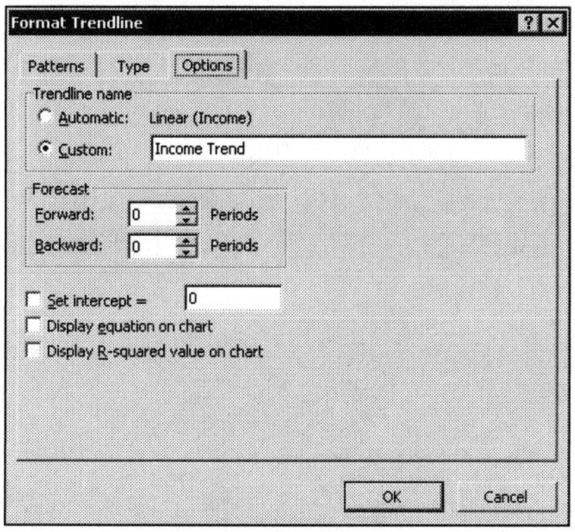

Figure 5-6: The Options tab in the Add Trendline dialog box

◆ **Trendline name:** If you choose Custom, you can provide a different caption for the trendline. This is the text that appears in the legend. If you do not specify a custom name, the legend text consists of the trendline type, followed by the series name in parentheses.

◆ **Forecast:** These options enable you to extend the trendline either forward, backward, or in both directions. You specify the number of periods to forecast.

◆ **Set intercept:** Enables you to specify the point on the value axis where the trendline crosses the axis.

◆ **Display equation on chart:** If checked, the regression equation for the trendline will be displayed on the chart.

◆ **Display R-squared value on chart:** If checked, the R-squared value for the trendline will be displayed on the chart.

 A single series can have more than one trendline associated with it. For example, you may want to add two different trendlines to determine which type better fits the data.

Formatting a trendline

When Excel inserts a trendline, it may look like a new data series, but it's not. It's a new chart element with a name, such as Series 1 Trendline 1. And, of course, it does not have a corresponding SERIES formula. Double-click a trendline to display the Format Trendline dialog box, which enables you to change its formatting or its options (the same options that were available when you added the trendline).

Formatting a trendline "data label"

If you choose either of the options that display a trendline equation or the R-squared value, the trendline will be accompanied by a text item that displays the requested information (see Figure 5-7). Excel refers to this as a data label — although, strictly speaking, it's not.

When the data changes, the data label is updated automatically to display the recalculated equation. To move the data label, just drag it. To change the formatting, select it and choose Format→Selected Data Labels.

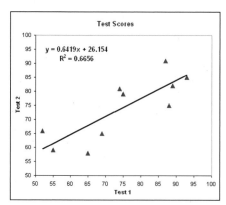

Figure 5-7: When you add a trendline, you have an option to include the equation and R-squared value.

TIP To display more or fewer decimal places in the equation and R-squared value, select the box and click the Increase Decimal or Decrease Decimal button on the Formatting toolbar.

NOTE You can edit the text contained in a trendline data label, but be aware that Excel will no longer update an edited data label if the data is changed. Therefore, it will display an incorrect equation. To make the trendline equation dynamic again, delete it and then add it again using the Format Trendline dialog box.

Linear Trendlines

A linear trend describes data in which two variables are related in a linear manner, or in which one variable changes steadily over time. Figure 5-8 shows an XY chart that plots the height and weight for 15 individuals. A linear trendline has been added to the chart.

The chart also uses the options to display the equation and the R-squared value for the trendline. In this example, the equation is

```
y = 4.2827x - 122.78
```

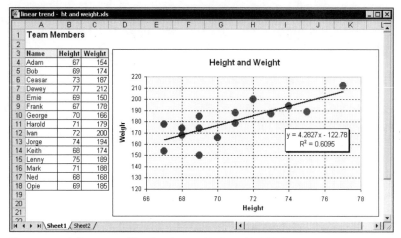

Figure 5-8: A linear trendline has been added to this XY chart.

The R-squared value is 0.6095.

What do these numbers mean? You may remember from algebra classes that a straight line can be described with an equation of the form:

```
y = mx +b
```

The variable m represents the slope of the line and b represents the y-intercept. The slope of a line is the amount by which the y value changes for a 1-unit change in x. The y-intercept is the value at which the line crosses the y-axis.

In the preceding example, the y-intercept is –122.78. However, the trend line *appears* to intersect the y-axis at (approximately) the 160 value. This apparent discrepancy is due to the fact that the scale values for the x-axis does not begin with 0. If you change the axis scaling and extend the trendline, you'll see that it meets the y-axis at the –122.78 value.

For each value of x (in this case, column B), you can calculate the predicted value of y (the value that falls on the trendline) by using the trendline equation. For example, Adam has a height (x) of 67 inches and a weight (y) of 154 pounds. Adam's *predicted* weight (y), using the following formula, is 164.16:

```
y = 4.2827 * (67) - 122.78
```

In other words, 164.16 is the y value on the linear trend line when x is 67. If a new 6'0" member were recruited for the team, the best guess of his weight would 185.57, as calculated by this formula:

```
y = 4.2827 * (72) - 122.78
```

The R-squared value, sometimes referred to as the *coefficient of determination*, ranges in value from 0 to 1. This value indicates how closely the estimated values for the trendline correspond to the actual data — a "goodness of fit" measure of the overall reliability of the trend. A trendline is most reliable when its R-squared value is near 1, and is least reliable when it's near 0. If all the data points fell exactly on the trendline, the R-squared value would be 1.0.

A much simpler way to generate the predicted y values for a linear trend line is to use the TREND function in a multicell array formula. Using the preceding example, select D4:D18 and enter the following array formula:

```
=TREND(C4:C18,B4:B18)
```

Enter the formula with Ctrl+Shift+Enter. The range will display the predicted y values for the data in B4:B18.

Linear forecasting

Thus far, the discussion has focused on making predictions for data that falls within the existing numerical range (*interpolation*). In addition, it's possible to make estimates for data that falls outside the existing range of data. This is known as *forecasting* or *extrapolation*.

When your chart contains a trendline, you can instruct Excel to extend the trendline to forecast additional values of x. You do this on the Options tab in the Format Trendline dialog box (or the Options tab in the Add Trendline dialog box). Just specify the number of periods to forecast (either forward or backward in time).

Figure 5-9 shows a line chart with monthly sales data for 21 months, along with a trendline that forecasts results for three subsequent months. The forecasted data is derived by simply extending the linear trendline to cover three additional periods.

Keep in mind that, because the category axis displays non-numeric data, Excel uses consecutive integers in place of the month names.

Figure 5-9: Using a trendline to forecast sales for three additional periods of time

Getting the trendline values

The preceding example leads, of course, to the question, *What are the actual forecasted sales values?* As described previously, you can use the slope and y-intercept values to calculate the predicted y value for a given value of x. It's a fairly simple exercise to create formulas to perform these calculations.

One approach is to copy the slope and y-intercept values displayed in the trendline's equation, and use these values to calculate the predicted y values (this is the method used earlier in this chapter to predict a person's weight, based on his or her height). For increased accuracy, you can calculate the slope and y-intercept and use these values to calculate the predicted values (see the sidebar, "Calculating the slope and y-intercept"). The simplest approach (for linear trendlines only) is to use Excel's FORECAST function.

Figure 5-10 shows the data from the sales forecast chart. Column A contains the month names (for reference only), and column B contains consecutive month numbers. The actual sales figures are in column C. Column D contains formulas that return the predicted y values displayed in the trendline.

The formula in cell D2 is:

```
=FORECAST(B2,$C$2:$C$25,$B$2:$B$25)
```

This formula was copied to the 24 cells below. As you can see, values for the final three months are forecast, based on the trend for the first 21 months.

The calculated values in column D, if plotted on a chart, would display a line that's identical to the linear trendline.

	A	B	C	D	E
1	Month	Month No.	Sales	Predicted	
2	Jan	1	146,899	147,426	
3	Feb	2	147,456	148,386	
4	Mar	3	141,865	149,346	
5	Apr	4	153,690	150,306	
6	May	5	153,554	151,266	
7	Jun	6	151,644	152,226	
8	Jul	7	158,500	153,186	
9	Aug	8	153,780	154,147	
10	Sep	9	154,834	155,107	
11	Oct	10	151,391	156,067	
12	Nov	11	155,012	157,027	
13	Dec	12	162,688	157,987	
14	Jan	13	161,601	158,947	
15	Feb	14	161,203	159,907	
16	Mar	15	168,586	160,867	
17	Apr	16	156,097	161,827	
18	May	17	162,608	162,787	
19	Jun	18	163,089	163,747	
20	Jul	19	161,577	164,707	
21	Aug	20	167,043	165,668	
22	Sep	21	164,445	166,628	
23	Oct	22		167,588	
24	Nov	23		168,548	
25	Dec	24		169,508	

Figure 5-10: Column D uses the FORECAST function to calculate points on a trendline.

Calculating slope, y-intercept, and R-squared

As described in this chapter, you can use the FORECAST function to calculate the points on a linear trendline and forecast other values. Alternatively, you can calculate the slope and y-intercept for the best-fit line, and then use these values to calculate the data points.

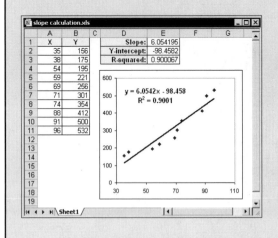

	A	B	C	D	E	F	G
1	X	Y		Slope:	6.054195		
2	35	156		Y-intercept:	-98.4582		
3	38	175		R-squared:	0.900067		
4	54	195					
5	59	221					
6	69	256					
7	71	301					
8	74	354					
9	88	412					
10	91	500					
11	96	532					

Chart: $y = 6.0542x - 98.458$, $R^2 = 0.9001$

Continued

Calculating slope, y-intercept, and R-squared *(Continued)*

Assume that the y values are in B2:B11 and the x values are in A2:A11. To calculate the slope, you can use the SLOPE function, as below:

```
=SLOPE(B2:B11,A2:A11)
```

Use the following formula to calculate the y-intercept:

```
=INTERCEPT(B2:B11,A2:A11)
```

Once you know the values for the slope and the y-intercept, you can calculate the predicted y value for each x using a formula in the form of

```
y = mx +b
```

The accuracy of forecasted values depends on how well the linear trendline fits your actual data. The value of R-squared represents the degree of fit. R-squared values closer to 1 indicate a better fit and will yield more accurate predictions. Statistically speaking, you can interpret R-squared as the proportion of the variance in y that is attributable to the variance in x.

To calculate R-squared, you can use the RSQ function, as in this formula:

```
=RSQ(B2:B11,A2:A11)
```

Or, calculate the correlation coefficient and square it:

```
=CORREL(B2:B11,A2:A11)^2
```

Keep in mind that the value of R-squared calculated by the RSQ function or CORREL function is valid only for a linear trendline.

Nonlinear Trendlines

Although linear trendlines are most common, an Excel chart can display nonlinear trendlines of the following types:

- ◆ **Logarithmic:** Used when the rate of change in the data increases or decreases quickly and then flattens out.

- ◆ **Power:** Used when the data consists of measurements that increase at a specific rate. The data cannot contain zero or negative values.

♦ **Exponential:** Used when data values rise or fall at increasingly higher rates. The data cannot contain zero or negative values.

♦ **Polynomial:** Used when data fluctuates in an orderly pattern. You can specify the order of the polynomial (from 2 to 6) depending on the number of fluctuations in the data.

The Type tab in the Trendline dialog box offers the option of Moving Average, which really isn't a trendline. This option, however, can be useful for smoothing out "noisy" data. Moving averages are discussed later in this chapter.

Earlier in this chapter, I noted that the equation for a straight line uses the slope and y-intercept. Nonlinear trendlines also have equations, but these equations are more complex. The following sections cover the nonlinear trendlines available in Excel, and I provide the equations for each type.

Logarithmic trendline

A logarithmic trendline may be appropriate for data that follows a logarithmic curve: It increases or decreases quickly and then levels out. A logarithmic trendline appears as a straight line on a chart with a linear y-axis scale and a logarithmic x-axis scale. The equation for a logarithmic trendline is

```
y = (c * LN(x)) - b
```

Figure 5-11 shows a chart with a logarithmic trendline added. The formula in cell E2, which follows, calculates c.:

```
=INDEX(LINEST(B2:B11,LN(A2:A11)),1)
```

The formula to calculate b, in cell F2, is

```
=INDEX(LINEST(B2:B11,LN(A2:A11)),2)
```

Column C shows the predicted y values for each value of x, using the calculated values for b and c. For example, the formula in cell C2 is

```
=($E$2*LN(A2))+$F$2
```

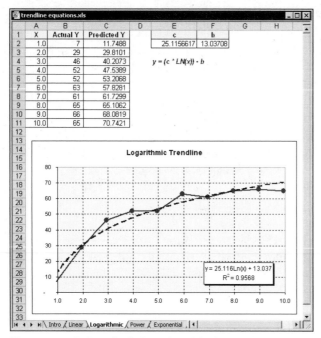

Figure 5-11: A chart displaying a logarithmic trendline

Power trendline

A power trendline describes data that increases (or accelerates) at a specific rate. A power law trendline appears as a straight line on a chart with a logarithmic y-axis and a logarithmic x-axis scale. This trendline is limited to positive values. The equation for a power trendline looks like this:

```
y = c * x^b
```

Figure 5-12 shows a chart with a power trendline added. Cell E2 contains the following formula, which calculates c:

```
=EXP(INDEX(LINEST(LN(B2:B11),LN(A2:A11)),1,2))
```

The value for b is calculated in F2, using this formula:

```
=INDEX(LINEST(LN(B2:B11),LN(A2:A11)),1)
```

Column C shows the predicted y values for each value of x, using the calculated values for b and c. For example, the formula in cell C2 is

```
=$E$2*(A2^$F$2)
```

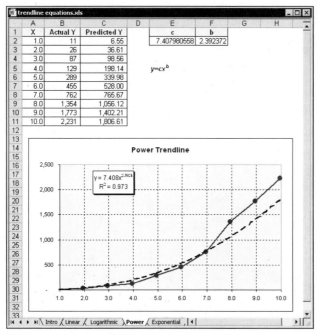

Figure 5-12: A chart displaying a power trendline

Exponential trendline

An exponential trendline is used for data that rises or falls at an increasing rate. An exponential trendline appears as a straight line on a chart with a logarithmic y-axis scale and a linear x-axis scale. As with the power trendline, the exponential trendline does not work with data that contains 0 or negative values. The equation for an exponential trendline looks like this:

```
y = c * EXP(b * x)
```

Figure 5-13 shows a chart with an exponential trendline added. The value for c is calculated in cell E2, which contains this formula:

```
=EXP(INDEX(LINEST(LN(B2:B11),A2:A11),1,2))
```

Cell F2 contains this formula, which calculates the value for b:

```
=INDEX(LINEST(LN(B2:B11),A2:A11),1)
```

Column C shows the predicted y values for each value of x, using the calculated values for b and c. For example, the formula in cell C2 is

```
=$E$2*EXP($F$2*A2)
```

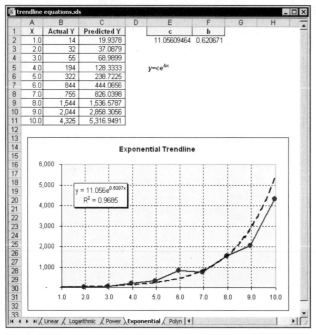

Figure 5-13: A chart displaying an exponential trendline

Polynomial trendline

A polynomial trendline defines a curved line and describes data that fluctuates in an orderly pattern. When you request a polynomial trendline, you also need to specify the order of the polynomial (ranging from 2 through 6). The equation for a polynomial trendline depends on the order of the polynomial.

SECOND-ORDER TRENDLINE

A second-order trendline (also known as a quadratic trendline) describes data that resembles a U or an inverted U. Following is the equation for a second-order polynomial trendline:

```
y = (c2 * x^2) + (c1 * x^1) + b
```

Notice that there are two c coefficients (one for each order).

Figure 5-14 shows a chart with a second-order polynomial trendline added. Formulas entered in E2:G2 calculate the values for each of the c coefficients and the b constant. The formulas are as follows:

```
E2:    =INDEX(LINEST(B2:B11,A2:A11^{1,2}),1)
F2:    =INDEX(LINEST(B2:B11,A2:A11^{1,2}),1,2)
G2:    =INDEX(LINEST(B2:B11,A2:A11^{1,2}),1, 3)
```

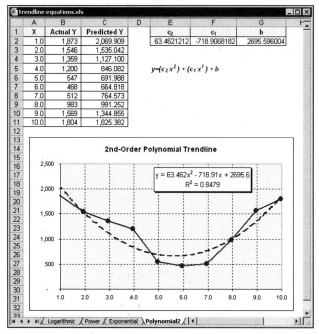

Figure 5-14: A chart displaying a second-polynomial trendline

Column C shows the predicted y values for each value of x, using the calculated values for b and the three c coefficients. For example, the formula in cell C2 is

```
=($E$2*A2^2)+($F$2*A2^1)+$G$2
```

HIGHER-ORDER POLYNOMIAL TRENDLINES

A polynomial trendline can use between two and six coefficients. Higher-order trendlines are often able to describe data sets that have complex or multiple curves. Figure 5-15 shows a chart with a third-order polynomial trendline. The equation for this trendline is similar to the second-order polynomial trendline equation, but with an additional coefficient:

```
y = (c3 * x^3) + (c2 * x^2) + (c1 * x^1) + b
```

Formulas in E2:H2 calculate the values for each of c coefficients and the b constant. The formulas are as follows:

```
E2:    =INDEX(LINEST(B2:B11,A2:A11^{1,2,3}),1)
F2:    =INDEX(LINEST(B2:B11,A2:A11^{1,2,3}),1,2)
G2:    =INDEX(LINEST(B2:B11,A2:A11^{1,2,3}),1,3)
H2:    =INDEX(LINEST(B2:B11,A2:A11^{1,2,3}),1,4)
```

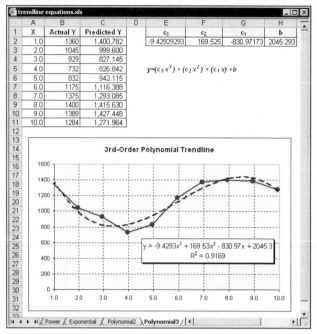

Figure 5-15: A chart displaying a third-polynomial trendline

Formulas to generate the values for other orders of polynomial trendlines follow a pattern similar to the formulas listed previously. For example, a fifth-order polynomial has five coefficients and one constant. The first coefficient for a fifth-order polynomial is calculated with the following formula:

```
=INDEX(LINEST(B2:B11,A2:A11^{1,2,3,4,5}),1,1)
```

Displaying a Moving Average

The Add Trendline dialog box lists Moving Average as an option. But as I noted earlier, a moving average is not really a trendline. A moving average displays a line that depicts the data series, averaged over a specified number of data points.

Adding a moving average line

To add a moving average line, select the chart series and choose Chart→Add Trendline. Click the Type tab, choose the Moving Average option, and specify a period. The period is the number of consecutive data points that are averaged. If you like, click the Options tab and enter a name for the moving average line. This is the text that will be displayed in the chart's legend.

A moving average is useful for smoothing out noisy data; it may also help to uncover trends that may otherwise be difficult to spot. Figure 5-16 shows a line chart with 50 data points, along with a moving average line with a period of 7 (it displays the average of every seven data points). As you can see, the moving average line is much smoother and clearly depicts the general upward trend in the data.

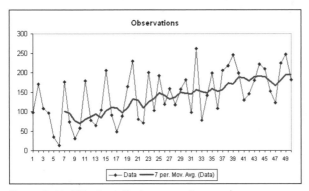

Figure 5-16: This chart displays a moving average.

Notice that the moving average line does not begin with the first data point. In this case, the line begins at the seventh data point because the period is 7. The beginning of the line is the average of the first seven data points. The second point is the average of data points 2 through 8, the third point is the average of data points 3 through 9, and so on. Generally, using a larger period will result in a smoother line – but the line gets shorter as the period increases.

Creating your own moving average data series

You can, of course, create formulas to calculate a moving average for a data series, and then plot the moving average as a separate chart series. For example, assume that your data is in the range A1:A50. To create a moving average with a period of 7, enter this formula into cell B7:

```
=AVERAGE(A1:A7)
```

Then, copy the formula down the column, ending with cell B50. Add B1:B50 as a new data series and the result will be identical to adding a moving average line via the Add Trendline dialog box.

This technique offers two advantages: You can add a moving average line to chart types that don't support trendlines, and you have more control over the appearance of the moving average line.

Figure 5-17, for example, shows a 3-D line chart (this type of chart does not support trendlines). The chart displays an additional series with a calculated moving average.

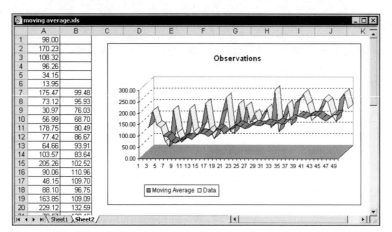

Figure 5-17: This 3-D line chart uses a data series in place of a moving average line.

Using Error Bars in a Chart Series

A chart series can include error bars to convey additional information about the data. For example, you might use error bars to indicate the amount of error or uncertainty associated with each data point.

Figure 5-18 shows a line chart with error bars above and below each data point, to indicate an error range for each data point. In this case, the error bars are based on percentage: The value plus or minus 10 percent. The error bars for the first data point (100) extend from 90 to 110.

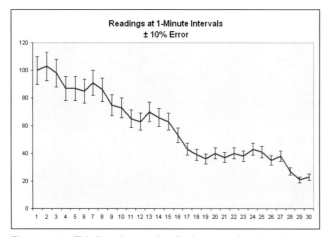

Figure 5-18: This line chart series displays error bars based on percentage.

Chart types that support error bars

Error bars are available for chart series of the following 2-D chart types:

◆ Area charts

◆ Bar charts

◆ Column charts

◆ Line charts

◆ XY charts

◆ Bubble charts

Because XY charts and bubble charts each have two value axes, you can display error bars for the x values, the y values, or both.

Adding error bars to a series

To add error bars, select the data series in the chart, access the Format Data Series dialog box, and select the Y Error Bars tab (see Figure 5-19). If the chart is an XY chart or a bubble chart, the dialog box will display an additional tab: X Error Bars.

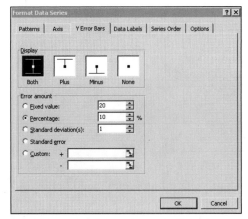

Figure 5-19: The Y Error Bars tab of the Format Data Series dialog box

First, choose the display type for the error bars. Y error bars display above each data point, below each data point, or both above and below each data point. X error bars offer the same options, but in the horizontal direction.

Next, select one of the following error amount options:

◆ **Fixed value:** The error bars will be offset from each data point by a fixed amount that you specify. Each error bar will be the same height (or same width, for X error bars).

◆ **Percentage:** The error bars will be offset from each data point by a percentage of the data point's value. For example, if you specify 5 percent as the percentage, a data point at 100 would display error bars at values 95 and 105. Error bars based on percentage will vary in size.

◆ **Standard deviation(s):** The error bars will be centered along an invisible line that represents the average of the data series values, plus or minus the number of standard deviations specified. For this option, the error bars are fixed in size, do not vary with each data point, and are always parallel to an axis.

◆ **Standard error:** The error bars will be offset from each data point by the standard error. The standard error is the standard deviation, divided by the square root of the sample size. Each error bar will be the same height (or same width, for X error bars).

◆ **Custom:** The error bars will be determined by the values in a range you specify. Usually, this range contains formulas.

Figure 5-20 shows a chart that uses error bars to indicate sampling error in a poll. Note that, in this example, the error bars use the Fixed Value option, with a value of .035 to represent a sampling error of 3.5 percent. It does *not* use the Percentage option, which displays as a percentage of each data point.

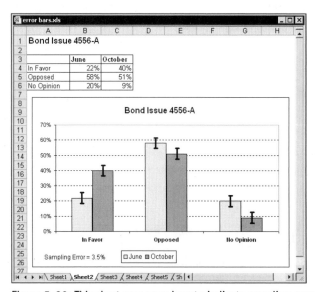

Figure 5-20: This chart uses error bars to indicate sampling error in a poll.

Figure 5-21 shows an XY chart that displays Y error bars using the Standard Deviation option. Unlike other error bar options, error bars that use the Standard Deviation option are displayed relative to the average of the data values. In this example, the 100 data points have a mean of 11.67 and a standard deviation of 4.69. Therefore, the error bars display the mean, plus or minus 4.69. Using error bars in this chart makes it clear that the majority of the data points fall within one standard deviation of the mean.

Because the x values for this chart are consecutive values, the data points (and the error bars) are equally spaced in the horizontal direction. This spacing creates a useful banding effect.

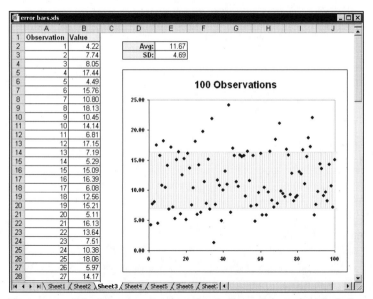

Figure 5-21: This chart uses error bars that indicate the standard deviation.

Figure 5-22 shows an XY chart that uses both Y error bars and X error bars. Both sets of error bars display the corresponding value plus or minus 10 percent. The X error bars and Y error bars are independent of each other and can use different options.

Formatting or modifying error bars

To change the formatting of error bars, double-click any error bar to display the Format Error Bars dialog box. In terms of formatting, you can change the line style and adjust the marker style (either on or off).

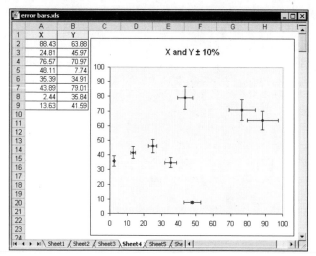

Figure 5-22: This XY chart uses X error bars and Y error bars.

The Format Error Bars dialog box also contains a Y Error Bars tab that enables you to change the options you set when you created the error bars. For XY charts and bubble charts, the dialog box also has an X Error Bars tab.

Using custom error bars

The Custom option for error bars is useful because it enables you to create error bars that aren't otherwise available. In most cases, you'll need first to create formulas that use the data and then to specify those formula cells as the range(s) for the error bars.

The chart in Figure 5-23 shows a line chart that plots monthly sales. It uses error bars to depict the relative sales volume for the *previous* year. In this case, an error bar that appears above a data point indicates that the previous year's sales were higher in that month. When it appears below the data point, the prior year's sales were lower for that month. This chart represents an alternative to displaying an additional data series. In this case, adding another series would make the chart cluttered and less legible.

Column D contains a simple formula that calculates the difference between the data in columns B and C. The range D2:D13 was used as the "+" range for the Custom error bar option, and the Plus display mode was selected.

Another example of a chart that uses custom error bars is shown in Figure 5-24. This column chart plots the average daily call volume for each of six weeks. The error bars depict the daily minimum and maximum for each week. For example, in Week-1 the average call volume was 77.71 calls per day. The maximum for the week was 116 and the minimum was 32.

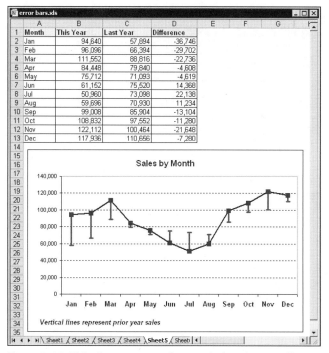

Figure 5-23: This chart uses error bars to depict corresponding monthly sales from the previous year.

The daily data appears in range A1:A9. Additional calculations were made for the data that appears in the chart. Row 13 contains the calculated average, which is the data used for the columns in the chart. Formulas in rows 14 and 15 calculate the maximums and minimums. Formulas in rows 16 and 17 calculate the data that's used for the error bars. The formulas in row 16 subtract the average from the maximum, to yield the values used in the "+" range for the error bars. The formulas in row 17 subtract the minimum from the average to get the values used in the "–" range for the error bars.

Connecting series points to a trendline

If you add a trendline to a chart, you can use error bars to indicate the deviations between the actual and the predicted values. Figure 5-25 shows an example.

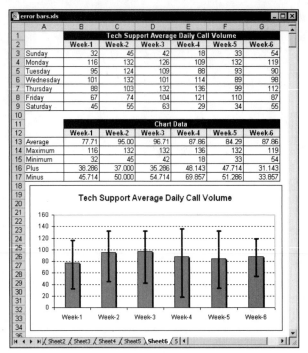

Figure 5-24: The columns depict the weekly average; the custom error bars show the minimum and maximum for the week.

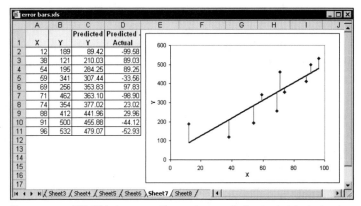

Figure 5-25: This XY chart uses Y error bars to indicate the deviation between the actual Y values and the predicted Y values on the trendline.

The first step is to add a trendline to the XY chart. Then, create formulas to calculate the predicted Y values (the values along the trend lines). For this example, the range C2:C11 contains the following array formula (entered using Ctrl+Shift+Enter):

```
=TREND(B2:B11,A2:A11)
```

Next, create formulas to calculate the difference between each predicted Y value and each actual Y value. In this example, cell D2 contains the following formula, which was copied down to cell D11:

```
=C2-B2
```

The final step is to add Y error bars to the chart, using the Y Error Bars tab of the Format Data Series dialog box. For this example, the Plus display option is used, along with a Custom + error amount. The values used for the custom error bars are in range D2:D11.

For data points in which the predicted Y value is greater than the actual Y value, the error bar extends upward from the data point. For data points in which the predicted Y value is less than the actual Y value, the error bar extends downward from the data point. The sum of these deviations will always be 0.

Error bar alternatives

In some cases you may prefer to "roll your own" error bars by adding one or two additional series to your chart. Figure 5-26 shows two charts. The chart on the top uses standard error bars to display one standard deviation. The chart on the bottom uses two additional series to plot lines that represent plus and minus one standard deviation.

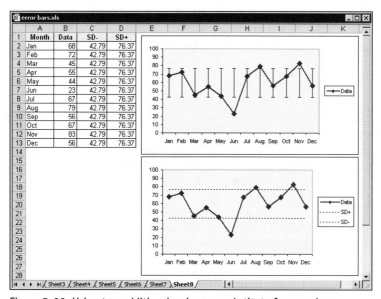

Figure 5-26: Using two additional series as a substitute for error bars

The data for the additional ranges used in the second chart are in columns C and D. The formula in C2, which was copied to the cells below, is

```
=AVERAGE($B$2:$B$13)-STDEV($B$2:$B$13)
```

The formula in D2, also copied to the cells below, is

```
=AVERAGE($B$2:$B$13)+STDEV($B$2:$B$13)
```

One advantage to these additional series is that you have more control over the formatting. Y Error bars, for example, always appear as vertical lines and cannot be connected horizontally. In addition, using a series for error bars enables you to display a description in the legend. Most would agree that the bottom chart is less cluttered and more legible.

Other Series Enhancements

So far, this chapter has covered trendlines and error bars. These are, essentially, two ways to augment a chart data series. In addition, some chart series can be enhanced with:

- ◆ Drop lines
- ◆ High-low lines
- ◆ Up/down bars
- ◆ Varied colors

These features are discussed in the sections that follow.

Series lines

A series line is applicable only for the 2-D variants of stacked-bar charts and stacked-column charts. Figure 5-27 shows an example of a stacked-column chart with the series line option enabled. As you can see, the series lines simply connect the top of each data point with the next data point in the series.

To turn series lines on or off, access the Format Data Series dialog box for any series in the chart. Click the Options tab and adjust the Series lines check box.

 TIP   For a single-series bar chart or column chart, the Series lines check box is disabled. If you would like to display a series line on such a chart, you need to change the chart type to a stacked-column chart.

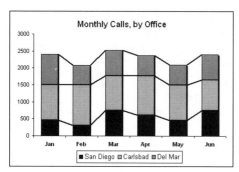

Figure 5-27: This stacked-column chart uses series lines.

To change the appearance of a series line, double-click it and use the Format Series Line dialog box. Formatting changes apply to all the series lines in the chart.

Drop Lines

Line charts and area charts can display drop lines, as shown in Figure 5-28. When this option is in effect, a line drops from each data point to the category axis.

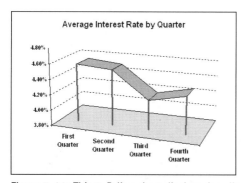

Figure 5-28: This 3-D line chart displays drop lines.

To turn drop lines on or off, access the Format Data Series dialog box for any series in the chart. Click the Options tab and adjust the Drop lines check box. All series that use the value axis for the selected series will be affected.

TIP Although XY charts do not support drop lines, you can get the same effect by using custom negative Y error bars. Set the error bar range equal to the y values range.

TIP

To apply drop lines to only one series in a multiseries chart, specify a secondary value axis for the series before you apply the drop lines. For details regarding secondary axes, refer to Chapter 4.

High-low lines

High-low lines are most often used in stock market charts. In fact, when you create a stock market chart, high-low lines are added automatically. However, this feature can be used in any line chart that has at least two series.

The high-low lines connect the maximum data point in the category with the minimum data point in the category. Figure 5-29 shows an example that uses two data series. The high-low lines depict the difference between the sales goal and the actual sales made.

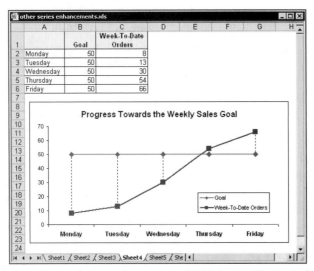

Figure 5-29: High-low lines connect the highest and lowest points within a category.

To add high-low lines to a line chart, access the Format Data Series dialog box for any series. Select the Options tab and place a checkmark next to the High-Low Lines check box.

To change the formatting, double-click a high-low line to access the Format High-Low Lines dialog box.

Up/down bars

As with high-low lines, up/down bars are commonly used in stock market charts. Up/down bars are available only with 2-D line charts that have at least two series.

In a stock market chart, up/down bars (sometimes referred to as *candlesticks*) connect the day's opening price with the closing price. If the closing price is higher than the opening price, then the bar is hollow (white). Otherwise, the bar is black. These are default colors; you can format up/down bars any way you like.

HOW UP/DOWN BARS WORK

If you plan to use up/down bars in a chart, you need to understand how they work. Up/down bars rely on the plot order of the series. The up/down bars always connect the first series with the last series. If a line chart has six data series, the up/down bars will connect the first and the sixth. The only way to control which series get connected is to change the series plot order. You can do this by using the Series Order tab of the Format Data Series dialog box for any data series.

Refer to Chapter 3 for more information about changing the plot order for data series.

To add up/down bars to a line chart, access the Format Data Series dialog box for any series. Select the Options tab and place a checkmark next to the Up/Down Bars check box. If the up/down bars do not connect the desired series, adjust the plot order.

To change the formatting, double-click an up/down bar to access the Format Up Bars dialog box. Also, note that when a chart has up/down bars, the Options tab of the Format Data series dialog box includes an option to change the gap between the bars.

USING UP/DOWN BARS IN NON-STOCK MARKET CHARTS

Figure 5-30 shows a line chart with up/down bars. The first series plots income and the second plots expenses. The up/down bars connect each corresponding data point and represent the net profit for the month. Note that, in January, expenses exceeded income, so the up/down bar for that month displays in a different color.

Another example of up/down bars is shown in Figure 5-31. This is a line chart with two series that display the normal high and low temperatures, by month. The lines are connected by up/down bars.

You'll notice, however, that the lines are invisible. This effect was done using the Patterns tab of the Format Data Series dialog box – the Line option was set to None. The result is a "floating column" chart that is not obscured by lines.

Varied colors for data points

Some chart types have an option that enables you to vary the color for each data point. Contrary to what you might expect, this option does not allow any type of conditional color formatting based on values.

For charts that support this option, it is turned on and off in the Options tab of the Format Data Series dialog box.

Except for pie charts and doughnut charts, this option is turned off by default. You'll find that this feature has quite a few limitations. For example, it is available only when the chart has one series. And for an XY chart, the feature works only with the default marker sizes. But, remember that you can format individual data points within a series. Refer to Chapter 4 for more details.

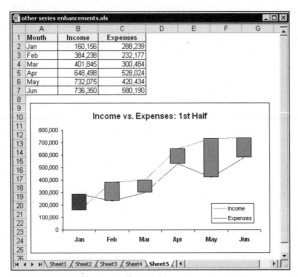

Figure 5-30: This chart uses up/down bars to depict net profit by month.

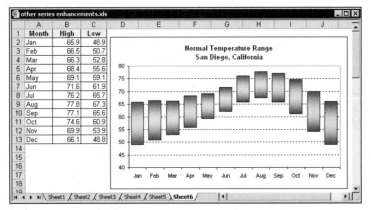

Figure 5-31: Using up/down bars to create floating columns

Chapter 6

Working with AutoShapes and Other Graphics

WHEN IT COMES TO VISUAL presentation, Excel has a lot more up its sleeve than charts. As you probably know, you can insert a wide (very wide) variety of graphic images into your worksheet to add pizzazz to an otherwise boring report. And, as you'll see, you can even combine these graphics with your charts.

This chapter describes the nonchart-related graphic tools available in Excel. These consist of AutoShapes, diagrams, and imported or pasted images.

Using AutoShapes

The Microsoft Office applications, including Excel, provide access to a variety of customizable graphic images known as *AutoShapes*. You can add an AutoShape to a worksheet's drawing layer or to a chart.

Access these AutoShapes using either of two methods:

♦ Choose Insert→Picture→AutoShapes to display the AutoShapes toolbar.

♦ Use the AutoShapes menu item on the Drawing toolbar.

The AutoShapes toolbar

The AutoShapes toolbar is shown in Figure 6-1.

Figure 6-1: The AutoShapes toolbar

Drawing objects with the AutoShapes tool is easy and very intuitive. The AutoShapes toolbar contains the following buttons, each of which represents a category of AutoShapes.

- **Lines:** Six styles of lines, including arrows and freehand drawing.

- **Connectors:** Nine styles of lines designed to indicate connections between other objects. These connectors automatically "snap to" other objects and maintain the connection when the objects are moved.

- **Basic Shapes:** Thirty-two basic shapes, including standard shapes such as rectangles and circles, plus nonstandard shapes such as a smiley face and a heart.

- **Block Arrows:** Twenty-eight arrow shapes.

- **Flowchart:** Twenty-seven shapes suitable for flowchart diagrams.

- **Stars and Banners:** Sixteen stars and banners.

- **Callouts:** Twenty callouts, suitable for annotating cells or chart elements.

- **More AutoShapes:** In case the supplied AutoShapes aren't enough, you can get more. Click this button and the Task Pane displays additional AutoShapes in a scrolling list. This option is not available in versions prior to Excel 2000.

You may find it convenient to "tear off" one or more of the AutoShape categories and create new toolbars. To do so, just drag the tiny title bar and move it away. The effect will be a free-floating toolbar that displays the icons for the AutoShapes in the category.

Inserting AutoShapes

An AutoShape can be added to a worksheet's drawing layer or added to a chart. To insert an AutoShape on a worksheet, start by selecting any cell. To insert an AutoShape into a chart, start by activating the chart. Next, click the category (for example, Basic Shapes), click a shape, and then drag in the worksheet (or chart) to create the AutoShape. When you release the mouse button, the object is selected and its name appears in the Name box (see Figure 6-2).

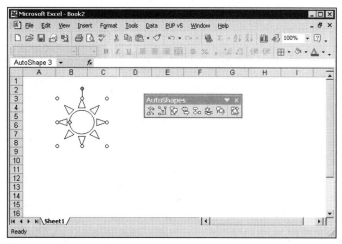

Figure 6-2: This AutoShape was drawn on the worksheet. Its name (AutoShape 3) appears in the Name box.

If a chart is not activated when you insert the AutoShape, you can still insert an AutoShape on *top* of a chart. The AutoShape may appear to be added to the chart, but it will actually reside on the worksheet's drawing layer (this is usually not what you want). Consequently, it will not be moved or resized with the chart.

A few of the AutoShapes require a slightly different approach. For example, when adding a FreeForm AutoShape (from the Lines category), you can click repeatedly to create lines. Or, click and drag to create a nonlinear shape. Double-click to finish drawing and create the AutoShape. The Curve AutoShape (also in the Lines category) also requires several clicks while drawing.

Following are a few tips to keep in mind when creating AutoShapes.

◆ AutoShapes are given names in the form of *AutoShape 1*, *AutoShape 2*, and so on. Some, however, are given more descriptive names. For example, if you create a rectangle AutoShape, it will be named *Rectangle n*, where n represents the next AutoShape number. To change the name of an AutoShape: Select it, type a new name in the Name box, and press Enter. Oddly, Excel allows multiple AutoShapes to have the same name.

◆ When you create an AutoShape by dragging, you can hold down the Shift key to maintain the object's default proportions. For example, the Rectangle AutoShape will be rendered as a perfect square. To constrain a line or arrow object to angles that are divisible by 15 degrees, press Shift while you draw the object.

◆ You can control how objects appear on-screen by using the View tab of the Options dialog box. Normally, the Show All option is selected. You can hide all objects by choosing Hide All or display objects as placeholders by choosing Show Placeholders (this may speed things up if you have complex objects that take a long time to redraw).

Adding text to an AutoShape

Many of the AutoShape objects support text. To add text to such an AutoShape, right-click it and then choose Add Text from the shortcut menu. Or, just select the object and start typing the text. Either of these actions puts the object into Edit mode, which allows you to enter and edit text. When an object is in Edit mode, the word *Edit* appears at the left side of the status bar.

 TIP   When an AutoShape contains text, clicking the object will put it into Edit mode. To select the object itself, press Escape to exit Edit mode. Alternatively, you can press Ctrl while you click the AutoShape, or click the edge of the AutoShape.

To change the formatting for all of the text in an AutoShape, select the AutoShape object. You can then use the Formatting toolbar buttons, or use the Format AutoShape dialog box. To change the formatting of specific characters within the text, select only those characters, and use the toolbar buttons or the Format AutoShape dialog box.

Formatting AutoShape objects

It should come as no surprise that you can change the formatting of AutoShapes at any time. First, you must select the AutoShape object. If the object is filled with a color or pattern, you can click anywhere on the object to select it. If the object is not filled (formatted with "No Fill" to make it transparent), you must click the object's border.

About the Drawing Layer

Every worksheet and chart sheet has what's known as a *drawing layer*. This invisible surface can hold AutoShapes, graphic images, embedded charts, inserted objects, and so on.

Objects placed on the drawing layer can be moved, resized, copied, and deleted — with no effect on any other elements in the worksheet. Objects on the drawing layer have properties that relate to how they are moved and sized when underlying cells are moved and sized. When you right-click on a graphic object and choose Format Object from the shortcut menu, you get a tabbed dialog box (see the accompanying figure). Click the Properties tab to adjust how the object moves or resizes with its underlying cells. Your choices are as follows:

◆ Move and size with cells: If this option is selected, the object appears to be attached to the cells beneath it. For example, if you insert rows above the object, the object moves down. If you increase the column width, the object gets wider.

◆ Move but don't size with cells: If this option is checked, the object moves if rows or columns are inserted, but it never changes its size if you change row heights or column widths.

◆ Don't move or size with cells: This option makes the object completely independent of the underlying cells.

The preceding options control how an object is moved or sized with respect to the underlying cells. Excel also lets you "attach" an object to a cell. In the Edit panel of the Options dialog box, place a checkmark next to the check box labeled Cut, Copy, and Sort Objects with Cells. After you do so, graphic objects on the drawing layer are attached to the underlying cells.

Because a chart sheet doesn't have cells, objects placed on a chart sheet don't have these options. Chart sheets, however, also have a drawing layer, and objects placed on the drawing layer float above the other chart elements. Objects on a chart sheet's drawing layer have a property that relates to how the object is sized if the chart size is changed. By default, objects within a chart are sized with the chart. You can change this so that the object size is not adjusted when the chart is resized.

You can make some basic formatting changes using the buttons on the Formatting or Drawing toolbars. For example, you can change the color by using the Fill Color button. Other modifications require that you use the Format AutoShape dialog box. After selecting one or more objects, you can display this dialog box by using any of the following techniques:

- ◆ Choose the Format→AutoShape command.

- ◆ Press Ctrl+1.

- ◆ Double-click the AutoShape.

- ◆ Right-click the AutoShape and choose Format AutoShape from the short-cut menu.

The Format AutoShape dialog box has several tabs, the number of which depends on the type of object and whether it contains text. I discuss each of the tabs in the following sections.

THE COLORS AND LINES TAB

Figure 6-3 shows the Colors and Lines tab of the Format AutoShape dialog box. This tab is used to adjust the colors, lines, and arrow styles used in the object. Depending on the type of AutoShape selected, some of the controls may be disabled. For example, the controls that adjust the arrowhead styles will not be available for an AutoShape that does not have arrows.

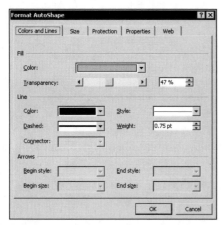

Figure 6-3: The Colors and Lines tab of the Format AutoShape dialog box

There is more to this dialog box than meets the eye, and it can lead to other dialog boxes. For example, click the Color drop-down list and you can select Fill Effects, which brings up another multitabbed dialog box that lets you specify a wide variety of fill effects, including colored gradients and pictures.

THE SIZE PANEL

The Size panel of the Format AutoShape dialog box enables you to precisely adjust the size, rotation, and scale of the object. If the object is a picture, you can use the Reset button to return the object to its original dimensions and rotation. Oddly,

Excel provides no direct way to precisely specify an object's *position* (its top and left coordinates).

 Contrary to what you might expect, if you rotate an AutoShape that contains text, the text *will not* be rotated along with the object.

You can also change the object's size directly by dragging one of the handles of the AutoShape. You can change the rotation directly by clicking the small green circle and then dragging. Note, however, that not all AutoShapes can be rotated.

If multiple objects of different sizes are selected, the Height and Width fields will be blank. You can then enter values, which will be applied to all the selected objects — a quick way to force all the objects to be the same size.

THE PROTECTION TAB
The Protection tab determines whether the object is "locked." Locking has no effect, however, unless the worksheet is protected. You can protect the worksheet with the Tools→Protection→Protect Sheet command.

THE PROPERTIES TAB
The Properties tab of the Format AutoShape dialog box determines how an object is moved and sized with respect to the underlying cells or chart. See the sidebar "About the Drawing Layer," earlier in this chapter.

THE FONT, ALIGNMENT, AND MARGINS TABS
These three tabs appear only if the shape contains text.

The Font tab should be familiar because its options are the same as those for formatting cells.

The controls in the Alignment tab enable you to specify the vertical and horizontal alignment of the text and choose the orientation. Unlike text contained in cells, you cannot specify an angle for the orientation (you're limited to four orientation options). If you choose the Automatic size option, the shape's size adjusts to fit the text that it contains.

The controls in the margins tab allow you to adjust the amount of space along the sides of the text.

THE WEB TAB
If you plan to save your worksheet as a Web page, you can specify some alternative text for the object in this tab. The alternative text appears when the user hovers the mouse pointer over the image in a Web browser. This option is available in Excel 2000 and later.

Selecting multiple objects

In many cases, you may want to work with several AutoShapes at one time. Excel provides several methods that enable you to select multiple objects on a worksheet or chart.

- ◆ Press Ctrl while you click the objects.

- ◆ Click the Select Objects tool on the Drawing toolbar. The mouse pointer turns into an arrow. Click and "lasso" the objects that you want to select. To return to normal selection mode, press Esc or click the Select Objects tool again.

- ◆ To select all objects on the worksheet, choose Edit→Go To (or press Ctrl+G) to display the Go To dialog box. Click Special, choose the Objects option button, and click OK. This method is particularly useful if you want to delete all objects on a worksheet. When the objects are selected, press Del.

Moving objects

To move an object, select it and drag one of its borders. For more precise control, use the arrow keys to move the selected object one pixel at a time.

Copying objects

You can use Excel's standard Copy and Paste operations to copy graphic objects on a worksheet or within a chart. Another alternative is to select one or more objects and then press Ctrl while you drag in the worksheet.

To copy an object from the worksheet's drawing layer into a chart, select the object and choose Edit→Copy. Then activate your chart and choose Edit→Paste.

Changing the stack order of objects

As you add objects to the drawing layer of a worksheet (or to a chart), you'll find that objects are "stacked" on top of each other in the order in which you add them. New objects are stacked on top of older objects.

In some case, an object may be partially or completely hidden by an object higher in the stack. You can change the order in this stack. Right-click the object and select Order from the shortcut menu. This command leads to a submenu with the following choices:

- ◆ **Bring to Front:** Brings the object to the top of the stack.

- ◆ **Send to Back:** Sends the object to the bottom of the stack.

- ◆ **Bring Forward:** Brings the object one step higher toward the top of the stack.

- ◆ **Send Backward:** Sends the object one step lower toward the bottom of the stack.

Embedded charts are stored on the drawing layer, and you can take advantage of the stack order to overlay one chart on top of another. Figure 6-4 shows an example. The smaller chart is higher in the stack order than the larger chart, so it appears on top. Note that the plot area of the larger chart is reduced in size and moved to the far left of the chart area, leaving room for the smaller chart.

For more examples of combining charts by stacking, refer to Chapter 8.

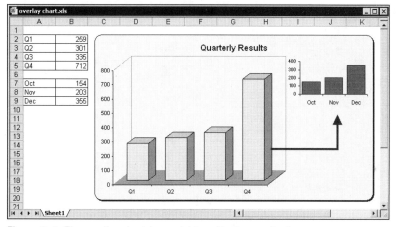

Figure 6–4: The smaller chart is overlaid on the larger chart.

Grouping objects

Excel lets you combine two or more objects into a single object. This feature is known as *grouping*. For example, if you create a design that uses four separate AutoShapes, you can combine them into a group. Then you can manipulate this group as a single object (move it, resize it, and so on).

To group two or more objects, select all the objects and then right-click. Choose Grouping→Group from the shortcut menu. Later, if you need to modify one of the objects in the group, you can ungroup them by right-clicking and selecting Grouping→Ungroup from the shortcut menu. This command breaks the object into its original components.

You can also group one or more embedded charts. Doing so ensures that the charts stay together and enables you to move and resize them together.

Using the Drawing Toolbar

To display the Drawing toolbar, click the Drawing button on Excel's Formatting toolbar. This button serves as a toggle, so clicking it again hides the Drawing toolbar. Normally, the Drawing toolbar appears at the bottom of Excel's window, but you can place it anywhere you like.

Figure 6-5 shows the Drawing toolbar. As you'll see, there is more to this toolbar than meets the eye.

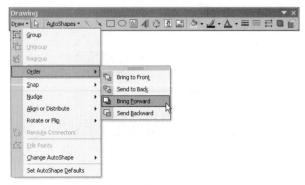

Figure 6-5: The Drawing toolbar

Table 6-1 describes the tools in the Drawing toolbar. The tools are listed in the order in which they appear. These tools are for Excel 2002. Some of these tools are not available in earlier versions of Excel.

TABLE 6-1 THE TOOLS ON THE DRAWING TOOLBAR

Tool Name	What the Tool Does
Draw	Displays a menu with choices that let you manipulate objects.
Select Objects	Selects one or more graphic objects. If you have several objects and you want to select a group of them, use this tool to drag the outline so that it surrounds all the objects. Click the button again (or press Esc) to return to normal selection mode.
AutoShapes	Displays a menu of seven categories of shapes. Drag this menu to create an AutoShapes toolbar. You also can display the AutoShapes toolbar with the Insert→Picture→ AutoShapes command.

Tool Name	What the Tool Does
Line	Inserts a line.
Arrow	Inserts an arrow.
Rectangle	Inserts a rectangle or square.
Oval	Inserts an oval or a circle.
Text Box	Inserts a free-floating box into which you type text.
Insert WordArt	Displays the WordArt Gallery dialog box, which lets you create attractive titles using text. You also can display this dialog box with the Insert→Picture→WordArt command.
Insert Diagram or Organization Chart	Displays the Diagram Gallery dialog box. You can also display this dialog box with the Insert→Diagram command.
Insert Clip Art	Displays the Insert ClipArt dialog box. You can also display this dialog box with the Insert→Picture→Clip Art command.
Insert Picture From File	Displays the Insert Picture dialog box. You can also display this dialog box with the Insert→Picture→From File command.
Fill Color	Lets you select a fill color or fill effect for an object.
Line Color	Lets you select the line color for an object.
Font Color	Lets you select a font color for text objects.
Line Style	Lets you specify the width of the lines in an object.
Dash Style	Lets you specify the style of the lines in an object.
Arrow Style	Lets you specify the arrow style for arrows.
Shadow Style	Lets you specify the type of shadow for an object and settings for the shadow.
3-D Style	Lets you specify the type of perspective effect for an object and settings for the effect.

Aligning objects

When you have several objects on a worksheet, you may want to align these objects with each other. Or, you may want to align objects with cell borders.

You can drag the objects (which isn't very precise). Or, you can use the keyboard arrow keys to move a selected object one pixel at a time. The fastest way to align objects is to let Excel do it for you.

To align multiple objects, start by selecting them. Then click the Draw tool on the Drawing toolbar. This tool expands to show a menu. Select the Align or Distribute menu option, followed by any of the six alignment options: Align Left, Align Center, Align Right, Align Top, Align Middle, or Align Bottom.

Unfortunately, you cannot specify which object is used as the basis for the alignment. When you're aligning objects to the left (or right), they are always aligned with the left- (or right-) most object that's selected. When you're aligning objects to the top (or bottom), they are always aligned with the top- (or bottom-) most object. Aligning the centers (or middles) of objects will align them along an axis halfway between the left and right (or top and bottom) extremes of the selected shapes.

To align objects to the cell grid when you create, resize, or move them, you need to turn on the "snap to grid" option. In the Drawing toolbar, choose Draw→Snap→To Grid. When that option is in effect, all objects that are created or resized will be aligned with the cell borders. And when you move an object, its upper-left corner will always be at a cell intersection.

You might find it easier to work with objects if you turn off the worksheet grid lines. The snap to grid features work, even if the cell grid lines aren't visible.

You can override the current snap to grid setting by pressing the Alt key while you move or resize an object.

Spacing objects evenly

You can instruct Excel to "distribute" three or more objects such that they are equally spaced horizontally or vertically. Select the objects and then click the Draw tool on the Drawing toolbar. This tool expands to show a menu. Select the Align or Distribute menu option, followed by either Distribute Horizontally or Distribute Vertically.

Changing an AutoShape to a different AutoShape

You can easily change an AutoShape to a different AutoShape. Select it and then click the Draw tool on the Drawing toolbar. Choose Change AutoShape, select the category for the new AutoShape, and then select the AutoShape. Any formatting applied to the AutoShape will remain.

This procedure does not work with AutoShapes from the Lines or Connectors category. AutoShapes in these categories cannot be changed to a different type.

Adding shadows and 3-D effects

You can apply attractive shadow and 3-D effects to AutoShapes (except for those in the Line and Connectors categories). Use the Shadow and 3-D tools on the Drawing toolbar to apply these effects. Shadows and 3-D effects are mutually exclusive. In other words, you can apply either a shadow or a 3-D effect – not both – to an AutoShape.

To apply either of these effects, select an AutoShape that you've drawn on a worksheet or chart, and then click either the Shadow or the 3-D tool. The tool expands to show a list of options. Select an option, and it's applied to the selected shape. Figure 6-6 shows some AutoShapes that have been formatted with shadows or 3-D effects.

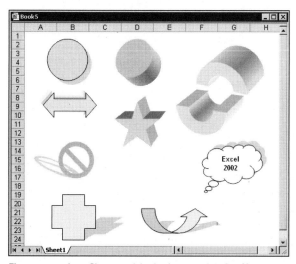

Figure 6-6: AutoShapes with shadows and 3-D effects

You can adjust the Shadow or 3-D settings by clicking the appropriate tool and then selecting the Shadow Settings or 3-D Settings option. Both these options display a toolbar that lets you fine-tune the effect. You'll find that there are *lots* of options available, and they're all quite straightforward. The best way to become familiar with these effects is to experiment.

Changing the AutoShape defaults

You can change the default settings for the AutoShapes that you draw. For example, if you prefer a particular text color or fill color for your AutoShapes, you can set these as the defaults for all new AutoShapes that you insert.

To change the default settings, create an AutoShape and format it as you like. You can change colors, fill effects, line widths and styles, font settings, and shadow or 3-D effects. Then select the formatted object, right-click, and select Set AutoShape Defaults from the shortcut menu. You can also access this command from the Draw tool on the Drawing toolbar.

Printing objects

By default, objects are printed along with the worksheet. If you don't want the objects to print, access the Sheet panel of the Page Setup dialog box and select the Draft option. Or right-click the object, select Format from the shortcut menu, and uncheck the Print Object check box in the Properties panel.

Working with Other Graphic Types

Excel can import a wide variety of graphics into a worksheet. You have several choices:

◆ Use the Microsoft Clip Organizer to locate and insert an image.

◆ Import a graphic file directly.

◆ Copy and paste and image using the Windows Clipboard.

◆ Obtain the image directly from a digital camera or scanner.

◆ Use any of several special-purpose "applets" provided with Microsoft Office.

About graphics files

Graphics files come in two main categories: *bitmap* and *vector* (picture). Bitmap images are made up of discrete dots. They usually look pretty good at their original size but often lose clarity if you increase or decrease the size. Vector-based images, on the other hand, retain their crispness regardless of their size. Examples of common bitmap file formats include BMP, PCX, DIB, JPG, and GIF. Examples of common vector file formats include CGM, WMF, EPS, and DRW.

Bitmap files vary in the number of colors they use (even "black-and-white" images use multiple colors, because these are usually gray-scale images). If you view a high-color bitmap graphic using a video mode that displays only 256 colors, the image usually doesn't look very good.

You can find thousands of graphics files free for the taking on the Internet. Be aware, however, that some files have copyright restrictions.

 Using bitmap graphics in a worksheet can dramatically increase the size of your workbook, resulting in more memory usage and longer load and save times. If you're using Excel 2002, you can compress the graphics files. To do so, select an image and choose Compress Pictures from the Picture toolbar.

The most common graphics file formats are GIF, JPG, and BMP, but Excel supports many other formats. Table 6-2 lists the graphics file types supported by Excel 2002. Earlier versions of Excel do not support all these formats.

TABLE 6-2 GRAPHICS FILE FORMATS SUPPORTED BY EXCEL 2002

File Type	Description
BMP, DIB, RLE, BMZ	Windows bitmap
CDR	CorelDRAW graphics
CGM	Computer Graphics Metafiles
DRW	Micrografx Designer/Draw
DXF	AutoCAD Format 2-D
EMF	Windows Enhanced Metafile
EMZ	Compressed Windows Enhanced Metafile
EPS	Encapsulated PostScript
FPX	FPX Format
GIF, GFA	Graphic Interchange Format*
HGL	HP Graphics Language
JPG, JPEG, JFIF, JPE	JPEG File Interchange Format
MIX	Picture It! Format
PCT, PICT	Macintosh PICT
PCD	Kodak Photo CD
PCG, PRG, PSG	Print Shop Graphics

Continued

TABLE 6-2 GRAPHICS FILE FORMATS SUPPORTED BY EXCEL 2002 *(Continued)*

File Type	Description
PCZ	Compressed Macintosh PICT
PCX	PC Paintbrush
PNG	Portable Network Graphics
TGA	Targa graphics format
TIF, TIFF	Tagged Image File Format
WMF	Windows Metafile
WMZ	Compressed Windows Metafile
WPG	WordPerfect Graphics

Excel supports animated GIF files — sort of. If you insert an animated GIF file, the image will be animated only if you save your workbook as a Web page and then view it in a Web browser.

Using the Microsoft Clip Organizer

The Clip Organizer is a shared program that is also accessible from other Microsoft Office applications. In some versions of Office, this is known as the Clip Gallery. Besides providing an easy way to locate and insert images, the Clip Organizer lets you insert sound and video files. This tool also gives you direct access to Microsoft's Design Gallery Live on the Web.

You access the Clip Organizer by selecting the Insert→Picture→Clip Art command. In Excel 2002, this displays the Insert Clip Art Task Pane. You can search for clip art using the controls at the top of the Task Pane. Figure 6-7 shows the thumbnail images resulting from a search for "car." To insert an image into the active worksheet, just click the thumbnail. For additional options, right-click the thumbnail image.

Want a Great Graphics File Viewer?

Many users are content to use the graphics file-viewing capabilities built into Windows. But if you do a lot of work with graphics files, you owe it to yourself to get a "real" file-viewing program.

Many graphics viewers are available, but one of the best products in its class is IrfanView. It enables you to view just about any graphics file you throw at it, and has features and options that will satisfy even hard-core graphics mavens. Best of all, it's free! To download a copy, visit www.irfanview.com.

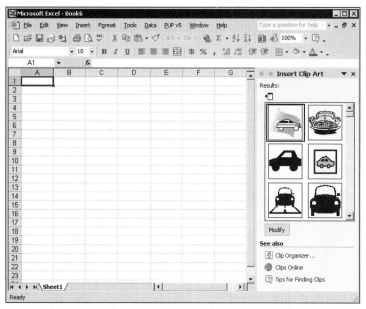

Figure 6-7: Use Excel 2002's Task Pane to search for clip art and other multimedia files.

You may prefer to use the Clip Organizer to access image files. To display the Clip Organizer, click the Clip Organizer hyperlink at the bottom of the Task Pane.

TIP   You can also add new files to the Clip Organizer. You might want to do this if you tend to insert a particular graphic file into your worksheets (such as your company logo). Use the File→Add Clips to Organizer→On My Own command to select the file. These images will be listed in the Unclassified Clips section. To place it in a different category, just drag the image to the category. You can also use the Edit→Keywords command to associate words with your imported image. Doing this will enable you to locate the image when searching.

If you can't find a suitable image, you can go online and browse through the extensive clip art at Microsoft's Clip Gallery Live Web site. Click the Clips Online button, and your Web browser will be activated, at which point you can view the images (or listen to the sounds) and add those you want to your Clip Organizer.

Inserting graphics files

If the graphic image that you want to insert is available in a file, you can easily import the file into your worksheet. Choose the Insert→Picture→From File command. Excel displays its Insert Picture dialog box, which enables you to browse for the file. Figure 6-8 shows a worksheet after importing a JPG photograph.

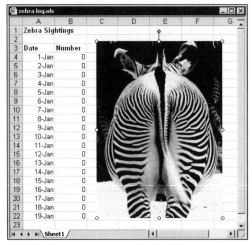

Figure 6–8: This photo was added to the worksheet.

Copying graphics by using the Clipboard

In some cases, you may want to use a graphic image that is not stored in a separate file or is in a file that Excel can't import. For example, you may have an obscure drawing program that uses a file format that Excel doesn't support. You may be able to export the file to a supported format, but it may be easier to load the file into the drawing program and copy the image to the Clipboard (using that program's Edit→Copy command). Then you can activate Excel and paste the image to the drawing layer, using Edit→Paste.

A graphic copied from an OLE-enabled application will retain a link to the originating application. Double-clicking the imported graphic will open the source application to edit the graphic. To disable this link, and possibly shrink the Excel file containing the graphic, use Edit→Paste Special and choose a format that doesn't create a link.

Suppose that you see a graphic displayed on-screen but you can't select it – it may be part of a program's logo, for example. In this case, you can copy the entire screen to the Clipboard and then paste it into Excel. To copy all or part of the screen, use the following keyboard commands:

◆ **PrintScreen:** Copies the entire screen to the Clipboard

◆ **Alt+PrintScreen:** Copies the active window to the Clipboard

Most of the time, you don't want the entire screen — just a portion of it. The solution is to crop the image using Excel's Crop tool (in the Picture toolbar). Versions prior to Excel 2000 do not have a Crop tool, so you'll need to crop the picture in a graphics program before pasting it.

Importing from a digital camera or scanner

Another option lets you bring in an image directly from a digital camera or a scanner. To use this feature, make sure that your device is connected and set up properly. Then choose Insert→Picture→From Scanner or Camera. The exact procedure will vary, depending on your camera or scanner. In most cases, the image will appear in Microsoft Photo Editor. You can adjust the image, if necessary, and then select File→Exit and Return to Excel.

NOTE   Many digital cameras use a USB port to transfer images. When that's the case, the digital camera's memory will be seen as a storage device located under "My Computer" and accessible with the normal Insert→Picture→From File command.

Displaying a worksheet background image

If you want to use a graphic image for a worksheet's background (similar to wallpaper on the Windows desktop), use the Format→Sheet→Background command and select a graphics file. The selected graphics file is tiled on the worksheet. Unfortunately, worksheet background images are for on-screen display only. These images do not appear when the worksheet is printed.

Modifying pictures

When you insert a picture on a worksheet, you can modify the picture in a number of ways using the Picture toolbar, shown in Figure 6-9. This toolbar appears automatically when you select a picture object. The Excel 2002 tools are described in Table 6-3. Note that some of these tools are not available in earlier versions of Excel.

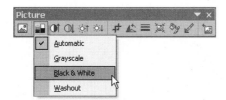

Figure 6-9: The Picture toolbar lets you adjust a picture.

TABLE 6-3 THE TOOLS ON THE PICTURE TOOLBAR

Tool Name	What the Tool Does
Insert Picture from File	Displays the Insert Picture dialog box.
Color	Lets you change a picture to gray scale, black and white, or "washout" (perhaps suitable for a watermark).
More Contrast	Increases the contrast of the picture.
Less Contrast	Decreases the contrast of the picture.
More Brightness	Increases the brightness of the picture.
Less Brightness	Decreases the brightness of the picture.
Crop	Crops the picture. After clicking this tool, drag any of the picture's handles to make the picture smaller.
Rotate Left	Rotates the picture 90 degrees counter-clockwise
Line Style	Selects a border for the picture.
Compress Pictures	Displays the Compress Pictures dialog box, which enables you to reduce the size of the image.
Format Picture	Displays the Format Picture dialog box, which provides options for modifying the picture.
Set Transparent Color	Selects a color that will be transparent. Underlying cell contents appear through the selected transparent color. This option is not available for all types of pictures.
Reset Picture	Returns the picture to its original state.

Using the Office Applets

Microsoft Office ships with a few graphics-related tools that, for lack of a better term, I refer to as applets. If you use Excel 2002, you'll have access to the following:

- Diagrams and Organization Charts
- Word Art

Creating diagrams and org charts

Excel 2002 introduced an interesting new feature that enables you to insert a variety of (possibly) useful diagrams into a worksheet. These diagrams are made up of AutoShapes that are enclosed in a "shell" so that they work together as a group.

To insert a diagram, choose Insert→Diagram and you'll see the dialog box shown in Figure 6-10.

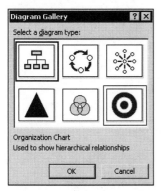

Figure 6-10: The Diagram Gallery dialog box is available in Excel 2002 only.

This dialog box offers the following diagram types:

◆ Organizational Chart

◆ Cycle Diagram

◆ Radial Diagram

◆ Pyramid Diagram

◆ Venn Diagram

◆ Target Diagram

Choose a diagram type, click OK, and Excel inserts a diagram template, ready to be customized. Use the Diagrams toolbar to customize your diagram. Don't hide this toolbar! It's the only source for the tools you need to customize the diagrams.

With the exception of the organizational chart, these diagrams are interchangeable. After a diagram is customized, you can convert it to a different type by using the Change To button on the Diagrams toolbar.

Perhaps the most useful diagram choice is the organization chart. You'll notice that an organizational chart diagram displays its own toolbar (not the Diagram toolbar). Figure 6-11 shows an example of a simple org chart.

Noticeably absent is a diagram type for creating flow charts. You can, however, create flow charts by using the standard AutoShapes (see "Creating a flow chart," later in this chapter).

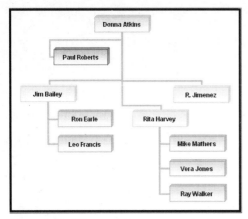

Figure 6-11: This org chart was created using
Excel 2002's Diagram Gallery.

 If you use a version prior to Excel 2002, you'll still be able to create organization
charts, but the procedure will be quite a bit different because Excel uses a
different tool. The Insert→Picture→Organizational Chart will insert a new
embedded object into your worksheet, and you can customize it to your liking.

Working with these diagrams takes a bit of practice, but after you get the hang
of it, you'll find that they can be customized in many ways. The best way to
become familiar with diagrams is to experiment. However, you should be aware of
these general tips:

◆ **The Organization Chart and Diagram toolbars both have a button labeled
Layout.** When you click this button, you see an AutoLayout menu item.
This is actually a toggle. When AutoLayout is turned on, you can't move
the diagram elements around. For fine-tuning the position of the items in
your diagram, you'll want to make sure that AutoLayout is turned off. But
be careful. If you turn AutoLayout back on, the diagram will revert to its
unedited state!

◆ **You can change the AutoShape used by an element in a diagram.** First,
right-click the diagram and turn off the AutoFormat option (by default,
this option is turned on). Then select the element, click the Draw item on
the Drawing toolbar, and choose Change AutoShape. To revert back to the
original shapes, turn the AutoFormat option back on.

◆ **To change the diagram background, right-click the background of the
diagram and choose Format Diagram.**

Creating WordArt

The WordArt applet enables you to create a graphic image from text. You can insert a WordArt image by using the WordArt tool on the Drawing toolbar or by selecting the Insert→Picture→WordArt command. Either method displays the WordArt Gallery dialog box. Select a style and then enter your text in the next dialog box. Click OK, and the image is inserted in the worksheet.

When you select a WordArt image, Excel displays the WordArt toolbar. Use these tools to modify the WordArt image. You'll find that you have *lots* of flexibility with this tool. In addition, you can use the Shadow and 3-D tools to further manipulate the image. Figure 6-12 shows a few examples of WordArt images inserted on a worksheet.

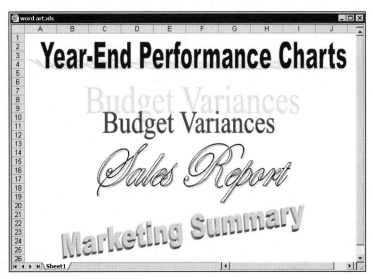

Figure 6-12: WordArt examples

A Gallery of Graphic Examples

In this section, I provide you with some examples of using Excel's drawing tools. Perhaps these examples will get your own creative juices flowing.

All the examples in this section, and others, are available on the companion CD-ROM.

Using AutoShapes and pictures with charts

Combining AutoShapes and other graphics with charts opens the door to some interesting visual effects. The examples in this section demonstrate a few possibilities. Have fun experimenting, but when other eyes will view your work, be careful not to overdo these effects. Whereas one or two embellishments can drive a point home, too many can obscure the chart's meaning.

ANNOTATING CHARTS

A common use for AutoShapes is to annotate a chart. For example, you can use AutoShapes from the Callout category to add descriptive text that calls attention to a particular data point. This technique works for both embedded charts and charts on chart sheets. Figure 6-13 shows an example of an embedded chart that has been annotated with a Text Box and an AutoShape from the Callouts category.

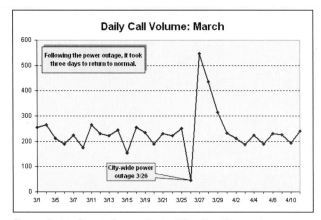

Figure 6-13: Annotating a chart with a Text Box and an AutoShape

Another example of chart annotation is shown in Figure 6-14. This pie chart is actually grouped with a Rectangle AutoShape that displays text. The text, which summarizes the chart, is aligned to the upper-right corner of the rectangle. The image also includes a small clip art logo in the bottom-right corner, which is grouped with the chart and AutoShape.

USING AUTOSHAPES IN LIEU OF A LEGEND

Figure 6-15 shows another example of AutoShapes from the Callout category. This chart displays two lines, and AutoShapes are used to identify the lines. This technique is often useful when charts are printed in black and white. In such a case, the line colors are often difficult or impossible to ascertain.

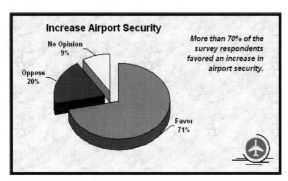

Figure 6-14: Annotating a chart with a Rectangle
AutoShape that includes text

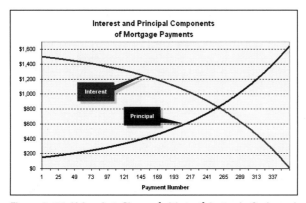

Figure 6-15: Using AutoShapes (with text) instead of a legend

USING AN AUTOSHAPE AS A CHART BACKGROUND

Figure 6-16 shows a rectangle AutoShape with 3-D formatting applied. The chart
was positioned on top of the rectangle, and then the two objects were grouped. This
creates an interesting alternative to using a standard data table.

Another example of using an AutoShape for a background for charts is shown in
Figure 6-17. This AutoShape is named *Film* and was taken from the "More
AutoShapes" category. It is used as a backdrop to display three pie charts. After
positioning the charts, all four objects were grouped together.

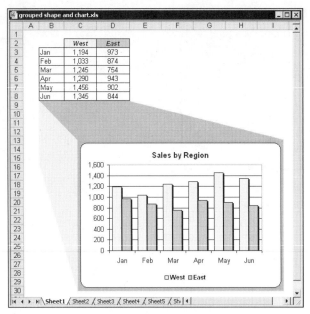

Figure 6-16: A chart placed on top of an AutoShape

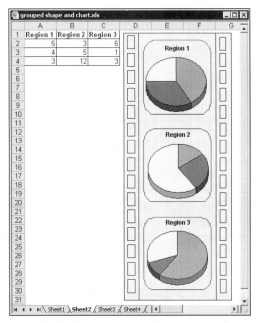

Figure 6-17: Three pie charts placed on top of
an AutoShape

USING GRAPHICS IN A CHART SERIES

Excel offers a wide variety of chart types, but sometimes you may want something else for added impact. One of the easiest ways to make a chart more interesting is to replace the series elements (bars, columns, areas, pie slices or line markers) with a graphic image.

For some reason, Excel is not consistent in this area. You can replace bars, columns, or line markers simply by pasting a copied image. But for an area chart or pie slice, the image must exist in a file (pasting doesn't work). To paste an image into a bar series, column series, or pie chart, the procedure is simple: Copy the image to the clipboard, select the data series or single data point, and choose Edit→Paste. The AutoShapes provide many images to work with, and you can also use WordArt. Figure 6-18 shows a standard column chart (left), and the same chart using an arrow-shaped AutoShape (with a shadow effect) for the columns.

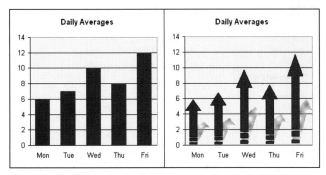

Figure 6-18: A column chart, before and after replacing the columns with an AutoShape

You can also use this procedure with standard text entered into a cell. It works best with markers in a line chart. The trick is to copy the cell as a picture. After formatting the cell to your liking, select it, press Shift, and choose Edit→Copy→Picture. Then select the line (or an individual marker on the line) and choose Edit→Paste. Figure 6-19 shows an example. Each of the line markers was replaced by a different graphic, generated with the Wingdings font.

If the graphic image exists in a file, you can use the following procedure. This method applies to bars, columns, line markers, area charts, and pie chart slices.

1. Click to select the series in the chart. To modify a single data point, click that data point when the series is selected.

2. Access the Format Data Series dialog box and select the Patterns tab.

3. Click the Fill Effects button to display the Fill Effects dialog box.

4. Select the Picture tab.

5. Click the Select Picture button and choose an image file.

6. Choose a format for the picture: Stretch, Stack, or Stack and Scale To.

7. Click OK.

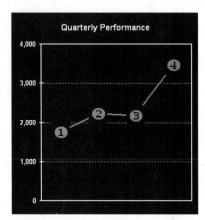

Figure 6–19: Each line marker was replaced
by text in a cell, copied as a picture.

The example in Figure 6-20 uses images that are stacked and scaled, with each image representing two units. In this chart, the data series was given the name *= 2 Tons* so that the legend would serve an additional purpose.

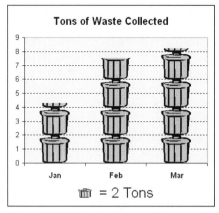

Figure 6–20: This chart uses an image scaled
to represent two units.

TIP Charts that use series which have been customized using an image can be saved as a user-defined custom format. See Chapter 4 for more information about user-defined chart formats.

CREATING SEMITRANSPARENT BARS OR COLUMNS

You may have noticed that the Colors and Lines tab of the Format AutoShape dialog includes an option labeled Transparency. This enables you to make an AutoShape semitransparent (that is, a see-through object). The transparency is specified as a percentage.

Although the columns and bars in an Excel chart do not support transparency, you can make them transparent by copying and pasting a transparent shape. Figure 6-21 shows an example. The top chart is a combination chart (area and columns), and the series plotted as an area is almost obscured by the columns. In the second chart, the columns are replaced with a transparent shape so that both series are clearly visible.

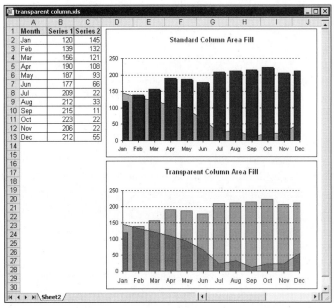

Figure 6-21: Copying a transparent AutoShape to columns makes the area portion of the chart more visible.

To replace bars or columns with a transparent shape:

1. Add a rectangle AutoShape to the worksheet.

2. Double-click the AutoShape and select the Colors and Lines tab in the Format AutoShape dialog box.

3. Select a Fill Color and specify a Transparent setting (the example chart uses 75%). For best results, set the Line Color to No Line. Click OK to close the Format AutoShape dialog box.

4. Select the AutoShape, press Shift, and choose Edit→Copy Picture. Accept the default settings in the Copy Picture dialog box.

5. Select the bar or column series in your chart and choose Edit→Paste.

6. If you like, you can then add a border around the bars or columns by using the Patterns tab of the Format Data Series dialog box.

Chapter 16 contains a VBA macro that simplifies the processes of making bars or columns semitransparent.

USING A PICTURE IN A CHART'S PLOT AREA OR CHART AREA

Every chart has two background elements: the Plot Area and the Chart Area. By default, these areas display a single fill color. You can, however, insert a graphic image for visual appeal.

To add a graphics image to a chart's plot area or chart area, the image must be in a file. It is not possible to copy an image and paste it to either of these areas. To use an AutoShape in a chart's plot area or chart area, you must first save the AutoShape to a file (see the sidebar "Saving an AutoShape to a File").

To add a graphic image, select either the plot area or the chart area of your chart. Display the Format dialog box for the element and click the Patterns tab. Then click the Fill Effects button. Click the Picture tab in the Fill Effects dialog box, and click Select Picture to choose the file that contains the image.

Figure 6-22 shows a pie chart that uses a clip art image in its chart area.

Charts that have been customized using an image for the plot area or chart area can be saved as a user-defined custom format. See Chapter 4 for more information about user-defined chart formats.

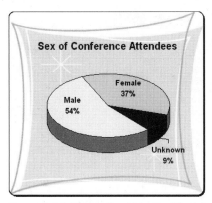

Figure 6-22: Using clip art in the Chart Area
adds visual appeal to an otherwise dull chart.

Figure 6-23 shows another example. This column chart uses clip art in the Plot Area, and the chart columns have been made transparent by using the technique described in the previous section. The effect is that the clip art background is not obscured by the columns.

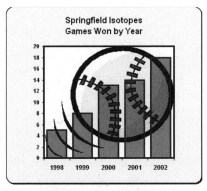

Figure 6-23: The clip art in the Plot Area
shows through the transparent columns.

Figure 6-24 shows another example. The plot area uses a picture of a dollar bill. This chart is actually a 100% stacked-line chart. The chart consists of six series, each of which displays a single data point (contained in column C). The series lines are not displayed, and each data marker was replaced by a wide AutoShape that extends across the entire plot area and matches the chart area's color. The effect is a "broken" dollar bill that depicts relative expenses.

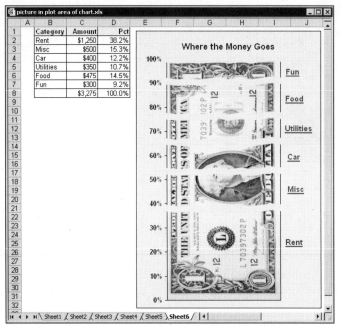

Figure 6-24: This chart depicts the relative expenses by using a 100% stacked-line chart with custom data markers.

Saving an AutoShape to a File

There are several ways to create a GIF file from an AutoShape. The following procedure is a simple technique that requires no additional software. This method works with Excel 2000 or later.

1 Start with an empty single-sheet workbook.

2. Create any number of AutoShapes on the worksheet and format them to your liking.

3. Choose File→Save as Web Page.

4. Specify a directory and filename. The location and filename are not important. This is just a temporary file that can be deleted.

5. Click OK.

The workbook will be saved in HTML format and a new directory will be created. That directory will hold the AutoShapes, each in a separate GIF file.

Alternatively, you can copy the AutoShape as a bitmap, paste it to a graphics program, and then save the file. To copy an AutoShape as a bitmap, select the object, press Shift and choose Edit→Copy Picture, and choose the Bitmap option.

Calling attention to a cell

Many of the AutoShapes — particularly those in the Callouts and the Stars and Banners categories — are useful for calling attention to a particular cell or range to make it stand out from the others. Figure 6-25 shows two examples of how you can make a cell's value stand out.

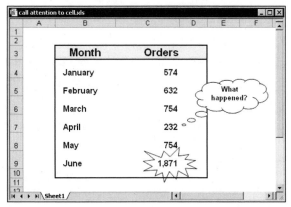

Figure 6-25: Two ways of making a particular cell stand out

Changing the look of cell comments

If a cell contains a cell comment, you can replace the normal comment box with any of the AutoShapes in the Callouts category. Select the cell comment and then click the Draw tool on the Drawing toolbar. This tool expands to show a menu. Select the Change AutoShape→Callouts command, followed by the desired callout shape.

TIP

You can also display an image in a cell comment. Access the Format Comment dialog box, select the Colors and Lines tab, click the Color drop-down list, and select Fill Effects. Click the Picture tab in the Fill Effects dialog box and select a graphics file. By storing an image in a cell comment, you make the graphic visible only when the mouse pointer is over the cell.

Linking text in an object to a cell

As an alternative to typing text directly into an AutoShape, you can create a link to a cell. After you do so, the text displayed in the object will reflect the current contents of the linked cell.

To link an AutoShape to a cell, select the object and then click in the Formula bar. Enter an equal sign, click the cell to be linked, and press Enter. You can format the text in the shape independently of the format of the cell. For best results, access the shape's Format dialog box and change the following settings:

- ◆ Automatic margins (Margins tab)
- ◆ Automatic size (Alignment tab)
- ◆ Center Horizontal alignment and Center Vertical alignment (Alignment tab)

Creating flow diagrams

A flow diagram (also known as a flow chart) is often used to depict how a process or system works. You might expect that the Diagram dialog box would provide an option for flow diagrams — but it doesn't. That doesn't mean that you can't use Excel to create your flow charts. In fact, one of the AutoShape categories is named Flowchart and has all the standard flow diagram shapes. Combine these with objects from the Connectors category and you have all the tools required to create great-looking flow charts.

Figure 6-26 shows an example of a flow diagram created with AutoShapes — with help from the Align and Distribute options on the Drawing toolbar. After creating the diagram, I selected all the objects and grouped them together so that the diagram could be moved as a single unit.

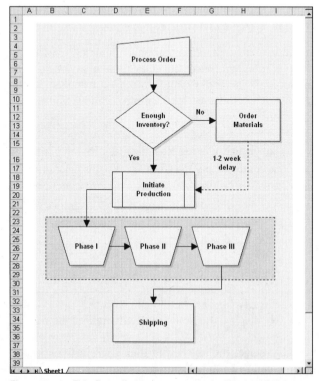

Figure 6-26: This flow diagram was created with AutoShapes.

Pasting pictures of cells

One of Excel's best-kept secrets is its ability to copy and paste pictures of cells. You can copy a cell or range and then paste a picture of the cell or range on any worksheet or chart. The picture can be static or linked. With a linked picture, the link is to the cells. In other words, if you change the contents of a cell that's in a picture, the picture changes.

To create a picture of a cell or range, select a range and choose Edit→Copy. Then press Shift and click the Edit menu. Choose Paste Picture to create a static picture, or choose Paste Picture Link to paste a linked picture of the selection.

You can paste a picture of a range into a chart, but Excel does not allow you to paste a *linked* picture of a range into a chart.

TIP

If you're a risk-taker, you can try this. Paste a picture of a range into a chart. Then select the picture and enter a formula into the Formula bar. For example, if your picture is a picture of range A1:C8 on Sheet1, enter this formula:

`=Sheet1!A1:C8`

This will convert the picture into a linked picture. However, it may be accompanied by some strange behavior when the chart is activated. I give no guarantees that this technique won't crash your system!

Figure 6-27 shows an example of a picture of a range pasted into a chart. This technique can be a good alternative to using a data table.

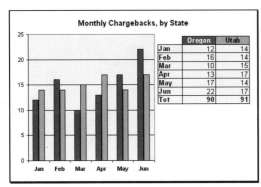

Figure 6-27: The chart contains a picture of the cells in A6:C8.

Part II

Mastering Charts

Chapter 7

Creating Interactive Charts

IN THIS CHAPTER

- ◆ Introducing the concept of interactive charts

- ◆ Creating a self-expanding chart – a chart that updates automatically when data is added or deleted

- ◆ Using a scrollbar to specify the data in a series

- ◆ Using a drop-down list to choose a beginning point and an end point for a series

- ◆ Plotting the last *n* data points in a series

- ◆ Plotting every *n*th data point in a series

- ◆ Plotting a series based on the active cell

- ◆ Using a check box or a drop-down list to select a series to plot

THE TERM INTERACTIVE CHART, as used in this book, refers to a chart that changes automatically, based on the worksheet environment. In a sense, all charts are interactive because charts series are linked to ranges, and the chart updates automatically when the data is changed. This is *not* the type of interactivity covered in this chapter.

Introducing Interactive Charts

If you create spreadsheets that are used by others, you'll probably find several useful techniques in this chapter. Many of these examples have a single goal: to make it easier for users (especially novice users) to deal with a workbook that contains charts.

A few examples of interactive charts include:

- ◆ A chart that updates itself to use newly added data

- ◆ A chart that updates itself when data is deleted

- ◆ A chart that limits the amount of data displayed in a series (for example, the last 12 data points)

♦ A chart that displays a series based on a value entered into a cell or an item chosen from a drop-down list.

♦ A chart that displays a series based on the location of the active cell

This chapter provides the information you need to create several types of charts that update automatically based on information contained in the workbook. You'll also discover how to use dialog box controls (such as check boxes and drop-down lists) to make your charts interactive.

Another way to create an interactive chart is to use a pivot chart. Refer to Chapter 9 for information about creating and using pivot charts.

All the examples discussed in this chapter are available on the companion CD-ROM.

Hands-On: Creating a Self-Expanding Chart

One of the most common questions related to charting is, "How can I create a chart that will expand automatically when I add new data to the worksheet?"

To understand this issue, examine Figure 7-1, which shows a worksheet set up to store sales information that is updated daily. The chart displays all the data in the worksheet. When new data is entered, the chart series must be expanded to include the new data. On the other hand, if data is deleted, the chart series should also be contracted to exclude the deleted cells.

Wouldn't it be nice if the chart series would expand and contract automatically? Excel doesn't provide a direct way to create such a self-expanding chart. But, as you'll see, it's certainly possible – if you're willing to do a little up-front work.

Chapter 3 describes several ways to change the source data used in a chart series. Although none of those techniques is particularly difficult, each requires manual intervention. Creating a self-expanding chart makes the process completely automatic.

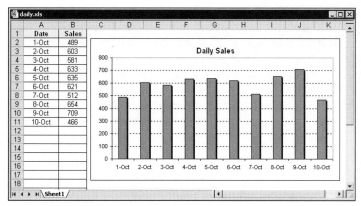

Figure 7-1: If this were a self-expanding chart, it would update automatically when new data is entered.

One option, of course, is to specify a larger-than-required range for the data series. Figure 7-2 shows an example in which the data series includes empty cells that will eventually be filled. The result is a lopsided chart that displays lots of empty space. In the majority of situations, this solution is not satisfactory.

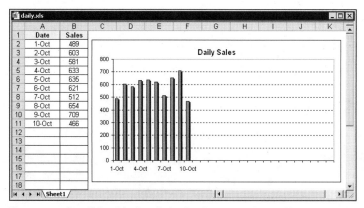

Figure 7-2: Specifying blank cells in the data range is usually not a viable solution.

As an introduction to the world of interactive charts, this section presents a hands-on, step-by-step example. You'll create a standard chart and then make the changes necessary to make the chart expand automatically when new data is added, and contract when data is deleted.

The example makes use of a simple worksheet that has dates in column A and sales amounts in column B. The assumption is that a new date and sales figure are each added daily, and the chart should display all the data.

Creating the chart

The first step is to create a standard chart, using the data that currently exists. Figure 7-1, presented earlier, shows the data and a column chart created from the data. The chart contains a single series and its SERIES formula is as follows:

```
=SERIES(Sheet1!$B$1,Sheet1!$A$2:$A$11,Sheet1!$B$2:$B$11,1)
```

This SERIES formula specifies that:

- ◆ The series name is in cell B1.
- ◆ The category labels are in A2:A11.
- ◆ The values are in B2:B11.

So far, this is just a common chart. If you add a new date and value, the chart will not display the new data. But that will soon change.

Creating named formulas

In this step, you create two named formulas. The names will eventually serve as arguments in the SERIES formula. In case you're not familiar with the concept of a named formula, it is explained later in this section. To create the named formulas:

1. Select Insert→Name→Define to bring up the Define Name dialog box.

2. In the Names in workbook field, enter **Date**. In the Refers to field, enter this formula:

   ```
   =OFFSET(Sheet1!$A$2,0,0,COUNTA(Sheet1!$A:$A)-1,1)
   ```

3. Click Add to create the formula named *Date*.

   Notice that the OFFSET function refers to the first category label (cell A2) and uses the COUNTA function to determine the number of labels in the column. Because column A has a heading in row 1, the formula subtracts 1 from the number.

4. Type **Sales** in the Names in workbook field. Enter this formula in the Refers to field:

   ```
   =OFFSET(Sheet1!$B$2,0,0,COUNTA(Sheet1!$B:$B)-1,1)
   ```

   In this case, the OFFSET function refers to the first data point (cell B2). Again, the COUNTA function is used to get the number of data points, and it is adjusted to account for the label in cell B1.

5. Click Add to create the formula named *Sales*.

6. Click Close to close the Define Name dialog box.

After you perform these steps, the workbook contains two new names, *Date* and *Sales*.

Modifying the series

The final step is to modify the chart so that it makes use of the two new names rather than the "hard-coded" range references.

1. Activate the chart and select Chart→Source Data to bring up the Source Data dialog box.

2. In the Values field, enter **Sheet1!Sales**.

3. In the Category (x) axis labels field, enter **Sheet1!Dates**.

4. Verify that the dialog box looks like Figure 7-3 and then click OK.

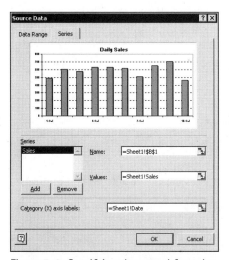

Figure 7-3: Specifying the named formulas in the Source Data dialog box

In Steps 2 and 3, note that the name was preceded by the worksheet name and an exclamation point. Because named formulas are workbook-level names (as opposed to sheet-level names), you should (technically) enter the *workbook* name, an exclamation point, and the name. However, Excel is very accommodating in this regard, and changes it for you. If you access the Source Data dialog box again, you'll discover that Excel substituted the workbook's name for the sheet reference you entered:

```
=daily.xls!Sales
```

Bottom line? When using these named formulas, you can precede the name with either the worksheet name or the workbook name (I find it easier to use the worksheet name). But keep in mind that if the sheet name or workbook name includes a space character, you must enclose it in single quotation marks, like this:

```
='daily sales.xls'!Sales
```

or

```
='sales data'!sales
```

For more information about names, refer to the sidebar "How Excel Handles Names."

 An alternative to using the Source Data dialog box is to edit the chart's SERIES formula directly.

How Excel Handles Names

Excel supports two types of names: workbook-level names and worksheet-level names. The scope of a workbook-level name is the entire workbook. Normally, when you create a name for a cell or range, that name can be used in any worksheet.

You can also create sheet-level names. A sheet-level name incorporates the sheet name as part of its name. For example, *Sheet1!Data* is a sheet-level name. When you create this name, you can use it in formulas in Sheet1 without the sheet qualifier. For example:

```
=Data*4
```

But if you enter this formula in a different worksheet, Excel will not recognize the name unless you fully qualify it:

```
=Sheet1!Data*4
```

Sheet-level names are useful because they enable you to use the same name on different worksheets. For example, you might create sheet-level names such as *Sheet1!Interest, Sheet2!Interest,* and *Sheet3!Interest.* Each name refers to a cell on its own sheet. A formula that uses the name *Interest* uses the definition for its own sheet.

The named formulas used in this chapter are workbook-level names because they are not preceded by a sheet name. But when you enter a name in a field in the Source Data dialog box, Excel (for some reason) requires that you qualify the name with either the sheet name or the workbook name.

Testing it

To test the results of your efforts, enter new data in columns A and B, or delete data from the bottom of the columns. If you performed the preceding steps correctly, the chart will update automatically. If you receive an error message or the chart doesn't update itself, review the preceding steps carefully. This method *does* work!

Understanding how it works

Many people use this self-expanding chart technique without fully understanding how it works. There's certainly nothing wrong with that. If you go through the hands-on exercise described previously, you should be able to adapt the procedures to your own charts. But understanding *how* it works will make it possible to go beyond the basic concept and create more powerful types of dynamic charts.

ABOUT NAMED FORMULAS

Many of the interactive chart techniques described in this chapter take advantage of a powerful feature called *named formulas*. You're probably familiar with the concept of named cells and ranges. But did you know that naming cells and ranges is really a misnomer? When you create a name for a range, you are really creating a *named formula*.

When you work with the Define Name dialog box, the Refers to field contains the formula, and the Names in workbook field contains the formula's name. You'll find that the contents of the Refers to field always begin with an equal sign — a sure sign that it's a formula.

Unlike a normal formula, a named formula doesn't exist in a cell. Rather, it exists in Excel's memory and does not have a cell address. But you can access the result of a named formula by referring to its name, either in a standard formula or in a chart's SERIES formula.

After defining the two named formulas, Excel evaluates these formulas every time the worksheet is calculated. But these named formulas aren't used in any cells, so there is no visible effect of creating these named formulas — until you use them to define the chart series.

To get a better handle on named formulas, use the Define Name dialog box to create the following formula, and name it *Sum12Cells*.

```
=SUM($A$1:$A$12)
```

After you've created the named formula, enter the following formula into any cell:

```
=Sum12Cells
```

This formula will return the sum of A1:A12.

Normally, cell and range addresses used in named formulas are absolute addresses — the row and column references are preceded by a dollar sign. If you use standard relative addresses, the result returned by the named formula will vary, depending on the location of the cell pointer. As you'll see later in this chapter, you can use this to your benefit (see "Plotting a Series Based on the Active Cell").

ABOUT THE OFFSET FUNCTION

The key to mastering self-expanding charts is understanding the OFFSET function. This function returns a range that is "offset" from a specified reference cell. Arguments for the OFFSET function let you specify the distance from the reference cell and the dimensions of the range (the number of rows and columns).

The OFFSET function has five arguments, as follows:

♦ *reference:* The first argument for the OFFSET function is essentially the "anchor" cell, used by the second and third argument.

♦ *rows:* This argument indicates how many rows to move from the reference address to begin the range.

♦ *cols:* This argument indicates how many columns to move from the reference address to begin the range.

♦ *height:* This argument indicates the number of rows to be included in the range.

♦ *width:* The final argument indicates the number of columns to be included in the range.

If the columns used for the data contain any other entries, COUNTA will return an incorrect value. To keep things simple, don't put any other data in the column. If the column contains additional information, you'll need to adjust the *height* argument in the COUNTA function.

Recall that the named formula *Sales* was defined as

```
=OFFSET(Sheet1!$B$2,0,0,COUNTA(Sheet1!$B:$B)-1,1)
```

If there are 11 entries in column B, the COUNTA function returns 11. This result is adjusted by one to account for the column heading. Therefore, the named formula can be expressed as

```
=OFFSET(Sheet1!$B$2,0,0,10,1)
```

This formula uses cell B2 as the anchor cell and returns a reference to the range that is

♦ Offset from cell B2 by 0 rows (second argument, *rows*)

♦ Offset from cell B2 by 0 columns (third argument, *cols*)

♦ Ten cells high (fourth argument, *height*)

♦ One cell wide (fifth argument, *width*)

In other words, the OFFSET function returns a reference to range B2:B11, and this is the range used by the chart series. When a new data point is added, the OFFSET function returns a reference to range B2:B12.

Subsequent examples in this chapter use the same basic concept but vary in the arguments supplied to the OFFSET function.

> To keep things simple, the charts in this chapter make use of a single data series. However, these techniques can be applied to charts with any number of data series. You will, however, have to make the necessary adjustments for each series.

Controlling a Series with a Scroll Bar

The example in this section demonstrates another type of interactivity. Figure 7-4 shows a chart that uses a Scroll Bar control to specify the number of months (from 1 to 12) to display.

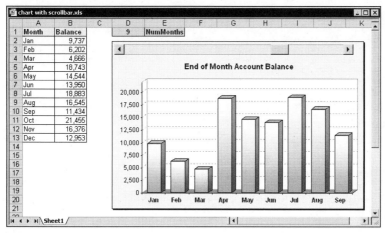

Figure 7-4: The scroll bar at the top of the chart controls how many months are displayed.

Creating the chart

Refer to Figure 7-4 and use the data in columns A:B to create a chart (the example uses standard 3-D column chart). Because the number of data points will vary, it's a good idea to turn off automatic scaling for the value axis. Set the Maximum scale value to a large enough value to accommodate all the data. Doing this keeps the value axis constant, regardless of the number of data points displayed.

Defining the names

This example uses several names, which are described in this section.

Cell D1 contains a value that determines the number of months displayed in the chart. For convenience, this cell is named *NumMonths*.

In addition, the workbook has two named formulas, which are used in the chart's series. *Months* is defined as

```
=OFFSET(Sheet1!$A$2,0,0, NumMonths,1)
```

Balance is defined as

```
=OFFSET(Sheet1!$B$2,0,0,NumMonths,1)
```

If you understand how the named formulas worked in the previous example, you should have no problem understanding this variation. As you can see, the OFFSET functions use *NumMonths* for their height argument. The result is that the *NumMonths* cell controls how many data points are displayed in the chart.

> **TIP**
>
> Another approach, which is a bit simpler, is to define *Balance* as an offset from the *Months* range. Using this approach, the definition for *Balance* would be:
>
> =OFFSET(Months,0,1)

As in the previous example, these two named formulas are then used for the category labels and values range for the chart series. This is done by using the Series tab of the Source Data dialog box. The net effect? Change the value in cell D1, and the chart updates immediately.

Adding the Scroll Bar control

The Scroll Bar control isn't really necessary, but it does add a touch of convenience. Moving the scroll bar with the mouse is a bit easier than changing the value in cell D1.

The Scroll Bar control can be added to the worksheet or to the chart itself. Adding it to the chart offers an advantage: If the chart is moved, the scroll bar will move with it. The following instructions add the Scroll Bar control to the chart.

1. Select View→Toolbars→Forms to display the Forms toolbar.

2. Click the chart to activate it.

3. On the Forms toolbar, click the Scroll Bar control and then drag in the chart to create the control. You can size and position it just as you can any other graphic object.

4. Right-click the Scroll Bar and choose Format Control from the shortcut menu. This displays the Format Control dialog box.

5. In the Format Control dialog box, click the Control tab (see Figure 7-5).

6. Enter 1 n the Minimum value field. In the Maximum value field, enter 12 (the maximum number of data points for the chart).

7. Set the Incremental change field to 1 and the Page change field to 3.

8. In the Cell link field, enter **NumMonths**. This will link the Spinner control with cell D1.

9. Click OK to close the dialog box.

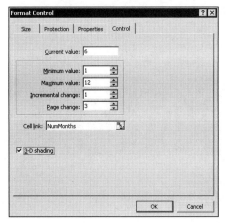

Figure 7-5: Linking a Scroll Bar control to a cell

After performing these steps, the value in D1 will be controlled by the Scroll Bar and will have a numeric range of 1–12. This value, in turn, will control the number of data points shown in the chart.

Excel offers two general types of controls: those from the Forms toolbar and those from the Control Toolbox toolbar. Controls in the Forms toolbar are easier to use, but they don't offer as much flexibility as the Control Toolbox controls. For example, the controls on the Forms toolbar offer virtually no formatting options. All the examples in this chapter use controls from the Forms toolbar.

Specifying the Beginning and End Point for a Series

If a chart uses a lot of data, you may want to be able to limit the data that's displayed in the chart. Figure 7-6 shows an example.

Cell D2 contains a value that represents the first row to be plotted, and cell D4 contains a value that represents the last row to be plotted. The chart is displaying the data in rows 6 through 13. If cells D2 or D4 are changed, the chart adjusts accordingly. This example uses Spinner controls linked to cells D2 and D4. These controls make it easy to change the values in these cells.

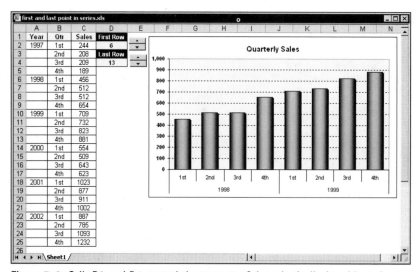

Figure 7-6: Cells D2 and D4 control the amount of data that's displayed in a chart.

Creating the chart

Refer to Figure 7-6 and create a chart from the data in columns A:C. The chart in this example is a standard column chart. It uses two columns (A:B) for the category axis labels, which results in having two rows of category labels in the chart.

Defining the names

For convenience, cell D2 is named *FirstRow* and cell D4 is named *LastRow*.
In addition, the workbook has two named formulas. *Date* is defined as

```
=OFFSET(Sheet1!$A$2,FirstRow-2,0,LastRow-FirstRow+1,2)
```

Because the category labels occupy two columns, the OFFSET function uses 2 as its final argument. In other words, the function returns a range that's two columns wide.

Sales is defined as

```
=OFFSET(Sheet1!$C$2,FirstRow-2,0,LastRow-FirstRow+1,1)
```

After creating these named formulas, they are then specified as the category labels and values range for the chart's series, using the Series tab of the Source Data dialog box (or by editing the SERIES formula directly). For more information about using named formulas for a chart series, refer to "Modifying the Series," earlier in this chapter.

 This technique offers no error handling. For example, entering a non-numeric value in cell D2 causes the named formulas to return error values. Excel displays the rather uninformative error message shown in Figure 7-7.

Figure 7-7: Entering a value that causes an error in the named formulas results in an error message.

Adding Spinner controls

For additional convenience, you may wish to add Spinner controls to the worksheet to make it easier to adjust the *FirstRow* and *LastRow* values. To do so:

1. Select View→Toolbars→Forms to display the Forms toolbar.

2. On the Forms toolbar, click the Spinner control and then drag in the worksheet to create the control. You can size and position it just as you can any other graphic object.

3. Right-click the Spinner and choose Format Control from the shortcut menu. This displays the Format Control dialog box.

4. In the Format Control dialog box, click the Control tab.

5. In the Minimum value field, enter 2.

6. In the Maximum value field, enter 25 (or a number that corresponds to the row that contains the last data point for the chart).

7. In the Cell link field, enter **FirstRow**. This will link the Spinner control with cell D2.

8. Click OK to close the dialog box.

9. Repeat Steps 3–8 to add another Spinner for the *LastRow* cell. In Step 7, specify **LastRow** as the Cell link.

After performing these steps, you can use the linked Spinners to quickly adjust the values that control the first and last data points in the chart.

Specifying the Beginning and Number of Points for a Series

The example in this section is similar to the previous example. Rather than enabling the user to specify the first row and last row to be plotted, this example allows the user to specify the first row (as a meaningful date) and the number of data points.

Figure 7-8 shows a worksheet that contains daily sales information. Cell C2 contains the first date to be plotted, and cell C4 contains the number of data points to appear in the chart.

This example utilizes two (optional) user interface enhancements: a drop-down list to select the start day, and a Spinner control to specify the number of days. The drop-down list (not visible in the figure) is accomplished with Excel's Data Validation feature.

Creating the chart

Use the data in columns A:B to create a chart. The chart in the figure is a standard line chart but this technique will work with any chart type.

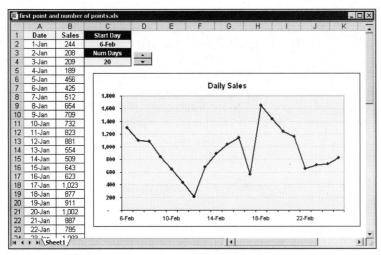

Figure 7-8: Cell C2 contains the start day and cell C4 contains the number of days to be plotted.

Defining the names

In this example, cell C2 is named *StartDay*, and cell C4 is named *NumDays*. The workbook has two named formulas. *Date* is defined as

```
=OFFSET(Sheet1!$A$2,MATCH(StartDay,Sheet1!$A:$A,1)-2,0,NumDays,1)
```

Sales is defined as

```
=OFFSET(Sheet1!$A$2,MATCH(StartDay,Sheet1!$A:$A,1)-2,1,NumDays,1)
```

The second argument for the OFFSET function uses the MATCH function. The MATCH function returns the relative position of an item in a range. In this case, it returns the position of the date in column A that matches the date in the *StartDay* cell. This, of course, is just another way of determining the first row to include in the chart.

As in the previous example, these two named formulas are then used for the category labels and values range for the chart series. For more information about using named formulas for a chart series, refer to "Modifying the Series," earlier in this chapter.

Adding the user interface elements

The *NumDays* cell has a linked Spinner control to make it easier to specify the number of days to include in the chart (see the previous section for information about adding a linked Spinner control).

Using a Spinner control isn't possible for the *StartDay* cell because it needs to display dates, and the Spinner control has a maximum value of 30,000 (the date values exceed this number). A scroll bar is an option, but a drop-down list of available dates would be perfect. Fortunately, Excel's Data Validation feature makes adding a drop-down list to a cell very easy. To do so:

1. Select cell C2 and make sure that it's formatted to display a date.

2. Choose Data→Validation to display the Data Validation dialog box (see Figure 7-9).

3. In the Data Validation dialog box, click the Settings tab.

4. In the Allow field, choose List.

5. In the Source field, enter =$A$2:$A$60, which is the worksheet range that contains the dates.

6. Click OK to close the Data Validation dialog box.

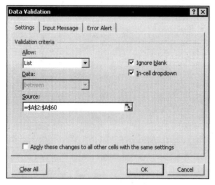

Figure 7-9: Specifying a range of dates for the drop-down Data Validation list

After entering the Data Validation settings, you can then select a date when cell C2 is activated. The selected date will be the first date in the chart. The Spinner control determines how many total data points appear in the chart.

TIP In Step 5 in the preceding list, you can take a different approach. Rather than enter the range address into the Source field, you can enter the following formula, which adjusts automatically if additional dates are added:

```
=OFFSET($A2,0,0,COUNTA($A:$A)-1,1)
```

Plotting the Last n Data Points in a Series

Another interactive chart variation is to make a chart show only the most recent n data points in a column. For example, you can create a chart that always displays the most recent six months of data (see Figure 7-10). In this example, cell F1 holds the number of data points to display in the chart.

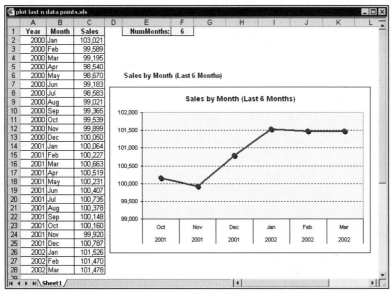

Figure 7-10: This chart displays the six most recent data points. The number plotted is controlled by the value in cell F1.

Creating the chart

Create a chart using the data in columns A:C. The chart in this example is a standard line chart, but this technique will work with any chart type. The category axis uses two columns (A and B).

Defining the names

In this example, cell F1 is named *NumMonths*. The workbook has two other named formulas. *Date* is defined as

```
=OFFSET(Sheet1!$A$2,COUNTA(Sheet1!$B:$B)-NumMonths-1,0,NumMonths,2)
```

Sales is defined as

```
=OFFSET(Sheet1!$C$2,COUNTA(Sheet1!$C:$C)-NumMonths-1,0,NumMonths,1)
```

The chart title uses a link to cell E6, which contains the following formula:

```
="Sales by Month (Last " & NumMonths &" Months)"
```

This formula uses the cell name *NumMonths* to ensure that the chart title always displays the number of months plotted.

After you create the names, you use these two named formulas for the category labels and values range for the chart series. For more information about using named formulas for a chart series, refer to "Modifying the Series," earlier in this chapter. The number of data points in the chart will then be controlled by the value in cell F1. New data added to the worksheet will be accommodated automatically.

Plotting Every nth Data Point in a Series

Suppose that you have a lot of data in a column, and you want to plot only every 10th data point. This section presents two techniques that enable you to do just that.

Using AutoFiltering

One way to plot every *n*th data point in a range is to use AutoFiltering in conjunction with a formula. AutoFiltering allows you to hide rows that don't meet a specified criteria. Excel, by default, doesn't plot data that resides in a hidden row. Therefore, the trick is to create formulas that return a specific value based on the data's row number and then use the results of these formulas as the basis for AutoFiltering.

Figure 7-11 shows a worksheet with AutoFiltering in effect. Cell B1 contains a value that represents *n*. For example, when B1 contains 10, the chart displays every 10th data point: the value in rows 4, 14, 24, and so on.

Column A contains 365 dates and column B contains 365 corresponding data points. Column C contains formulas that return a value which is used to determine whether the row should be hidden. The formula in cell C4, which is copied to the cells below, is

```
=MOD(ROW()-ROW($B$4),$B$1)
```

This formula uses the MOD function to calculate the remainder when the row number (minus the row number of the first row) is divided by the value in B1. As a result, every *n*th cell contains 0.

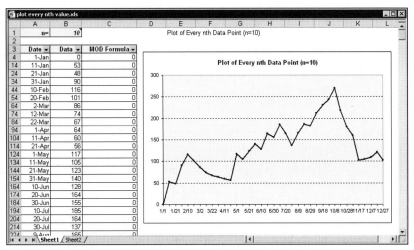

Figure 7–11: This chart plots every nth data point (specified in B1) by ignoring data in the rows hidden by AutoFiltering.

Use the Data→Filter→AutoFilter command to turn on AutoFiltering. Use the drop-down arrow in cell C3 to display only the rows that contain a 0 in column C. This technique will not work if the Plot Visible Cells Only option is not in effect for the chart. By default, this setting is in effect. To check (or change) this setting, select the chart, choose Tools→Options, and click the Chart tab.

The main problem with this technique is that it's not fully automatic. When you change the value in cell B1, you need to re-specify the AutoFilter criteria for column C. The rows will not hide automatically.

Using array formulas

The preceding technique works well, but it would be nice to make it fully automated. Tushar Mehta, an Excel charting expert, developed a clever technique that uses named formulas. The example in this section is an adaptation of his method.

Figure 7-12 shows the same data used in the previous example. This workbook uses three named ranges: *Nth* (cell B1), *Dates* (range A4:A368), and *Data* (range B4:B368). The *Nth* cell is linked to a Spinner control.

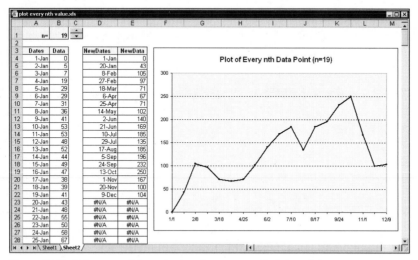

Figure 7-12: Using named formulas to return every nth data point

You'll notice two additional columns of formulas (columns D and E). Both of these are multicell array formulas. The array formula in D4:D368 is

```
=N(OFFSET(Dates,(ROW(OFFSET($A$1,0,0,ROWS(Dates)/Nth))-1)*Nth,0))
```

This formula returns an array that consists of every *n*th row in the *Dates* range.
    The array formula in E4:E368 is very similar and returns an array that consists of every *n*th row in the *Data* range:

```
=N(OFFSET(Data,(ROW(OFFSET($A$1,0,0,ROWS(Data)/Nth))-1)*Nth,0))
```

These array formulas are complex, and a complete explanation is beyond the scope of this book. However, it's not necessary that you fully understand them in order to use them. They can easily be adapted to other data sets. Be aware that the reference to cell $A$1 must remain intact. This cell is used to generate a series of offsets that reference cells within the original range.

Creating named formulas

If you created a chart from the data in columns D:E, the result would not be very satisfactory. Every *n*th value would be plotted, but the chart would display a lengthy series of empty (#NA) cells.

The solution is to call upon the named formulas technique to substitute for the two array formulas. These named formulas are identical to the array formulas listed in the previous section.

Define *NewDates* as

```
=N(OFFSET(Dates,(ROW(OFFSET(Sheet2!$A$1,0,0,ROWS(Dates)/Nth))-1)*Nth,0))
```

Define *NewData* as

```
=N(OFFSET(Data,(ROW(OFFSET(Sheet2!$A$1,0,0,ROWS(Data)/Nth))-1)*Nth,0))
```

After you create the names, you use these two named formulas for the category labels and values range for the chart series. For more information about using named formulas for a chart series, refer to "Modifying the Series," earlier in this chapter. The result? The arrays used by the charts consist only of the values (no #NA values).

Because the named formulas substitute for the array formulas, the formulas in columns D:E are no longer needed.

Plotting a Series Based on the Active Cell

Another type of interactive chart is one that plots a series based on the user's selection in the worksheet. Figure 7-13 shows an example. This worksheet contains the results of a customer survey and is set up such that the chart displays the data in the row that contains the cell pointer. When you press F9 (to calculate the workbook), a named formula is calculated, and that named formula is used in the chart's SERIES formula.

ON THE CD   The CD-ROM contains two versions of this example. The version described in the preceding paragraph requires a press of the F9 key to update the chart. The other version uses a simple event macro that is executed whenever the selection changes. The macro-driven version is completely automatic.

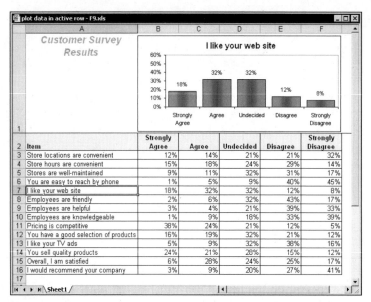

Figure 7-13: Pressing F9 displays the data in the row that contains the cell pointer.

Creating the chart

The chart is a standard column chart, created using the data in rows 2 and 3. Notice that the height of row 1 has been increased to accommodate the chart. The workbook uses "frozen panes" to keep row 1 in view at all times. To freeze the panes, select cell A2 and choose Window→Freeze Panes.

Defining the names

The chart uses two named formulas. Unlike the other named formulas in this chapter, these formulas are defined using "mixed" cell references (the column part of the reference is absolute, but the row part is relative). Using non-absolute cell references adds a new twist to named formulas, because the formula evaluates differently, depending on the active cell at the time the sheet is calculated.

In fact, the location of the active cell is critical when you *create* the named formulas. The following names assume that cell A3 (in the first data row) was active when the names were created.

ChartTitle is defined as

```
=OFFSET($A3,0,0)
```

ChartData is defined as

```
=OFFSET($A3,0,1,1,5)
```

As with the previous examples, the SERIES formula for the chart's data series uses these named formulas. The SERIES formula looks like this:

```
=SERIES(Sheet1!ChartTitle,Sheet1!$B$2:$F$2,Sheet1!ChartData,1)
```

Notice that a named formula is not required for the second argument (category labels). These labels do not change. When the worksheet is recalculated, the named formulas are updated based on the active cell.

If the cell cursor is not within the data range, the chart displays an empty series.

Using a macro to force a recalculation

An alternative version of this example uses a simple VBA macro to calculate the sheet when the selection changes. This macro eliminates the need to press F9 to calculate the sheet and update the chart.

To add this macro:

1. Right-click the worksheet tab and choose View Code from the shortcut menu. This activates the VBA Editor and displays an empty code module for the worksheet.

2. Enter the following code:

   ```
   Private Sub Worksheet_SelectionChange(ByVal Target As Range)
       If ActiveCell.Row > 2 And ActiveCell.Row < 17 Then _
           ActiveSheet.Calculate
   End Sub
   ```

3. Press Alt+F11 to return to Excel.

This VBA macro is executed whenever the range selection is changed on the worksheet. The code checks the location of the active cell. If the active cell is in a row greater than 2 but less than 17, it executes a statement that calculates the worksheet.

Chapter 16 contains additional examples of macros that execute when a particular event occurs.

Defining a Series Based on the Active Cell

As with the previous example, the example in this section (see Figure 7-14) uses the active cell. But in this case, the active cell determines the extent of a series. The data displayed in the chart starts with the row of the active cell and extends for a number of data points defined by the value in cell B2. Pressing F9 (or clicking the Spinner control) calculates the sheet and updates the chart.

ON THE CD

The CD-ROM contains two versions of this example. The version described in the preceding paragraph requires a press of the F9 key to update the chart. The other version uses a simple event macro that is executed whenever the selection changes. The macro-driven version is completely automatic.

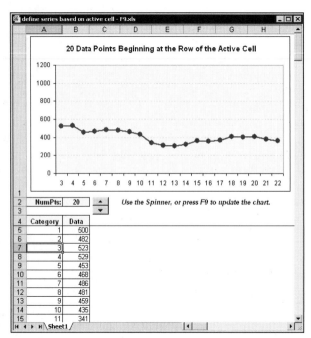

Figure 7-14: This chart displays n data points relative to the active cell.

Creating the chart

The chart in this example is a standard line chart. As with the previous example, this workbook uses frozen panes to ensure that the chart is visible when the worksheet is scrolled vertically. In this case, the first four rows remain visible.

The chart title is linked to a cell that contains the following formula, which refers to a cell named *NumPoints*:

```
=NumPoints &" Data Points Beginning at the Row of the Active Cell"
```

Defining the names

Cell B2, named *NumPoints*, stores the number of data points to be displayed in the chart series. The example also uses a linked Spinner to make changing the value of *NumPoints* easy.

The chart's SERIES formula uses two named formulas and, as in the previous example, these formulas use mixed references. The following names assume that cell A5 (in the first data row) was active when the names were created.

Category is defined as

```
=OFFSET(Sheet1!$A5,0,0,NumPoints)
```

Data is defined as

```
=OFFSET(Sheet1!$B5,0,0,NumPoints)
```

When the worksheet is recalculated, the named formulas are updated based on the active cell.

Using a macro to force a recalculation

To make the calculation occur automatically when the cell pointer is moved, you can add a simple VBA macro. To add this macro:

1. Right-click the worksheet tab and choose View Code from the shortcut menu. This activates the VBA Editor and displays an empty code module for the worksheet.

2. Enter the following code:

   ```
   Private Sub Worksheet_SelectionChange(ByVal Target As Range)
       ActiveSheet.Calculate
   End Sub
   ```

3. Press Alt+F11 to return to Excel.

Using Check Boxes to Select Series to Plot

The example shown in Figure 7-15 displays a line chart with three series. The number of series that are actually displayed is controlled by three Check Box controls. When all three check boxes are checked, the chart displays data for Product A, Product B, and Product C. Uncheck a check box and the corresponding series disappears from the chart.

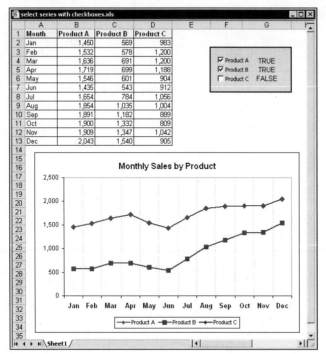

Figure 7-15: The series displayed in the chart are controlled
by check boxes.

Creating the chart

The chart in this example is a standard line chart that uses the data in A1:D13.

Adding the Check Box controls

To add the check boxes to the worksheet:

1. Select View→Toolbars→Forms to display the Forms toolbar.

2. On the Forms toolbar, click the Check Box control and then drag in the worksheet to create the control.

3. Right-click the Check Box and choose Format Control from the shortcut menu. This displays the Format Control dialog box.

4. In the Format Control dialog box, click the Control tab.

5. In the Cell link field, enter $G$4. This will link the Check Box control with the cell G4, which will display either TRUE or FALSE, depending on the state of the Check Box control.

6. Click OK to close the dialog box.

7. Repeat Steps 2–6 to add two more Check Box controls, linked to cells G5 and G6.

Defining the names

This example uses quite a few names, which are listed in Table 7-1. Note that SeriesA, SeriesB, and SeriesC are named formulas. The other names all refer to cells or ranges. Also, note that range E2:E13 is empty. This is the range that will be used if a series is not selected.

TABLE 7-1 DEFINED NAMES

Name	Refers to
Month	=Sheet1!$A$2:$A$13
ProductA	=Sheet1!$B$2:$B$13
ProductB	=Sheet1!$C$2:$C$13
ProductC	=Sheet1!$D$2:$D$13
BlankRange	=Sheet1!$E$2:$E$13
ShowProductA	=Sheet1!$G$4
ShowProductB	=Sheet1!$G$5
ShowProductC	=Sheet1!$G$6
SeriesA	=IF(ShowProductA,ProductA,BlankRange)
SeriesB	=IF(ShowProductB,ProductB,BlankRange)
SeriesC	=IF(ShowProductC,ProductC,BlankRange)

The three named formulas are quite a bit different from the previous examples in the chapter. These formulas use an IF function that checks the corresponding check box value (stored in a cell in column G). If it's TRUE, then the named formula returns the range reference for the corresponding product's data. If the check box is not checked, the named formula returns a reference to the blank range (E2:E13).

Modifying the chart series

The final step is to modify the three chart series, so they use the named formulas for the values range. The easiest way to do this is to use the Series tab of the Source Data dialog box. For example, the Values range for the Product A series is

```
=Sheet1!SeriesA
```

The Product B and Product C series are modified in a similar manner.

Creating a Very Interactive Chart

The final example, shown in Figure 7-16, is a useful application that allows the user to choose two U.S. cities (from a list of 284 cities) and view a chart that compares the cities by month in any of the following categories: average precipitation, average temperature, percent sunshine, and average wind speed.

The interactivity is provided using by using Excel's built-in features — no macros required. The cities are chosen from a drop-down list, using Excel's Data Validation feature, and the data option is selected using four Option Button controls. The pieces are all connected using a few formulas.

 This example uses some named ranges. But, unlike the previous examples in this chapter, it does *not* use named formulas. Rather, the chart uses data that is retrieved by using VLOOKUP formulas.

This example demonstrates that it is indeed possible to create a user-friendly, interactive application without the assistance of macros.

The following sections describe the steps I took to set up this application.

Getting the data

I did a Web search and spent about five minutes locating the data I needed at the National Climatic Data Center. I copied the data from my browser window, pasted it to an Excel worksheet, and did a bit of clean up work. The result was four 13-column tables of data, which I named *PrecipitationData, TemperatureData, SunshineData,* and *WindData.* To keep the interface as clean as possible, I put the data on a separate sheet (named Data).

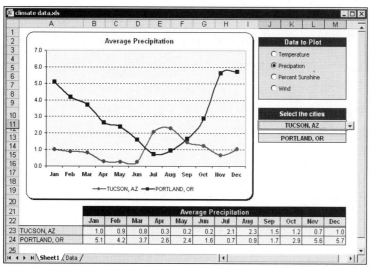

Figure 7-16: This application uses a variety of techniques to plot monthly climate data for two selected U.S. cities.

Creating the Option Button controls

I needed a way to allow the user to select the data to plot and decided to use Option Button controls from the Forms toolbar. Because option buttons work as a group, the four Option Button controls are all linked to the same cell (cell O3). Cell O3, therefore, contains a value from 1 to 4, depending on which option button is selected.

I needed a way to obtain the name of the data table based on the numeric value in cell O3. The solution was to write a formula (in cell O4) that uses Excel's CHOOSE function:

```
=CHOOSE(O3,"TemperatureData","PrecipitationData","SunshineData","WindData")
```

Therefore, cell O4 displays the name of one of the four named data tables. I then did some cell formatting behind the Option Button controls to make them more visible.

Creating the city lists

Next step in setting up the application: Create drop-down lists to enable the user to choose the cities to be compared in the chart. Excel's Data Validation feature makes creating a drop-down list in a cell very easy. First, I did some cell merging to create a wider field. I merged cells J11:M11 for the first city list and gave them the name *City1*. I merged cells J13:M13 for the second city list and gave them the name *City2*.

To make working with the list of cities easier, I created a named range, *CityList*, which refers to the first column in the *PrecipitationData* table.

Following are the steps I used to create the drop-down lists:

1. Select J11:M11 (remember, these are merged cells).

2. Choose Data→Validation to display Excel's Data Validation dialog box.

3. Select the Settings tab in the Data Validation dialog box.

4. In the Allow field, choose List.

5. In the Source field, enter =CityList.

6. Click OK.

7. Copy J11:M11 to J13:M13. This duplicates the Data Validation settings for the second city.

Figure 7-17 shows the result.

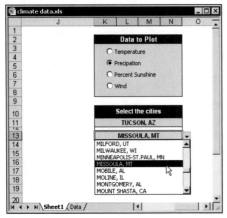

Figure 7-17: Using the Data Validation
drop-down to select a city

Creating the chart's data range

The key to this application is that the chart uses data in a specific range. The data in this range is retrieved from the appropriate data table using formulas that utilize the VLOOKUP function. Figure 7-18 shows the range of data that is used by the chart.

The formula in cell A23, which looks up data based on the contents of *City1*, is

```
=VLOOKUP(City1,INDIRECT(DataTable),COLUMN(),FALSE)
```

The formula in cell A24 is the same, except that it is looking up data based on the contents of *City2*:

```
=VLOOKUP(City2,INDIRECT(DataTable),COLUMN(),FALSE)
```

climate data.xls													
	A	B	C	D	E	F	G	H	I	J	K	L	M
22													
23					Average Temperature								
24		Jan	Feb	Mar	Apr	May	Jun	Jul	Aug	Sep	Oct	Nov	Dec
25	TUCSON, AZ	51.7	55.0	59.2	66.0	74.5	84.1	86.5	84.9	80.9	70.5	58.7	51.9
26	SAN DIEGO, CA	57.8	58.9	60.0	62.6	64.6	67.4	70.9	72.5	71.6	67.6	61.8	57.6
27													
28													

Sheet1 / Data /

Figure 7-18: The chart uses the data retrieved by formulas in A22:M24.

After entering these formulas, I simply copied them across to the next 12 columns.

You may be wondering about the use of the COLUMN function for the third argument of the VLOOKUP function. This function returns the column number of the cell that contains the formula. This is a convenient way to avoid hard-coding the column to be retrieved and allows the same formula to be used in each column.

The label above the months is generated by a formula that refers to the DataTable cell and constructs a descriptive title: The formula is

```
="Average " &LEFT(DataTable,LEN(DataTable)-4)
```

Creating the chart

After completing the previous tasks, the final step — creating the actual chart — is a breeze. The line chart has two data series and uses the data in A22:M24. The chart title is linked to cell A21. The data in A22:M24 changes, of course, whenever an Option Button control is selected or a new city is selected from either of the Data Validation lists.

Chapter 8

Charting Techniques and Tricks

IN THIS CHAPTER

◆ Adding lines and background elements to a chart

◆ Working with single-point charts that resemble a thermometer or gauge

◆ Using an XY series to simulate an axis

◆ Creating specialty charts that make use of a variety of tricks

◆ Creating charts for mathematical and statistical applications

◆ Stacking and overlaying charts

◆ Using an add-in to create an alternative to Excel's contour chart

◆ Making non-chart charts

THIS CHAPTER MIGHT BEST BE described as the catch-all chapter. You'll find a wide variety of useful charting examples that incorporate various tricks of the trade. These examples may give you some new ideas and stimulate your imagination.

Many of the examples in this chapter assume that you're familiar with the material presented in previous chapters. In other words, I focus on the general technique and assume that you know the basic procedures.

 All the examples described in this chapter are available on the companion CD-ROM. The CD also contains some examples that are not discussed in this chapter.

Adding Lines and Backgrounds to a Chart

This section presents examples of charts that have been augmented in a number of ways to display various types of lines and background elements. Several of the examples involve "tricks" that make use of combination charts.

241

Adding horizontal reference lines to a chart

Many charts benefit from adding one or more reference lines. Figure 8-1 shows an area chart that depicts a product's defect rate over a 20-day period. This chart displays an additional line, which indicates the "acceptable" defect rate. Data points that appear above this line represent an unacceptable level.

Adding a reference line is very simple. Just add a new series to the chart that displays as a straight horizontal line. In this case, the line uses the data column C, which consists of a single value repeated for each data point.

This is just a simple combination chart. The chart started as a line chart, and then I converted the Defect Rate series to an area chart series. I removed the gridlines to make the line more prominent. You can, of course, add any number of reference lines to a chart. Each will require a new data series.

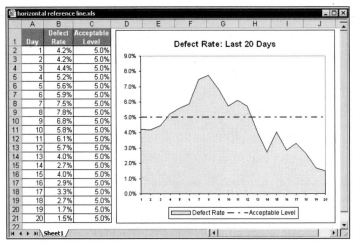

Figure 8-1: This combination chart displays a comparison line.

Adding a vertical line to a chart with an XY series

The previous section describes how to display a horizontal line to a chart. Adding a *vertical* line to a chart is a bit more challenging. Figure 8-2 shows a chart that displays monthly sales. The vertical line represents the date of a merger and provides a reference point for comparing pre-merger and post-merger sales.

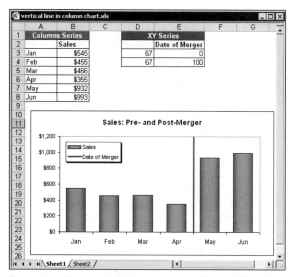

Figure 8-2: The vertical line is generated by an XY series.

To create this chart, use the following steps:

1. Create a standard column chart using the data in range A2:B8.

2. Select the range D2:E4 and choose Edit→Copy.

3. Select the chart and choose Edit→Paste Special. In the Paste Special dialog box, select New series, Values (Y) in Columns, Series Names in First Row, and Category (X Labels) in First Column.

4. Select the new series (a column series with two data points) and change the chart type for the series to XY. Use the "lines without markers" subtype. Excel will display two additional value axes in the chart (at the top and right).

5. For each of the two new value axes, access the Format Axis dialog box, click the Scale tab, and change the Minimum value to 0 and the maximum value to 100. Then select the Patterns tab and set all options to None (this hides the axes).

6. Add a title and apply other cosmetic formatting as desired.

You can use a similar procedure to create a horizontal line in a chart. Although the process described in the previous section is simpler, it may not be suitable for a column chart because the horizontal line does not extend all the way to the vertical borders of the plot area.

The XY series uses an arbitrary scale of 0–100. This scale could be anything because the scale values are not shown. Using 0–100 enables you to specify the line location in terms of a percentage. In this case, the value 67 (in D3:D4) specifies a line that begins at 67% of the length of the category axis.

Using background columns to represent a vertical line

The example in this section uses the same data as the previous example, but the approach to generating the vertical line is different. In this combination chart, the vertical line is created with an additional column chart series. The line is formed by using different colors for the bars (see Figure 8-3).

 Even though both series use columns, a secondary axis is necessary in order to control the gap width of the series independently. Technically, this is still classified as a combination chart: a column - column combination chart.

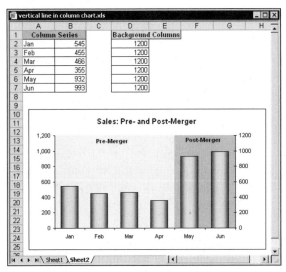

Figure 8-3: The vertical line is generated by colored columns.

Creating this chart involved the following steps:

1. Create a standard column chart using the data in range A2:B7. Delete the legend.

2. Select D2:D7 and choose Edit→Copy.

3. Select the chart and choose Edit→Paste Special. In the Paste Special dialog box, select New series and Values (Y) in Columns.

4. Click the original series (not the newly added series) and access the Format Data Series dialog box. Select the Axis tab and choose the Secondary axis option.

5. Click the newly added series and access the Format Data Series dialog box. Click the Options tab and set the Gap width to 0. Click the Patterns tab and set the Border to None. Change the Area to some light color such as yellow. The columns will appear as a single background block.

6. Click the fifth bar in the series and change the fill color. Repeat these actions for the sixth bar in the series.

7. Access the Format Axis dialog box for the left value axis (the axis associated with the background series). Click the Scale tab and set the Maximum scale value to 1200 (which is the maximum scale value for the right value axis).

8. Access the Format Axis dialog box for the right value axis. Select the Patterns tab and set all options to None (this hides the axis).

9. Add a title and descriptive labels to indicate the Pre-Merger and Post-Merger sections of the chart.

If you followed the previous steps, you've realized that the value axis on the left is actually associated with the background column series. This is necessary because a column series plotted on the secondary axis always appears in front of a column series plotted on the primary axis.

This procedure can easily be adapted to other situations — for example, dividing a chart into three vertical sections. Just change the colors of the appropriate background bars. In most cases, you'll want the background series to contain the same number of data points as the actual data series.

Adding horizontal or vertical "bands"

The examples in this section demonstrate a variation on the previous concept. Figure 8-4 shows a chart that displays vertical bands. Again, it's a combination chart — this time an XY series combined with a column chart series.

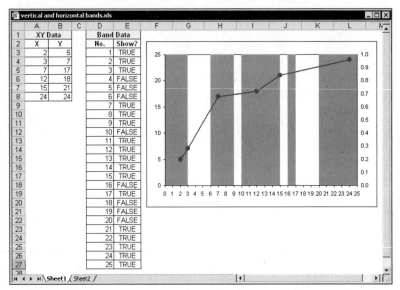

Figure 8-4: The vertical bands are provided by a column series that uses the secondary value axis.

The column chart series, which uses the data in columns D:E, is associated with the secondary value axis and has a scale range from 0 to 1. Normally, you would hide the secondary axis, but it's shown here for clarity. Note that the data consists of TRUE and FALSE values that determine whether the band is visible. In Excel, TRUE has the value 1 and FALSE has the value 0. Therefore, these Boolean values map perfectly to the chart's scale.

The companion CD-ROM contains a practical example of this technique. A line chart plots 100 data points, and the background vertical band displays only if the data point is greater than the previous one (see Figure 8-5).

Figure 8-6 shows another example. In this case, the "band" series consists of 50 bars rather than columns. The result is a column chart that shows horizontal bars in the background. The visibility of each of the 50 bars is controlled by changing the Boolean values in a range of 50 cells. The axes for the bars are displayed in the figure, but you would normally hide these axes.

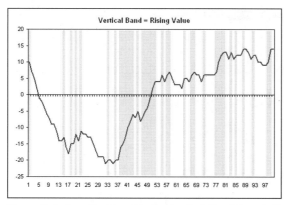

Figure 8-5: A vertical band indicates that the data point's value is greater than the previous point.

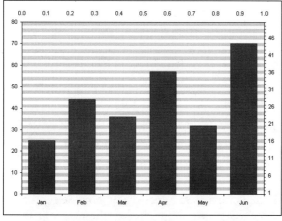

Figure 8-6: The horizontal bands are provided by a bar series that uses the secondary value axis.

Creating an XY chart with colored quadrants

Figure 8-7 shows an XY chart that plots 10 data points. Notice the two value axes cross in the center of the chart, forming four equal-size quadrants. Each of these quadrants is a different color — thanks to the assistance of a stacked-column chart series.

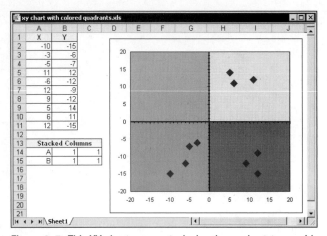

Figure 8-7: This XY chart uses a stacked-column chart to provide four different colors in the background.

Here's how it's done:

1. Create a standard XY chart using the data in range A2:B11. Delete the legend.

2. Select A14:C15 and choose Edit→Copy.

3. Select the chart and choose Edit→Paste Special. In the Paste Special dialog box, select New series, Values (Y) in Columns, and Categories (X Values) in First Column. The chart now has three XY series named Series 1, Series 2, and Series 3.

4. Select Series 2 and access the Format Data Series dialog box. Select the Axis tab and choose the Secondary axis option. Repeat these actions for Series 3.

5. Select Series 2 and change it to 1 100% Stacked Column chart. Repeat for Series 3.

6. Access the Chart Options dialog box, click the Axes tab, and make sure that all four axes are displayed.

7. Select either Series 2 or Series 3 and access the Format Data Series dialog box. Click the Options tab and set the Gap width to 0.

8. Select each of the four individual data points in the column chart and change its color. Remember, the first click selects the series and the second click selects the data point within the series.

9. Select the axis on top, access its Format Axis dialog box, select the Patterns tab, and set all options to None. Repeat these actions for the axis on the right.

10. The axis labels for the XY chart are next to their respective axis. You may prefer to set the Tick mark labels option to Low, using the Patterns tab of the Format Axis dialog box.

 TIP Another way to get a four-color background effect is to create an image file that consists of four colored quadrants. Then you can use the Format Plot Area dialog box to specify this file to be used as the Plot Area background.

Charts That Use a Single Data Point

The two examples in this chapter demonstrate how to display a single value in a chart. This is done by using metaphors such as a thermometer, a speedometer, or a tachometer.

Creating a thermometer chart

You're probably familiar with a "thermometer" type display that shows the percentage of a task that's completed. Creating such a display in Excel is very easy. The trick involves creating a chart that uses a single cell (which holds a percentage value) as a data series.

Figure 8-8 shows a worksheet set up to track daily progress toward a goal: 1,000 new customers in a 15-day period. Cell B18 contains the goal value, and cell B19 contains a simple sum formula:

```
=SUM(B2:B16)
```

Cell B21 contains a formula that calculates the percent of goal:

```
=B19/B18
```

As you enter new data in column B, the formulas display the current results.

To create the chart, select cell B21, click the Chart Wizard button, and create a column chart. Notice the blank row before cell B21. Without this blank row, Excel uses the entire data block for the chart, not just the single cell. Because B21 is isolated from the other data, the Chart Wizard uses only the single cell. Other changes required are the following:

◆ Remove the category (x) axis.

◆ Remove the legend.

◆ Add data labels.

♦ Set the Gap width to 0 (this makes the column occupy the entire width of the plot area).

♦ In the Format Axis dialog select Scale tab, set the Minimum to 0 and the Maximum to 1.

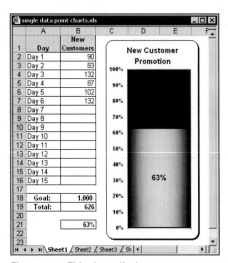

Figure 8-8: This chart displays progress toward a goal.

Figure 8-9 shows a variation on this theme. In this case, the chart is a line chart, with a single data point. The series marker has been replaced by an AutoShape in the form of a double-headed arrow.

Refer to Chapter 6 for more information about copying AutoShapes and pasting them as series markers.

Creating a gauge chart

Figure 8-10 shows a pie chart set up to resemble a gauge. Although this chart displays a single value (entered in cell B1), it actually uses three data points (in A4:A6).

One slice of the pie – the slice at the bottom – always consists of 50%, and that slice is hidden (the slice's Area and Border were set to None). The other two slices are apportioned based on the value in B1. The formula in cell B4 is

```
=MIN(B1,100%)/2
```

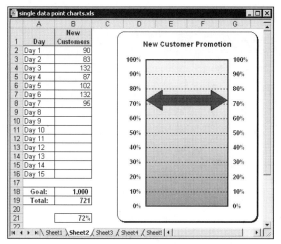

Figure 8-9: This single-value line chart uses an AutoShape for the series marker.

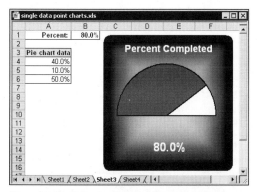

Figure 8-10: This chart resembles a speedometer gauge and displays a value between 0 and 100%.

This formula uses the MIN function to display the smaller of two values: the value in cell B1, or 100%. It then divides this value by 2 because you're dealing only with the visible half of the pie chart. Using the MIN function prevents the chart from displaying more than 100%.

The formula in A6, which follows, simply calculates the remaining part of the pie — the part to the right of the gauge's "needle."

```
=50%-A5
```

Figure 8-11 shows a variation that uses a doughnut chart with two series. Again, the lower portions of the two series are hidden. The outer series colors (red, yellow, and green) use data labels to indicate the meaning of various ratings.

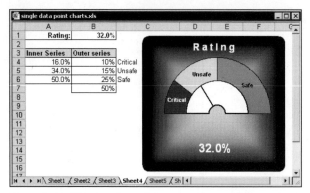

Figure 8-11: This doughnut chart resembles a tachometer and displays a value between 0 and 100%.

Using a Dummy Axis

This section describes a very useful trick that can be applied in a variety of situations. The trick involves using an XY series that simulates a value axis.

An introductory example

A common use for a dummy value axis is to provide descriptive labels. As you probably know, it is not possible to change the text used in the value axis labels – they are always values derived from the numbers in the chart series. You can control the number formatting and font attributes, but the actual contents of these labels are determined by Excel and cannot be changed.

Figure 8-12 shows a chart that seems to defy this rule. This chart displays the results of ten tests, and the value axis shows letter grades (A–F), not values.

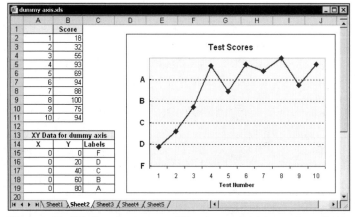

Figure 8-12: This line chart uses an XY series to simulate a value axis.

ABOUT THIS CHART

Following are a few key points regarding this chart:

- The chart is actually a combination chart that combines a standard line chart with an XY chart.

- The "real" value axis is hidden. In its place is an XY series that is formatted to look like an axis.

- The data for the XY series is stored in A14:B18. The Y values represent the scores for each letter grade category. For example, an *F* is 0–19, a *D* is 20–39, and so on.

- The axis labels (the letters A–F) are custom data labels for the XY series.

To get a better feel for how a dummy value axis is set up, refer to Figure 8-13. This is a standard XY chart, with the data points connected by lines, and series markers set to display a horizontal tick. It uses the five data points specified in A2:B6. Because each X value is the same (1), the series displays as a vertical line. This XY series uses custom data labels to identify each "tick." As you can see, this data series look very much like a vertical axis.

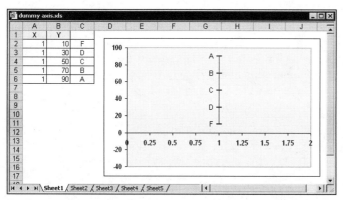

Figure 8-13: This XY series displays as a vertical line with tick marks and uses custom data labels.

CREATING THE CHART

Following are the steps required to create the line chart pictured at the beginning of this section.

1. Select the data in A1:B11 and create a standard line chart. Delete the legend.

2. Select A15:B19 and choose Edit→Copy.

3. Select the chart and choose Edit→Paste Special. Specify New series, Values (Y) in Columns, and Category (X Labels) in First Column. Doing so adds a new line series to the chart.

4. Select the new line series and choose Chart→Chart Type. Specify an XY (Scatter) chart using the subtype that displays lines and markers. The XY series will appear on top of the chart's value axis. The X value axis for the new series appears on the top, and its Y value axis appears on the right.

5. Select the XY series and access the Format Data Series dialog box. In the Patterns tab, make the line color black and specify a tick as the marker style. In the Data Labels tab, specify any option (the labels will be changed later).

6. Select the data labels for the XY series and access the Format Data Labels dialog box. In the Alignment tab, specify Left for the Label Position. You will need to adjust the size and position of the Plot Area to accommodate the left-positioned labels.

7. Now it's time to clean up the axes. Select the *real* value axis on the left (this is the axis for the line series). Access the Format Axis dialog box, select the Scale tab, and set Minimum to 0, the Maximum to 100, and the Major Unit to 20. These selections create gridlines that divide the chart into five vertical sections to correspond to the five letter grades. Then select the Patterns tab and set all options to None (to hide the axis).

8. Select the X value axis for the XY series (it will be at the top of the chart) and access the Format Axis dialog box. In the Patterns tab, set all options to None. Doing so hides the axis.

9. Select the Y value axis for the XY series (it will on the right side of the chart). Access the Format Axis dialog box. In the Scale tab, set the Minimum to 0, the Maximum to 100, and the Major Unit to 20. In the Patterns tab, set all options to None.

10. Finally, select each individual data label for the XY series and change the text to correspond to the letter grade labels in column C.

TIP   To apply the data labels automatically, refer to the sidebar "Applying Custom Data Labels," in this chapter.

Labeling an axis with non-equal intervals

In the previous example, the dummy axis had equal-intervals: Each y value was separated by 20. Figure 8-14 shows another chart that uses a dummy value axis, but this time the scale intervals on the value axis vary in size. Essentially, this chart makes it easy to translate the monthly numeric rating values into descriptive text. As you can see from the chart, June is the only month in which a "Good" rating was attained.

Applying Custom Data Labels

Several of the examples in this chapter use custom data labels. You may have discovered that Excel's data label feature has a serious limitation: You can't specify a range of cells to be used as data labels for a chart series.

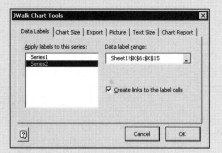

You can, of course, add data labels to a series and then select each data label and edit it manually. A better approach is to use a VBA macro. The author's JWalk Chart Tools add-in (available on the companion CD-ROM) provides such a macro.

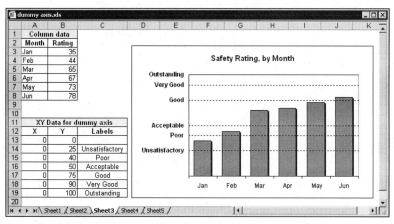

Figure 8-14: This chart uses an XY series to simulate a value axis.

This chart is very similar to the previous example but has one additional twist: It simulates gridlines by using X error bars for the XY series. The normal gridlines for the column chart series are not displayed.

Column and Bar Chart Variations

This section contains a number of examples that demonstrate how to create charts that you may have thought were impossible. As you'll see, the key is applying a few charting tricks – and being creative.

Stacked-column chart variations

A stacked-column chart enables you to compare relative proportions of individual items across categories. But this type of chart sometimes doesn't quite do the job. Figure 8-15 demonstrates the problem. The goal is to facilitate comparisons by month, across the two years (compare January '01 with January '02, and so on). Because of the data arrangement, this comparison is difficult to do. For example, the January data is separated by five columns.

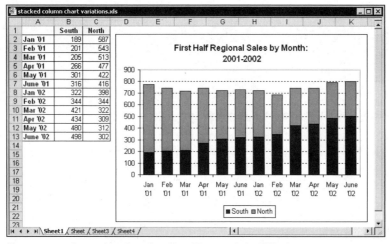

Figure 8-15: Comparing data for a specific month is difficult.

Figure 8-16 shows an improved version of this chart. Rearranging the data so that the same months are contiguous, as well as inserting blank rows, solves the problem. This chart also has its gap width set to 0. You may prefer to include an additional blank row at the top and bottom of the series. Doing so would display a gap before the January columns and after the June columns.

In some cases, you may want to compare a single-value column with a stacked column. The chart in Figure 8-17, for example, displays Orders for each item, along with a corresponding stacked column that depicts the Inventory amount with the In Production amount.

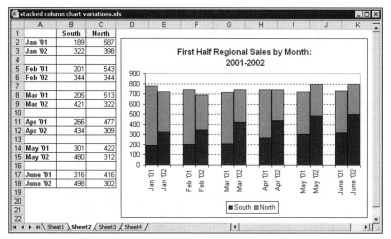

Figure 8-16: Rearranging the data and inserting blank rows facilitates comparisons of the same month.

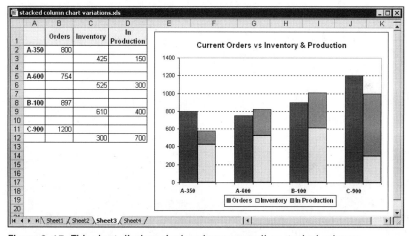

Figure 8-17: This chart displays single columns as well as stacked columns.

Excel doesn't provide a direct way to do this, but it's fairly easy to do if you arrange your data properly. This is a standard stacked-column chart generated from the data in A1:D12. The gap width was set to 0. The chart actually has 11 categories, although it appears to have only four.

Figure 8-18 shows a variation on the previous chart. In this case, the data need not be arranged in any special way (as in the previous example). This is actually a combination chart that uses two value axes. The Orders series is assigned to the left value axis, and the other two series are assigned to the right value axis.

Because the series use different value axes, you can adjust the gap width independently for the Orders series. In this example, the gap width is set to 50.

It's critical that both value axes use the same scale. Excel's automatic scaling may cause the value axes to use different scales. In such a case, you will need to adjust one or both of the axis scales manually.

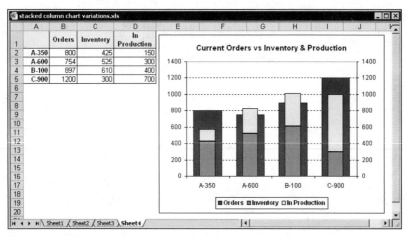

Figure 8-18: This chart displays stacked columns in front of single columns.

Creating a step chart

A "step" chart is similar to a hybrid column/line chart. Figure 8-19 shows two charts that use the data in columns A and B. The top chart is a standard line chart, and the bottom chart is a column chart – modified to have a gap width of 0 and no border colors. A typical step chart is similar to the column chart, but the columns are not visible. Rather, a step chart depicts a single line with the data points connected at right angles. Excel does not provide a step chart type, but you can create such a chart by using an XY chart, along with X error bars and Y error bars. Figure 8-20 shows an example of this type of chart. Column A and B contain the same data used in the previous charts. In addition, this chart uses the data in columns C and D as the source for the X error bars and Y error bars.

Refer to Chapter 5 for more information about using error bars.

Column C contains simple formulas that calculate the difference between the dates in column A. For example, cell C3 contains this formula:

```
=A3-A2
```

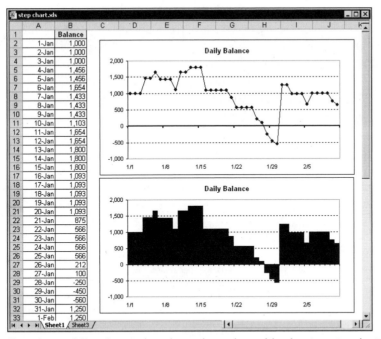

Figure 8-19: A line chart and a column chart — but neither is a true step chart.

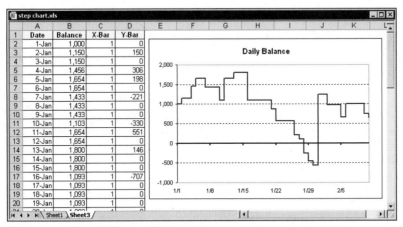

Figure 8-20: This XY chart, which resembles a step chart, uses the data in columns C and D for X error bars and Y error bars.

The formulas in column D are similar and calculate the difference between the Balance data in column B. The formula in D3, for example, is as follows:

```
=B3-B2
```

Although the chart is an XY chart, the series line and series markers are both hidden (formatted as None). Therefore, the line is composed entirely from the X error bars (column C) and Y error bars (Column D). The error bars are formatted as heavy lines, with no crosses at their ends.

A bar-line combination chart

It's easy to create a column-line combination chart. You either can use the custom chart type in the Chart Wizard, or you can start with a standard column chart and change one of the series to a line chart type. Figure 8-21 shows a simple example. The columns represent sales, and the line depicts projected sales. But if you've ever needed to create a combination bar-line chart, you may have concluded that Excel does not allow it.

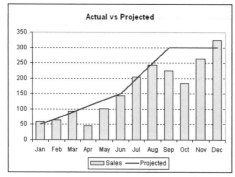

Figure 8-21: A column–line combination chart is easy to create.

Technically, Excel does not support a combination bar-line chart. The category axis for a bar chart extends in the vertical direction. The category axis for a line chart, on the other hand, must always be the horizontal axis. The solution is to use an XY chart type instead of the line chart type. Figure 8-22 shows an example.

To create this chart:

1. Create a standard bar chart using the data in A1:A13.

2. Select range D1:E13 and choose Edit→Copy.

3. Activate the chart and choose Edit→Paste Special. Choose New series, Values (Y) in Columns, Series Names in First Row, and Category (X Labels) in First Column. Note that the data is arranged opposite of what you might expect: The x values consist of the Project Sales amounts, and the y values consist of consecutive integers.

4. Select the newly added series (it will be a bar series) and access the Format Data Series dialog box. In the Axis tab, select Secondary axis.

5. Change the chart type of the new series to an XY chart with the data points connected by lines.

6. Adjust the secondary Y axis. The default Minimum and Maximum values are 1 and 12, respectively. Change these to 0.5 (Minimum) and 12.5 (Maximum). This change makes the line begin at the midpoint of the Jan bar and end at the midpoint of the Dec bar.

7. If you prefer that the months begin at the top of the chart, select the Category axis (on the left) and access the Format Axis dialog box. Select Categories in Reverse Order, and Value (Y) Axis Crosses at Maximum category.

8. Repeat Step 7 for the Secondary Value axis on the right side of the chart.

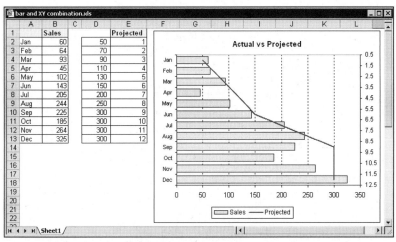

Figure 8-22: A bar-line combination chart is possible if you create the line with an XY series.

Varying column widths

The column chart shown in Figure 8-23 is a bit unusual: The width of the columns is not the same! The chart displays the Units Sold data on the value axis, and the width of each column is proportional to the Total Income for the product. In other words, this column chart is conveying more information than a typical column chart.

Although you can control the width of all columns by using the gap width setting, Excel does not provide an option to vary the width of individual columns. This chart is not actually using the data in A1:D7. Rather, the chart consists of six series, each with 100 data points. A portion of the data is shown in Figure 8-24.

The cells in column J contain formulas that determine the number of columns to show for each of the six series, using the values in column D (Total Income). Remember, this chart contains 100 data points. These data points are allocated among the six series. Formulas in columns K:L determine the starting row and the ending row for the data in each series. For example, Series A will display 12 of the

100 columns. Its 12 data points will be in rows 2–13. Series B will display five of the 100 columns, and its five data points will be in rows 14–18.

The formulas are relatively complex, but you can easily modify this example to handle other types of data.

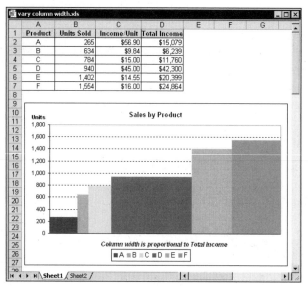

	A	B	C	D	E	F	G
1	Product	Units Sold	Income/Unit	Total Income			
2	A	265	$56.90	$15,079			
3	B	634	$9.84	$6,239			
4	C	784	$15.00	$11,760			
5	D	940	$45.00	$42,300			
6	E	1,402	$14.55	$20,399			
7	F	1,554	$16.00	$24,864			

Figure 8-23: Producing this comparative histogram chart requires a few tricks.

vary column width.xls

	I	J	K	L	M	N	O	P	Q	R	S
1	Series	# Cols	1st Row	Last Row		A	B	C	D	E	F
2	A	12	2	13		265					
3	B	5	14	18		265					
4	C	10	19	28		265					
5	D	35	29	63		265					
6	E	17	64	80		265					
7	F	21	81	101		265					
8						265					
9						265					
10						265					
11						265					
12						265					
13						265					
14							634				
15							634				
16							634				
17							634				
18							634				
19								784			
20								784			
21								784			
22								784			
23								784			
24								784			
25								784			
26								784			
27								784			
28								784			
29									940		

Figure 8-24: Some of the 100 rows of data used to generate the chart

Conditional colors

You're probably familiar with Excel's Conditional Formatting feature, which enables you to modify cell formatting based on the value contained in the cell. Unfortunately, Excel does not provide an analogous feature for charts. If you would like to display different colors in a chart based on values, you can use the technique described here.

Figure 8-25 shows a column chart that appears to display the data in column B, and the columns are colored based on the values. For example, data that is less than or equal to 0 displays in yellow. Data that is between 0–33 displays in purple, and so on.

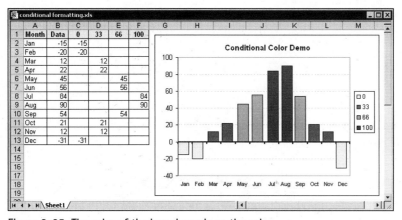

Figure 8-25: The color of the bars depends on the value.

Actually, this chart consists of four series (each using a different fill color), and uses the data in columns C:F. The cells in these columns contain formulas that reference the data in column B, and use the values in row 1 to determine whether the cell should contain the data value or display an empty string.

The formula in cell C2, for example, which follows this paragraph, examines the value in cell B2. If it's less than the value in C1 (0), the value from column B is displayed. Otherwise, the formula returns an empty string.

```
=IF(B2<=$C$1,B2,"")
```

The formulas in column D:F are a bit more complex because they need to determine whether the value in column B falls between two values. The formula in D3, for example is

```
=IF(AND($B2>C$1,$B2<=D$1),$B2,"")
```

TIP

If you would like to use this technique for an XY chart, you need to adjust the formulas so that they return #NA instead of an empty string (which is interpreted as 0). For example:

```
=IF(B2<=$C$1,B2,NA())
```

Creating a column chart from the data in columns C:F produces a chart with four data series, and the chart will contain gaps for the blank cells. To eliminate the gaps, adjust the gap width and overlap. The chart shown has a gap width of 0 and an overlap of 90.

You can adjust the values in row 1 to create different numeric ranges for the colors. And, of course, you can add more series to display more than four conditional colors.

Creating a population pyramid chart

A population pyramid chart, sometimes known as a comparative histogram, compares two groups using horizontal bars. Figure 8-26 shows an example, which depicts the age distribution, by sex, of the United States. Although this type of chart is often used with population data, it can be used in a variety of other situations.

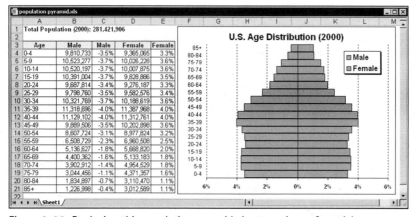

Figure 8-26: Producing this population pyramid chart requires a few tricks.

Excel does not provide this type of chart, but you can convert a standard bar chart using the following steps:

1. Create a stacked-bar chart with two series, using column A for the category labels, and columns C and E for the data. Note that the percentages for Males are calculated as negative numbers.

2. Select the value axis (on the bottom) and access the Format Axis dialog box. Select the Number tab and apply the following custom number format:

   0%;0%;0%

   This custom format eliminates the negative signs in the percentages.

3. Select the category axis (in the middle of the chart) and access the Format Axis dialog box. Click the Patterns tab and remove all tick marks. Set the Tick Mark Labels option to Low. This keeps the axis in the center of the chart, but displays the axis labels at the left side.

4. Select either of the data series and then access the Format Data Series dialog box. Click the Options tab and set the Gap width to 0.

Creating Gantt charts

A Gantt chart is a horizontal bar chart often used in project management applications. Although Excel doesn't support Gantt charts per se, you can fairly easily create a simple Gantt chart. The key is getting your data set up properly.

Figure 8-27 shows a Gantt chart set up to depict the schedule for a project, in range A1:C13. The horizontal axis represents the total time span of the project, and each bar represents a project task. The viewer can quickly see the duration for each task and identify overlapping tasks.

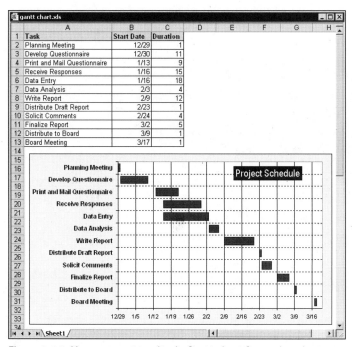

Figure 8-27: You can create a simple Gantt chart from a bar chart.

Column A contains the Task name, column B contains the corresponding Start Date, and column C contains the duration of the task, in days.

Follow these steps to create this chart:

1. Use the Chart Wizard to create a stacked-bar chart from the range A2:C13.

2. In Step 3 of the Chart Wizard, remove the legend and then click Finish to create an embedded chart.

3. Adjust the height of the chart so that all the axis labels are visible. You can also accomplish this by using a smaller font size for the category axis labels.

4. Access the Format Axis dialog box for the value (horizontal) axis. Adjust the horizontal axis Minimum and Maximum scale values to correspond to the earliest and latest dates in the data (note that you can enter a date into the Minimum or Maximum box). You also may want to set the Major unit to 7, to indicate weeks.

5. Access the Format Axis dialog box for the category (vertical) axis. In the Scale tab, select the option labeled Categories in Reverse Order, and set the option labeled Value (Y) Axis Crosses at Maximum Category.

6. Select the first data series and access the Format Data Series dialog box. On the Patterns tab, set Border to None and Area to None. This makes the first data series invisible.

7. Apply other formatting as desired.

TIP If you have many tasks, you may find it impossible to force Excel to display all the category names. In such a case, you can use a dummy series along the vertical axis with task names for data labels. Refer to "Using a Dummy Axis," earlier in this chapter.

Identifying the maximum and minimum values in a series

Figure 8-28 shows a line chart that has its maximum and minimum values identified with a circle and a square, respectively. These identifiers are the result of using two additional series in the chart. You can achieve this effect manually, by adding two AutoShapes, but using the additional series makes it fully automated.

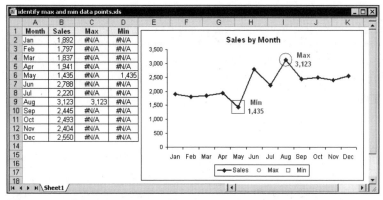

Figure 8-28: This chart uses two XY series to highlight the maximum and minimum data points in the line series.

To create this chart using the data in range A1:B13:

1. Enter the following formula in cell C2:

   ```
   =IF(B2=MAX($B$2:$B$13),B2,NA())
   ```

2. Enter this formula in cell D2:

   ```
   =IF(B2=MIN($B$2:$B$13),B2,NA())
   ```

3. Copy range C2:D2 down, ending in row 13. These formulas display the maximum and minimum values in column B, and all other cells display #NA.

4. Select C1:D13 and choose Edit→Copy.

5. Select the chart and choose Edit→Paste Special. In the Paste Special dialog box, choose New series, Values (Y) in Columns, and Series Names in First Row. This adds two new series, named Max and Min.

6. Select the Max series and access the Format Data Series dialog box. In the Patterns tab, set the Line to None, and change the marker to a large hollow circle. To create a hollow circle, select the circle style, set the Marker Background to No Color, and increase the Size.

7. Repeat Step 6 for the Min series, but use a large, hollow square for the marker.

8. Add data labels to the Max and Min series (the #NA values will not appear).

9. Apply other cosmetic formatting as desired.

The formulas entered in Steps 1 and 2 display #NA if the corresponding value in column B is not the maximum or minimum. In a line chart, an #NA value causes a gap to appear in the line — which is exactly what is needed. As a result, only one data point is plotted (or more, if there is a tie for the maximum or minimum).

Shading between two series in a line chart

The example in this section describes how to apply shading to the region between two lines in a line chart. Figure 8-29 shows a line chart with two series. The area between the lines is shaded with a fill color.

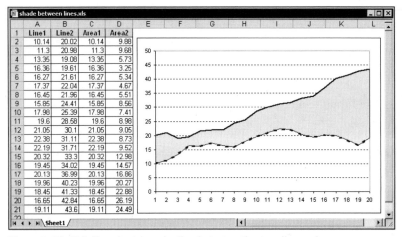

Figure 8-29: This line chart has shading between the two line series.

This type of chart requires two additional series, formatted as area chart series. One area chart series uses the data in column C. These values are the same as those in column A. You can, in fact, simply create the area chart series from the data in column A. The second area chart series uses the values in column D. These values are generated with a formula that calculates the difference between the first line and the second line data point. For example, the formula in D2 is

```
=B2-A2
```

After adding these two new area chart series, you need to hide the Area1 series. Do this by accessing the Format Data Series dialog box. Select the Patterns tab, and set the Border and Area to None.

XY Chart Variations

This section presents several examples of XY charts, with various accoutrements.

Drawing with an XY chart series

You can use an XY chart series to "draw" 2-D outline images as a chart. Figure 8-30 shows a simple example. This XY chart uses nine data points to draw an arrow.

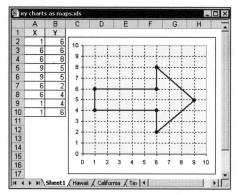

Figure 8-30: An XY chart that displays a simple drawing

How complex can you make an XY chart drawing? Take a look at Figure 8-31 This XY chart uses more than 3,000 data points to display a drawing of the state of California. An additional data series (with markers only) displays the location of various cities. The data was obtained from the Digital Chart of the World Data Server Web site, which provides latitude and longitude data that define the outline for hundreds of geographic locations.

The companion CD-ROM contains additional XY charts that depict other geographic areas.

Drawing a circle with an XY series

You can create an XY chart that draws a perfect circle. To do so, you need two ranges, one for the x values and another for the y values. The number of data points in the series determines the smoothness of the circle.

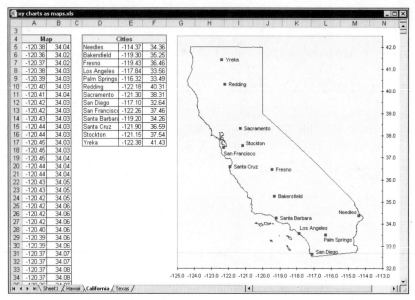

Figure 8-31: An XY chart that displays a map of California

The example in Figure 8-32 uses 13 points to create a circle with an origin of 0,0 and a radius of 1. This series uses the Smoothed line option (in the Patterns tab of the Format Data Series dialog box). When this option is not set, the circle is not very smooth, and its component lines are clearly visible.

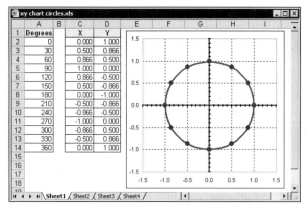

Figure 8-32: This XY chart uses 13 data points to define a circle.

To draw a circle in a chart, generate a series of values such as the ones shown in column A. The numeric series starts with 0 and has 30-degree increments. The ranges that are used in the chart are in columns C and D. The formula in C2 is

```
=SIN(RADIANS(A2))
```

The formula in D2 is

```
=COS(RADIANS(A2))
```

The formulas in C2 and D2 are copied down to subsequent rows.

> **NOTE** To plot a circle with more data points, you need to adjust the increment value in column A (the final value should always be 360). The increment is 360 divided by the number of data points minus 1. The more data points used, the smoother the circle.

Drawing a circle around data points

The example in this section, which builds on the previous example, demonstrates how to use an XY chart series to draw circles around data points in a chart. Figure 8-33 shows an XY chart that contains four series: the first series (range A2:B4) plots the three data points (as markers only; no line). Three additional series (ranges B9:C21, D9:E21, and F9:G21) plot a circle around each point (as lines, not markers).

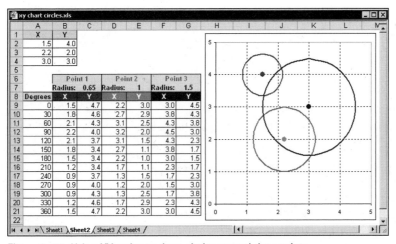

Figure 8-33: Using XY series to draw circles around data points

The three circle series use formulas similar to those described in the previous section, but these formulas allow for a specific origin and radius. The radius of each circle is defined by the entries in row 7.

The companion CD-ROM contains an additional example that draws squares around data points.

Connecting data points to the axes with error bars

The example in Figure 8-34 shows an XY chart in which each data point is projected to the x and y axis. These lines are created with error bars. Access the Format Data series dialog box and use the X Error Bars tab and the Y Error Bars tab to add the error bars.

In this example, X error bars are set to use the X data range (Custom negative option), and the Y error bars are set to use the Y data range (Custom positive option).

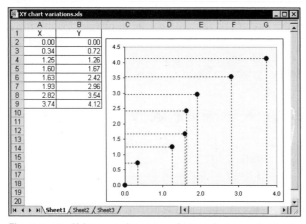

Figure 8-34: Using error bars to project each data point to the axes

Connecting XY points to the origin

The chart in Figure 8-35 shows an XY chart in which each data point is connected to the origin. This type of chart requires an additional series for each data point. The chart shown in the figure displays five data points, and the chart has six data series.

The first series uses the data in B3:C7, and this series is set to display markers (but no line) and data labels. Each data point has an additional series displayed as a dashed line. For example, the first data point uses the values in B10:C11. Note that each of these additional series consists of two data points that connect the original data point with the chart's origin (0,0). You can, of course, use any other XY pair in place of 0,0.

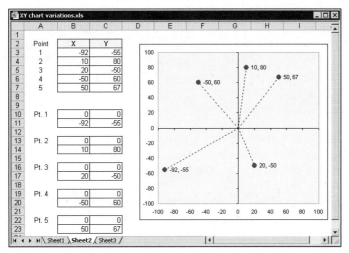

Figure 8-35: Using additional data series to connect each data point with the chart's origin

Displaying data points on axes

The example in this section was inspired by a chart depicted in Edward Tufte's *The Visual Display of Quantitative Information* book. Tufte starts with a standard XY chart and then systematically removes all nonessential elements. What remains is a minimalist chart with two axes that display the data values (see Figure 8-36).

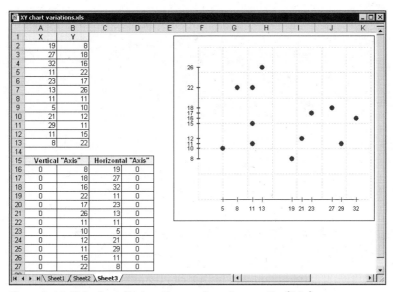

Figure 8-36: This chart displays the x and y values on the (fake) axes.

The data for the chart is in A2:B13. The axes in this chart are actually additional XY data series, formatted to look like axes (the "real" axes are hidden). Data that generates the vertical axis is in A16:B27. Data for the horizontal axis is in C16:D27. Both of these are XY series that display lines and markers. For details on using dummy axes, refer to "Using a Dummy Axis," earlier in this chapter.

Creating a timeline

Figure 8-37 shows an XY chart, set up to display a timeline of events. The chart uses the data in columns A and B, and the series uses Y error bars to connect each marker to the timeline (the X value axis). The text consists of customized data labels. The Y value axis for the chart is hidden, but it is set to display Values in reverse order so that the earliest events display higher in the vertical dimension.

This type of chart is limited to relatively small amounts of text — otherwise, the data labels wrap and the text may be obscured.

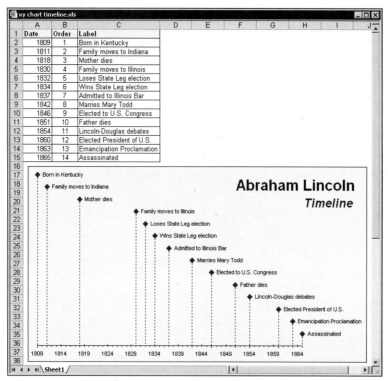

Figure 8-37: This XY chart uses data labels and Y error bars to connect its points to the X value axis.

Mathematics and Statistics Applications

The examples in this section may appeal to those involved with mathematical and statistical applications.

Creating frequency distributions and histograms

A frequency distribution is a summary table that shows the frequency of each value in a range. For example, an instructor may create a frequency distribution of test scores. The table would show the count of test scores in various numeric ranges. A chart created from a frequency distribution is often referred to as a *histogram*.

Excel provides a number of ways to create frequency distributions. You can

◆ Use the FREQUENCY function

◆ Use the Analysis ToolPak add-in

◆ Use a pivot table

This section covers the FREQUENCY function and the Analysis ToolPak options. Refer to Chapter 9 for examples of using a pivot table to create a histogram.

USING THE FREQUENCY FUNCTION

Using Excel's FREQUENCY function is probably the easiest way to create a frequency distribution. This function always returns an array, so you must use it in an array formula entered into a multicell range.

Figure 8-38 shows a workbook with data in range A2:1001 (named *Data*). These values range from 43 to 100. The range C5:C14 contains the *bins* used for the frequency distribution. Each cell in this bin range contains the upper limit for the bin. In this case, the bins consist of <=55, 56–60, 61–65, and so on. See the sidebar "Creating Bins for a Frequency Distribution" to discover an easy way to create a bin range.

To create the frequency distribution, select a range of cells that correspond to the number of cells in the bin range — in this example, range D5:D14. Then enter the following array formula:

```
=FREQUENCY(Data,C5:C14)
```

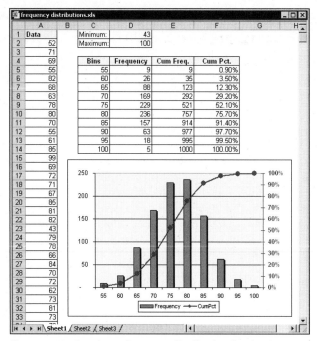

Figure 8-38: Creating a frequency distribution for the data in column A

Enter an array formula by pressing Ctrl+Shift+Enter.

The array formula is entered into all the selected cells and returns the count of values in the *Data* range that fall into each bin. You can then create other formulas that make use of the frequencies. For example, column E displays cumulative frequencies, and column F shows cumulative percent.

The combination chart was created using the frequency data in column D (the column series) and the cumulative percent data in column F (the line series). The histogram suggests that the data approximates a normal distribution.

USING THE ANALYSIS TOOLPAK TO CREATE A FREQUENCY DISTRIBUTION

If you install the Analysis ToolPak add-in, you can use the Histogram option to create a frequency distribution. Select Tools→Data Analysis to display the Data Analysis dialog box. Next, select Histogram and click OK. You should see the Histogram dialog box shown in Figure 8-39.

Creating Bins for a Frequency Distribution

When creating a frequency distribution, you must first enter the values into the bin range. The number of bins determines the number of categories in the distribution. Most of the time, each of these bins will represent an equal range of values.

To create 10 evenly spaced bins for values in a range named *Data*, enter the following array formula into a range of 10 cells in a column:

```
=MIN(Data)+(ROW(INDIRECT("1:10"))*(MAX(Data)-MIN(Data))/10)
```

To enter a multicell array formula, select the range, type the formula, and press Ctrl+Shift+Enter.

This formula creates 10 bins, based on the values in the *Data* range. The upper bin will always equal the maximum value in the range.

To create more or fewer bins, use a value other than 10 and enter the array formula into a range that contains the same number of cells. For example, to create five bins, enter the following array formula into a five-cell vertical range:

```
=MIN(Data)+(ROW(INDIRECT("1:5"))*(MAX(Data)-MIN(Data))/5)
```

Figure 8-39: The Analysis ToolPak's
Histogram dialog box

Specify the range for your data (Input Range). If you've created a bin range, specify that range — otherwise, leave it blank and the program will generate bins automatically. Specify the upper-left cell for the results (Output Range) and then select any options. Figure 8-40 shows a frequency distribution (and chart) created with the Histogram option.

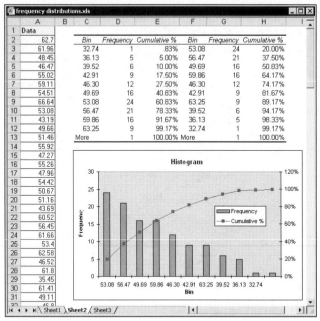

Figure 8–40: A frequency distribution (and chart) generated by the Analysis ToolPak's Histogram option

A potential problem with using this technique is that the frequency distribution consists of values, not formulas. Therefore, if you make any changes to your input data, you need to rerun the Histogram procedure to update the results.

USING ADJUSTABLE BINS TO CREATE A HISTOGRAM

Figure 8-41 shows a worksheet with student grades listed in column B (67 students total). Columns D and E contain formulas that calculate the upper and lower limits for bins, based on the entry in cell E1 (named *BinSize*). For example, if *BinSize* is 10 (as in the figure), then each bin contains 10 scores (1–10, 11–20, and so on).

The chart uses two named formulas. The name *Categories* is defined as

```
=OFFSET(Sheet3!$E$4,0,0,ROUNDUP(100/BinSize,0))
```

The name *Frequencies* is defined as

```
=OFFSET(Sheet3!$F$4,0,0,ROUNDUP(100/BinSize,0))
```

The net effect is that the chart adjusts automatically when you change the *BinSize* cell. Figure 8-42 shows the chart when the bin size is 6.

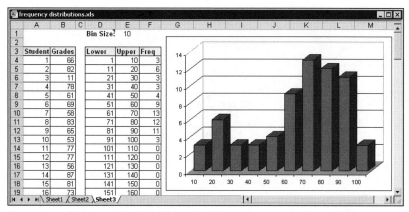

Figure 8-41: The chart displays a histogram; the contents of cell E1 determine the number of categories.

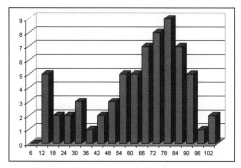

Figure 8-42: The previous chart, after changing the bin size

 See Chapter 7 for more about creating charts that use named formulas in their SERIES formulas.

Plotting a normal curve

Figure 8-43 shows two XY charts that display a normal distribution and the cumulative normal distribution. The top chart uses the data in columns A and B. The bottom chart uses the data in columns A and C. Cell B1, named *Mean*, controls the mean of the distribution, and cell B2, named *SD*, controls the standard deviation.

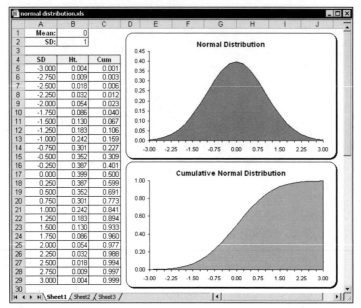

Figure 8-43: The XY charts display the normal distribution and the cumulative normal distribution.

Column A contains formulas that generate values ranging from –3 SD units to +3 SD units. The formula in cell A5, which was copied to the cells below, is

```
=(-SD*3)+Mean
```

Column B contains formulas that generate the height of the curve for a given mean and standard deviation. The formula in cell B5 is

```
=NORMDIST(A5,Mean,SD,FALSE)
```

The formulas in column C also use the NORMDIST function, but the fourth argument is set to TRUE. The formula in C5 is

```
=NORMDIST(A5,Mean,SD,TRUE)
```

In some cases, you may want to compare a histogram created from your data with the theoretical normal distribution. Figure 8-44 shows an example of how this can be done. The chart is a combination with two value axes. The data consist of 2,600 data points (not shown). Simple formulas in column D calculate key statistics for the data.

The histogram is generated from the data in column G, using the FREQUENCY function (see the previous section). The normal distribution curve uses the data in column H. The formula in cell H2, which is copied to the cells below, is

```
=NORMDIST(F2,$D$4,$D$5,FALSE)
```

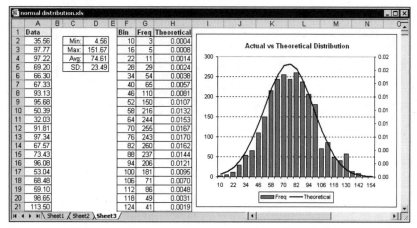

Figure 8-44: This combination chart displays a histogram (columns) along with the normal distribution curve.

 ON THE CD The companion CD-ROM contains another example that applies a scaling factor to the theoretical values. The theoretical data is multiplied by the number of data points (2600) times the bin size (6). After this transformation, both data series can use a single value axis.

Plotting z-scores with standard deviation bands

Figure 8-45 shows an XY chart that plots 1,000 values. Each data point in column A has been converted to a z-score (column B), and that's the data actually used in the chart. A z-score is a way of standardizing data, such that the transformed data has a mean of 0 and a standard deviation of 1. The midpoint on the vertical axis corresponds to the average data value, and the gridlines correspond to standard deviation units.

Formulas calculate the mean and standard deviation of the data, and these cells are given names (*Mean* and *SD*). The z-score calculation is done with simple formulas. Cell B2, for example, contains this formula:

```
=(A2-Mean)/SD
```

The shaded bands are generated by a bar chart series with eight data points (in the range D2:E9). The bar chart series uses the value axis at the bottom of the chart, and each bar has been manually formatted to display a graduated color effect. Because the chart plots transformed data, the chart can be used for any data set without modification.

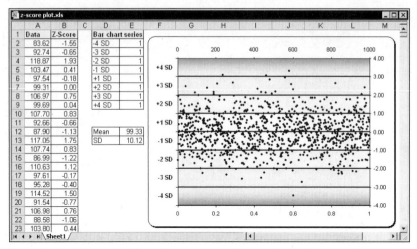

Figure 8-45: This combination chart uses a bar chart series to display horizontal bands that correspond to standard deviation units.

Calculating the area under a curve

If you use an XY chart to generate a curve, you may need to calculate the area under the curve. I'm starting with an elementary example, shown in Figure 8-46. The gridlines in this chart are separated by one unit, so calculating the area under this curve can be done manually. It consists of 10.5 square units (nine complete squares plus three half squares).

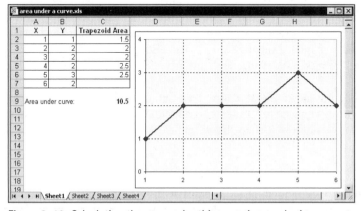

Figure 8-46: Calculating the area under this curve is a no-brainer.

If you don't feel like counting squares, you can take a more calculated approach and use formulas. This is known as the "trapezoid" method. A trapezoid, as you may recall, is a four-sided figure with two parallel sides. This method essentially divides the area under the curve into a series of trapezoids and then calculates the area of each one. The area under the curve is the sum of the trapezoid areas.

The general formula to calculate the area of a trapezoid is to multiply the "average" height by the base. In the preceding example, the left side of the first trapezoid has a height of 1 and the right side has a height of 2. The average height is 1.5. The base is one unit, so the area of the first trapezoid is 1.5. The area of the second trapezoid is 2, and so on.

The formulas in column C calculate the area for each trapezoid. Cell C2, for example, contains the following formula:

```
=((B2+B3)/2)*(A3-A2)
```

This formula is copied down to accommodate the number of data points. Note that the last cell (cell C7) is empty. That's because each formula refers to the subsequent row, and the formula is not valid for the last row of data. The formula in C9 simply adds these segment areas together.

This formula works fine — except when negative values are involved. In such a case, the formula gets much more complex because triangles (as well as trapezoids) enter the picture. The curve shown in Figure 8-47 presents more of a challenge because it has negative values. Using the previous formula to calculate trapezoid areas for this chart, the result is 3.5, which is clearly incorrect.

When negative numbers are involved, a more complex formula is required. The formula below is a general-purpose formula that works in all situations.

```
=IF(B2*B3>=0,ABS(((B2+B3)/2)*(A3-A2)),ABS(((B2^2+B3^2)/(B2-B3)/2)*(A3-A2)))
```

The formula uses an IF function that determines whether the calculation returns the area of a trapezoid, of the area of two triangles. In this example, the formula is used four times to yield the final result. The first, second, and third calculations compute the area of a trapezoid. The fourth calculation, however, computes the area of the two triangles that result from the line crossing the x axis. The sum of the areas of these two triangles is 0.83. The total area under the curve is 4.83.

It's important to understand that the area calculation is *approximate.* Generally, the accuracy of the calculation increases with the number of data points that define the curve. Figure 8-48 shows three charts, all of which plot a sine curve. The charts vary, however, in the number of data points used and, subsequently, in the number of area calculations performed. The calculated area under the curve ranges from 220.01 to 229.16, the latter being the most accurate.

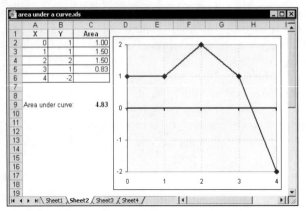

Figure 8-47: Calculating the area under this curve requires complex formulas.

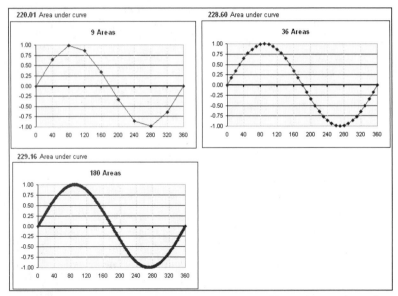

Figure 8-48: Calculating the area under a sine curve, with varying numbers of data points

Creating a box plot

A box plot (sometimes known as a *quartile plot* or a *box and whisker plot*) is often used to summarize data. Figure 8-49 shows a box plot created for four groups of data. Each group has a diagram, the height of which represents the numerical range of the data (minimum and maximum values). The "boxes" represent the 25th through the 75th percentile. The horizontal line inside the box is the median value (or 50th percentile). This type of chart enables the viewer to make quick comparisons among groups of data.

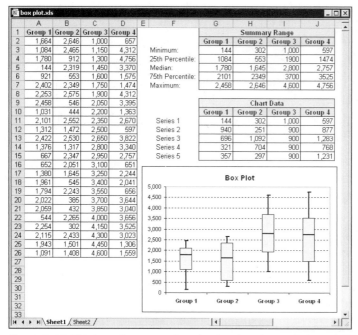

Figure 8-49: This box plot summarizes the data in columns A through D.

The raw data appears in columns A:D. The data is summarized in range F1:J7, with simple formulas. The following table lists the formulas for Group 1 (G3:G7). These formulas were copied to the three columns to the right.

Cell	Calculation	Formula
G3	Minimum	=MIN(A$2:A$26)-
G4	25th Percentile	=PERCENTILE(A$2:A$26,0.25)
G5	Median	=MEDIAN(A$2:A$26)
G6	75th Percentile	=PERCENTILE(A$2:A$26,0.75)
G7	Maximum	=MAX(A$2:A$26)

The summary data must be transformed in order to create the box plot. This is done in the section labeled Chart Data (G11:J15). This range contains simple formulas that calculate the difference between the row values in the Summary Range. For example, the formula in cell G12 is

```
=G4-G3
```

Follow these steps to create the box plot:

1. Select the range F10:J15 and use the Chart Wizard to create a stacked-column chart.

2. In Step 2 of the Chart Wizard, select the Rows option. Click Finish to create the chart.

3. Select Series 1 and access the Format Data Series dialog box. In the Patterns tab, set the Border to None and the Area to None.

4. Select Series 2 and access the Format Data Series dialog box. In the Patterns tab, set the Border to None and the Area to None. In the Y Error Bars tab, specify Minus error bars, with an Error amount of 100%.

5. Select Series 4 and access the Format Data Series dialog box. In the Y Error Bars tab, specify Plus error bars, with the custom range: G15:J15 (the Series 5 range).

6. Select Series 5 and access the Format Data Series dialog box. In the Patterns tab, set the Border to None and the Area to None.

7. You'll probably want to delete the legend because it provides no meaningful information.

The only two bars that remain visible are Series 3 and Series 4. Vertical error bars extend to cover the space occupied by the hidden Series 2 and Series 5. You can adjust the Gap width to adjust the width of the boxes.

You can also create a horizontal box plot by starting with a stacked-bar chart and using the same series of steps.

The companion CD-ROM contains an additional example that creates a vertical box plot using a line chart with high-low lines and up/down bars.

Plotting mathematical functions

The examples in this section demonstrate how to plot mathematical functions that use one variable (a 2-D line chart) and two variables (a 3-D surface chart).

The examples make use of Excel's Data Table feature, which enables you to evaluate a formula with varying input values. Coverage of this feature is beyond the scope of this book. Excel's Help provides a good overview.

PLOTTING FUNCTIONS WITH ONE VARIABLE

An XY chart is useful for plotting various mathematical and trigonometric functions. For example, Figure 8-50 shows a plot of the SIN function. The chart plots y for values of x (expressed in radians) from –5 to +5 in increments of 0.5. Each pair of x and y values appears as a data point in the chart, and the points connect with a line.

The function is expressed as

```
y = SIN(x)
```

The corresponding formula in cell B2 (which is copied to the cells below) is

```
=SIN(A2)
```

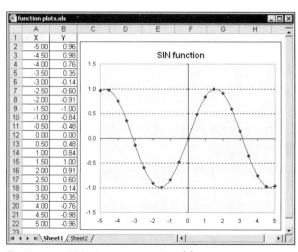

Figure 8-50: This chart plots the SIN(x).

Figure 8-51 shows a general-purpose, single-variable plotting application. The data for the chart is calculated by a Data Table in columns J:K and is not shown in the figure. To use this application:

1. Enter a formula in cell B3. The formula should contain at least one "x" variable. In the figure, the formula in cell B3 is

   ```
   =SIN(PI()*x)*(PI()*x)
   ```

2. Enter the minimum value for x in cell B4.

3. Enter the maximum value for x in cell B5.

The formula will display the value of y for the minimum value of x. The Data Table, however, evaluates the formula for 200 equally spaced values of x, and these values appear in the chart. In addition, the chart's title displays the function that plotted.

 This worksheet is protected to allow input only in cells B3:B5. It does not use a password, however, so you can unprotect and modify the sheet.

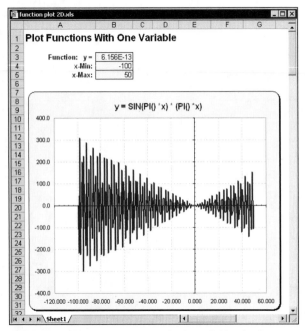

Figure 8-51: A general-purpose, single-variable plotting workbook

Plotting functions with two variables

The preceding section describes how to plot functions that use a single variable (x). You also can plot functions that use two variables. For example, the following function calculates a value of z for various values of two variables (x and y):

```
z = SIN(x)*COS(y)
```

Figure 8-52 shows a surface chart that plots the value of z for 21 x values ranging from 2 to 5, and for 21 y values ranging from –3 to 0.

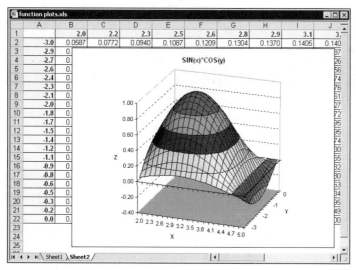

Figure 8-52: Using a surface chart to plot a function with two variables

Figure 8-53 shows a general-purpose, two-variable plotting application, similar to the workbook described in the previous section. The data for the chart is a 25 x 25 Data Table range in columns L:AK (not shown in the figure). To use this application:

1. Enter a formula in cell B3. The formula should contain at least one x variable and at least one y variable. In the figure, the formula in cell B3 is

```
=SIN(SQRT(x^2 + y^2))
```

2. Enter the minimum x value in cell B4, and the maximum .x value in cell B5.

3. Enter the minimum y value in cell B6, and the maximum .y value in cell B7.

The formula in cell B3 will display the value of z for the minimum values of x and y. The Data Table evaluates the formula for 25 equally spaced values of x and 25 equally spaced values of y. These values are plotted in the surface chart.

This worksheet is protected to allow input only in cells B3:B7. It does not use a password, however, so you can unprotect and modify the sheet. In addition, the workbook contains simple macros that enable you to easily change the rotation and elevation of the chart. To use these macros, you'll need to unprotect the sheet.

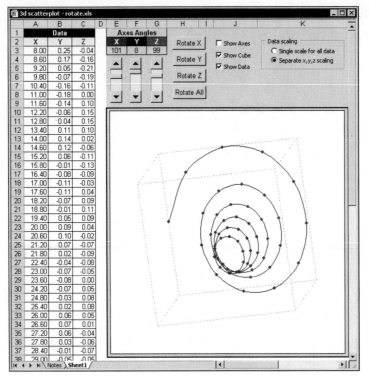

Figure 8-53: A general-purpose, two-variable plotting workbook

Creating a 3-D scatter plot

One of the most requested chart types for Excel is a 3-D scatter plot. Unfortunately, however, Microsoft has not paid attention to these requests. This type of chart is like an XY chart but with an added "depth" dimension (Z).

Andy Pope, a charting expert from the UK, sent me an interesting workbook that simulates a 3-D scatter plot. Each data point is entered as three coordinate values (x, y, and z). Formulas then transform the data to make it appear in a 3-D space. The chart includes additional series to display the x, y, and z axes, as well as the cube that encompasses the 3-D space.

I took Andy's idea and spent many hours refining it and (I hope) making it easier to understand. The result, shown in Figure 8-54, has quite a few accoutrements. The three scroll bars control the angle of each of the three axes, and the buttons perform animations.

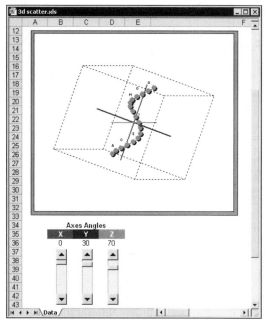

Figure 8-54: A simulated 3-D scatter plot

Creating "Impossible" Charts by Stacking and Overlaying

This section presents a few examples of what might be considered "impossible" charts – charts that were created by combining two or more charts. The examples in this section are not combination charts. Rather, they are two (or more) separate charts that have been combined either by stacking or overlaying.

Stacking charts

Figure 8-55 shows a simple example of combining charts. I simply stacked these three single-series line charts vertically. I removed the category axis from the top two charts, so they appear to share a single category axis.

After creating the charts, use the Align or Distribute tools on the Drawing toolbar to assist with positioning the charts. After they have been positioned, you may want to group the charts into a single object. Press Ctrl while you select each chart; then, right-click and choose Group from the shortcut menu. After the charts are grouped, you can move and resize them as a single object.

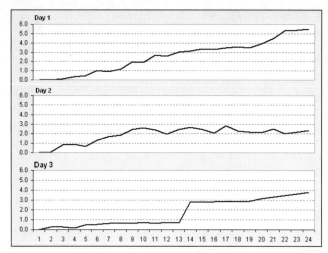

Figure 8-55: Three line charts, stacked and grouped

Figure 8-56 shows another example of stacked charts, this time with different chart types. The charts share a common category axis but use different value axes. Each chart has its own title, and I added a text box to provide a descriptive title of the collection.

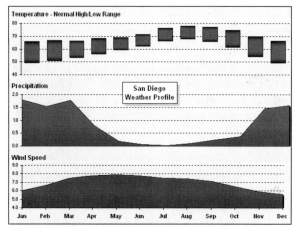

Figure 8-56: Three charts, stacked and grouped with a text box

Overlaying charts

The examples in this section demonstrate chart overlays — charts that are positioned on top of other charts.

A 2-D CHART COMBINED WITH A 3-D CHART

If you attempt to create a combination chart that uses any of the 3-D chart types, you'll find that Excel does not allow this. If you *must* create such a chart, the only option is to create separate charts and overlay one on top of the other.

Figure 8-57 shows an example of a 2-D line chart overlaid on a 3-D column chart. I stripped the line chart of all elements (except the line itself) and made the Plot Area and Chart Area transparent. I then carefully sized and positioned the line chart so that it aligned properly with the cone chart.

When overlaying charts, the stack order of the objects is very important. The top chart in the stack must be higher in the stack order. To change the stack order of objects on a worksheet, select the object, right-click, and use the Order menu on the shortcut menu. When working with charts, you must select the chart object (not the chart). To select the chart object, press Ctrl or Shift while you click the chart.

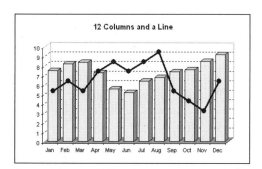

Figure 8-57: A 2-D line chart on top of a 3-D column chart

When overlaying charts, it's important that you keep the value scales identical. In this case, I set the value scale for both charts manually. It was still necessary to adjust the height of the line chart to force the axes to line up. Letting Excel adjust the scaling often results in mismatched scales and an inaccurate chart.

Overlaying charts is a manual task and will almost always require a bit of trial and error to get things looking right. It can also be a frustrating experience because Excel has a tendency to resize chart elements automatically when you make changes to a chart.

COMBINING TWO CHARTS IN ONE FRAME

Figure 8-58 shows a 3-D pie chart and a 3-D column chart, presented as a single unit. These are, in fact, two separate charts. The "frame" effect results from adding a border around a range of cells. Both charts have a transparent Chart Area and

Plot Area, and they were positioned over the bordered range. The title is actually text entered into in a cell.

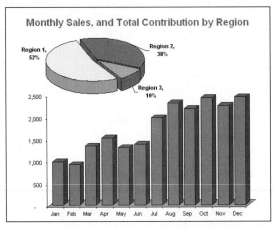

Figure 8-58: These two charts appear to be a single object.

CREATING A STACKED 3-D COLUMN CHART

You may have discovered a limitation with Excel's 3-D stacked-column charts: You can't plot additional series in the depth dimension. In other words, Excel does not provide the option of creating a "true" 3-D stacked-column chart. When dealing with Excel, workarounds are often possible. Figure 8-59 shows three stacked 3-D column charts (one for each year), combined to display a depth dimension. This chart allows comparisons by region, month, and year.

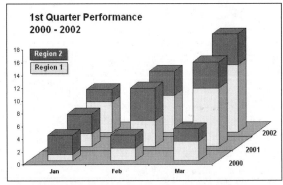

Figure 8-59: Some careful overlaying makes these three charts appear to be a single chart.

I removed the walls from all charts, and only the frontmost chart has a value axis. The title, legend, and year labels are text boxes that I added separately. When you're combining charts like this, it's very important that the value axes use identical scaling. Also, any modification to the 3-D view (for example, rotation) must be applied to all the charts.

SIMULATING A "BROKEN" VALUE AXIS

The final example, in Figure 8-60, shows a standard column chart, along with another chart that simulates a "broken" value axis. This type of chart is often used when a few data points greatly exceed the others. In the example, the value for June is much larger than the other values. When plotted on a standard chart, the other values are dwarfed.

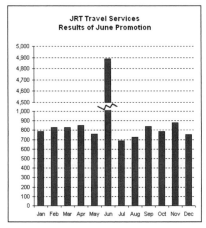

Figure 8-60: Two charts are combined to simulate a broken axis.

The chart on the right consists of two charts, shown in Figure 8-61. Both charts use the same data but different value axis scaling. The main chart (on the left) contains the title and lots of white space above the Plot Area. The value axis Maximum is set to 1,000. The secondary chart has a transparent Chart Area with no border, and its value axis ranges from 4,500 to 5,000. An AutoShape is used to indicate the fact that the column is not continuous.

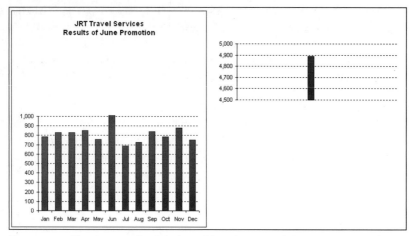

Figure 8-61: The chart on the right is positioned on top of the chart on the left.

Creating this type of chart is a manual process and will likely require a fair amount of tweaking.

 An example on the companion CD-ROM demonstrates a simpler approach that uses a single chart, with the Maximum value for the value axis set manually. An AutoShape is placed over the "outlier" column, along with a text box that contains the value for this column.

A Gradient Contour Chart

Excel's contour chart (a subtype of the surface chart) is essentially a surface chart viewed from above. To control the number of gradients used, you must modify the Major Unit value for the value axis (a smaller value results in more gradients). Because each gradient uses an arbitrary color, discerning the actual gradients is not always easy.

I created an add-in designed to overcome some of the limitations in the contour chart. Figure 8-62 shows a standard contour chart along with a gradient contour chart created with this add-in.

The Gradient Contour Chart add-in offers many options. For example, you can specify the number of colors to use (from 2 to 56), and you can choose the beginning and ending color for the gradient – including two rainbow options. The Gradient Contour Chart dialog box is shown in Figure 8-63.

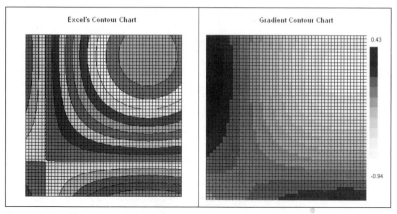

Figure 8-62: The chart on the right was created using the author's Gradient Contour Chart add-in.

 The add-in works by creating a picture and then pasting the picture to the column in a single data point column series. Because of this, the chart that's generated is not dynamic. If your data changes, you must recreate the chart.

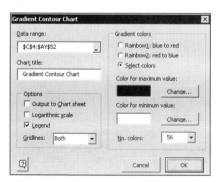

Figure 8-63: The Gradient Contour Chart add-in dialog box

Plotting Data without a Chart

How is it possible to plot data without a chart? You can use the worksheet cells to display quantitative information visually. This section presents two methods of creating chartless charts. As you'll discover, these types of charts do not offer the level of precision available in a "real" chart.

Plotting with ASCII characters

Figure 8-64 shows a chart that consists of text characters that comprise horizontal bars. Columns E and G contain formulas that graphically depict monthly budget variances by displaying a series of characters in the Wingdings font. The number of characters displayed is determined by an IF function.

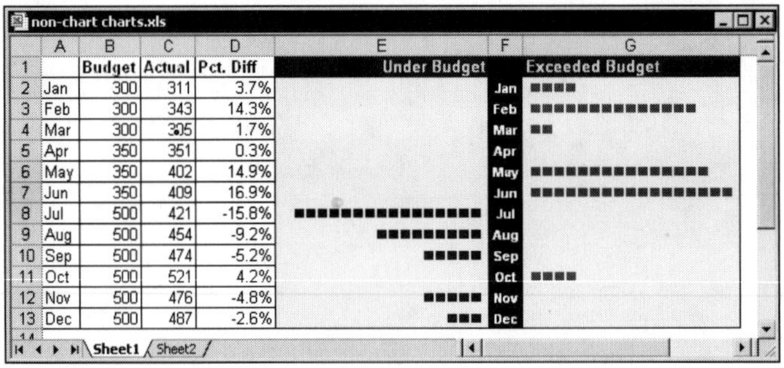

Figure 8-64: This chart is made up of text characters displayed in cells.

The data used in this chart are in columns A:C. Formulas in column D calculate the percent difference between the Budget and Actual amounts. Columns E and G contain formulas that use the value in column D. The formulas for columns E and G follow. I copied these formulas down to accommodate the 12 rows of data.

```
E2: =IF(D2<0,REPT("n",-ROUND(D2*100,0)),"")
G2: =IF(D2>0,REPT("n",-ROUND(D2*-100,0)),"")
```

The key to this technique is the use of the REPT function, which displays a character (specified in the function's first argument) the number of times specified in the function's second argument. The cells that display the bars use the Wingdings font – the letter n in this font produces a square block. In column E, the text is aligned to the right. In column G, the text is aligned to the left.

Depending on the numerical range of your data, you may need to change the scaling. Experiment by replacing the "100" value in the formulas. You can, of course, substitute any character you like for the n in the formulas to produce a different character in the chart.

Plotting with conditional formatting

Excel's conditional formatting feature is a handy tool that enables you to format cells based on their content. Many users don't realize it, but conditional formatting can also be used to format cells based on types of conditions rather than just on the contents of the cells.

Figure 8-65 shows an example that takes advantage of conditional formatting to produce a crude bar chart, displayed directly in worksheet cells. Note that the column widths in this worksheet are very narrow, producing square cells (except for columns C and D, which store data used by the chart).

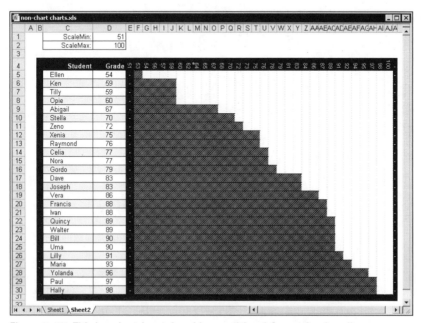

Figure 8-65: This bar chart is produced by conditional formatting in cells.

The worksheet uses two named cells: D1 (named *ScaleMin*) and D2 (named *ScaleMax*). These cells control the upper and lower limits for the "axis" scale, in row 4. Cell E4 simply contains a reference to the *ScaleMin* cell. Cell F5 contains the following formula, which is copied across to cell AJ4:

```
=((ScaleMax-ScaleMin)/COLUMNS(F$1:AJ$1))*(COLUMN()-5)+ScaleMin
```

This formula generates the intervals displayed in row 4. It uses the COLUMNS function (rather than a literal value) to return the number of columns used in the chart. Using this function enables the user to insert additional columns without the need to modify the formula.

The conditional formatting is applied to range F5:AJ30. Figure 8-66 shows the Conditional Formatting dialog box. As you can see, the condition is based on a formula:

```
=$D5>=F$4
```

When this formula returns TRUE, conditional formatting (cell shading) is applied to the cell. This formula compares the value in column D with the interval value in row 4. If the value is greater than or equal to the interval value, shading is applied to the cell.

Figure 8-66: This conditional formatting formula determines whether shading is applied to each cell.

Chapter 9

Using Pivot Charts

MANY PEOPLE (AUTHOR INCLUDED) consider pivot tables to be the most innovative and powerful analytical feature in Excel. A pivot table can instantly convert a mass of data into a nicely summarized table. Pivot tables have been around since Excel 5. Beginning with Excel 2000, this feature was augmented to include charting capabilities.

 If you're using Excel 97 or earlier, much of the information in this chapter does not apply.

This chapter starts out with an introductory overview of pivot tables and then moves on to cover pivot charts.

What Is a Pivot Table?

A *pivot table* is essentially a dynamic summary report generated from a database. The database can reside in a worksheet or in an external file.

A pivot table can create frequency distributions and cross-tabulations of several different data dimensions. In addition, you can display subtotals and any level of detail that you want. Perhaps the most innovative aspect of a pivot table is its interactivity. After you create a pivot table, you can rearrange the information in almost any way imaginable. You can even create custom groupings of summary items (for example, combine Northern Region totals with Western Region totals).

As far as I can tell, the term *pivot table* is unique to Excel. The name stems from the fact that you can rotate (that is, pivot) the table's row and column headings around the core data area to give you different views of your summarized data.

One minor drawback to using a pivot table is that, unlike a formula-based summary report, a pivot table does not update automatically when you change the source data. This drawback does not pose a serious problem, however, because a single click of the Refresh toolbar button forces a pivot table to update and use the latest data.

A pivot table example

Perhaps the best way to understand the concept of a pivot table is to see one. Start with Figure 9-1, which shows a portion of the data that I'm using to create a pivot table.

	A	B	C	D	E	F
1	Date	AcctType	Amount	Branch	OpenedBy	Customer
2	2-Sep	Checking	2,100.00	Central	Teller	New
3	2-Sep	Savings	8,320.13	N. County	New Acct	Existing
4	2-Sep	Checking	3,773.58	N. County	New Acct	Existing
5	2-Sep	Checking	2,909.81	Westside	New Acct	Existing
6	2-Sep	Checking	2,715.34	N. County	New Acct	New
7	2-Sep	Checking	4,200.10	Westside	New Acct	New
8	2-Sep	IRA	4,474.76	Central	New Acct	New
9	2-Sep	Savings	5,903.94	N. County	New Acct	Existing
10	2-Sep	Checking	3,570.90	Central	Teller	Existing
11	2-Sep	Checking	968.75	Central	Teller	Existing
12	2-Sep	Checking	4,000.00	Central	New Acct	Existing
13	2-Sep	Checking	3,561.85	Central	New Acct	Existing
14	2-Sep	CD	7,500.00	Central	Teller	New
15	2-Sep	Savings	7,306.83	Central	New Acct	Existing
16	2-Sep	Savings	7,230.93	N. County	New Acct	Existing
17	2-Sep	Checking	3,902.03	Central	New Acct	Existing
18	2-Sep	Checking	2,895.28	Central	Teller	Existing
19	2-Sep	Savings	6,123.89	Central	Teller	Existing

Figure 9-1: This database is used to create a pivot table.

This database consists of daily new-account information for a three-branch bank. The database contains 1,908 records (rows), representing the new accounts opened in one month. Each record contains information for the new account that was opened. The data collected consists of the following:

◆ The date that the account was opened

◆ The account type (CD, Checking, Savings, or IRA)

◆ The opening dollar amount

- ◆ The branch at which it was opened (Central, Westside, or N. County)

- ◆ The type of employee who opened the account (a teller or a new-account representative)

- ◆ Whether the account holder is a new customer or an existing customer

The bank accounts database contains quite a bit of information, but in its current form the data does not reveal much. To make the data more useful, you need to summarize it. Summarizing a database is essentially the process of answering questions about the data. Following are a few questions that may be of interest to the bank's management:

- ◆ What is the total deposit amount for each branch, broken down by account type?

- ◆ How many accounts were opened at each branch, broken down by account type?

- ◆ What's the dollar distribution of the different account types?

- ◆ What types of accounts do tellers open most often?

- ◆ How does the Central branch compare to the other two branches?

- ◆ Which branch opens the most accounts for new customers?

If you're proficient with formulas, you could write formulas to answer these questions. Often, however, a pivot table is a better choice. Creating a pivot table takes only a few seconds and doesn't require a single formula. And, as you'll see, a single button click is all it takes to convert the data into an interactive chart.

Figure 9-2 shows a pivot table created from the database displayed in Figure 9-1. This pivot table shows the amount of new deposits, broken down by branch (a Column field) and account type (a Row field). It also displays grand totals for rows and for columns. This particular summary represents one of dozens of summaries that you can produce from this data.

bank data.xls					
	A	B	C	D	E
1					
2					
3	Sum of Amount	Branch ▼			
4	AcctType ▼	Central	N. County	Westside	Grand Total
5	CD	1,342,877.09	506,594.30	377,128.15	2,226,599.54
6	Checking	2,069,135.99	949,639.24	481,621.85	3,500,397.08
7	IRA	478,377.19	280,482.69	111,619.23	870,479.11
8	Savings	2,211,305.75	933,963.59	582,570.65	3,727,839.99
9	Grand Total	6,101,696.02	2,670,679.82	1,552,939.88	10,325,315.72
10					
11					
◄ ► ►I \Sheet1 / Sheet2 / Data /			◄		►

Figure 9-2: A simple pivot table generated from the bank account data

Figure 9-3 shows another pivot table generated from the bank data. This pivot table differs from the previous one in several ways:

◆ The AcctType field appears as a Column Field, and the Branch field appears as a Row field.

◆ An additional Row field (OpenedBy) was added.

◆ A Page field (Customer) was added.

◆ The pivot table is formatted (using an AutoFormat) to make it more readable.

In the figure, the pivot table displays the data only for existing customers (the user could also select New or All from Page field list).

	A	B	C	D	E	F	G
	bank data.xls						
1	Customer	Existing					
2							
3	Amount		AcctType				
4	Branch	OpenedBy	CD	Checking	IRA	Savings	Grand Total
5	Central	New Acct	795,647.54	1,183,391.02	265,947.43	1,261,294.82	3,506,280.81
6		Teller	328,670.06	570,951.61	150,456.60	604,163.11	1,654,241.38
7	Central Total		1,124,317.60	1,754,342.63	416,404.03	1,865,457.93	5,160,522.19
8							
9	N. County	New Acct	351,827.89	587,091.36	151,290.26	520,439.82	1,610,649.33
10		Teller	93,383.64	248,289.94	88,315.60	310,916.67	740,905.85
11	N. County Total		445,211.53	835,381.30	239,605.86	831,356.49	2,351,555.18
12							
13	Westside	New Acct	254,519.72	268,815.23	42,424.78	350,060.83	915,820.56
14		Teller	78,635.12	140,706.73	49,803.46	141,210.53	410,355.84
15	Westside Total		333,154.84	409,521.96	92,228.24	491,271.36	1,326,176.40
16							
17	Grand Total		1,902,683.97	2,999,245.89	748,238.13	3,188,085.78	8,838,253.77
18							

Figure 9-3: Another pivot table generated from the bank account data

Data appropriate for a pivot table

The data that you summarize in a pivot table must start out in the form of a database table. You can store the database in either a worksheet or an external database file. Although Excel can generate a pivot table from any database, not all databases benefit.

Generally speaking, fields in a database table can consist of two types:

◆ **Data:** Contains a value or data to be summarized. In Figure 9-1, the Amount field is a data field.

◆ **Category:** Describes the data. In Figure 9-1, the Date, AcctType, OpenedBy, Branch, and Customer fields are category fields because they describe the data in the Amount field.

A single database table can have any number of data fields and category fields. When you create a pivot table, you usually want to summarize one or more of the data fields. Conversely, the values in the category fields appear in the pivot table as rows, columns, or pages.

Exceptions exist, however, and you may find Excel's pivot table feature useful even for databases that don't contain actual numerical data fields. Figure 9-4, for example, shows a three-column database that consists only of text data. The pivot table counts the items in fields rather than sums them. This pivot table cross-tabulates the Month Born field by the Sex field; the intersecting cells show the count for each combination of month and gender.

employee list.xls								
	A	B	C	D	E	F	G	H
1	Employee	Month Born	Sex					
2	Anthony Taylor	July	Male					
3	Charles S. Billings	February	Male		Count of Employee	Sex		
4	Christine Poundsworth	January	Female		Month Born	Female	Male	Grand Total
5	Clark Bickerson	February	Male		January	1	3	4
6	Douglas Williams	March	Male		February	0	6	6
7	Janet Silberstein	April	Female		March	3	1	4
8	James Millen	May	Male		April	1	3	4
9	Jeffrey P. Jones	June	Male		May	1	4	5
10	Joan Morrison	July	Female		June	1	4	5
11	John T. Foster	August	Male		July	1	5	6
12	Kurt Kamichoff	January	Male		August	1	4	5
13	Michael Hayden	February	Male		September	0	5	5
14	PhyllisTodd	March	Female		October	1	4	5
15	Richard E. Card	April	Male		November	1	4	5
16	Rick Fogerty	May	Male		December	1	5	6
17	Robert H. Miller	June	Male		Grand Total	12	48	60
18	Stephen C. Carter	July	Male					

Figure 9-4: This database doesn't have any numerical fields, but you can use it to generate a pivot table.

In fact, you can create a pivot table from a database that contains only a single column of data. See "Creating a quick frequency distribution chart," later in this chapter.

Creating a Pivot Table

You create a pivot table by using the PivotTable and PivotChart Wizard. You access this wizard by choosing Data→PivotTable and PivotChart Report. Then, carry out the steps outlined in the following sections.

This discussion assumes that you use Excel 2000 or later. The procedure differs slightly in earlier versions of Excel.

Pivot Table Terminology

Understanding the terminology associated with pivot tables is the first step in mastering this feature. Refer to the accompanying figure to get your bearings.

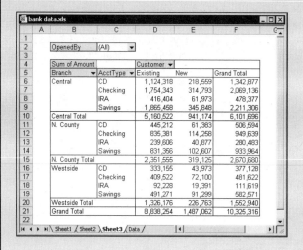

◆ **Column field:** A field that has a column orientation in the pivot table. Each item in the field occupies a column. In the figure, Customer represents a column field that contains two items (Existing and New). You can have nested column fields.

◆ **Data area:** The cells in a pivot table that contain the summary data. Excel offers several ways to summarize the data (sum, average, count, and so on). In the figure, the Data area includes D6:F21.

◆ **Grand totals:** A row or column that displays totals for all cells in a row or column in a pivot table. You can specify that grand totals be calculated for rows, columns, both, or neither. The pivot table in the figure shows grand totals for both rows and columns.

◆ **Group:** A collection of items treated as a single item. You can group items manually or automatically (group dates into months, for example). The pivot table in the figure does not have any defined groups.

◆ **Item:** An element in a field that appears as a row or column header in a pivot table. In the figure, Existing and New are items for the Customer field. The Branch field has three items: Central, N. County, and Westside. AcctType has four items: CD, Checking, IRA, and Savings.

◆ **Page field:** A field that has a page orientation in the pivot table — similar to a slice of a three-dimensional cube. You can display only one item (or all items) in a page field at one time. In the figure, OpenedBy represents a page field that displays the New Accts item; the pivot table shows data only for New Accts.

◆ **Row field:** A field that has a row orientation in the pivot table. Each item in the field occupies a row. You can have nested row fields. In the figure, Branch and AcctType both represent row fields.

◆ **Source data:** The data used to create a pivot table. It can reside in a worksheet or an external database.

◆ **Subtotals:** A row or column that displays subtotals for detail cells in a row or column in a pivot table. The pivot table in the figure displays subtotals for each branch.

Step 1: Specifying the data location

The first dialog box presented by the PivotTable and PivotChart Wizard is shown in Figure 9-5. In this step, you identify the data source. Excel is quite flexible in the data that you can use for a pivot table. This example uses a worksheet database.

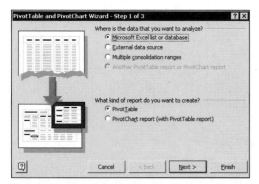

Figure 9–5: The first of three PivotTable and PivotChart Wizard dialog boxes

 You see different dialog boxes while you work through the wizard, depending on the location of the data that you want to analyze. The following sections present the wizard's dialog boxes for data located in an Excel list or database.

Step 2: Specifying the data

To move on to the next step of the wizard, click the Next button. Step 2 of the PivotTable and PivotChart Wizard prompts you for the data. Remember, the dialog box varies depending on your choice in the first dialog box; Figure 9-6 shows the dialog box that appears when you select an Excel list or database in Step 1.

Figure 9-6: In Step 2, you specify the data range.

If you place the cell pointer anywhere within the worksheet database when you select Data→PivotTable Report, Excel identifies the database range automatically in Step 2 of the PivotTable and PivotChart Wizard. You can use the Browse button to open a different workbook and select a range. To move on to Step 3, click the Next button.

If the source range for a pivot table is named *Database*, you can use Excel's built-in Data Form to add new data to the range. The named range will extend automatically to include the new records.

Step 3: Completing the pivot table

Figure 9-7 shows the dialog box for the final step of the PivotTable and PivotChart Wizard. In this step, you specify the location for the pivot table. If you select the New worksheet option, Excel inserts a new worksheet for the pivot table. If you select the Existing worksheet option, the pivot table appears on the current work-sheet (you can specify the starting cell location).

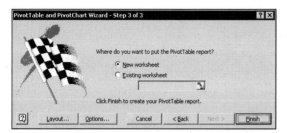

Figure 9-7: In Step 3, you specify the pivot table's location.

At this point, you can click the Options button to select some options that deter-mine how the table appears. (Refer to the sidebar "Pivot Table Options.") You can set these options at any time after you create the pivot table, so you do not need to do so before creating the pivot table.

You can set up the actual layout of the pivot table by using either of two techniques:

◆ Clicking the Layout button in Step 3 of the PivotTable and PivotChart Wizard. You then can use a dialog box to lay out the pivot table.

◆ Clicking the Finish button to create a blank pivot table. You then can use the PivotTable Field List toolbar to lay out the pivot table.

I describe both of these options in the following subsections.

USING A DIALOG BOX TO LAY OUT A PIVOT TABLE

When you click the Layout button of the wizard's last dialog box, you get the dialog box shown in Figure 9-8. The fields in the database appear as buttons along the right side of the dialog box. Simply drag the buttons to the appropriate area of the pivot table diagram (which appears in the center of the dialog box).

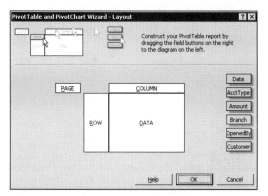

Figure 9–8: Specify the table layout.

 For versions prior to Excel 2000, this dialog box appears as Step 3 of the wizard. For these versions, using the Layout dialog box is the only way to lay out a pivot table.

The pivot table diagram has four areas:

◆ **Page:** Values in the field appear as page items in the pivot table.

◆ **Row:** Values in the field appear as row items in the pivot table.

◆ **Data:** The field is summarized in the pivot table.

◆ **Column:** Values in the field appear as column items in the pivot table.

You can drag as many field buttons as you want to any of these locations, and you don't have to use all the fields. Any fields that you don't use simply don't appear in the pivot table.

When you drag a field button to the Data area, the PivotTable and PivotChart Wizard applies the Sum function if the field contains numeric values; it applies the Count function if the field contains non-numeric values.

While you set up the pivot table, you can double-click a field button to customize it. You can specify, for example, to summarize a particular field as a Count or other function. You also can specify which items in a field to hide or omit. If you drag a field button to an incorrect location, just drag it off the table diagram to get rid of it. Note that you can customize fields at any time after you create the pivot table; I demonstrate this later in the chapter.

Figure 9-9 shows how the dialog box looks after dragging some field buttons to the pivot table diagram. This pivot table displays the sum of the Amount field, broken down by AcctType (as rows) and Customer (as columns). In addition, the Branch field appears as a page field. Click OK to redisplay the PivotTable and PivotChart Wizard – Step 3 of the dialog box.

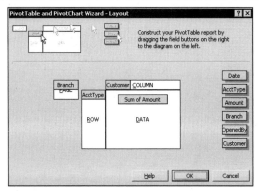

Figure 9-9: The table layout after dragging field buttons to the pivot table diagram

USING THE PIVOTTABLE FIELD LIST TOOLBAR TO LAY OUT A PIVOT TABLE

You may prefer to lay out your pivot table directly in the worksheet, using the PivotTable Field List toolbar. The technique closely resembles the one just described, because you still drag and drop fields. But in this case, you drag fields from the toolbar into the worksheet.

You cannot use this technique with versions prior to Excel 2000. Also, note that Excel 2000 doesn't have a PivotTable Field List toolbar. Rather, the fields are displayed as buttons on the PivotTable toolbar.

Complete the first two steps of the PivotTable and PivotChart Wizard. If desired, set options for the pivot table by using the Options button that appears in the third dialog box of the wizard. Don't bother with the Layout button, however. Select a location for the pivot table and choose Finish. Excel displays a pivot table template similar to the one you see in Figure 9-10. The template provides you with hints about where to drop various types of fields.

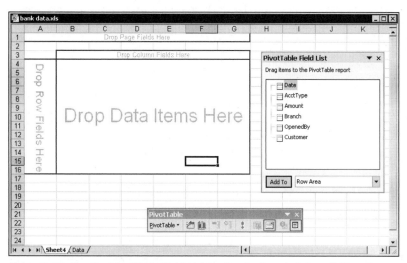

Figure 9-10: Use the PivotTable Field List toolbar to drag and drop fields onto the pivot table template that Excel displays.

Drag and drop fields from the PivotTable Field List toolbar onto the template. Or select the field name, choose the location from the drop-down list, and click the Add To button. Excel continues to update the pivot table as you add or remove fields. For this reason, you'll find this method easiest to use if you drag and drop *data* items last. In other words, set up the field items and then specify the data to summarize.

If you make a mistake, simply drag the field off the template and drop it onto the worksheet — Excel removes it from the pivot table template. All fields remain on the PivotTable Field List toolbar, even if you use them.

THE FINISHED PRODUCT

Figure 9-11 shows the result of this example. Notice that the page field displays as a drop-down box. You can choose which item in the page field to display by choosing it from the list. You also can choose an item called All, which displays all the data.

	A	B	C	D	E
	bank data.xls				
	A	B	C	D	E
1	Branch	(All)			
2					
3	Sum of Amount	Customer			
4	AcctType	Existing	New	Grand Total	
5	CD	1,902,683.97	323,915.57	2,226,599.54	
6	Checking	2,999,245.89	501,151.19	3,500,397.08	
7	IRA	748,238.13	122,240.98	870,479.11	
8	Savings	3,188,085.78	539,754.21	3,727,839.99	
9	Grand Total	8,838,253.77	1,487,061.95	10,325,315.72	
10					
11					

Figure 9-11: The pivot table created by the PivotTable and PivotChart Wizard

TIP   Excel's AutoFormat feature works well with pivot tables. Select any cell in your pivot table and then choose Format→AutoFormat. Use the AutoFormat dialog box to select a format. The first 10 AutoFormats are listed as Reports and the remainder are listed as Tables. AutoFormats in Report category may change the layout of your pivot table. If you don't like the result, choose Edit→Undo to revert to the previous formatting.

Pivot Table Options

Excel provides plenty of options that determine how your pivot table looks and works. To access these options, click the Options button in the final step of the PivotTable and PivotChart Wizard to display the PivotTable Options dialog box. You also can access this dialog box after you create the pivot table. Right-click any cell in the pivot table and then select Table Options from the shortcut menu. Following are the options in the PivotTable Options dialog box:

◆ **Name:** You can provide a name for the pivot table. Excel provides default names in the form of PivotTable1, PivotTable2, and so on.

◆ **Grand totals for columns:** Check this box if you want Excel to calculate grand totals for items displayed in columns.

◆ **Grand totals for rows:** Check this box if you want Excel to calculate grand totals for items displayed in rows.

◆ **AutoFormat table:** Check this box if you want Excel to apply one of its AutoFormats to the pivot table. Excel uses the AutoFormat even if you rearrange the table layout.

◆ **Subtotal hidden page items:** Check this box if you want Excel to include hidden items in the page fields in the subtotals.

◆ **Merge labels:** Check this box if you want Excel to merge the cells for outer row and column labels. Doing so may make the table more readable.

◆ **Preserve formatting:** Check this box if you want Excel, when it updates the pivot table, to keep any of the formatting that you applied.

◆ **Repeat item labels on each printed page:** Check this box to set row titles that appear on each page when you print a PivotTable report.

◆ **Mark Totals with *:** Available only if you generated the pivot table from an OLAP data source. If checked, displays an asterisk after every subtotal and grand total to indicate that these values include any hidden items as well as displayed items.

◆ **Page layout:** You can specify the order in which you want the page fields to appear.

◆ **Fields per column:** You can specify the number of page fields to show before starting another row of page fields.

◆ **For error values, show:** You can specify a value to show for pivot table cells that display an error.

◆ **For empty cells, show:** You can specify a value to show for empty pivot table cells.

◆ **Set print titles:** Check this box to set column titles that appear at the top of each page when you print a PivotTable report.

◆ **Save data with table layout:** If you check this option, Excel stores an additional copy of the data (called a *pivot table cache*), enabling Excel to recalculate the table more quickly when you change the layout. If memory is an issue, you should keep this option unchecked (which slows updating a bit).

◆ **Enable drill to details:** If checked, you can double-click a cell in the pivot table to view the records that contributed to the summary value.

◆ **Refresh on open:** If checked, the pivot table refreshes whenever you open the workbook.

◆ **Refresh every x minutes:** If you are connected to an external database, you can specify how often you want the pivot table refreshed while the workbook is open.

◆ **Save password:** If you use an external database that requires a password, you can store the password as part of the query so that you don't have to reenter it.

◆ **Background query:** If checked, Excel runs the external database query in the background while you continue your work.

◆ **Optimize memory:** This option reduces the amount of memory used when you refresh an external database query.

Grouping Pivot Table Items

One of the more useful features of a pivot table is the ability to combine items into groups. To group items in a pivot chart, select them, right-click, and choose Group and Outline→Group from the shortcut menu.

When a field contains dates, Excel can create groups automatically by month, quarter, and year. Figure 9-12 shows part of a simple database table with two fields: Date and Mileage. This table has weekly mileage data for four years (210 data points). The goal is to summarize the mileage data by month.

	A	B	C
	Date	Mileage	
1	Date	Mileage	
2	1/1/1999	21	
3	1/8/1999	98	
4	1/15/1999	105	
5	1/22/1999	104	
6	1/29/1999	97	
7	2/5/1999	145	
8	2/12/1999	129	
9	2/19/1999	145	
10	2/26/1999	158	
11	3/5/1999	114	
12	3/12/1999	91	
13	3/19/1999	163	
14	3/26/1999	71	
15	4/2/1999	127	
16	4/9/1999	139	
17	4/16/1999	74	

Figure 9-12: You can use a pivot table to summarize the data by month.

Figure 9-13 shows a pivot table created from the data. This pivot table displays one row for each date and looks exactly like the original data. To group the rows by month, right-click the Date heading and select Group and Show Detail→Group. You'll see the Grouping dialog box shown in Figure 9-14. In the list box, select Months and Years, and verify that the starting and ending dates are correct. Click OK. The Date items in the pivot table are grouped by years and by months (see Figure 9-15).

If you select only Months in the Grouping list box, months in different years combine. For example, the June item would display mileage data for June of all four years. The pivot table would contain only 12 rows.

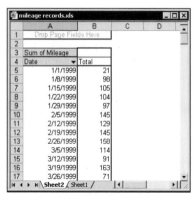

Figure 9-13: The pivot table, before grouping by month

Figure 9-14: Use the Grouping dialog box
to group items in a pivot table.

Copying a Pivot Table

A pivot table is a special type of object, and you cannot perform many standard range operations with it. For example, you can't insert a new row or enter formulas within a pivot table. If you want to manipulate a pivot table in ways not normally permitted, you can make a copy of it.

To copy a pivot table, select the table (or the part that you're interested in) and choose Edit→Copy. Then activate a new worksheet and choose Edit→Paste Special. Select the Values option and click OK. The contents of the pivot table are copied to the new location so that you can do whatever you like to them.

Keep in mind that the copied information is no longer linked to the source data, and cannot be refreshed. If the source data changes, your copied pivot table does not reflect these changes.

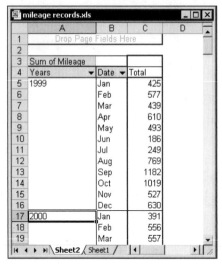

Figure 9-15: The pivot table, after grouping by month and year

Working with Pivot Charts

This section discusses pivot charts and assumes that you're familiar with the material already presented in this chapter.

Creating a pivot chart

After you've created a pivot table, a pivot chart is one click away. First, make sure that your pivot table contains at least one row field. Then, select any cell in the pivot table and click the Chart Wizard button in either the PivotTable toolbar or the Standard toolbar. Alternatively, you can right-click any cell in the pivot table and choose PivotChart from the shortcut menu. Or, just select any cell in the pivot table and press F11. The pivot chart is always created on a new Chart sheet.

Figure 9-16 shows a pivot chart created from the mileage data pivot table presented in the previous section.

Although the button on the PivotTable toolbar is named Chart Wizard, clicking the button invokes the Chart Wizard only if a pivot chart is active when you click the button. And then, the Chart Wizard skips over Step 2 (Chart Source Data). When you use this button to create a pivot chart, the pivot chart is created with a single click, bypassing the Chart Wizard.

When you select the Data→PivotTable and PivotChart Report command, the first step of the PivotTable and PivotChart Wizard contains an option that enables you to create a pivot chart along with the pivot table. If you choose this option, the pivot chart is created at the same time as the pivot table.

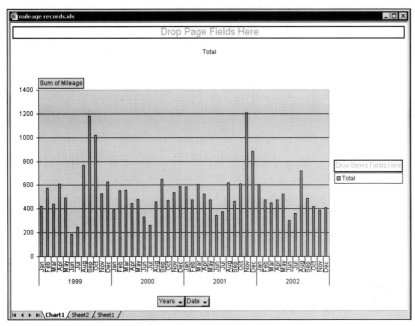

Figure 9-16: A pivot chart that displays monthly mileage data

Understanding pivot charts

It's important to understand that a pivot chart is essentially a graphic representation of a pivot table, and the two items are linked together. A pivot chart always shows exactly the same data that's displayed in its corresponding pivot table.

Figure 9-17 shows a pivot table, along with its corresponding pivot chart (the pivot chart was converted to an embedded chart). When comparing the pivot table with the pivot chart, you'll notice the following:

◆ All the field buttons present in the pivot table are also present in the pivot chart. Furthermore, the setting for each field button is identical.

◆ The Page field button (in this case, labeled *Product*) appears in the upper-left corner in both the pivot table and the pivot chart.

◆ Each pivot table data column appears as a separate data series in the pivot chart.

◆ Total and subtotal rows and column in the pivot table do not appear in the pivot chart.

◆ The Column field buttons correspond to the legend in the pivot chart.

◆ The Row field buttons in the pivot table appear below the category axis in the pivot chart.

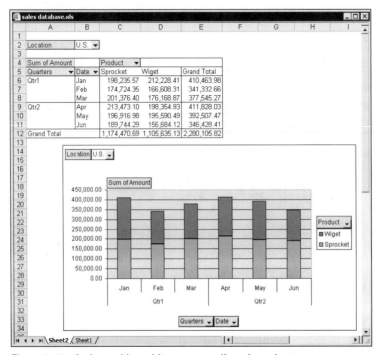

Figure 9-17: A pivot table and its corresponding pivot chart

Modifying the data displayed in a pivot chart

As described earlier in this chapter, a pivot table is dynamic: You can easily change the layout of the pivot table and adjust the field buttons to show different data. The same holds true for a pivot chart. A pivot chart contains interactive controls, exactly like those in a pivot table. Because a pivot chart is always linked to an associated pivot table, if you change the pivot chart, the pivot table also changes – and vice versa.

Formatting a pivot chart

With a few exceptions, you can format a pivot chart just as you can a standard chart. But you may be surprised to discover that formatting applied to chart series will be lost when a pivot chart is refreshed, or when you change the display using the field buttons! For example, if you change the colors of the columns in a column chart, they will revert to the default colors when the pivot chart is refreshed. In addition, features such as trendlines and data labels will also be wiped out.

 Microsoft acknowledged this problem after Excel 2000 was released, but did not correct it in Excel 2002.

Pivot charts versus standard charts

Pivot charts differ from standard charts in a number of ways. I summarize these differences in the following list.

◆ Pivot charts contain field buttons, which are used to change the layout or data used in the pivot chart. Standard charts do not have field buttons.

◆ A pivot chart is always created on a Chart sheet. After the chart is created, however, you can convert it into an embedded chart. To do so, use the Chart→Location command.

◆ When you create a pivot chart, Excel ignores the default chart type. Pivot charts always start out as a stacked-column chart. After the pivot chart is created, you can change it to any other chart type except XY, stock, or bubble.

◆ Standard charts are linked directly to worksheet cells. Data used by a pivot chart is linked to a pivot table — which summarizes data that can come from a number of sources. Unlike a standard chart, you cannot change the data source used by a pivot chart (the Chart→Data Source command is not available, and the SERIES formulas in a pivot chart cannot be edited).

◆ You cannot change the series plot order for a pivot chart. You can, however, drag the series labels in the pivot table to change the order in which the data appears in the pivot chart.

◆ Many formatting changes applied to a pivot chart are lost when the chart is refreshed. A standard chart always maintains the formatting you apply.

◆ In a pivot chart, you cannot move or resize the Plot Area or titles. In addition, you cannot move the legend manually — although you can choose from among the preset positions.

Hiding the pivot chart field buttons

Pivot charts contain controls (known as *field buttons*) that enable you to manipulate the information displayed. These controls are analogous to the similar controls used in a pivot table. As you've probably noticed, these field buttons can make a chart look terrible. If you would like to hide these controls, right-click any one of them and then choose Hide PivotChart Field Buttons from the shortcut menu.

To re-display the hidden field buttons, you need to make sure that the PivotTable toolbar is displayed. Then, click the PivotChart button and select Hide PivotChart Field Buttons (this menu item is a toggle). Keep in mind that there is usually no need to display the pivot chart field buttons. If you need to change the layout or adjust the data, you can do so in the corresponding pivot table.

Creating multiple pivot charts from a pivot table

In some cases, creating multiple pivot charts from a pivot table might be desirable. You can create as many pivot charts as you like. Unfortunately, however, doing so is of limited value. If you make a layout change to one of your pivot charts or to the pivot table itself, that change will be reflected in all your pivot charts. In other words, you can't have multiple pivot charts that display different data summaries.

You can, however, create multiple pivot charts and assign a different chart type to each one. Figure 9-18 shows four pivot charts created from a pivot table.

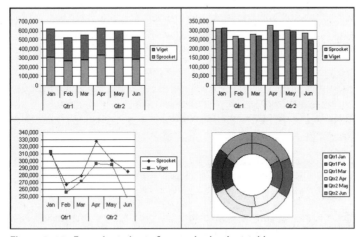

Figure 9-18: Four pivot charts from a single pivot table

 You can create any number of pivot tables from a single database. Therefore, it is possible to create multiple pivot charts that display different summaries — but each different pivot chart must have its own pivot table.

Unlinking a pivot chart from a pivot table

In some cases, you may want to create a permanent copy of your pivot chart – a chart that is no longer attached to a pivot table. One option is to create a picture of the chart (refer to Chapter 3). The resulting picture will be a static object that cannot be edited as a chart.

Another option is to delete the associated pivot table. You must do this by deleting the sheet or by deleting entire rows or columns (simply deleting the cells in a pivot table won't work). When the pivot chart's source data is no longer available, Excel converts the pivot chart to a standard chart and each data series in the chart uses arrays (not ranges).

 If you delete a pivot table and the associated pivot chart contains a large number of data points, Excel may display a confusing message: *The text string you entered is too long. Reduce the number of characters used or cancel the entry.* You'll get this message every time you click the chart's series. This error is due to the fact that a chart SERIES formula is limited to 1,024 characters. The chart continues to display all the data, but the annoying error message never goes away.

Creating a standard chart from a pivot table

Some users are frustrated by the fact that Excel does not allow you to create a standard chart from the data in a pivot table. Even if you select a portion of the data before you create a chart, Excel *still* creates a pivot chart. Why is this an issue? Pivot charts have some limitations. For example, a pivot chart cannot be an XY chart or a bubble chart. And, you don't have as much control over formatting. This section describes four methods that you can use to create a standard chart from the data in a pivot table.

Method 1: Copy the pivot table data to another part of your worksheet

If you select an entire pivot table and then use standard copy/paste techniques, the result will be another pivot table. One alternative is to select only a *portion* of the pivot table before you copy it. The result will be a static range of cells, and you can use this range to create a chart.

If you would like to duplicate all of the data in a pivot table, use these steps:

1. Select the cells that make up the pivot table.

2. Choose Edit→Copy.

3. Activate a cell in an empty area of a worksheet.

4. Choose Edit→Paste Special.

5. In the Paste Special dialog box, select the Values option.

The result will be an exact duplicate of the pivot table, but this will be a static range – not an actual pivot table. You can then create your chart from this new range.

Method 2: Destroy the pivot table

If you no longer need the interactivity of a pivot table, you can convert it to a standard range of cells:

1. Select the cells that make up the pivot table.

2. Choose Edit→Copy.

3. Choose Edit→Paste Special.

4. In the Paste Special dialog box, select the Values option.

The pivot table will no longer be a pivot table, and you can create your chart.

Method 3: Drag or copy data into an empty chart

This method requires an empty chart. To create an empty embedded chart:

1. Select any blank cell near the pivot table.

2. Click the Chart Wizard button.

3. Click Finish.

You can then select some of the data in the pivot table and drag or copy it into the chart. In most cases, the result will be a standard chart. You'll find, however, that selecting too much of the pivot table may result in a pivot chart that uses all the data in the pivot table. It's not clear (at least to me) how much is "too much."

 Keep in mind that the chart you create still depends on the data in the pivot chart. Consequently, if the layout of the pivot table is changed, your chart will continue to use the original range locations — and your chart will (probably) get very messed up.

Method 4: Copy the pivot chart to a different workbook

Activate your chart and choose Edit→Copy. Then activate a worksheet in a different workbook and choose Edit→Paste. The pasted chart will be unlinked from the pivot table. If you examine the chart's SERIES formulas, you'll find that they contain arrays, not cell references. Because there is a limit to the length of a SERIES formula, this technique may not work if the chart uses a large amount of data.

Pivot Chart Examples

This section presents three additional examples of pivot tables and pivot charts.

Pivot charts, by their very nature, are interactive charts. Chapter 7 discusses other ways to create interactive charts.

Creating a quick frequency distribution chart

The example in this section describes how to use a pivot table to create a frequency distribution chart, sometimes known as a histogram. This technique works with values and text.

Figure 9-19 shows a workbook with ratings from a survey item. Column A consists of the respondent number (from 1 to 192), and column B contains the rating. The objective is to create a frequency distribution chart that shows the number of each Rating response.

To create the frequency distribution chart:

1. Select any cell in columns A or B.

2. Start the PivotTable and PivotChart Wizard and then choose the option to create a pivot table and a pivot chart.

3. In Step 3, click the Layout button.

4. Drag the Rating button to the Row field and to the Data field.

5. Click Finish to create the pivot table and the pivot chart.

Figure 9-20 shows the pivot table and pivot chart (the field buttons are removed from the pivot chart). Note that the Rating items are listed in alphabetical order in the pivot table. To change the order of the items, you can just click an item and drag it to a new position. The pivot chart will adjust accordingly.

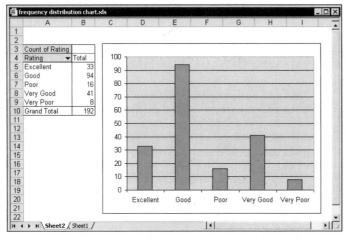

Figure 9-19: A pivot chart will display the frequency
of each response in column B.

Figure 9-20: The pivot chart displays the frequency of each response.

TIP

To display the data in percentages, double-click the Count of Rating button
to display the PivotTable Field dialog box. Click the Options button and
select % of Column in the field labeled Show Data As.

If the data consists of numerical values, you may want to create groups. To do so, right-click the field button in the pivot table and choose Group. Then specify the parameters for the grouping. Figure 9-21 shows a frequency distribution for numeric data, with the results grouped. Note that the pivot table displays a count of the values. By default, the pivot table will display the sum. You'll need to change this.

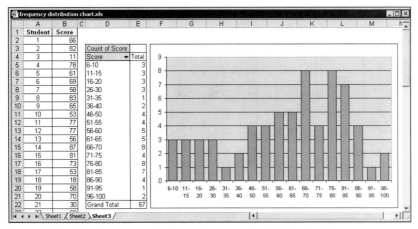

Figure 9-21: This pivot chart displays a frequency distribution for the data in column B, in groups of five.

Selecting a row to plot

Although pivot tables are often used to summarize large data sets, they can also be useful for small amounts of data. Figure 9-22 shows a range of data (in range A3:D17), with a pivot table and a pivot chart. The pivot table (and the pivot chart) contains a Page field (Year), and three Data fields (CA, WA, and Other).

To create this pivot chart:

1. Select any cell within the data range.

2. Start the PivotTable and PivotChart Wizard, and choose the option to create a pivot table and a pivot chart.

3. In Step 3, click the Layout button.

4. Drag the Year button to the Page field.

5. Drag the other three buttons (CA, WA, and Other State) to the Data area.

6. Click Finish to create the pivot table and the pivot chart.

After creating this chart, you can quickly change the year displayed in the chart by using the Year field button.

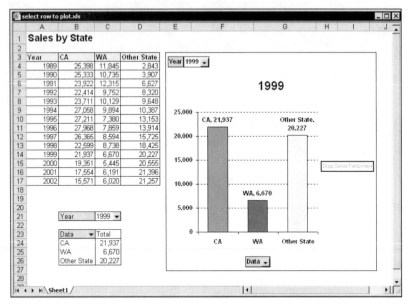

Figure 9-22: This pivot chart displays the data selected in the Year control.

Chapter 7 describes other examples of interactive charts that do not use a pivot table.

Using data from multiple sheets

Often, you'll have data in multiple worksheets within a workbook. Figure 9-23, for example, shows a workbook that contains three sheets, named Yr2000, Yr2001, and Yr2002. Each sheet contains data for a year, and each has a similar four-column range of cells. This is a simple example. In actual practice, the sheets would probably contain much more data. Also, keep in mind that the data can come from different workbooks.

You can create a pivot table to combine the information from these three sheets, although the procedure may not be immediately obvious. The following steps describe how to create a pivot table and pivot chart to summarize the data in these three sheets.

1. Activate the Yr2000 worksheet.

2. Start the PivotTable and PivotChart Wizard. Choose the option labeled Multiple Consolidation Ranges, and the option to create a pivot table and a pivot chart.

3. In Step 2, choose the option labeled Create a Single Page Field for Me.

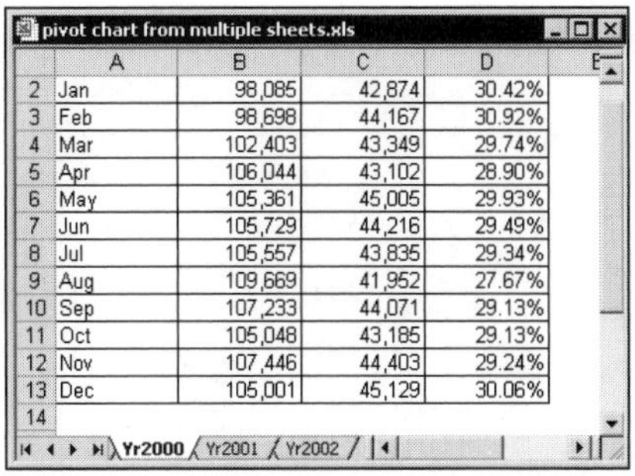

pivot chart from multiple sheets.xls

	A	B	C	D
2	Jan	98,085	42,874	30.42%
3	Feb	98,698	44,167	30.92%
4	Mar	102,403	43,349	29.74%
5	Apr	106,044	43,102	28.90%
6	May	105,361	45,005	29.93%
7	Jun	105,729	44,216	29.49%
8	Jul	105,557	43,835	29.34%
9	Aug	109,669	41,952	27.67%
10	Sep	107,233	44,071	29.13%
11	Oct	105,048	43,185	29.13%
12	Nov	107,446	44,403	29.24%
13	Dec	105,001	45,129	30.06%
14				

Yr2000 Yr2001 Yr2002

Figure 9-23: This workbook contains data in three worksheets.

4. In Step 2b, you specify the ranges. Select range A1:D13 in the first worksheet and click Add. Repeat this step for the other sheets. The All ranges box should display three ranges.
5. In Step 3, specify New worksheet and click Finish. In the pivot table, notice that the Page field displays generic item names (Item1, Item2, and Item3).
6. Drag the Page field button to the left of the pivot chart. Doing so converts the Page field to a Row field. You can now change the item's names to more meaningful text: 2000, 2001, and 2002.
7. The grand total column is not meaningful, so delete it. Right-click, choose Table Options, and remove the checkmark from the Grand Total for Rows checkbox.

Figure 9-24 shows the pivot table and pivot chart after making these changes.

Now it's time to fix the pivot chart. Excel creates a stacked-column chart, which is not at all appropriate. Start by selecting only one year to display – year 2000. Then:

1. Select the chart and convert it to a clustered column chart.
2. Access the Format Data Series dialog box for the Ratio series and assign it to the secondary axis.
3. Select the Ratio series and change the chart type to a line chart.

Now the pivot chart is looking good (see Figure 9-25).

But wait: Change the Year field so that the chart displays a different year's data, and you'll discover that the Ratio series reverts back to a column series, and the secondary axis is gone! You've just experienced a serious problem with pivot charts. Changes made to a data series are not maintained when the chart layout is changed or when the pivot table is refreshed.

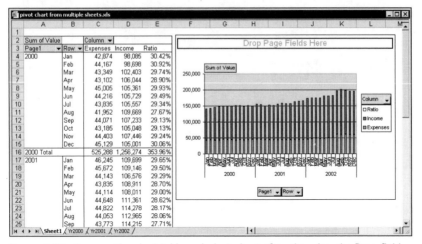

Figure 9-24: Here are the pivot table and pivot chart after changing the Page field to a Row field, changing the item names, and removing the grand totals.

 In this particular case, there is a partial solution: use the "Line - Column on 2 Axes" custom chart type. As luck would have it, this custom chart type displays the Ratio series as a line that uses the secondary axis. But you'll notice that a custom chart type is not maintained when the pivot table's layout is changed or when it's refreshed. However, re-specifying the chart type is much easier than performing the individual customizations described previously.

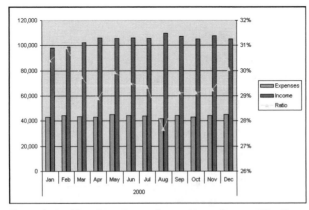

Figure 9-25: The pivot chart, after making some modifications

Chapter 10

Using Excel Charts in Other Applications

IN THIS CHAPTER

- ◆ Understanding basic copy and paste techniques
- ◆ Exporting a chart as a GIF file
- ◆ Using Excel charts in PowerPoint and Word

THE APPLICATIONS IN MICROSOFT OFFICE are designed to work together. These programs have a common look and feel. Sharing data among these applications is relatively easy and, for the most part, reliable.

This chapter describes techniques that enable you to display your Excel charts in other applications.

Basic Copy and Paste Techniques

Most computer users understand the concept of copy and paste. Basically, it works like this:

1. Select something – a cell, a range, some text, a picture, a chart, for example.

2. Choose Edit→Copy (or use the Ctrl+C shortcut). This command copies the selected information to the Windows Clipboard.

3. Activate something else, such as a different location in the current document or a location in a different document (which could also be in a different application).

4. Choose Edit→Paste (or use the Ctrl+V) shortcut). This command pastes the information on the Clipboard into the document.

Many applications (including the Microsoft Office apps) also have an Edit→Paste Special command. This command displays a dialog box providing some options that determine how the information is pasted. This topic, as it relates to sharing information between applications, is explained later in this chapter.

Excel Copy and Paste options

If you're working with Excel, you'll want to keep these additional copy and paste options in mind:

◆ After you copy a cell or range, you can move the cell pointer to a different cell and press Enter. This pastes the copied range as well as clears the Clipboard.

◆ You can use the Edit→Paste Special command to specify additional options for the pasted information. For example, you can use this command to convert formulas to values, or to copy the formatting from one chart to another chart.

◆ You can use the Edit→Copy Picture command rather than the Edit→Copy command. To access this command, you must press Shift when you click the Edit menu. This command, which copies the selection as a *picture*, displays the Copy Picture dialog box, which presents some options.

◆ You can use the Edit→Paste Picture command rather than the Edit→Paste command. To access this command, you must press Shift when you click the Edit menu. This command pastes a *picture* of the original selection.

◆ When copying a cell or range, you can use the Edit→Paste Picture Link command rather than the Edit→Paste command. To access this command, you must press Shift when you click the Edit menu. This command pastes a *linked picture* of the original range (if you modify the copied range, the link picture reflects those changes).

The Copy Picture dialog box

In some cases, you may want to copy a chart as a picture: Activate the chart, press Shift, and choose Edit→Copy Picture. The Copy Picture dialog box pops up with some potentially confusing choices (see Figure 10-1), described next.

◆ **Appearance:** This option (supposedly) affects the appearance of the chart. But it's not at all clear what this option really does. The online help is no help.

◆ **Size:** If you choose the As Shown When Printed option, the size of the pasted chart will be different from the size of the original chart. For an embedded chart, the pasted copy is sized to print as if it were on a chart sheet. If the chart is on a Chart sheet, this option is available only if the Sized with Window setting is in effect.

◆ **Format:** The choices are Picture and Bitmap. If you choose Picture, the chart is copied as an "Enhanced Metafile." The Bitmap option causes the chart to be saved in Bitmap format (a raster graphic file). This option is available only when the Appearance option is set to As Shown on Screen.

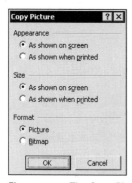

Figure 10-1: The Copy Picture dialog box

Your choices in the Copy Picture dialog box depend on what you will be doing with the copied chart picture. When pasting it to Excel or to another Office application, I've found that the best-looking image is the picture that results from Appearance – As Shown When Printed, and Size – As Shown on Screen. But your mileage may vary. You'll probably want to experiment with these settings to determine which combination produces the best picture for your particular application.

Not all software applications can receive pasted metafile pictures, but most can receive pasted bitmaps.

The companion CD-ROM contains a workbook that demonstrates the result of using all possible combinations of Copy Picture dialog box options.

Exporting a Chart to a GIF File

The GIF file format is a very commonly used format for graphic images, and this file format works well for exported charts. Virtually all graphics programs can open GIF files, and most of the images that appear in Web pages are GIF files.

You may want to save one or more charts as GIF files so that you can use them in other software or on a Web page. This section presents three ways to accomplish this.

Copy and paste to a graphics application

This technique requires some type of graphics application. Just about any application that enables you to work with graphic files will be sufficient. My preference is a freeware program called IrfanView (available for download at www.irfanview.com).

1. Create your chart and format it as you like.

2. Launch your graphics software.

3. Re-activate Excel and then activate your chart (or chart sheet).

4. Press Shift and choose Edit→Copy Picture.

5. In the copy picture dialog box, select an option that allows copying in Bitmap format. Click OK.

6. Re-activate your graphics software and select Edit→Paste.

7. Perform any additional manipulations and then save the file in GIF format (or any other supported format).

Export your file in HTML format

The procedure outlined in this section requires Excel 97 or later. It's a simple technique that requires no additional software or macros.

1. Create any number of embedded charts, and format and size them as you like.

2. Save your workbook file.

3. Choose File→Save as Web Page (in Excel 97, use File→Save as HTML)

4. Specify a directory and filename. The location and filename are not important. This is just a temporary file that can be deleted later.

5. Click OK.

The workbook will be saved in HTML format, and a new directory will be created. That directory will contain all your charts, each in a separate GIF file. They will be named image001.gif, image002.gif, and so on.

After retrieving your GIF files, you can delete the HTML file and its directory.

Use a simple VBA macro

Another way to save charts as GIF files is to use a VBA macro. The following macro, for example, saves all embedded charts on the active worksheet as GIF files. The files are saved in the current directory, and the filenames include the worksheet name and the chart name.

```
Sub SaveChartsAsGIF ()
    Dim ChtObj As ChartObject
    Dim Counter As Long
    For Each ChtObj In ActiveSheet.ChartObjects
        With ChtObj
            .Chart.Export .Parent.Name & " " & .Name & ".gif", "GIF"
        End With
        Counter = Counter + 1
    Next ChtObj
    MsgBox Counter & " charts were saved in " & CurDir
End Sub
```

This macro is very rudimentary and does no error checking. In addition, it will overwrite existing files with the same name. Refer to Chapter 16 for additional macros that export charts.

 The author's JWalk Chart Tools, available on the companion CD-ROM, includes a more versatile utility to save charts as GIF, JPEG, TIF, or PNG files.

Using Excel Charts in PowerPoint or Word

This section describes how to use Excel charts in Microsoft PowerPoint. Although the examples use PowerPoint, the same procedures work in Word.

Creating charts in PowerPoint

If you use PowerPoint to prepare presentations, you may be familiar with PowerPoint's built-in chart feature. Well, it's not really built in. It makes use of Microsoft Graph, an "embeddable OLE applet" that is also available in other Microsoft Office applications, including Word.

The version of MS Graph that's included with Office XP creates charts that are virtually identical to those created in Excel. There are some limitations, however. For example, every series in an XY chart must use the same set of X values. Figure 10-2 shows a PowerPoint slide with an embedded MS Graph object.

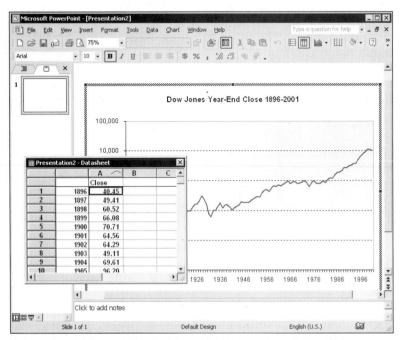

Figure 10-2: A Microsoft Graph object embedded in a PowerPoint slide

Use PowerPoint's Insert→Chart command to insert an MS Graph object. For other Office application, use Insert→Object and select Microsoft Graph Chart from the list of objects. You can insert a Microsoft Graph object into an Excel worksheet – but there's really no reason that you would need to.

The data used by the chart is stored in a DataSheet window. When the MS Graph object is activated, the host application's menus and toolbars will display commands relevant to editing the MS Graph object. Click outside the object to de-activate it.

This book doesn't cover MS Graph, but the applet has a reasonably thorough Help file. If you understand Excel's chart-making techniques, you should have no problems using MS Graph. I mention it only because using MS Graph is an alternative to pasting Excel charts into your PowerPoint presentation or Word document.

Importing an Excel chart into MS Graph

If you don't want to use MS Graph to *create* a chart, you may want to use it to import an existing Excel chart. Although this technique won't work for all Excel charts, it will work in the majority of cases.

1. Start by creating and formatting your chart in Excel. For best results, make sure that it's in a Chart sheet, not an embedded chart. Save the workbook.

2. Activate your PowerPoint slide and choose Insert→Chart to create the default chart.

3. Activate the MS Graph DataSheet window. If it's not visible when the chart object is activated, choose View→DataSheet.

4. Select the upper-left cell in the Data sheet and choose Edit→Import File.

5. In the Import File dialog box, select your Excel workbook and click Open.

6. In the Import Data Options dialog box, select the Chart sheet and click OK (see Figure 10-3).

The chart will be displayed, and the DataSheet will display the source data for the chart. Note that the cells do not contain formulas—just the values that were saved with the file. And, of course, there is no link to the original data.

Figure 10-3: Importing an Excel Chart sheet into MS Graph

Pasting Excel charts into a PowerPoint slide

There are several ways to paste a chart into a PowerPoint slide, but I'm starting with the most straightforward approach: a simple copy and paste operation.

1. Create an Excel chart.

2. Activate the chart and choose Edit→Copy.

3. Activate PowerPoint and select a slide.

4. Choose Edit→Paste.

The Excel chart is copied to the slide, and everything appears perfect.

But wait! You may not realize it, but the preceding steps cause a copy of your entire Excel workbook to be embedded in the PowerPoint presentation. If the chart you're copying happens to be contained in a 10-megabyte workbook file, all 10 of those megabytes come along for the ride. Even worse, if you copy and paste another chart from that workbook into your presentation, another copy of the entire workbook is embedded!

To demonstrate that your entire workbook is embedded, double-click the pasted chart in PowerPoint. This will activate the Excel workbook object and you can examine it. You'll also discover that if you pasted an embedded chart, it is converted to a Chart sheet in the embedded workbook.

TIP If you use Office XP, you may see a SmartTag at the lower-right corner when you paste the chart into your PowerPoint slide. Click the SmartTag and you'll see the options shown in Figure 10-4. These options provide you with two ways to paste: embed the entire workbook, or paste a picture of the chart.

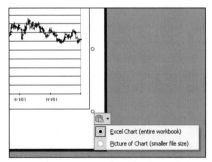

Figure 10-4: In Office XP, a SmartTag lets you choose how the Excel chart is pasted.

It's important to understand that the Excel workbook that's embedded in the PowerPoint presentation is not linked to the original Excel workbook. It's a completely separate copy, stored inside your PowerPoint file. Consequently, if you modify the chart in your workbook, those changes will not be reflected in the PowerPoint slide. You can, however, double-click the Excel object in the PowerPoint slide, and you can work with the Excel embedded object using all of Excel's commands.

Office applications vary in their default handling of data that's copied and pasted. For example, if you copy a paragraph of text from a Word document and paste it into a PowerPoint slide or an Excel worksheet, a Word object is *not* embedded by default. You can, however, use Edit→Paste Special and choose an option to paste the paragraph as an embedded Word document. But even then, the entire document is not embedded – only the copied paragraph.

So why does an entire Excel workbook get embedded? The most likely reason is that Excel workbooks are complex documents and contain many internal links (charts are linked to cells, cells contain formulas that reference other cells, and so on). A paragraph in a Word document, by comparison, is an entity that can stand alone.

If your PowerPoint presentation contains embedded Excel charts, use caution when sending the presentation to someone else. You may think you're sending only the chart — but you're actually sending the entire workbook — which may contain proprietary data.

Using Paste Special for more control

For optimal control over your pasted chart, choose the application's Edit→Paste Special command (if it has one). This will display a list of all available paste formats, and you can choose the most appropriate one.

Figure 10-5 shows the PowerPoint Paste Special dialog box when an Excel chart has been copied. The paste options are as follows:

- **Microsoft Excel Chart Object:** Embeds a copy of the entire Excel workbook (the default).

- **Picture:** Pastes the chart as a picture.

- **Picture (Enhanced Metafile):** Pastes the chart as a picture. This option produces the same result as the previous one.

  When you select the Paste Link option in the Paste Special dialog box, you get this option:

- **Microsoft Excel Chart Object:** This creates a link to the original Excel workbook. The chart will always reflect the current data in the workbook. Double-clicking such a linked object will activate Excel with the original workbook opened.

You'll notice that the Paste Special dialog box does not provide an option to paste the chart as a bitmap. The Bitmap option is available only if the chart was copied as a picture, with the Bitmap option selected in Excel's Copy Picture dialog box.

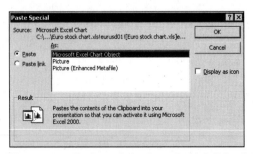

Figure 10-5: The PowerPoint Paste Special dialog box

Deciding which method is best

The preceding sections discuss several ways to get an Excel chart into PowerPoint (or Word). Which is the preferred method? You'll have to decide the answer to that. All of the various paste methods exist because they are useful in some situations.

- ◆ If your chart is relatively simple, consider creating it directly with MS Graph.

- ◆ If you're certain that your chart is finalized (and the data will not change), pasting the chart as a picture is probably the best choice.

- ◆ If your data is continually changing (and the original workbook is always available), creating a link to the workbook is a good option. One potential drawback is that the link will be severed if the source workbook is moved or the name is changed.

- ◆ Probably the least desirable technique is the default paste operation: embedding a copy of the workbook in your PowerPoint presentation. This method can significantly increase the size of your file. Use this option only if your workbook is small and contains no extraneous information.

Chapter 11

Avoiding Common Chart-Making Mistakes

IN THIS CHAPTER

◆ Various ways in which a chart can be inaccurate

◆ Potential problems related to using an inappropriate chart type

◆ Chart complexity

◆ Stylistic and aesthetic considerations

◆ A chart-maker's checklist

IN A PERFECT WORLD, EVERY chart you create is a work of art that communicates a message clearly and efficiently. In the real world, of course, charts are subject to a wide variety of problems.

This chapter discusses some frequent problems related to charts, and it may help you avoid some common pitfalls – and create more effective charts.

Know Your Audience

Every chart has an audience or a potential audience. In some cases, the audience is only yourself. But in the majority of cases, the charts you produce will be viewed by others – in the context of your Excel workbook, or perhaps in the form of a PowerPoint presentation or as part of a printed report. The finished product (that is, the chart) should be geared toward its intended audience.

Key points that you need to consider include:

◆ **The accuracy of the data.** A chart can present data that is perfectly accurate, yet can be very misleading in a number of different ways.

◆ **The complexity of the information presented.** A general rule of thumb: Those higher in the corporate pecking order typically desire simple information. When you're faced with a decision to make a simple chart or a complex chart, a simpler chart is almost always a better option.

◆ **The appropriateness of the chart type.** Just about everyone can under-stand a simple column chart, but nontechnical types usually cringe at the sight of a radar chart.

◆ **The overall "style" of the chart, ranging on a scale from informal to formal.** A chart intended for an employee newsletter will probably look much different than a chart prepared for a Board of Directors meeting.

◆ **The choice of colors used in the chart.** A chart that looks great in color may be incomprehensible when printed on a black-and-white printer, photocopied, or faxed.

The sections that follow expand upon these general points.

Chart Accuracy

When people view a chart, they make the implicit assumption that the chart reflects the truth. In fact, an attractive chart may even *create* a sense of accuracy. After all, the chart-maker surely wouldn't go through all that work if the numbers weren't accurate!

But, of course, truth is relative. The accuracy of the data that comprises the chart is a key consideration. Inaccurate data comes from measurement error and human error (including incorrect formulas in your worksheet). Only you can determine whether your data (and calculations that use the data) are accurate.

There are a number of ways in which a chart can present a less-than-truthful pic-ture. The remainder of this section presents examples that demonstrate various ways in which charts can mislead the viewer and possibly lead to incorrect conclusions.

Plotting data out of context

Typically, data that's presented in a chart should be presented in its proper context. Figure 11-1 shows an example. The top chart displays data for three months and leaves the impression that there is a downward trend in the numbers. But, when viewed in the context of the entire year, the last three data points do not seem at all out of the ordinary.

Plotting percent change versus actual change

Time-based data is often summarized by calculating a percent change from one period to another. These percentage calculations do not take into account the mag-nitude of the values and can therefore mislead the viewer.

The chart in Figure 11-2 displays the percentage change for three products. Product C, of course, stands out in the chart – even though its total values are almost insignificant when compared to the other products. The data is completely accurate, yet the chart is very misleading. Creating a chart from the data in column D would be a much better choice.

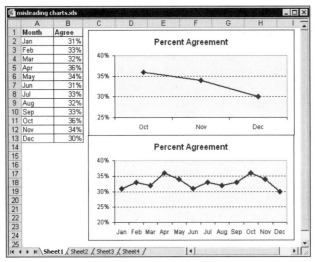

Figure 11-1: Plotting only the last three data points does not tell the entire story.

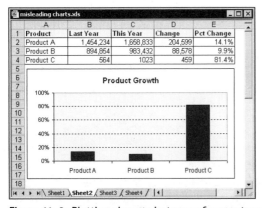

Figure 11-2: Plotting changes in terms of percentage can lead to incorrect conclusions.

Exaggerating differences or similarities

The scale settings for the value axis of a chart can have a tremendous effect on a chart's overall impact. Figure 11-3 shows two charts. Both charts display the same data, but they present dramatically different messages.

In the top chart, the value axis has a range of 15,000 units. In the bottom chart, the axis has a range of only 160 units, which causes the minor deviations in the data to be magnified.

Is a Chart Really Necessary?

Before you create a chart, you might ask yourself a simple question: Is a chart really necessary? The purpose of a chart is to present information. But, depending on your audience, a chart may not always be the *best* way to present your information. Before you assume that a chart is required, consider the alternatives and then make a decision.

For simple data, a nicely formatted text table may be a better option. The data in the accompanying figure, for example, does not reveal any significant changes over time, and it does not benefit by being viewed in the form of a chart.

Also, keep in mind that creating too many charts may simply overwhelm the audience. Viewing an endless series of charts that don't have a compelling message may even disrupt the viewers' attention and cause them to overlook the charts that *do* have a message.

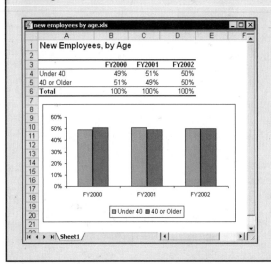

A chart's aspect ratio can also affect the chart's overall message. The term *aspect ratio* refers to the chart's width-to-height relationship. A "normal" aspect ratio is 4:3, which means that the chart is four units wide and three units high (this also corresponds to common computer display resolutions).

Figure 11-4 shows three line charts that display the same data. Even though the value axis scale is identical for the three charts, they present very different impressions of the data.

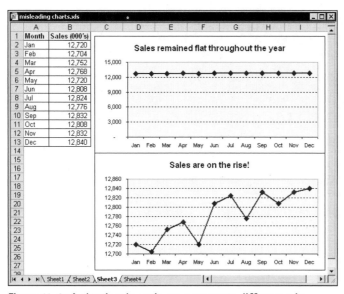

Figure 11-3: A chart's value axis can exaggerate differences in data points.

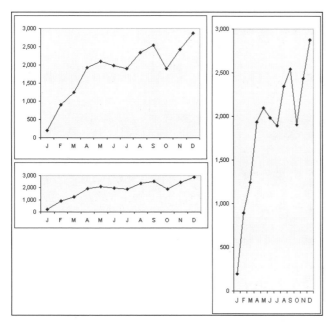

Figure 11-4: A chart's aspect ratio can affect the viewer's perception of the data.

Problems with Chart Type Selection

As you know, Excel offers a wide variety of chart types. Selecting the most appropriate chart type for a particular set of data is sometimes difficult. This section presents examples of potential problems that stem from using an incorrect chart type.

Category versus value axis

A common problem with charts stems from confusion between a category axis and a value axis. This topic is covered in Chapter 4, but it's worth revisiting.

Common chart types such as a column chart, line chart, area chart, and bar chart all use a standard category axis. A category axis does not convey any numerical information. An XY chart, on the other hand, uses two value axes, both of which convey numerical information.

Figure 11-5 shows a worksheet with a company's net income data for six periods of time, along with a line chart that plots the numbers. Note that the increments are not equal (the last two periods are one-year intervals). The chart is misleading because the last two data points use a different time scale, and the chart suggests that net income growth has slowed considerably. The use of a line chart usually implies a continuous stream of data – which is not the case with this chart.

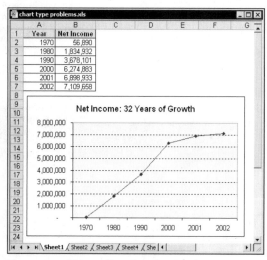

Figure 11-5: Using a line chart for this data presents an incorrect picture of the growth.

Figure 11-6 presents a more accurate picture of the growth. The chart in this figure is an XY chart that treats the horizontal scale as numeric. Yet another solution is to eliminate any source of confusion: remove the last two data points from the series, and use a column chart (see Figure 11-7).

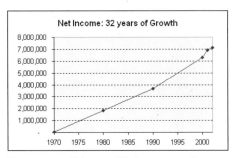

Figure 11-6: Using an XY chart treats the years as values.

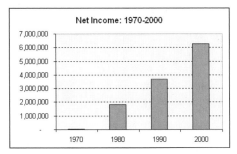

Figure 11-7: Eliminating the last two data points makes the chart more accurate.

Problems with pie charts

For some reason, pie charts are one of the most commonly used chart types. A single pie chart is often acceptable, as long as the number of categories is kept to a reasonable number. Often, however, people present multiple pie charts in order to make a comparison.

Figure 11-8 shows an example. This group of charts suffers from several problems. The charts essentially look identical. With no numerical labels, the viewer cannot draw any conclusions. But more important, the charts provide no clue as to the total "value" of each pie.

Two alternatives are shown in Figure 11-9. Either one of these charts is vastly superior to the four pie charts. The stacked column chart provides all the information in the pie charts; it also allows the viewer to make overall comparisons by year.

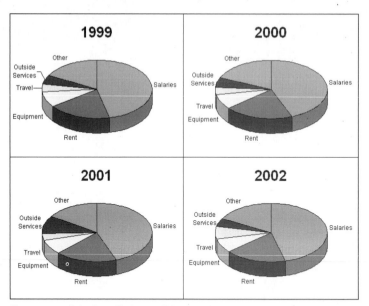

Figure 11-8: It's virtually impossible to make comparisons by using multiple pie charts.

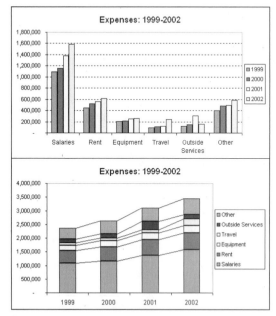

Figure 11-9: These two column chart variations are preferable to four pie charts.

Figure 11-10 shows a pie chart that was actually published by a state government agency (the state will remain nameless). This chart has 18 slices and is pretty much incomprehensible. If the goal was to present an accurate picture of how lottery funds are disbursed, this chart fails miserably. Using a more appropriate chart type (see Figure 11-11) converts this mess into a comprehensible and informative chart.

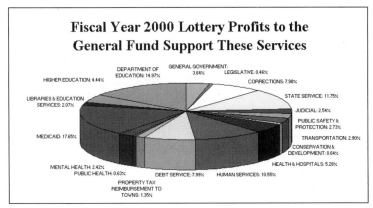

Figure 11-10: Violation: Inappropriate use of a pie chart. Guilty as charged.

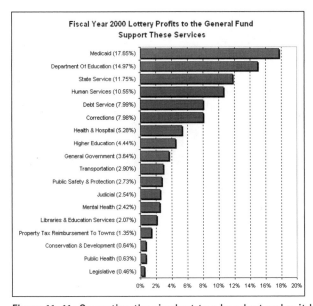

Figure 11-11: Converting the pie chart to a bar chart makes it legible.

Problems with negative values

Some chart types don't handle negative numbers as you might expect. For example, a pie chart (or a doughnut chart) simply converts all negative values to positive values. This, of course, is rarely what you want. Figure 11-12 shows a pie chart that presents an incorrect view of the data. Note that the data label for Net Domestic Migration doesn't even display a negative sign.

Figure 11-13 shows the same data presented in a stacked-column chart and in a standard column chart. Although the stacked-column chart does put the negative value below the category axis scale, the chart is still *somewhat* misleading because the stacked columns imply that the total is just under 200,000. The clustered column chart clearly presents the most accurate picture of this data.

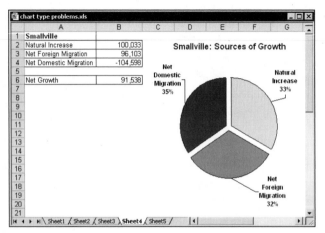

Figure 11-12: The pie chart converts negative values to positive values.

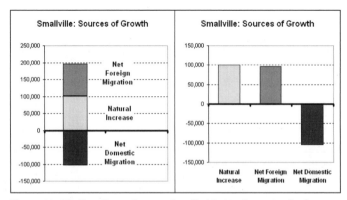

Figure 11-13: Negative values are handled better by a standard column chart (right).

XY charts with the Smoothed Line option

When you create an XY chart, you have an option to connect the points with a line. Another option is to create a "smoothed line." When the Smoothed Line option is in effect, the data markers are connected with a line that contains curves. Figure 11-14 shows an example of an XY chart with straight lines (top) and an XY chart with smoothed lines. Note that the chart on the right can be deceiving. The chart shows the data extending below zero, even though none of the Y data values is less than zero. Also, notice that using smoothed lines without data markers makes it impossible to determine how many data points are used.

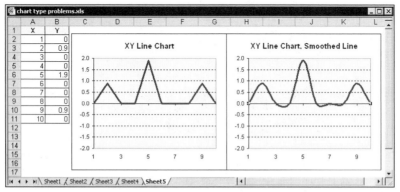

Figure 11-14: The Smoothed Line option can distort the data.

Don't be tempted by 3-D charts

Excel's 3-D charts have a special appeal because they often seem more artistic. But, when all is said and done, 3-D charts offer few real advantages — and lead to quite a few potential problems. I won't say that you should *never* use 3-D charts, but it is important that you understand their weaknesses.

3-D charts are usually acceptable if your goal is to show general relationships. But for technical charts in which the viewer may want to make detailed comparisons, a 2-D chart will always be preferable. Figure 11-15 shows a 3-D line chart with three data series. What's the value of the Qtr-3 data point for the WA series? Which series has the highest value in Qtr-2? These questions cannot be answered by looking at the chart.

With 3-D charts, there's always the possibility of hidden data (see Figure 11-16). You can rotate the chart or change the order of the series, but changing the chart type is probably the best solution — unless, of course, your goal is to keep the data hidden!

And for those who really want to obscure their data, Excel enables you to add perspective distortion, as in Figure 11-17. This setting, in effect, displays the chart as if viewed through a very wide-angle lens.

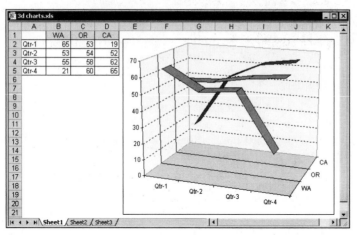

Figure 11-15: A 3-D chart can depict general relationships — sometimes.

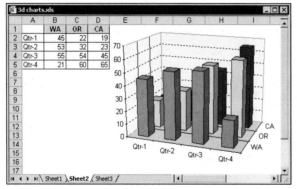

Figure 11-16: 3-D charts have a tendency to obscure data.

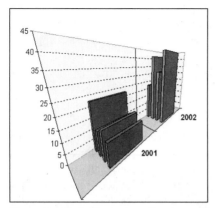

Figure 11-17: Adding perspective to a 3-D chart makes it even more difficult to understand.

Chart Complexity

The KISS principle (*Keep It Simple, Stupid*) is particularly applicable to charts. The main purpose of a chart, after all, is to present information in a manner that makes the information easy to understand. A chart that is unnecessarily complex defeats the purpose.

Just plain bad

We've all seen charts like the one in Figure 11-18. This chart is so bad that it doesn't even deserve further discussion.

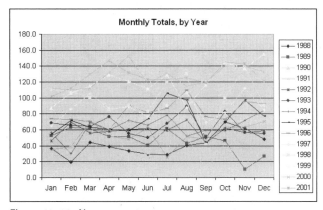

Figure 11-18: No comment.

Maximizing "data ink"

Edward R. Tufte, author of several books that deal with the visual presentation of data, refers to the principle of *data ink maximization*. Simply put, this principle states that the most effective charts use their "ink" to display data – not chart accoutrements such as grid lines and labels. Consequently, nonessential chart elements can often be deleted with little or no adverse effect on the readability of the chart.

Figure 11-19 shows a typical column chart on the left and a "minimalist" version of the chart on the right. There's certainly nothing wrong with the original version of this chart. The chart on the right, however, removes all nonessential elements – and the basic message remains. The chart on the right underwent the following modifications:

♦ The Chart Area border was removed.

♦ The Plot Area was made transparent.

♦ The grid lines were removed.

◆ The category axis was hidden.

◆ Data labels were added to the bottom of the columns.

◆ The value axis number format was simplified and minor unit tick marks were displayed.

◆ The chart's title was changed to reflect the scale units and eliminate the superfluous reference to the years.

◆ The chart's title was moved into the Plot Area.

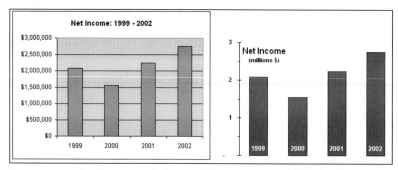

Figure 11-19: A column chart before and after removing all nonessential elements.

Another chart makeover is shown in Figure 11-20. This chart started as an area chart, and the modified version is a line chart. Adding color to the area below each line really adds nothing to the chart. Other modifications include:

◆ The Chart Area border was removed.

◆ The Plot Area was made transparent.

◆ The grid lines were removed.

◆ The value axis was moved to the right side of the chart, closer to the line segments that represent the more recent (and more relevant) data.

◆ The value axis number format was simplified.

◆ The legend was replaced with Text Boxes that identify each line.

◆ The category axis was simplified to display fewer labels.

◆ The title was simplified to eliminate the superfluous reference to the years and moved inside of the Plot Area.

The modified chart conveys all the information of the original chart in an (arguably) more efficient manner.

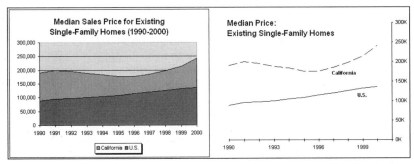

Figure 11-20: An area chart before and after removing all nonessential elements

Chart Style

When someone views a chart, they often have an immediate reaction to it, and that reaction is due in large part to the overall style or appearance of the chart. Does it look inviting, or is it a jumbled mess?

To paraphrase Plato, beauty is in the eye of the beholder. A chart that looks terrible to me may look great to you. That said, following are some general aesthetic guidelines to keep in mind when creating charts:

◆ Don't let design elements detract from the chart. For example, if you use a clip art image in a chart's Plot Area, make sure that the image is relevant to the chart's subject matter and is not overpowering

◆ For time-based data, the standard arrangement (at least for most Western cultures) is left to right. If you must use a bar chart with a vertical category axis, arrange the time-based categories from top to bottom.

◆ Excel offers a wide variety of patterns (available in the Pattern tab of the Fill Effects dialog box). These are essentially holdovers from very early versions of Excel, when color printers were a rarity. If you must use any of these patterns, do some print tests to ensure that they look good when printed.

◆ If possible, avoid using vertically oriented text.

◆ If you display gridlines, make sure that they don't overpower the chart. Often, using a gray dashed line is sufficient.

◆ If you're using multiple charts, it is critical that they all have the same "look." This includes elements such as color, font, number formatting, sizing, and so on.

Be aware of grayscale conversion

Not everyone has a color printer. And even if your chart is printed on a color printer, someone might photocopy or fax it. One way to determine how your colors will look when converted to grayscale is to use Excel's print preview feature (and make sure that a noncolor printer is selected).

For more information about Excel's color system and color-to-grayscale conversion, refer to the excel color system.htm document in the Bonus Material directory on the companion CD-ROM.

Text and font mistakes

Quite a few chart elements can contain text: titles, axis labels, legends, data labels, and so on. Perhaps the most common problem is too much text in a chart. A chart should stand on its own, and lengthy explanatory text should not be necessary (see Figure 11-21).

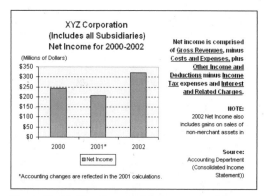

Figure 11-21: There's a chart in here somewhere.

A very common problem with Excel charts is displaying text correctly on the category axis. The problem is that lengthy text often doesn't fit, and Excel automatically rotates the text.

Figure 11-22 shows an example of a chart in which the category axis text has been rotated. The main problem is that the text takes up an inordinate amount of space in the chart, at the expense of the Plot Area. Although the rotated text often looks terrible on-screen, it looks much better when printed.

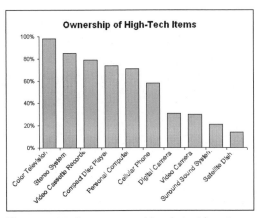

Figure 11-22: A common problem is text in category axis labels.

By default, axis text orientation is set to Automatic, so Excel adjusts the orientation based on its algorithms. For more control over the axis text, access the Format Axis dialog box and click the Alignment tab. You can then force the text alignment to be a specific angle (0 degrees results in normal horizontally oriented text).

After making this change, you may find that Excel skips some of the axis labels. You can force all axis labels to be displayed by using the Scale tab of the Format Axis dialog box. Specify a value of 1 for the Number of Categories Between Tick Mark Labels. Then, you can adjust the font size, Plot Area width, and chart width to ensure that all category axis labels are displayed properly (see Figure 11-23).

Depending on your Excel version, you may find that Excel sometimes overrides the Number of Categories Between Tick Mark Labels and continues to use its own best guess regarding how many labels to display.

Font mistakes generally fall into one or more of the following categories:

- **Too many different fonts faces.** One font per chart almost always works.

- **Poor choice of fonts.** When in doubt, use the Arial font.

- **Poor choice of font sizes.** All text should be large enough to be legible. Use bold or italic to draw attention to a particular element.

- **All uppercase or all lowercase text.** Text in a chart should generally be "proper" case.

The chart in Figure 11-24 demonstrates all these problems.

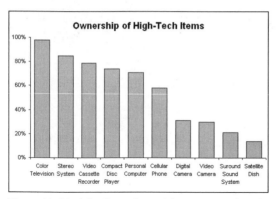

Figure 11-23: Adjusting a few settings ensures that the text is displayed horizontally.

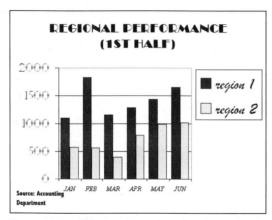

Figure 11-24: This chart has quite a few font-related problems.

A Chart-Maker's Checklist

You collected the data, sliced it and diced it, and summarized in it the form of several charts. Before you unleash your creation on the world (or your boss), take a minute to review the following items.

- ◆ Does the chart actually convey a message? If your boss asks you what the chart means, will you have an answer?

- ◆ On the "formality" scale, is the overall look and tone of the chart appropriate for its intended audience?

- ◆ Is the data accurate? Have you double-checked your formulas?

◆ Is the chart type the most appropriate chart type for the data? Have you even considered using another type?

◆ If it's a pie chart, have you considered any alternatives?

◆ If it's a 3-D chart, can the viewer actually derive the values for each data point?

◆ Is there anything about the chart that could possibly be misleading? Confusing? Not clear?

◆ Are your axes correct? If you use numerical values for a category axis, are the categories at equal intervals?

◆ Is there anything in the chart that isn't necessary?

◆ Is the chart legible when printed on a noncolor printer?

◆ Is the numeric scale of the value axis identified (for example, thousands or millions)?

◆ Is the measurement unit specified?

◆ If your chart uses two value axes, can the viewer easily identify the appropriate axis for each series?

◆ If you're creating multiple charts, do they all have a similar look? Do they use the same color scheme? Same fonts and text sizes?

◆ Is all the text readable?

◆ Is all the text necessary? Can it be shortened?

◆ Does the text use more than one type font? If so, consider using a single font such as Arial.

◆ Does the text used all uppercase or all lowercase?

◆ Are the words spelled correctly?

Chapter 12

Just for Fun

ALTHOUGH EXCEL IS USED primarily for serious applications, many users discover that this product has a lighter side. This is especially apparent in the area of charts and graphics. Although the topics discussed here deal with nonserious applications of graphics in Excel, you'll quite possibly discover some techniques that you can apply to your more serious charting efforts.

All the examples discussed in this chapter are available on the companion CD-ROM. Many of these examples use macros. I don't discuss the programming aspects in this chapter, but the files are all unprotected, so you can view and experiment with the VBA code.

Depending on your security setting, you may receive a macro virus warning when the workbook is opened. Be assured that these files are virus-free.

Animating Stuff

When people think of animation software, Excel certainly isn't the first application that comes to mind. But, with the aid of some relatively simple macros, you can coax some crude animations out of Excel.

If you're a VBA programmer, be aware that the "secret" to producing animations in Excel is to use the following VBA statement within a loop:

```
DoEvents
```

This statement causes a refresh of the screen. Without this statement, the results of your animation code are not displayed until the macro ends — which pretty much defeats the purpose of animation!

Animated AutoShapes

Chapter 6 covers the wonderful world of AutoShapes. If you've played around with AutoShapes, you may enjoy seeing them in action. Create an AutoShape, add a touch of 3-D formatting, and toss in a VBA macro. You've got a recipe for an animated AutoShape. The possibilities are, as they say, limited only by your imagination. The types of animations you can perform include:

◆ Moving an AutoShape from one location to another

◆ Rotating an AutoShape

◆ Changing the colors of an AutoShape

◆ Changing the shape of an AutoShape

The practical applications are limited or maybe even nonexistent. But most people are amazed to discover that you can do this sort of thing in Excel, and it's a good way to take a break from number crunching.

Figure 12-1 shows one of several examples that are available on the companion CD-ROM. Because we lack the technology to make moving images on a printed page, you'll need to open the actual file to experience the animation.

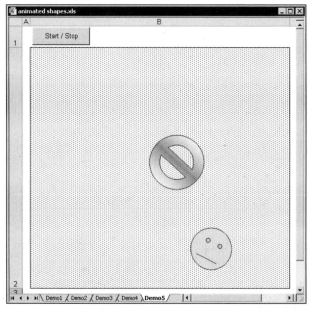

Figure 12-1: Click the button, and the AutoShapes rotate and bounce around inside the box.

Animated charts

When you get tired of watching the animated AutoShapes, you can turn your attention to animated charts. A relatively simple macro can convert a chart into an action-packed piece of entertainment. The macros in these examples increment the value in a cell. This cell is then used in formulas that are displayed in the chart.

Figure 12-2 shows an example of an animated chart. This is a 3-D line chart. When animated, the effect is reminiscent of bird wings in flight.

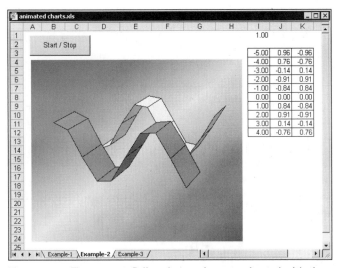

Figure 12-2: These two 3-D line chart series get animated with the help of a macro.

The companion CD-ROM includes a few other animated charts, including a mind-boggling rotating surface chart.

Doughnut chart wheel of fortune

Round and round it goes. Where it stops, nobody knows.

Figure 12-3 shows a doughnut chart with 12 data points, set up like a carnival wheel of fortune. The numbers are data labels, and the slices were formatted individually to get the alternating color effect.

Click the button to kick off a macro that systematically changes the angle of the first slice, which results in a rotating chart. The difficult part was programming the macro so that the spinning gradually slows down before the wheel comes to a final stop.

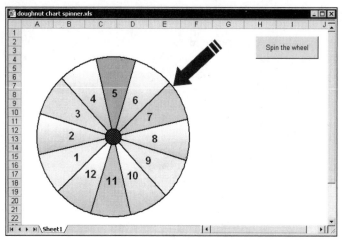

Figure 12-3: Spin the wheel — uh, doughnut chart.

Fun with Trigonometry

Charts that plot data generated by trigonometric functions can be stunning. Even if you don't know the difference between a SIN function and a stop sign, you can still create some incredible designs.

A simple sine versus cosine plot

I start with a simple example. The XY chart in Figure 12-4 plots the data in column B against the data in column C (the chart axes are hidden). Column A contains formulas that generate a sequence of numbers, using the increment value in cell A1.

The formula in B3, which is copied to 99 cells below it, is

```
=SIN(A3)
```

The formula in C3, which is also copied to the cells below, is

```
=COS(A3)
```

The chart will look dramatically different with various increment values in cell A1. Figure 12-5 shows the chart when cell A1 contains 2.1. To display various geometric shapes, use a formula in the form of the following, varying the value of n. For example, when n is 4, the chart displays an octagon.

```
=PI()/n
```

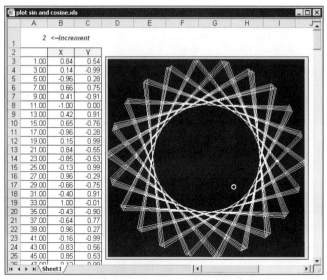

Figure 12-4: This XY chart plots various values generated with the SIN and COS functions.

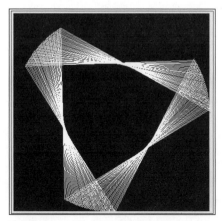

Figure 12-5: Changing the increment value causes a dramatic change in the chart.

Hypocycloid charts

Figure 12-6 shows an example of an XY chart that displays "hypocycloid" curves. A hypocycloid curve is defined as follows:

The curve produced by fixed point P on the circumference of a small circle of radius b rolling around the inside of a large circle of radius a > b.

In other words, this type of curve is the same as that generated by Hasbro's popular SpiroGraph toy, which you may remember from your childhood.

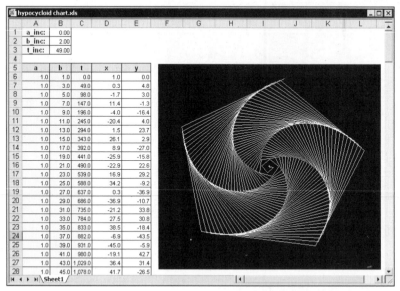

Figure 12-6: This hypocycloid chart is driven by the three parameters in column B.

The formulas that generate the data used in the series are rather complex, but they use three parameters, stored in B1:B3. Change any of these parameters and you get a completely different design. I guarantee that you will be amazed by the variety of charts that you can generate – some of them are simply stunning. Figure 12-7 shows a few more examples.

The companion CD-ROM contains two versions of this file. The first, shown in the figure, enables you to change the parameters manually. A more sophisticated version uses macros to randomly generate parameter values and even has an animation option.

Figure 12-7: Four examples of hypocycloid charts

Radar chart designs

The chart in Figure 12-8 is a radar chart with three series. The chart has 360 axes, which represent the degrees in a circle. The axes are hidden. If they were visible, they would completely overwhelm the chart.

Data for the three series is generated by formulas in column B:D. These formulas use trigonometric functions and depend on the values in column A and the three adjustment parameters in B1:B3. These cells are linked to Scroll Bar controls. Manipulating the scroll bars results in many variations on the design.

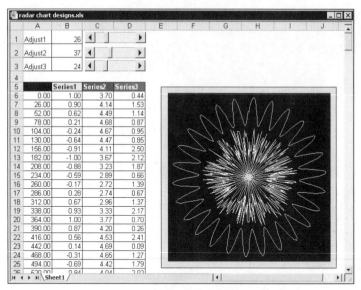

Figure 12-8: Creating designs with a radar chart

Chart Art

Sometimes a chart can resemble a picture. This section presents three examples of chart art (and I use the term *art* loosely).

A mountain range chart

One day I was working with an area chart, and it occurred to me that the chart resembled a mountain range. I quickly abandoned my original task and set out to create the ultimate mountain range chart. The result is shown in Figure 12-9 (it looks better in color). Okay, I cheated. The moon and stars are actually AutoShapes.

A bubble chart mouse head

Work with bubble charts long enough and you may start seeing faces take shape. Figure 12-10 shows a cartoon-like mouse face made up of a data series with nine data points. The data in column C controls the size of the bubbles. Each bubble was formatted separately, of course, to control the color and gradient effects.

The folks at Pixar Animation Studios have nothing to worry about.

Contour chart pattern generator

A contour chart is one of the chart subtypes of a surface chart. This chart type is basically a standard surface chart viewed from above. The contour chart in Figure 12-11 uses only a 7 x 7 range of cells, but it can display some awesome (and very colorful) symmetrical patterns.

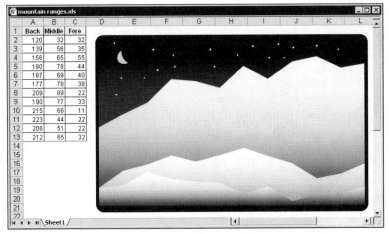

Figure 12-9: Creating a mountain out of an area chart

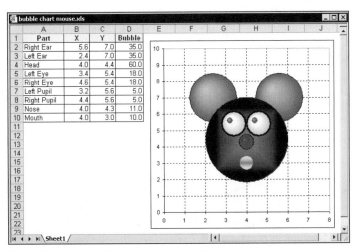

Figure 12-10: A bubble chart mouse head

The number of colors used in a surface chart depends on the Major Unit scale value. This example includes a Spinner control (linked to cell I3) that enables you to easily change the Major Unit value for the chart (this is done with a simple macro). Smaller Major Unit values produce more colors. Another spinner, linked to cell I6, feeds the formulas in the chart's source range (A1:G7). These formulas are color-coded to identify the cells that contain the same formula. Some of these formulas refer to a randomly generated value, which results in a wide variety of patterns.

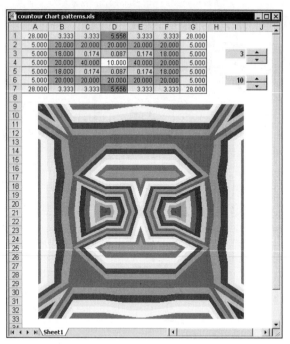

Figure 12-11: Patterns displayed in this contour chart are controlled by the two Spinner controls.

An Analog Clock Chart

Figure 12-12 shows an XY chart formatted to look like a clock. It not only *looks* like a clock but also functions like one. There is really no reason that anyone would need to display a clock such as this on a worksheet, but creating the workbook was challenging, and you may find it instructive.

The chart uses three data series for the clock hands: one for the hour hand, one for the minute hand, and one for the second hand. These series contain formulas that use Excel's NOW function (which returns the current time). The formulas use trigonometric functions to determine the angle of the hands for the time of day. A simple macro is executed once each second. This macro simply calculates the sheet, which updates the formulas and the clock.

The chart uses another series to display the numbers. This data series draws a circle with 12 data points. The numbers consist of manually entered data labels.

Uncheck the Analog clock checkbox to reveal a hidden digital clock (see Figure 12-13). This clock consists of 28 merged cells that contains a simple formula:

```
=NOW()
```

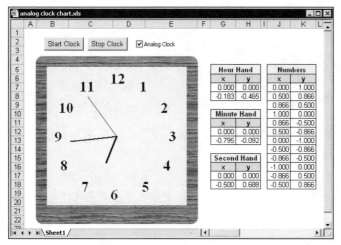

Figure 12-12: This fully functional clock is actually an XY chart in disguise.

Figure 12-13: The digital clock is much easier to create.

XY Sketch

The example in this section has absolutely no practical value – except, perhaps, to kill some time. The worksheet contains an XY chart, along with a number of controls from Excel's Forms toolbar. Clicking one of the arrow buttons draws a line in the chart, the size of which is determined by the step value, which is set with one of the Spinner controls. With a little practice (and patience), you can create simple sketches. Figure 12-14 shows an example.

Clicking an arrow button executes a macro that adds two values to a range in columns A and B. The chart series uses two named formulas:

```
=OFFSET(Sheet1!$A$1,0,0,COUNTA(Sheet1!$A:$A))
=OFFSET(Sheet1!$B$1,0,0,COUNTA(Sheet1!$B:$B))
```

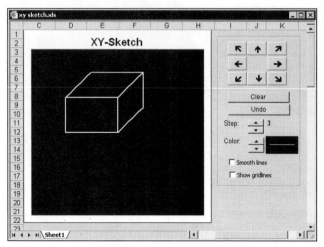

Figure 12-14: This drawing is actually an XY chart.

 For more information about using named formulas in a chart series, refer to Chapter 7.

You'll appreciate the multilevel Undo button. Clicking this button simply erases the last set of values in the chart range. Additional accoutrements include the capability to change the color of the lines, display smoothed lines, and toggle the display of chart gridlines.

Roll the Dice

The workbook shown in Figure 12-15 simulates rolling two dice. The outcome of each roll is stored in a range, which is displayed in a chart. The chart shows the actual distribution of the dice rolls, as well as the theoretical distribution of throwing two dice. This workbook may be useful for teaching elementary probability theory.

Following are a few points to keep in mind while you examine this workbook:

◆ A simple VBA macro, triggered by the Roll 'em button, is used to store the history of the dice rolls in column A:D. Another macro, which deletes the history, is attached to the Clear History button.

◆ The dice picture uses no graphics. The graphics are generated by IF functions that determine whether a particular dot should be visible, based on the randomly generated dice value. The dot is actually a Wingdings font character.

◆ The chart series that displays the theoretical distribution uses an array, not a range. Because the series never changes, you don't need to store the values in a range.

◆ A Text Box in the chart displays the number of dice rolls. This Text Box is linked to a cell that determines the number of items in the History area of the worksheet.

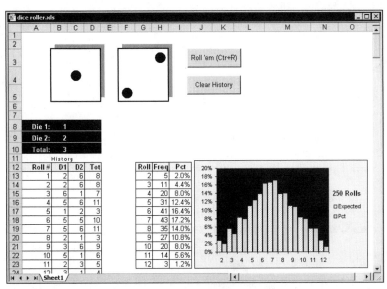

Figure 12-15: This workbook simulates rolling two dice.

Create Your Own Clip Art?

One day I received a package from someone named Debbie Gewand. The package contained a brief note and a floppy disk with an Excel workbook. Reading the note made me curious, so I opened the workbook — and was astounded by what I saw. The file contained hundreds of carefully crafted AutoShapes, combined to create amazing pictures.

It turns out that Debbie is an artist in New York. Amazingly, she uses Excel as her primary drawing software. Figure 12-16 shows an example (a simple example) of one of her creations. This butterfly is made up of 69 hand-crafted AutoShapes! Each AutoShape was drawn manually using the Freeform tool, and then coloring was applied using gradients.

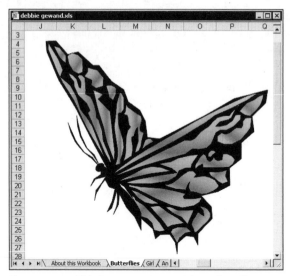

Figure 12-16: This image was created from AutoShapes.

Debbie's work falls into two categories: free-form artwork such as the butterfly, and copies of existing illustrations and photographs. In the latter case, she inserts a scanned picture into a worksheet and then adds AutoShapes on top of the image. Figure 12-17 shows an example. The girl on the right consists of about 120 AutoShapes.

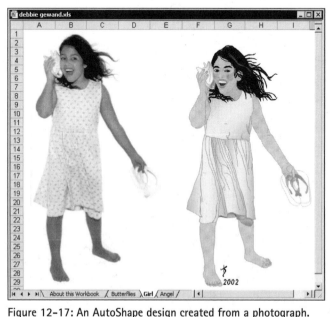

Figure 12-17: An AutoShape design created from a photograph.

Creating a complex image may take four or five hours, but she's become so proficient that she can whip up an impressive image in less than an hour. Figure 12-18 shows yet another example of Debbie's incredible skill. This angel consists of nearly 300 AutoShapes.

Figure 12-18: Another example of converting AutoShapes into art.

Part III

Using VBA with Charts

CHAPTER 13
Introducing VBA

CHAPTER 14
VBA Programming Concepts

CHAPTER 15
Understanding Objects, Collections,
Properties, and Methods

CHAPTER 16
Using VBA with Charts: Examples

Chapter 13

Introducing VBA

IN THIS CHAPTER

◆ An introduction to Visual Basic for Applications — Excel's macro programming language

◆ How to use the Visual Basic Editor

◆ How to work in the code windows of the Visual Basic Editor

THIS CHAPTER INTRODUCES YOU to Visual Basic for Applications (VBA). VBA is Excel's programming language and it is used to automate various aspects of Excel — including charts.

This chapter provides some basic background knowledge of VBA and the Visual Basic Editor and sets the stage for the information presented in subsequent chapters.

VBA in a Nutshell

VBA is best thought of as Microsoft's common application scripting language. VBA is included with all Office 2002 applications, and it's also available in applications from other vendors. You use VBA to write procedures, frequently known as macros.

Following is a quick-and-dirty summary of what VBA is all about.

You perform actions in VBA by executing VBA code.

You write (or record) VBA code, which is stored in a VBA module.

VBA modules are stored in an Excel workbook, but you view or edit a module using the Visual Basic Editor.

A VBA module consists of procedures.

A procedure is basically a unit of computer code that performs some action. Here's an example of a simple Sub procedure called Test. This procedure calculates a simple sum and then displays the result in a message box:

```
Sub Test()
    Sum = 1 + 1
""
    MsgBox "The answer is " & SumEnd Sub
```

In addition to Sub procedures, a VBA module can have Function procedures.

A Function procedure returns a single value. A function can be called from another VBA procedure, or used in a worksheet formula. This book does not cover Function procedures.

VBA manipulates objects contained in its host application (in this case, Excel is the host application).

Excel provides you with more than 100 classes of objects to manipulate. Examples of objects include a workbook, a worksheet, a range on a worksheet, a chart, and a shape. Many more objects are at your disposal, and you can manipulate them using VBA code.

Object classes are arranged in a hierarchy.

Objects can act as containers for other objects. For example, Excel is an object called Application, and it contains other objects, such as Workbook and CommandBar objects. The Workbook object can contain other objects, such as Worksheet objects and Chart objects. A Worksheet object can contain objects such as Range objects, PivotTable objects, embedded chart objects (called ChartObjects), and so on. The arrangement of these objects is referred to as Excel's *object model.*

Like objects form a *collection.*

For example, the Worksheets collection consists of all the worksheets in a particular workbook. The Charts collection consists of all Chart sheet objects. The ChartObjects collection consists of all embedded charts. Collections are objects in themselves.

When you refer to a contained or member object, you specify its position in the object hierarchy using a period (also known as a "dot") as a separator between the container and the member.

For example, you can refer to a workbook named Book1.xls as

```
Application.Workbooks("Book1.xls")
```

This refers to the Book1.xls workbook in the Workbooks collection. The Workbooks collection is contained in the Excel Application object. Extending this to another level, you can refer to Sheet1 in Book1 as

```
Application.Workbooks("Book1.xls").Worksheets("Sheet1")
```

You can take it to still another level and refer to a specific cell as follows:

```
Application.Workbooks("Book1.xls").Worksheets("Sheet1").Range
("A1")
```

If you omit a specific reference to an object, Excel uses the *active* objects.

If Book1 is the active workbook, the preceding reference can be simplified as

```
Worksheets("Sheet1").Range("A1")
```

If you know that Sheet1 is the active sheet, you can simplify the reference even more:

```
Range(""A1"")
```

Objects have *properties.*

A property can be thought of as a *setting* for an object. For example, a Range object has properties such as Value and Name. A Chart object has properties such as HasTitle and ChartType. You can use VBA to determine object properties and also to change them.

You refer to properties by combining the object with the property, separated by a period.

For example, you can refer to the value in cell A1 on Sheet1 as

```
Worksheets(""Sheet1").Range(""A1").Value
```

You can assign values to VBA variables.

Think of a variable as a name that you can use to store a particular value.

To assign the value in cell A1 on Sheet1 to a variable called *Interest*, use the following VBA statement:

```
Interest = Worksheets("Sheet1").Range("A1").Value
```

You can also assign a variable's value to a cell.

To assign a variable called *Interest* to cell A1 on Sheet1, use the following VBA statement:

```
Worksheets("Sheet1").Range("A1").Value = Interest
```

Objects have *methods.*

A method is an action that is performed with the object. For example, one of the methods for a Range object is ClearContents. This method clears the contents of the range.

You specify methods by combining the object with the method, separated by a period.

For example, to clear the contents of cell A1 on the active worksheet, use this:

```
Range("A1").ClearContents
```

VBA also includes all the constructs of modern programming languages, including arrays, looping, and so on.

Believe it or not, this summary pretty much describes VBA. Now it's just a matter of learning some details.

What You Can Do with VBA

VBA is an extremely rich programming language with thousands of uses. The following are just a few things that you can do with VBA macros:

◆ **Insert a text string or formula.** If you frequently need to enter your company name into worksheets, you can create a macro to do the typing for you. The AutoCorrect feature can also do this.

◆ **Automate a procedure that you perform frequently.** For example, you may need to create a series of charts to prepare a month-end summary. If the task is straightforward, you can develop a macro to do it for you.

◆ **Automate repetitive operations.** If you need to perform the same action in 12 different charts, you can record a macro while you perform the task once — and then let the macro repeat your action on the other charts.

◆ **Create a custom command.** For example, you can combine several of Excel's menu commands so that they are executed from a single keystroke or from a single mouse click.

◆ **Create a custom toolbar button.** You can customize Excel's toolbars with your own buttons to execute macros that you write.

◆ **Create a simplified "front end" for users who don't know much about Excel.** For example, you can set up a foolproof data entry template.

◆ **Develop a new worksheet function.** Although Excel includes a wide assortment of built-in functions, you can create custom functions that greatly simplify your formulas.

◆ **Create complete, turnkey, macro-driven applications.** Excel macros can display custom dialog boxes and add new commands to the menu bar.

◆ **Create custom add-ins for Excel.** The JWalk Chart Tools add-in (available on the companion CD-ROM) is an example of an add-in created with VBA.

Introducing the Visual Basic Editor

Before you can begin working with VBA, you need to become familiar with the Visual Basic Editor, or VB Editor for short. The VB Editor enables you to work with *VBA modules*, which are containers for your VBA code.

This chapter assumes that you use Excel 97 or a later version. Previous versions don't have a separate VB Editor.

Activating the VB Editor

When you work in Excel, you can switch to the VB Editor by using any of the following techniques:

◆ Press Alt+F11.

◆ Select Tools→Macro→Visual Basic Editor.

◆ Click the Visual Basic Editor button, located on the Visual Basic toolbar (not visible by default).

Figure 13-1 shows the VB Editor. Chances are that your VB Editor window won't look exactly like the window shown in the figure. This window is highly customizable. You can hide windows, change their sizes, "dock" them, rearrange them, and so on.

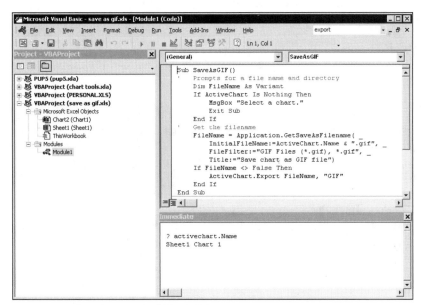

Figure 13-1: The Visual Basic Editor window

The VB Editor components

The VB Editor consists of a number of components. I briefly describe some of the key components in the following sections. Refer to Figure 13-1 to get your bearings.

MENU BAR

The VB Editor menu bar works like every other menu bar that you've encountered. It contains commands that you use to work with the various components in the VB Editor. The VB Editor also features shortcut menus. Right-click virtually anything in a VB Editor window, and you get a shortcut menu of common commands.

TOOLBARS

The standard toolbar, directly under the menu bar by default, is one of six VB Editor toolbars that are available. VB Editor toolbars work just like those in Excel: You can customize toolbars, move them around, display other toolbars, and so forth.

PROJECT WINDOW

The Project window displays an expandable list that consists of every workbook that's currently open in Excel (including add-ins and hidden workbooks). In the VB Editor, each workbook is known as a *project*. I discuss the Project window in more detail in the section "Using the Project Window." If the Project window is not visible, press Ctrl+R.

CODE WINDOW

A code window contains VBA code. Every item in a project has an associated code window. To view a code window for an object, double-click the object in the Project window. Or, select the item and click the View Code button at the top of the Explorer window.

For example, to view the code window for the Sheet1 object for a particular workbook, double-click Sheet1 in the Project window. Unless you've added some VBA code, the code window will be empty. I discuss code windows later in this chapter (see "Using Code Windows").

PROPERTIES WINDOW

The Properties window contains a list of all properties for the selected object. Use this window to examine and change properties. You can use the F4 shortcut key to display the Properties window. The Properties window is not shown in Figure 13-1.

IMMEDIATE WINDOW

The Immediate window is most useful for executing VBA statements directly, testing statements, and debugging your code. This window may or may not be visible. If the Immediate window isn't visible, press Ctrl+G. To close the Immediate window, click the Close button on its title bar.

Using the Project window

When you work in the VB Editor, each Excel workbook and add-in that's currently open is considered a *project*. You can think of a project as a collection of objects arranged as an outline. You can expand a project by clicking the plus sign (+) at the left of the project's name in the Project window. You contract a project by clicking the minus sign (–) to the left of a project's name. Figure 13-2 shows the Project window with three projects listed (one add-in and two workbooks).

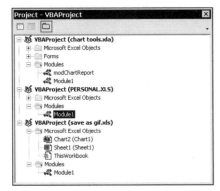

Figure 13-2: A Project window with three projects listed

If you try to expand a project that is protected with a password, you are prompted to enter the password.

Every project expands to show at least one "node" called "Microsoft Excel Objects." This node expands to show an item for each worksheet and chart sheet in the workbook (each sheet is considered an object) and another object called ThisWorkbook (which represents the Workbook object). If the project has any VBA modules, the project listing also shows a Modules node with the modules listed there. A project may also contain a node called Forms (which contains UserForm objects) and a node called Class Modules (which contain Class Module objects). This book doesn't cover the objects contained in the UserForms node or Class Modules node.

RENAMING A PROJECT

By default, all projects are named VBAProject. In the Project window, the workbook name appears (in parentheses) next to the project name. For example, a project may appear as

```
VBAProject (budget.xls)
```

You may prefer to change the name of your project to a more descriptive name. To do so, select the project in the Project window. Make sure that the Properties window is displayed (press F4 if it's not displayed) and change the name from

VBAProject to something else. After you make the change, the Project window displays the new name.

ADDING A NEW VBA MODULE
A new Excel workbook has no VBA modules. To add a VBA module to a project, select the project's name in the Project window and choose Insert→Module.

RENAMING A MODULE
VBA modules have default names, such as Module1, Module2, and so on. To rename a VBA module, select it in the Project window and then change the Name property by using the Properties window (a VBA module has only one property – Name). If the Properties window is not visible, press F4 to display it. Figure 13-3 shows a VBA module that is being renamed ChartMacros.

Figure 13-3: Use the Properties window to change the name of a VBA module.

REMOVING A VBA MODULE
If you want to remove a VBA module from a project, select the module's name in the Project window and choose File→Remove *xxx,* (where *xxx* is the name of the module). You are asked whether you want to export the module before removing it. Exporting a module makes a backup file of the module's contents. You can import an exported module into any other project.

Using code windows

Each object in a project has an associated code module, displayed in a code window. For example, the workbook itself has a code module named ThisWorkbook. Every worksheet and chart sheet also has a corresponding code module (for example, Sheet1 or Chart1). Each code module has its own code window.

MINIMIZING AND MAXIMIZING WINDOWS

At any given time, the VB Editor may have lots of code windows. Code windows are much like worksheet windows in Excel. You can minimize them, maximize them, hide them, rearrange them, and so on. Most people find that it's much easier to maximize the code window that they're working on. Sometimes, however, you may want to have two or more code windows visible. For example, you may want to compare the code in two modules, or copy code from one module to another.

Minimizing a code window gets it out of the way. You also can click the Close button in a code window's title bar to close the window completely. To open it again, just double-click the appropriate object in the Project window.

You can't close a workbook from the VB Editor. You must reactivate Excel and close it from there.

STORING VBA CODE

In general, a module can hold three types of code:

◆ **Sub procedures:** A *procedure* is a set of instructions that performs some action. For example, you may have a Sub procedure that combines various parts of a workbook into a concise report.

◆ **Function procedures:** A function is a set of instructions that returns a single value or an array. You can use Function procedures in worksheet formulas.

◆ **Declarations:** A *declaration* is information about a variable that you provide to VBA. For example, you can declare the data type for variables that you plan to use.

A single VBA module can store any number of procedures and declarations.

Entering VBA code

This section describes the various ways of entering VBA code in a code window. For Function procedures, the code window will always be a VBA module. You can add code to a VBA module in three ways:

◆ Use your keyboard to type it.

◆ Use Excel's macro-recorder feature to record your actions and convert them into VBA code.

◆ Copy the code from another module and paste it into the module that you are working on.

ENTERING CODE MANUALLY

Sometimes the most direct route is the best one. Type the code by using your keyboard. Entering and editing text in a VBA module works just as you expect. You can select text and copy it, or cut and paste it to another location.

Use the Tab key to indent the lines that logically belong together – for example, the conditional statements between an If and an End If statement. Indentation isn't necessary but makes the code easier to read.

A single instruction in VBA can be as long as you want. For the sake of readability, however, you may want to break a lengthy instruction into two or more lines. To do so, end the line with a space followed by an underscore character, and then press Enter and continue the instruction on the following line. The following code, for example, is a single statement split over three lines.

```
If IsNumeric(MyCell) Then _
    Result = "Number" Else _
    Result = "Non-Number"
```

Notice that I indented the last two lines of this statement. Doing this is optional, but it helps to clarify the fact that these three lines comprise a single statement.

After you enter an instruction, the VB Editor performs the following actions to improve readability:

◆ It inserts spaces between operators. If you enter **Ans=1+2** (without any spaces), for example, VBA converts it to

```
Ans = 1 + 2
```

◆ The VB Editor adjusts the case of the letters for keywords, properties, and methods. If you enter the following text:

```
user=application.username
```

VBA converts it to

```
user = Application.UserName
```

Automatic case adjustment is a handy debugging tool. Get into the habit of entering VBA code in lowercase. Then, if the VB Editor does not capitalize the keywords, it means you have entered something incorrectly.

◆ Because variable names are not case sensitive, the VB Editor adjusts the names of all variables with the same letters so that their case matches the case of letters that you most recently typed. For example, if you first specify a variable as myvalue (all lowercase) and then enter the variable as MyValue (mixed case), VBA changes all other occurrences of the variable to MyValue. An exception to this occurs if you declare the variable with Dim or a similar statement; in this case, the variable name always appears as it was declared.

◆ The VB Editor scans the instruction for syntax errors. If it finds an error, it changes the color of the line and may display a message describing the problem. You can set various options for the VB Editor in the Options dialog box (accessible by selecting Tools→Options).

As does Excel, the VB Editor has multiple levels of Undo and Redo. Therefore, if you find that you mistakenly deleted an instruction, you can click the Undo button (or press Ctrl+Z) repeatedly until the instruction returns. After undoing the action, you can select Edit→ReDo Delete (or click the ReDo Delete toolbar button) to redo previously undone changes.

USING THE MACRO RECORDER
Another way to get code into a VBA module is to record your actions by using Excel's macro recorder. In many cases, you can use the recorded macro as is. More often, however, you'll want to edit the recorded macro to make it more useful.

For more information about recording macros, refer to Chapter 15.

COPYING VBA CODE
This section has covered entering code directly and recording your actions to generate VBA code. The final method of getting code into a VBA module is to copy it from another module. For example, you may have written a macro for one project that would also be useful in your current project. Rather than reenter the code, you can open the workbook, activate the module, and use the normal Clipboard copy-and-paste procedures to copy it into your current VBA module.

You also can copy VBA code from other sources. For example, you may find a listing on a Web page or in a newsgroup. In such a case, you can select the text in your browser (or newsreader), copy it to the Clipboard, and then paste it into a module.

Saving your project

As with any application, you should save your work frequently while working in the VB Editor. To do so, use the File→Save command, press Ctrl+S, or click the Save button on the standard toolbar.

When you save your project, you actually save your Excel workbook. By the same token, if you save your workbook in Excel, you also save the changes made in the workbook's VB project.

The VB Editor doesn't have a File→Save As command. To save your project with a different name, activate Excel and use Excel's File→Save As command.

Chapter 14

VBA Programming Concepts

IN THIS CHAPTER

◆ Introducing an example Sub procedure

◆ Using comments in your code

◆ Understanding VBA's language elements, including variables, data types, and constants

◆ Using assignment expressions in your code

◆ Declaring arrays and multidimensional arrays

◆ Using VBA's built-in functions

◆ Using ranges in your code

THIS CHAPTER DISCUSSES SOME OF the key language elements and programming concepts in VBA. If you've used other programming languages, then much of this information may sound familiar. VBA has a few unique wrinkles, however, so even experienced programmers may find some new information.

VBA is a complex topic – far too complex to be covered completely in this book. Because this book deals with charts, I focus on the VBA elements that are relevant to creating and manipulating charts.

 If your goal is to become a VBA expert, this book nudges you in that direction, but it doesn't get you to your final destination. You may want to check out another book of mine: *Excel 2002 Power Programming with VBA,* published by Hungry Minds, Inc. That book covers all aspects of VBA programming for Excel.

An Introductory Example

To get the ball rolling, I begin with a simple example of a VBA procedure. This procedure, named CountCharts, displays a message box that tells you the name of the active sheet and the number of charts on the sheet. Figure 14-1 shows the message box that pops up when this macro is executed.

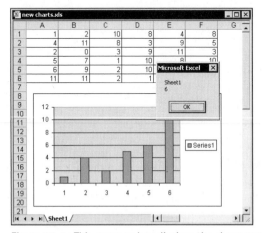

Figure 14-1: This message box displays the sheet name and the number of charts.

To create this procedure, insert a VBA module into a project and then enter the following VBA code into the code window of the module:

```
Sub CountCharts()
    'Counts the charts on the active sheet
    Dim Msg As String
    Msg = ActiveSheet.Name
    Msg = Msg & vbNewLine
    Msg = Msg & ActiveSheet.ChartObjects.Count
    MsgBox Msg
End Sub
```

To execute the macro, activate a worksheet and press Alt+F8 to display the Macro dialog box. Select CountCharts from the list and click Run. Or, you can execute directly from the VB Editor. Put the mouse cursor anywhere within the procedure and then press F5.

Look closely at the code line by line:

◆ The first line of the procedure is called the *declaration line*. Notice that the procedure starts with the keyword Sub, followed by the name of the procedure (CountCharts). This procedure uses no arguments, so it is followed by a set of empty parentheses.

◆ The second line is simply a comment (optional) that describes what the procedure does. The initial apostrophe designates this line as a comment.

◆ The next line uses the Dim keyword to declare a variable (named Msg) and its data type (String). Declaring variables isn't necessary, but (as you'll see later) it's an excellent practice.

◆ The procedure's next line assigns a value to the variable. It uses the Name property of the ActiveSheet. At this point, the Msg variable contains the name of the active sheet (such as *Sheet1*).

◆ The next statement uses the concatenation operator (&) to add a "new line" character to the end of the current contents of the Msg variable.

◆ The next statement counts the number of chart objects on the active sheet, and this value is appended to the contents of the Msg variable, again using the concatenation operator.

◆ The next statement uses VBA's MsgBox function to display the contents of the Msg variable. This appears in the form of a pop-up dialog box that the user must respond to.

◆ The procedure ends with an End Sub statement.

This simple macro uses some common VBA language elements, including:

◆ A comment (the line preceded by the apostrophe)

◆ A variable declaration

◆ Three assignment statements

◆ String concatenation (using the & operator)

◆ References to properties (Name and Count)

◆ The MsgBox function

Not bad for a first effort, eh? The remainder of this chapter provides more information on these (and many other) programming concepts.

About the MsgBox Function

Many of the examples in this chapter use VBA's `MsgBox` function. One of the uses for this function is to display a message to the user in a pop-up box. This is often useful for displaying the value of a variable at various points throughout your code.

For more details on the `MsgBox` function, consult VBA's help.

Using Comments in Your Code

A *comment* is descriptive text embedded within your code. VBA completely ignores the text of a comment. It's a good idea to use comments liberally to describe what you do (because the purpose of a particular VBA instruction is not always obvious).

You can use a complete line for your comment, or you can insert a comment *after* an instruction on the same line. A comment is indicated by an apostrophe. Following are examples of comments:

```
' Close the workbook without saving the changes
ActiveChart.Parent.Delete ' Delete the Chart object
```

VBA ignores any text that follows an apostrophe through to the end of the line. An exception occurs when an apostrophe is contained within quotation marks. For example, the following statement doesn't contain a comment, even though it has an apostrophe:

```
Result = "Can't create a chart."
```

Using Variables, Data Types, and Constants

A *variable* is a named storage location in your computer's memory. Variables can accommodate a wide variety of *data types* – from simple Boolean values (True or False) to large, double-precision values. You assign a value to a variable by using the assignment operator, which is an equal sign.

Following are some examples of assignment statements that use various types of variables. The variable names are to the left of the equal sign. Each statement assigns the value to the right of the equal sign to the variable on the left.

```
x = 1
SeriesCount = 4
```

```
LoanPayoffAmount = 243089
ChartHasATitle = False
x = x + 1
MyNum = YourNum * 1.25
TitleText = "4th Quarter Summary"
DateStarted = #4/1/2003#
```

Understanding data types

VBA makes life easy for programmers because it can automatically handle all the details involved in dealing with data. The term *data type* refers to how data is stored in memory — as integers, real numbers, strings, and so on.

Although VBA can take care of data typing automatically, it does so at a cost — slower execution and less efficient use of memory. If you want optimal speed for your code, you need to be familiar with data types. Generally, it's best to use the data type that uses the smallest number of bytes, yet still can handle all the data that will be assigned to it.

When VBA works with data, execution speed is a function of the number of bytes that VBA has at its disposal. In other words, the fewer bytes used by data, the faster VBA can access and manipulate the data. Table 14-1 lists VBA's assortment of built-in data types.

TABLE 14-1 VBA'S DATA TYPES

Data Type	Bytes Used	Range of Values
Byte	1 byte	0 to 255
Boolean	2 bytes	TRUE or FALSE
Integer	2 bytes	–32,768 to 32,767
Long	4 bytes	–2,147,483,648 to 2,147,483,647
Single	4 bytes	–3.402823E38 to –1.401298E–45 (for negative values); 1.401298E–45 to 3.402823E38 (for positive values)
Double	8 bytes	–1.79769313486231E308 to –4.94065645841247E–324 (negative values); 4.94065645841247E–324 to 1.79769313486232E308 (positive values)
Currency	8 bytes	–922,337,203,685,477.5808 to 922,337,203,685,477.5807

Continued

TABLE 14-1 VBA'S DATA TYPES *(Continued)*

Data Type	Bytes Used	Range of Values
Decimal	14 bytes	+/–79,228,162,514,264,337,593,543,950,335 with no decimal point; +/–7.9228162514264337593543950335 with 28 places to the right of the decimal
Date	8 bytes	January 1, 0100 to December 31, 9999
Object	4 bytes	Any object reference
String (variable-length)	10 bytes + string length	0 to approximately 2 billion
String (fixed-length)	Length of string	1 to approximately 65,400
Variant (with numbers)	16 bytes	Any numeric value up to the range of a double data type
Variant (with characters)	22 bytes + string length	0 to approximately 2 billion

Declaring variables

Before you use a variable in a procedure, you may want to *declare* it. Declaring a variable tells VBA its name and data type. You declare a variable by using the Dim keyword. For example, the following statement declares a variable named Count to be an integer.

```
Dim Count As Integer
```

You also can declare several variables with a single Dim statement. For example:

```
Dim x As Integer, UserName As String, Rate As Double
```

If you don't declare the data type for a variable that you use, VBA uses the default data type, variant. Data stored as a variant acts like a chameleon: It changes type depending on what you do with it.

Introducing object variables

An object variable is a variable that represents an entire object, such as a range or a chart. Object variables, as with normal variables, are declared with a Dim statement. For example:

```
Dim UserRange As Range
Dim CurrentChart As Chart
Dim MySeries As Series
```

To create an object variable, use the `Set` statement. Here are a few examples:

```
Set MyRange = Range("A1:A100")
Set CurrentChart = ActiveChart
Set MySeries = ActiveChart.SeriesCollection(1)
```

Using constants

A variable's value may — and often does — change while a procedure is executing (that's why it's called a *variable*). Sometimes, you need to refer to a named value or string that never changes; in other words, a *constant*.

DECLARING CONSTANTS

You declare a constant by using the `Const` statement. Here are some examples:

```
Const NumQuarters as Integer = 4
Const Rate = .0725, Period = 12
Const CompanyName as String = "Acme Snapholytes"
```

The second statement declares two constants with a single statement, but it doesn't declare a data type. Consequently, the two constants are variants. Because a constant never changes its value, you normally want to declare your constants as a specific data type.

The *scope* of a constant depends on where it is declared within your module:

◆ To make a constant available within a single procedure only, declare it after the `Sub` or `Function` statement to make it a local constant.

◆ To make a constant available to all procedures in a module, declare it before the first procedure in the module.

◆ To make a constant available to all modules in the workbook, use the `Public` keyword and declare the constant before the first procedure in a module.

Using constants throughout your code in place of hard-coded values or strings is a good programming practice. For example, if your procedure needs to refer to a specific value (such as an interest rate) several times, it's better to declare the value as a constant and use the constant's name rather than its value in your expressions. This technique makes your code more readable and makes it easier to change should the need arise — you have to change only one instruction rather than several.

Forcing Yourself to Declare All Variables

To force yourself to declare all the variables that you use, include the following as the first instruction in your VBA module:

```
Option Explicit
```

This statement causes your procedure to stop whenever VBA encounters an undeclared variable name. VBA issues an error message (Compile error: Variable not defined), and you must declare the variable before you can proceed.

Using an Option Explicit statement can prevent errors that might be very difficult to identify. For example, your procedure might use a variable named Interest. But what if you misspell the variable — for example, Intrest? VBA will consider it to be a new variable, with a value of 0, and no error will be generated. If an Option Explicit statement is present, this error will be flagged, and you can correct it.

To ensure that the Option Explicit statement appears in every new VBA module, enable the Require Variable Declaration option on the Editor tab of the VB Editor's Options dialog box.

USING BUILT-IN CONSTANTS

VBA has many built-in constants that you can use in your code. For example, the following statement changes the chart type of the active chart to a line chart:

```
ActiveChart.ChartType = 3
```

Many people find it difficult to remember that a value of 3 represents a line chart. Thankfully, you can use a built-in constant instead. The constant xlLine has a value of 3 and can be used as follows:

```
ActiveChart.ChartType = xlLine
```

When you record a macro, the macro recorder almost always uses built-in constants rather than the actual values.

Using dates

You can use a string variable to store a date, of course, but then you can't perform date calculations using the variable. Using the Date data type is a better way to work with dates.

A variable defined as a Date uses 8 bytes of storage and can hold dates ranging from January 1, 0100, to December 31, 9999. That's a span of nearly 10,000 years — more than enough for even the most aggressive financial forecast! The Date data type is also useful for storing time-related data. In VBA, you specify dates and times by enclosing them between pound signs (#).

The range of dates that VBA can handle is much larger than Excel's own date range, which begins with January 1, 1900. Therefore, be careful that you don't attempt to use a date in a worksheet that lies outside Excel's acceptable date range.

Here are some examples of declaring variables and constants as Date data types:

```
Dim Today As Date, StartTime As Date
Const FirstDay As Date = #1/1/2003#
Const Noon = #12:00:00#
```

Date variables display dates according to your system's short date format, and times appear according to your system's time format (either 12 or 24 hours). You can modify these system settings by using the Regional Settings option in the Windows Control Panel.

Using Assignment Statements

An *assignment statement* is a VBA instruction that evaluates an expression and assigns the result to a variable or an object. An *expression* is a combination of keywords, operators, variables, and constants that yields a string, number, or object. An expression can perform a calculation, manipulate characters, or test data.

If you know how to create formulas in Excel, you'll have no trouble creating expressions in VBA. You can assign a VBA expression to a variable or use it as a property value. VBA uses the equal sign (=) as its assignment operator. Note the following examples of assignment statements (the expressions are to the right of the equal sign):

```
x = 1
x = x + 1
x = (y * 2) / (z  * 2)
SheetHasCharts = True
```

Expressions often use functions. These can be VBA's built-in functions, Excel's worksheet functions, or custom functions that you develop in VBA. I discuss VBA's built-in functions later in this chapter.

Operators play a major role in VBA. Familiar operators describe mathematical operations, including addition (+), multiplication (*), division (/), subtraction (–), exponentiation (^), and string concatenation (&). Less familiar operators are the backslash (\) that's used in integer division, and the Mod operator that's used in modulo arithmetic.

VBA also supports the same comparative operators used in Excel formulas: equal to (=), greater than (>), less than (<), greater than or equal to (>=), less than or equal to (<=), and not equal to (<>). Additionally, VBA provides a full set of logical operators, such as And, Not, Or, and so on. The order of precedence for operators in VBA exactly matches that in Excel. Of course, you can add parentheses to change the natural order of precedence.

Using Arrays

An *array* is a group of elements of the same type that have a common name. You refer to a specific element in the array by using the array name and an index number. For example, you may define an array of 12 string variables so that each variable corresponds to the name of a different month. If you name the array MonthNames, you can refer to the first element of the array as MonthNames(0), the second element as MonthNames(1), and so on, up to MonthNames(11).

Declaring an array

You declare an array with a Dim or Public statement just as you declare a regular variable. You also can specify the number of elements in the array. You do so by specifying the first index number, the keyword To, and the last index number – all inside parentheses. For example, here's how to declare an array comprised of exactly 100 integers:

```
Dim MyArray(1 To 100) As Integer
```

When you declare an array, you need to specify only the upper index, in which case VBA (by default) assumes that 0 is the lower index. Therefore, the following two statements have the same effect:

```
Dim MyArray(0 to 100) As Integer
Dim MyArray(100) As Integer
```

In both cases, the array consists of 101 elements.

Declaring multidimensional arrays

The array examples in the preceding section are one-dimensional arrays. VBA arrays can have up to 60 dimensions. The following statement declares a 100-integer array with two dimensions:

```
Dim MyArray(1 To 10, 1 To 10) As Integer
```

You can think of the preceding array as occupying a 10 x 10 matrix. To refer to a specific element in a 2-D array, you need to specify two index numbers. For example, here's how you can assign a value to an element in the preceding array:

```
MyArray(3, 4) = 125
```

Arrays crop up later in this chapter in the sections that discuss looping.

Using VBA's Built-In Functions

VBA has a variety of built-in functions that simplify calculations and operations. Many of VBA's functions are similar (or identical) to Excel's worksheet functions. For example, the VBA function UCase, which converts a string argument to upper-case, is equivalent to the Excel worksheet function UPPER.

TIP

To display a list of VBA functions while writing your code, type **VBA** followed by a period (.). The VB Editor displays a drop-down list of all functions. In addition to functions, the displayed list also includes built-in constants. The VBA functions are all described in the online help. To view help, just move the cursor over a function name and press F1.

Here's a statement that calculates the square root of a variable by using VBA's Sqr function, and then assigns the result to a variable named x.

```
x = Sqr(MyValue)
```

You can use many (but not all) of Excel's worksheet functions in your VBA code. To use a worksheet function in a VBA statement, just precede the function name with WorksheetFunction and a dot. The following code demonstrates how to use Excel's MEDIAN worksheet function in a VBA statement.

```
x = WorksheetFunction.Median(Range("A1:A10"))
```

It's important to understand that you can't use worksheet functions that have an equivalent VBA function. For example, VBA can't access Excel's SQRT worksheet function because VBA has its own version of that function: Sqr. Therefore, the following statement generates an error:

```
x = Application.Sqrt(123)
```

Controlling Execution

Some VBA procedures start at the top and progress line by line to the bottom. Often, however, you need to control the flow of your routines by skipping over some statements, executing some statements multiple times, and testing conditions to determine what the routine does next.

This section discusses several ways of controlling the execution of your VBA procedures:

- `If-Then` constructs
- `Select Case` constructs
- `For-Next` loops
- `On Error` statements

The If-Then construct

Perhaps the most commonly used instruction grouping in VBA is the `If-Then` construct. This instruction is one way to endow your applications with decision-making capability. The `If-Then` construct executes one or more statements conditionally. The `Else` clause is optional. If included, it enables you to execute one or more instructions when the condition that you test is not true.

The following procedure demonstrates an `If-Then` structure without an `Else` clause. The example deals with time. VBA uses the same date-and-time serial number system as Excel. The time of day is expressed as a fractional value — for example, noon is represented as .5. VBA's `Time` function returns a value that represents the time of day. The following example uses an `If-Then` statement to check the time of day. If the time is before noon, the Then part of the statement executes and the procedure displays a `Good Morning` message.

```
Sub GreetMe()
    If Time < 0.5 Then MsgBox "Good Morning"
End Sub
```

The following procedure uses two `If-Then` statements. It displays either `Good Morning` or `Good Afternoon`:

```
Sub GreetMe()
    If Time < 0.5 Then MsgBox "Good Morning"
    If Time >= 0.5 Then MsgBox "Good Afternoon"
End Sub
```

Notice that the second `If-Then` statement uses >= (greater than or equal to). This covers the extremely remote chance that the time is precisely 12:00 noon when the function is executed.

Another approach is to use the `Else` clause of the `If-Then` construct. For example:

```
Sub GreetMe()
    If Time < 0.5 Then MsgBox "Good Morning" Else _
      MsgBox "Good Afternoon"
End Sub
```

Notice that the preceding example uses the line continuation sequence (a space followed by an underscore); `If-Then-Else` is actually a single statement.

The preceding examples all used a single statement for the Then clause of the `If-Then` construct. However, you often need to execute multiple statements if a condition is True. You can still use the `If-Then` construct, but you need to use an `End If` statement to signal the end of the statements that comprise the Then clause. Here's an example that executes two statements if the `If` clause is True:

```
If x > 0 Then
    y = 2
    z = 3
End If
```

You can also use multiple statements for an `If-Then-Else` construct. Here's an example that executes two statements if the `If` clause is True, and two other statements if the `If` clause is not True.

```
If x > 0 Then
    y = 2
    z = 3
Else
    y = -2
    z = -3
End If
```

The Select Case construct

The `Select Case` construct is useful for choosing among three or more options. This construct also works with two options and is a good alternative to If-Then-Else. The following example of a `Select Case` construct shows another way to code the `GreetMe` examples presented in the preceding section:

```
Sub GreetMe()
    Select Case Time
        Case Is < 0.5
            MsgBox "Good Morning"
        Case 0.5 To 0.75
```

```
            MsgBox "Good Afternoon"
        Case Else
            MsgBox "Good Evening"
    End Select
End Sub
```

Any number of instructions can be written below each Case statement; they all execute if that case evaluates to True.

Looping blocks of instructions

Looping is the process of repeating a block of VBA instructions within a procedure. You may know the number of times to loop, or it may be determined by the values of variables in your program. VBA offers a number of looping constructs, but I cover only two of them: For-Next loops and For Each-Next loops:

FOR-NEXT LOOPS

The following listing is an example of a For-Next loop. This procedure displays the sum of the first 100 integers:

```
Sub SumIntegers()
    total = 0
    For num = 1 To 100
        total = total + num
    Next num
    MsgBox total
End Sub
```

In this example, num (the loop counter variable) starts out with 1 and increases by 1 each time the loop repeats. The loop ends when num is equal to 100. The total variable simply accumulates the various values of num as it changes during the looping.

You also can use a Step value to skip some values in the loop. Here's the same procedure rewritten to sum *every other* integer between 1 and 100 (that is, 1, 3, 5, and so on):

```
Sub SumOddIntegers()
    total = 0
    For num = 1 To 100 Step 2
        total = total + num
    Next num
    MsgBox total
End Sub
```

The previous examples use relatively simple loops. But you can have any number of statements in the loop, and you can even nest For-Next loops inside other For-Next loops. The following is VBA code that uses nested For-Next loops to initialize a 10 x 10 x 10 array with the value –1. When the three loops finish executing, each of the 1,000 elements in MyArray contains –1.

```
Dim MyArray(1 To 10, 1 To 10, 1 To 10)
For i = 1 To 10
    For j = 1 To 10
        For k = 1 To 10
            MyArray(i, j, k) = -1
        Next k
    Next j
Next I
```

FOR EACH-NEXT LOOPS

Your procedures often need to loop various items in a *collection*. A collection is a group of related objects. For example, the Workbooks collection includes all the workbooks currently open. The Charts collection comprises all chart sheets in a workbook. The Sheets collection includes all worksheets and chart sheets. All series in a chart are included in the SeriesCollection collection.

The following example displays the names of all series in the active chart, each in a separate message box:

```
Sub ShowSeriesNames()
    Dim s As Series
    For Each s In ActiveChart.SeriesCollection
        MsgBox s.Name
    Next s
End Sub
```

 In the preceding example, *s* is a variable name. There's nothing special about this name; you can replace it with any valid variable name.

The following example loops through all cells in a range and displays the sum:

```
Sub AddCells()
    Dim c As Range
    Dim Total As Double
    Total = 0
    For Each c In Range("A1:C100")
        Total = Total + c
    Next c
    MsgBox Total
End Sub
```

Basic Error Handling

When VBA code executes, a number of errors can occur. You can write code to specify how these errors are handled. In some cases, you can safely ignore any errors that occur within your procedures. To force VBA to ignore errors, use the following statement:

```
On Error Resume Next
```

The following procedure attempts to delete a chart named Old Chart. If that chart doesn't exist, an error will occur. Using the On Error statement causes VBA to ignore that inconsequential error and not display an error message.

```
Sub DeleteCharts()
    On Error Resume Next
    ActiveSheet.ChartObjects("Old Chart").Delete
End Sub
```

In other cases, you want your code to know whether errors occurred and then do something about them. You can determine whether an error occurred by checking the Number property of the Err object. If this property is equal to zero, an error did not occur. If Err.Number is equal to anything else, an error *did* occur.

The following procedure attempts to activate Chart 1. If Chart 1 does not exist, Err.Number will be something other than zero and a message will be displayed.

```
Sub ActivateTheChart()
    On Error Resume Next
    ActiveSheet.ChartObjects("Chart 1").Activate
    If Err.Number <> 0 Then MsgBox "Chart does not exist"
End Sub
```

You can also specify that code execution continue at a different location when an error occurs. The following procedure uses an On Error statement that points to a code label called BailOut. If any error occurs in the procedure, execution stops and the code after the BailOut statement is executed.

```
Sub ActivateTheChart()
    On Error GoTo BailOut
    ActiveSheet.ChartObjects("Chart 1").Activate
    'Other code goes here
    Exit Sub
BailOut:
    MsgBox "Cannot continue"
End Sub
```

Using Ranges

Charts, of course, use data stored in ranges. Therefore, it's important that you understand how to work with ranges using VBA. The information in this section is intended to be practical rather than comprehensive. If you want more details, consult Excel's help system.

Referencing a range

VBA code can reference a range in a number of different ways:

- The `Range` property
- The `Cells` property
- The `Offset` property

THE RANGE PROPERTY

You can use the `Range` property to refer to a range directly, by using a cell address or name. The following example assigns the value in cell A1 to a variable named `Init`. In this case, the statement accesses the `Range` object's `Value` property.

```
Init = Range("A1").Value
```

In addition to the `Value` property, VBA enables you to access a number of other properties of a `Range` object. For example, the following statement counts the number of cells in a range and assigns the value to the `Cnt` variable.

```
Cnt = Range("A1:C300").Count
```

THE CELLS PROPERTY

Another way to reference a range is to use the `Cells` property. The `Cells` property accepts two arguments (a row number and a column number), and returns a single cell. The following statement assigns the value in cell A1 to a variable named `FirstCell`:

```
FirstCell = Cells(1, 1).Value
```

THE OFFSET PROPERTY

The `Offset` property (like the `Range` and `Cells` properties) also returns a `Range` object. The `Offset` property is used in conjunction with a range. It takes two arguments that correspond to the relative position from the upper-left cell of the specified `Range` object. The arguments can be positive (down or right), negative (up or left), or zero.

The following example returns the value one cell below cell A1 (that is, cell A2) and assigns it to a variable named `NextCell`:

```
NextCell = Range("A1").Offset(1,0).Value
```

Some useful properties of ranges

Previous sections give examples that used the `Value` property for a range. VBA gives you access to many additional range properties. Some of the more useful properties for function writers are briefly described in the following sections. For complete information on a particular property, refer to Excel's online help.

THE FORMULA PROPERTY

The `Formula` property returns the formula (as a string) contained in a cell. If you try to access the `Formula` property for a range that consists of more than one cell, you get an error. If the cell doesn't have a formula, this property returns the cell's value. The following statement simply displays the formula for cell A1 on the active worksheet:

```
MsgBox Range("A1").Formula
```

You can use the `HasFormula` property (which returns True or False) to determine whether a cell has a formula.

THE ADDRESS PROPERTY

The `Address` property returns the address of a range as a string. By default, it returns the address as an absolute reference (for example, $A$1:$C$12). The following statement displays the address of the range selection.

```
MsgBox Selection.Address
```

THE COUNT PROPERTY

The `Count` property returns the number of cells in a range. The following statement displays the number of cells in range A1:M200:

```
MsgBox Range("A1:M200").Count
```

THE COLUMNS AND ROWS PROPERTIES

The `Columns` and `Rows` properties work with columns or rows in a range. For example, the following statement displays the number of columns in a range by accessing the `Count` property:

```
MsgBox Range("B5:K32").Columns.Count
```

Chapter 15

Understanding Objects, Collections, Properties, and Methods

IN THIS CHAPTER

◆ An overview of objects, collections, properties, and methods

◆ An introduction to the `Chart` objects

◆ Understanding the benefits and limitations of Excel's macro recorder

◆ Various ways to execute macros

VBA ESSENTIALLY IS A PROGRAMMING language that manipulates objects contained in a host application such as Excel or PowerPoint. Excel provides a bewildering array of objects, and they can all be modified by using VBA macros.

This chapter focuses on one particular object: the `Chart` object. As you'll see, this object can contain many additional objects, which can also contain other objects. In other words, they comprise an object hierarchy.

Objects and Collections

This section presents a broad overview of Excel's objects and collections.

The object hierarchy

The `Application` object (that is, Excel) contains other objects. Here are a few examples of objects that may be contained in the `Application` object:

◆ A `Workbook` object

◆ A `Window` object

◆ An `AddIn` object

A group of similar objects is known as a *collection*. For example, the Workbooks collection consists of all the open workbooks. Each Workbook object in that collection can contain other objects, a few of which follow:

- A `Worksheet` object
- A `Chart` object (a Chart sheet, not an embedded chart)
- A `Name` object

As you might expect, these objects also form collections. All the `Worksheet` objects in a particular workbook make up the `Worksheets` collection. And these objects, in turn, can contain other objects. A `Worksheet` object, for example, can contain many other objects, which include the following:

- A `ChartObject` object (the container for an embedded chart)
- A `Range` object
- A `PageSetup` object
- A `PivotTable` object

If this seems confusing, trust me, it *will* make sense, and you'll eventually realize that this whole object hierarchy thing is quite logical and well structured. By the way, the complete Excel object model is diagrammed in the VBA help system. Figure 15-1 shows an example.

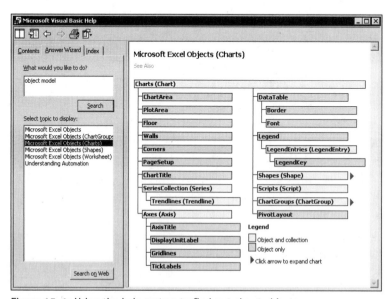

Figure 15-1: Using the help system to find out about objects

More about collections

As I noted, a collection is a group of objects of the same class. A collection is itself an object, and you can work with the entire collection or with an individual object in a collection. To reference a single object from a collection, you put the object's name or index number in parentheses after the name of the collection, like this:

```
Charts("Chart1")
```

If `Chart1` is the first Chart sheet in the collection, you may also use the following reference:

```
Charts(1)
```

You refer to the second Chart sheet in a Workbook as `Charts(2)`, and so on.

There is also a collection called `Sheets`, which is made up of all sheets in a workbook, whether they're worksheets or Chart sheets. If Chart1 is the first sheet in the workbook, you can reference it as follows:

```
Sheets(1)
```

Referring to objects

When you refer to an object using VBA, you often must qualify the object by connecting object names with a period (also known as a "dot operator"). What if you had two workbooks open and they both had a worksheet named `Sheet1`? The solution is to qualify the reference by adding the object's *container*, like this:

```
Workbooks("Book1").Worksheets("Sheet1")
```

Without the workbook qualifier, VBA would look for `Sheet1` in the active workbook.

To refer to a specific range (such as cell A1) on a worksheet named Sheet1 in a workbook named Book1, you can use the following expression:

```
Workbooks("Book1").Worksheets("Sheet1").Range("A1")
```

The fully qualified reference for the preceding example also includes the `Application` object, as follows:

```
Application.Workbooks("Book1").Worksheets("Sheet1").Range("A1")
```

Most of the time, however, you can omit the `Application` object in your references (it is assumed). If the `Book1` object is the active workbook, you can even omit that object reference and use this:

```
Worksheets("Sheet1").Range("A1")
```

And — I think you know where I'm going with this — if Sheet1 is the active worksheet, you can use an even simpler expression:

```
Range("A1")
```

 Contrary to what you might expect, Excel does not have a `Cell` object that refers to an individual cell. A single cell is simply a `Range` object that happens to consist of just one element.

Simply referring to objects (as in these examples) doesn't do anything. To perform anything meaningful, you must read or modify an object's properties, or specify a method to be used with an object.

Properties and Methods

This section discusses two key attributes of objects: their properties and their methods.

Object properties

Every object has properties, which you can think of as attributes. For example, a `Chart` object has a property called `HasTitle`. This property will be True if the chart contains a title, or False if it does not. You can write VBA code to display the value of the `HasTitle` property or write VBA code to set the `HasTitle` property to True or False.

You refer to a property in your VBA code by placing a period and the property name after the object's name. Here's a procedure that uses VBA's `MsgBox` function to display the `HasTitle` property of the chart on the chart sheet named Chart1.

```
Sub DoesChartHaveTitle()
    Msgbox Charts("Chart1").HasTitle
End Sub
```

The code in the preceding example displays the current setting of the `HasTitle` property of the chart on the chart sheet named Chart1. Note that if this particular chart sheet does not exist when this macro is executed, it will generate an error. In other words, this simple procedure contains no error-checking code.

To add a title to a chart, set the `HasTitle` property to True. When you do so, the chart's title consists of generic text: *Chart Title.* To actually provide the title text, you need to access the `Text` property of the `ChartTitle` object. The following procedure demonstrates.

```
Sub AddTitle()
    Charts("Chart1").HasTitle = True
    Charts("Chart1").ChartTitle.Text = "2003 Budget Summary"
End Sub
```

After executing this routine, the chart on the Chart1 sheet will display *2003 Budget Summary* as its title.

The `Application` object (that is, Excel) has several useful properties:

- `Application.ActiveWorkbook`: Returns the active workbook (a `Workbook` object) in Excel.

- `Application.ActiveSheet`: Returns the active sheet (a `Sheet` object) of the active workbook.

- `Application.ActiveChart`: Returns the active chart (a `Chart` object), if any.

- `Application.ActiveCell`: Returns the active cell (a `Range` object) object of the active window.

- `Application.Selection`: Returns the object that is currently selected in the active window of the `Application` object. This can be a range, a chart, a shape, or some other selectable object.

It's important to understand that properties can return objects. In fact, that's exactly what the preceding examples do. The result of `Application.ActiveChart`, for example, is a `Chart` object. Therefore, you can access properties by using a statement such as the following:

```
Application.ActiveChart.HasTitle = True
```

In this case, `Application.ActiveChart` is an object, and `HasTitle` is a property of the object. Because `Application` properties are so commonly used, you can omit the object qualifier (`Application`). For example, to access the `HasTitle` property of the active chart, you can use a statement such as the following:

```
ActiveChart.HasTitle
```

Object methods

In addition to properties, objects also have methods. A *method* is an action that is performed with an object. Here's a simple example that uses the `PrintPreview` method of a `Chart` object. When you execute this procedure, the active chart is displayed in Excel's print preview window.

```
Sub PreviewChart()
    ActiveChart.PrintPreview
End Sub
```

Most methods also use *arguments* to define the action further. Here's an example that uses the `Export` method of a `Chart` object to save the active chart to a GIF file. The `Export` method uses two arguments (both strings), which represent the filename and the type of file to export.

```
Sub ExportChart()
    ActiveChart.Export "mychart.gif", "GIF"
End Sub
```

Specifying Arguments for Methods and Properties

An issue that often leads to confusion among VBA programmers concerns arguments for methods and properties. Some methods use arguments to further clarify the action to be taken, and some properties use arguments to further specify the property value. In some cases, one or more of the arguments is optional.

If a method uses arguments, place the arguments after the name of the method, separated by commas. If the method uses optional arguments, you can insert blank *placeholders* for the optional arguments. Consider the `Protect` method for a workbook object. Check the online help and you'll find that the `Protect` method takes three arguments: `password`, `structure`, `windows`. These arguments correspond to the options in the Protect Workbook dialog box.

If you want to protect a workbook named MyBook.xls, for example, you might use a statement like this:

```
Workbooks("MyBook.xls").Protect "xyzzy", True, False
```

In this case, the workbook is protected with a password (argument 1). Its structure is protected (argument 2), but not its windows (argument 3).

If you don't want to assign a password, you can use a statement like this:

```
Workbooks("MyBook.xls").Protect , True, False
```

Notice that the first argument is omitted and I specified the placeholder using a comma.

Another approach, which makes your code more readable, is to use named arguments. Here's an example of how you use named arguments for the preceding example:

```
Workbooks("MyBook.xls").Protect Structure:=True, Windows:=False
```

Using named arguments is a good idea, especially for methods that have lots of optional arguments, and also when you need to use only a few of them. When you use named arguments, you don't need to use a placeholder for missing arguments.

For properties that use arguments, you must place the arguments in parentheses. For example, the Address property of a Range object takes five arguments, all of which are optional. The following statement is not valid because the parentheses are omitted:

```
MsgBox Range("A1").Address False    ' invalid
```

The proper syntax for such a statement requires parentheses, as follows:

```
MsgBox Range("A1").Address(False)
```

Or the statement could also be written using a named argument:

```
MsgBox Range("A1").Address(rowAbsolute:=False)
```

These nuances will become clearer as you gain more experience with VBA.

Learning more

With literally thousands of objects, properties, and methods at your disposal, how do you learn about them all? There are three general ways:

- ◆ Use the macro recorder (see the next section).

- ◆ Use the Help system. To get specific help about a particular object, property, or method, type the word in a VBA code window and press F1. Figure 15-2 shows an example of the help screen for the Series object. Notice that it contains links to display the properties and methods for the object.

- ◆ Study (or adapt) VBA code written by others. Chapter 16 is a good starting place.

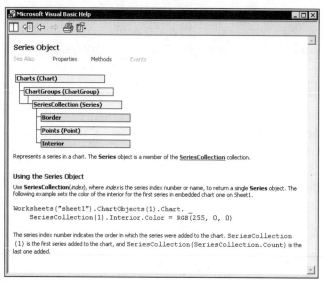

Figure 15-2: Using the help system to find properties and methods of objects

The Chart Object Model

When you use VBA to work with charts, you'll quickly discover that the `Chart` object model is very complex. First, keep in mind that a `Chart` object can have either of two different parent objects. The parent object of a chart on a Chart sheet is the `Workbook` object that contains the Chart sheet. The object hierarchy is

```
Workbook
  Chart
```

The parent object of an embedded chart is a `ChartObject` object. The parent of a `ChartObject` object is a `Worksheet`. The object hierarchy for an embedded chart is as follows:

```
Workbook
  Worksheet
    ChartObject
      Chart
```

Getting Help with Properties and Methods

When you're typing VBA code, you may want take advantage of a very useful feature known as Auto List Members. This feature helps you identify properties and methods for objects by displaying a list. The accompanying figure shows an example. The list appears as soon as you type the period after the object's name. You can then click an item in the list, and it will be entered for you. In the list, properties and methods are identified with different icons.

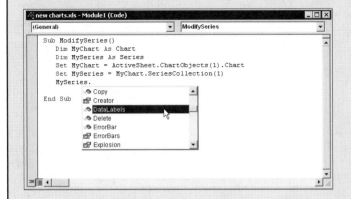

If this feature isn't working for you, select Tools→Options in the VB Editor. In the options dialog box, click the Editor tab, and make sure that there's a checkmark next to Auto List Members. Also, make sure that you've declared your variables as a specific data type.

A `Chart` object contains, of course, other objects. Following is a *partial* object hierarchy for a `Chart` object.

```
Chart
   ChartArea
   PlotArea
   ChartTitle
   Legend
   DataTable
   Axes (Collection)
   SeriesCollection (Collection)
```

These objects, in turn, can contain other objects. Consider the SeriesCollection, which is a collection of all Series objects in the chart. A Series object contains the following objects:

```
Series
   Border
   Points (Collection)
   Interior
```

Now consider the Points collection. Each Point object contains the following objects:

```
Point
   Border
   DataLabel
   Interior
```

Assume that you want to write code to set the text of a data label to *January*. Furthermore, assume that this data label belongs to the first point of the first series of the first chart in the first worksheet of the active workbook. Your VBA statement needs to traverse this object hierarchy and set the Text property of the appropriate DataLabel object.

```
Workbook
   Worksheet
      ChartObject
         Chart
            Series
               Point
                  DataLabel
```

Here's the statement that does the job (this is a single statement that spans two lines):

```
ActiveWorkbook.Worksheets(1).ChartObjects(1).Chart.SeriesCollection(1) _
   .Points(1).DataLabel.Text = "January"
```

 Actually, it's even a bit more complex. Setting the Text property for a DataLabel object will generate an error if the HasDataLabel property of the Point object is False (its default setting).

About Collection Names

As you know, a collection is an object that contains similar objects. Normally, the name of the collection consists of the plural form of the object. For example, the `Workbooks` collection contains all open `Workbook` objects, and the `ChartObjects` collection consists of all `ChartObject` objects on a worksheet. But what about the collection of `Series` objects? Because the singular and plural form of the word *Series* are identical, the designers deviated from this naming convention. Therefore, the collection of all `Series` objects is known as a `SeriesCollection` object (not a `Series` collection object).

Using the Macro Recorder

The macro recorder is a handy tool that converts your Excel actions into VBA code. However, this tool is not the ultimate solution to creating macros. It's important to remember the following points:

♦ The macro recorder is appropriate only for simple macros or for recording a small part of a more complex macro. You'll also find that examining recorded code is an excellent way to learn about objects, properties, and methods.

♦ The macro recorder cannot generate code that performs looping (that is, repeating statements), assigns variables, executes statements conditionally, displays dialog boxes, and so on.

♦ The code that is generated depends on certain settings that you specify.

♦ You'll usually want to clean up the recorded code to remove extraneous commands.

 Excel's Visual Basic toolbar has several useful buttons for you. On this toolbar you'll find the Run Macro, Record Macro, Stop Macro, and Visual Basic Editor buttons useful.

Hands-on: Recording a macro

This section introduces the macro recorder with a simple hands-on exercise. Start with a new workbook, enter some data, and create a default column chart. Figure 15-3 shows the data and chart that I created.

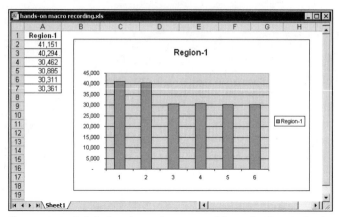

Figure 15-3: A default column chart created from the data in A1:A7

1. Activate the chart.

2. Select Tools→Macro→Record New Macro. This displays the Record Macro dialog box.

3. In the Record Macro dialog box, enter a name for the macro (no spaces allowed). For this example, enter **FormatChart** as the Macro name and choose This Workbook as the location for the macro.

4. Click OK to begin recording the macro. From this point, all your actions will be converted to VBA code. Also, notice the small floating toolbar that contains a blue square (the Stop Recording button). You can move this toolbar out of the way, but don't close it.

5. Change the Plot Area color to white.

6. Change the column color to red.

7. Change the gridlines to gray dashed lines.

8. Delete the legend.

9. Click the Stop Recording button in the floating toolbar. Or, choose Tools→Macro→Stop Recording.

Your workbook will now contain a VBA module with a macro named FormatChart. To view the macro, press Alt+F11 and double-click the workbook name in the Project window. Double-click the Modules node to display the Module (it will be named Module1). Figure 15-4 shows the macro that I recorded. Yours may look a bit different, depending on how you performed the formatting steps. For example, if you select the legend and press Del, the generated code will be different than if you deleted the legend by clicking the Legend button in the Chart toolbar.

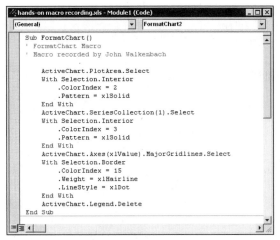

```
hands-on macro recording.xls - Module1 (Code)                    _ □ X
(General)                          ▼  FormatChart2                ▼

    Sub FormatChart()
    ' FormatChart Macro
    ' Macro recorded by John Walkenbach

        ActiveChart.PlotArea.Select
        With Selection.Interior
            .ColorIndex = 2
            .Pattern = xlSolid
        End With
        ActiveChart.SeriesCollection(1).Select
        With Selection.Interior
            .ColorIndex = 3
            .Pattern = xlSolid
        End With
        ActiveChart.Axes(xlValue).MajorGridlines.Select
        With Selection.Border
            .ColorIndex = 15
            .Weight = xlHairline
            .LineStyle = xlDot
        End With
        ActiveChart.Legend.Delete
    End Sub
```

Figure 15-4: A recorded macro

TIP

If you use the Formatting dialog boxes to record this macro, you'll find that Excel records quite a bit of extraneous code. Recording toolbar button clicks often produces more efficient code.

To try out the macro, create another chart using the same data or different data. Activate the chart and press Alt+F8 to display the Macro dialog box. Select the FormatChart macro and click Run. All the formatting changes will be applied in an instant.

XREF

For other ways to execute macros, refer to "Executing Macros," later in this chapter.

Cleaning up recorded macros

As you become more fluent with VBA, you'll realize that the macros generated by the macro recorder almost always need some additional work. For example, the macro may include extraneous commands, which you can delete, and you may want to add some error-checking code.

ELIMINATING SELECTIONS

It's also important to understand that the macro recorder doesn't always generate the most efficient code. If you examine the generated code, you'll see that Excel generally records what is selected (that is, an object) and then uses the generic Selection object in subsequent statements. For example, here's a portion of the macro recorded in the preceding section:

```
ActiveChart.PlotArea.Select
With Selection.Interior
    .ColorIndex = 2
    .Pattern = xlSolid
End With
```

It's not really necessary for a macro to select the PlotArea object. In fact, it's hardly ever necessary to select an object before you manipulate its properties in a macro. Selecting an object may even make the code run slower. The five statements in the preceding code block can be rewritten as follows:

```
With ActiveChart.PlotArea.Interior
    .ColorIndex = 2
    .Pattern = xlSolid
End With
```

USING THE WITH-END WITH CONSTRUCT

You'll notice that the macro recorder makes frequent use of the With-End With construct. In the preceding code, the object being manipulated is the Interior object of the PlotArea object. Specifically, the code is changing the ColorIndex property and the Pattern property.

The code can be rewritten so that it doesn't use the With-End With construct. Those four statements can be replaced by these two:

```
ActiveChart.PlotArea.Interior.ColorIndex = 2
ActiveChart.PlotArea.Interior.Pattern = xlSolid
```

If you need to change many properties of an object, using With-End With is usually a more efficient approach.

The Pattern property is assigned a built-in constant, xlSolid. The constant xlSolid has a value of 1. Using these built-in constants simply makes it easier to remember various arbitrary values.

ADDING ERROR-HANDLING CODE

If you use the FormatChart macro recorded in the previous section long enough, you'll discover that it will generate an error in a few situations. In particular, you'll get an error message if a chart is not active, or if the chart does not have a legend.

Following is the "cleaned up" `FormatChart` macro. I changed the code so that the objects were not selected; I incorporated some simple error-handling; I added some comments.

```
Sub FormatChart2()
'    Exit if a chart is not active
    If ActiveChart Is Nothing Then Exit Sub

'    Make plot area white
    With ActiveChart.PlotArea.Interior
        .ColorIndex = 2
        .Pattern = xlSolid
    End With

'    Make series interior red
    With ActiveChart.SeriesCollection(1).Interior
        .ColorIndex = 3
        .Pattern = xlSolid
    End With

'    Make gridlines dashed, light gray
    With ActiveChart.Axes(xlValue).MajorGridlines.Border
        .ColorIndex = 15
        .Weight = xlHairline
        .LineStyle = xlDot
    End With

'    Delete the legend
    ActiveChart.HasLegend = False
End Sub
```

You will, of course, need to understand VBA thoroughly before you start cleaning up your recorded macros. But for now, just be aware that recorded VBA code isn't always the best, most efficient code. But it is an excellent tool to help you learn about the various object, properties, and methods.

Watching the macro recorder

Excel's macro recorder translates your mouse and keyboard actions into VBA code. I could probably write several pages describing how this is done, but the best way to show you is by example. Follow these steps:

1. Start with a blank workbook.

2. Make sure that Excel's window is not maximized. You don't want it to fill the entire screen.

3. Press Alt+F11 to activate the VB Editor window, and make sure that *this* window is not maximized.

4. Resize and arrange Excel's window and the VB Editor window so that both are visible. For best results, minimize any other applications that are running.

5. Activate Excel, Choose Tools→Macro→Record New Macro, and click OK to start the macro recorder.

   Excel inserts a new module (named Module1) and starts recording.

6. Activate the VB Editor window.

7. In the Project Explorer window, double-click Module1 to display that module in the code window.

8. Close the Project Explorer window in the VB Editor to maximize the view of the code window.

Your screen should look something like the example in Figure 15-5. The size of the windows will depend on your video resolution.

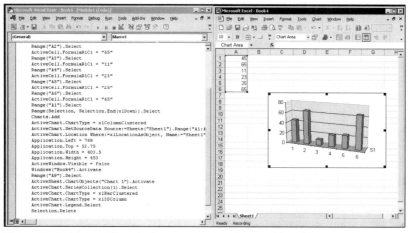

Figure 15-5: A convenient window arrangement for watching the macro recorder do its thing

Now, move around in the worksheet and select various Excel commands. Watch as the code is generated in the window that displays the VBA module. Select cells, enter data, format cells, use the menus and toolbars, create a chart, and so on. I guarantee that you'll be enlightened as you watch the code being spit out before your very eyes.

The Personal Macro Workbook

If you create some VBA macros that you find particularly useful, you may want to store these routines in your Personal Macro Workbook. This workbook, named Personal.xls, is stored in your Xlstart directory. Whenever you start Excel, this workbook is loaded. It's hidden, so it's out of your way. When you record a macro, one of your options is to record it to your Personal Macro Workbook. The Personal.xls file doesn't exist until you record a macro to it.

Recording options

When you record your actions to create VBA code, you have several options. Recall that the Tools→Macro→Record New Macro command displays the Record Macro dialog box before recording begins. This dialog box gives you quite a bit of control over your macro. The following paragraphs describe your options.

MACRO NAME

You can enter a name for the procedure that you are recording. By default, Excel uses the names Macro1, Macro2, and so on for each macro you record. I usually just accept the default name and change the name of the procedure later. You, however, may prefer to name the macro before you record it. The choice is yours.

SHORTCUT KEY

The Shortcut key option lets you execute the macro by pressing a shortcut key combination. For example, if you enter w (lowercase), you can execute the macro by pressing Ctrl+W. If you enter W (uppercase), the macro comes alive when you press Ctrl+Shift+W. You can add or change a shortcut key at any time, so you don't need to set this option while recording a macro.

STORE MACRO IN

The Store macro in option tells Excel where to store the macro that it records. By default, Excel puts the recorded macro in a module in the active workbook. If you prefer, you can record it in a new workbook (Excel opens a blank workbook) or in your Personal Macro Workbook.

DESCRIPTION

By default, Excel inserts five lines of comments (three of them blank) that list the macro name, the user's name, and the date. You can put anything you like here, or nothing at all. As far as I'm concerned, typing anything in is a waste of time, because I always delete these comments and add my own.

Executing Macros

Excel provides a number of ways to execute macros. These are described in the following sections.

Using the Macro dialog box

The Tools→Macro→Macros command (or Alt+F8) displays the Macro dialog box, which lists all available macros. To execute a macro, select it in the list and click Run.

Using a shortcut key

When you record a macro, the Record Macro dialog box offers the option to specify a shortcut key to be associated with that macro. You can, however, associate a shortcut key with any existing macro. To specify a shortcut key for a macro (or to change the existing shortcut key):

1. Select Tools→Macro→Macros (or Alt+F8) to display the Macro dialog box.

2. Select the macro from the list.

3. Click Options to display the Macro Options dialog box (see Figure 15-6).

4. Specify the shortcut key for the macro (an uppercase or lowercase letter).

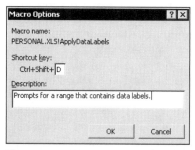

Figure 15-6: Using the Macro Options dialog box to specify a shortcut key for a macro

Assigning a macro to a toolbar button

If the macro is a general-purpose macro that you plan to use in more than one workbook, you may want to assign it to a button on a toolbar. First, ensure that the macro is stored in your Personal Macro Workbook so that it will always be available. Then:

1. Select View→Toolbars→Customize to display the Customize dialog box.

2. Select the Toolbars tab in the Customize dialog box, and make sure that the toolbar that is to contain the new button is visible. Or, click New to create a new toolbar.

3. Select the Commands tab in the Customize dialog box.

4. Choose the Macros category.

5. In the Commands list, drag the Custom Button icon to the toolbar.

6. Right-click the toolbar button and select Assign Macro from the shortcut menu. Excel displays its Assign Macro dialog box.

7. Select the macro name from the list and click OK.

8. At this point, you can right-click the button again to change its name and button image.

9. Click Close to exit the Customize dialog box.

Assigning a macro to an object

Many objects that are inserted on a worksheet can have a macro associated with them. For example, you may want to add a Button object from the Forms toolbar, and use the button to execute a macro. Or, you can assign a macro to AutoShape or even a ChartObject.

After adding the control or AutoShape, right-click the object and select Assign Macro to display the Assign Macro dialog box. Select the macro from the list and click OK.

When you add a Button object from the Forms toolbar, the Assign Macro dialog box appears automatically.

Chapter 16

Using VBA with Charts: Examples

IN THIS CHAPTER

- ◆ Macros to activate and deactivate charts
- ◆ Macros to determine whether a chart is selected
- ◆ Macros to count and loop through all charts
- ◆ Macros to delete charts and print charts
- ◆ Macros to format and customize charts
- ◆ Macros to apply data labels to a series
- ◆ Macros to export charts as GIF files
- ◆ Macros to identify and modify ranges used by a chart
- ◆ Macros that are triggered by events

THIS CHAPTER PRESENTS A WIDE variety of macros that manipulate charts in various ways. These examples are intended to demonstrate how to work with the objects that comprise a chart. You may be able to use some of these as written, but others may require some modification to make them more useful to you.

All the examples in this chapter are available on the companion CD-ROM.

Activating a Chart

Clicking an embedded chart "activates" the chart. Your VBA code can activate an embedded chart using the `Activate` method. Here's an example that activates the first embedded chart on the active sheet:

```
ActiveSheet.ChartObjects(1).Activate
```

Note that the `Activate` method applies to the `ChartObject` object — not the `Chart` object contained in the `ChartObject`. The following statement, for example, will generate an error:

```
ActiveSheet.ChartObjects(1).Chart.Activate
```

When a chart is on a Chart sheet, however, the `Activate` method does apply to the `Chart` object. To activate the chart on the first Chart sheet in the active workbook, use a statement like this:

```
ActiveWorkbook.Charts(1).Activate
```

After a chart is activated, you can refer to it in your code with the `ActiveChart` property, which returns a `Chart` object. For example, the statement below displays the name of the active chart. If there is no active chart, the statement generates an error:

```
MsgBox ActiveChart.Name
```

If you use the macro recorder to create chart-related macros, you'll find that the recorded code always activates the chart and then selects the objects that are manipulated. To modify a chart with VBA, it's not necessary to activate it or make any selections. In fact, it's usually more efficient if your code does *not* activate charts and select elements.

The following two procedures have exactly the same effect (they change the embedded chart named Chart 1 to an area chart). The first procedure activates the chart before performing the manipulations; the second one doesn't.

```
Sub ModifyChart1()
    ActiveSheet.ChartObjects("Chart 1").Activate
    ActiveChart.Type = xlArea
    ActiveChart.Deselect
End Sub


Sub ModifyChart2()
    ActiveSheet.ChartObjects("Chart 1").Chart.Type = xlArea
End Sub
```

The `ModifyChart1` procedure uses the `Deselect` method to "deactivate" a chart. This action is similar to pressing Esc when an embedded chart is activated. One key difference, however, is that the previously selected worksheet cell or range is not selected.

Determining the Context for a Macro

In many cases, your macros may require that a specific type of object be selected. For example, a macro may be written such that it requires that a chart be active or that a range is selected. The examples in this section demonstrate how to write code to ensure that the macro is running in the proper context.

Ensuring that a chart is selected

The simple macro that follows adds a title to the active chart (the title consists of the contents of cell A1). If a chart is not active when this macro is executed, you'll see the rather cryptic error message shown in Figure 16-1.

```
Sub AddTitle()
    With ActiveChart
        .HasTitle = True
        .ChartTitle.Text = Range("A1")
    End With
End Sub
```

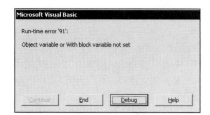

Figure 16-1: This error message appears if a chart is not active.

To prevent this error (and make the macro a bit more user friendly), add a few lines of code that check for the existence of an active chart. If there is no active chart, the user gets a message to that effect and the procedure ends. The `AddTitle` macro follows, showing the modification that checks for an active chart.

```
Sub AddTitle()
    If ActiveChart Is Nothing Then
        MsgBox "Select a chart."
        Exit Sub
    End If
    With ActiveChart
        .HasTitle = True
        .ChartTitle.Text = Range("A1")
    End With
End Sub
```

Determining whether the active chart is embedded

As you know, a chart can be either of two types: an embedded chart or a chart on a Chart sheet. In some cases, your macro may need to make this determination. The TypeOfSelection macro, which follows, displays one of three messages.

```
Sub TypeOfSelection()
    If ActiveChart Is Nothing Then
        MsgBox "No Chart"
        Exit Sub
    End If
    If TypeName(ActiveChart.Parent) = "Workbook" Then
        MsgBox "Chart Sheet"
        Exit Sub
    End If
    If TypeName(ActiveChart.Parent) = "ChartObject" Then
        MsgBox "Embedded Chart"
    End If
End Sub
```

The TypeOfSelection macro first checks for whether a chart is active. If not, it displays *No Chart* and the macro ends. The next two If statements use VBA's TypeName function to determine the object type of the active chart's "parent" object (an object's parent is the object that contains it). The Chart object in an embedded chart is contained in a ChartObject object. The ChartObject's parent is the worksheet on which it is embedded. The parent of a Chart sheet is the Workbook object that contains it.

Identifying the Selected Object

The WhatIsSelected macro, which follows, uses VBA's TypeName function to determine the type of object that is currently selected. For example, it will display

Range if a range is selected, *Series* if a chart series is selected, *PlotArea* if a chart's plot area is selected, and so on.

```
Sub WhatIsSelected1()
    MsgBox TypeName(Selection)
End Sub
```

This macro works fine — except when an embedded chart is selected and the macro is executed by clicking a button on a sheet. In such a case, the button temporarily gets the focus, and the chart is deactivated, leaving the ChartObject selected. Consequently, the message box always displays *ChartObject*.

Following is a modified version of this macro that works regardless of how the macro is executed (see Figure 16-2). If the macro detects that the type of selection is a ChartObject, it then activates the selection, which causes the previously selected chart element to be selected. This modification, however, introduces another minor problem: The macro cannot determine whether a ChartObject is selected (that is, the user selected the chart by using Ctrl+Click).

```
Sub WhatIsSelected2()
    If ActiveChart Is Nothing Then
        MsgBox TypeName(Selection)
    Else
        If TypeName(Selection) = "ChartObject" Then Selection.Activate
        MsgBox TypeName(Selection)
    End If
End Sub
```

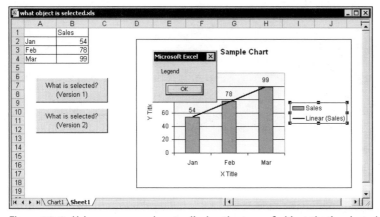

Figure 16-2: Using a message box to display the type of object that's selected

Counting and Looping through Charts

The examples in this section deal with various aspects of counting charts and looping through all charts in a worksheet or workbook.

Counting Chart sheets

To determine how many Chart sheets are in the active workbook, access the `Count` property of the `Charts` collection. For example, the following statement displays the number of Chart sheets in the active workbook:

```
MsgBox Activeworkbook.Charts.Count
```

Counting embedded charts

To count the number of embedded charts on a particular worksheet, access the `Count` property of the `ChartObjects` collection. The following statement, for example, displays the number of embedded charts on Sheet1 of the active workbook.

```
MsgBox ActiveWorkbook.Worksheets("Sheet1").ChartObjects.Count
```

Looping through all charts

A common task is to perform an operation on all existing charts. For example, you may want to write a macro to resize all embedded charts, or add the current date to each chart's title. The following macro loops through all embedded charts on the active worksheet and displays a list of their names.

```
Sub LoopThruChartObjects()
    Dim ChtObj As ChartObject
    Dim Msg As String
    Msg = ""
    For Each ChtObj In ActiveSheet.ChartObjects
        Msg = Msg & ChtObj.Name & vbNewLine
    Next ChtObj
    MsgBox Msg
End Sub
```

The `LoopThruChartObjects` macro uses a variable named `Msg` to store the names of the charts and then displays the list in a message box. `vbNewLine` is a built-in constant that adds a line break to the `Msg` variable.

The listing that follows is a modified version of the macro that uses two loops: One loop cycles through all worksheets, another loop cycles through all embedded charts. The result is a listing of all embedded charts on all worksheets. The result of running this macro is shown in Figure 16-3. This workbook contains seven embedded charts on three sheets.

Figure 16-3: Displaying the names of all embedded charts on all worksheets.

```
Sub LoopThruChartObjects2()
    Dim Wks As Worksheet
    Dim ChtObj As ChartObject
    Dim Msg As String
    Msg = ""
    For Each Wks In ActiveWorkbook.Worksheets
        For Each ChtObj In Wks.ChartObjects
            Msg = Msg & Wks.Name & " - " & ChtObj.Name & vbNewLine
        Next ChtObj
    Msg = Msg & vbNewLine
    Next Wks
    MsgBox Msg
End Sub
```

The previous examples looped through embedded charts. The following procedure is similar, but it loops through all Chart sheets in the active workbook.

```
Sub LoopThruChartSheets()
    Dim Cht As Chart
    Dim Msg As String
    Msg = ""
    For Each Cht In ActiveWorkbook.Charts
        Msg = Msg & Cht.Name & vbNewLine
    Next Cht
    MsgBox Msg
End Sub
```

Changing the location of all charts

The Location method of a Chart object moves a chart. You can use this method to convert embedded charts to Chart sheets (and vice versa).

The following macro loops through all embedded charts on the active sheet and moves each chart to a Chart sheet.

```
Sub ConvertToChartSheets()
    Dim ChtObj As ChartObject
    For Each ChtObj In ActiveSheet.ChartObjects
        ChtObj.Chart.Location Where:=xlLocationAsNewSheet
    Next ChtObj
End Sub
```

The macro that follows performs the opposite task: It loops through all Chart sheets and converts each chart to an embedded chart on the active sheet.

```
Sub ConvertToEmbeddedCharts()
    Dim Cht As Chart
    For Each Cht In ActiveWorkbook.Charts
        Cht.Location Where:=xlLocationAsObject, Name:=ActiveSheet.Name
    Next Cht
End Sub
```

After you run the ConvertToEmbeddedCharts macro, all the embedded charts are stacked on top of each other. You may want to modify this macro such that the embedded charts are better positioned. For more information, see "Sizing and Aligning Charts," later in this chapter.

Deleting Charts

To delete an embedded chart, you must delete its ChartObject container. The following statement, for example, deletes the chart named Chart 1 on the active sheet:

```
ActiveSheet.ChartObjects("Chart 1").Delete
```

To delete all embedded charts on the active sheet, use the Delete method of the ChartObjects collection:

```
Worksheets("Sheet1").ChartObjects.Delete
```

To delete a specific Chart sheet, use a statement like this:

```
ActiveWorkbook.Charts("Chart 1").Delete
```

To delete all Chart sheets in the active workbook, use the `Delete` method of the `Charts` collection:

```
ActiveWorkbook.Charts.Delete
```

When this statement is executed, you'll see the alert message displayed in Figure 16-4. To eliminate this message, set the `DisplayAlerts` property to False. Normally, you'll want to set this property back to True after the sheets are deleted. The following procedure demonstrates.

```
Sub DeleteAllChartSheets()
    Application.DisplayAlerts = False
    ActiveWorkbook.Charts.Delete
    Application.DisplayAlerts = True
End Sub
```

Figure 16-4: This message, which appears when a sheet is about to be deleted, can be avoided by setting the `DisplayAlerts` property to False.

Printing All Embedded Charts

As you know, printing a worksheet also prints the embedded charts on that worksheet. In some cases, you may prefer that each chart be printed on a separate page. The example in this section prints all embedded charts on the active sheet.

```
Sub PrintAllCharts()
    Dim ChtObj As ChartObject
    For Each ChtObj In ActiveSheet.ChartObjects
        ChtObj.Chart.PrintOut
    Next ChtObj
End Sub
```

This procedure loops through all `ChartObject` objects and uses the `PrintOut` method of the `Chart` object. If you would like to preview the charts, use the `PrintPreview` method instead of the `PrintOut` method.

Basic Formatting and Customizing Examples

A common use for a macro is to apply formatting or various customizations to a chart. This involves changing properties of the objects in the chart. The easiest way to determine which properties are appropriate is to record a macro while you make the changes to the chart. The macro may be usable as is. At the very least, the recorded macro will identify the relevant properties.

Changing colors

Following is a macro that sets the series colors for three series in the active chart.

```
Sub ChangeSeriesColors()
    If ActiveChart Is Nothing Then Exit Sub
    With ActiveChart
        .SeriesCollection(1).Interior.ColorIndex = 3
        .SeriesCollection(2).Interior.ColorIndex = 5
        .SeriesCollection(3).Interior.ColorIndex = 4
    End With
End Sub
```

The ChangeSeriesColors macro sets the ColorIndex property of the Interior object, which is contained in each of the three Series objects. These ColorIndex values correspond to red, blue, and green in the standard color palette. Note that this macro performs no error checking. In other words, it will generate an error if the chart doesn't have the referenced Series objects, or if the Series object does not have an Interior object – which is the case for a line chart series. To avoid these error messages, the simplest approach is to ignore them by adding the following statement at the top of the procedure:

```
On Error Resume Next
```

The ChangeSeriesColors macro originated as a recorded macro, which follows. The modified version is much simpler and is more efficient because it doesn't select the objects before setting the property values. Notice that the modified macro does not set the Pattern property. This property is rarely used and it will almost certainly be set to its default value (xlSolid).

```
Sub Macro1()
    ActiveChart.SeriesCollection(1).Select
    With Selection.Interior
```

```
        .ColorIndex = 3
        .Pattern = xlSolid
    End With
    ActiveChart.SeriesCollection(2).Select
    With Selection.Interior
        .ColorIndex = 5
        .Pattern = xlSolid
    End With
    ActiveChart.SeriesCollection(3).Select
    With Selection.Interior
        .ColorIndex = 4
        .Pattern = xlSolid
    End With
End Sub
```

Applying a random color gradient

The goal of this exercise is to create a macro that applies a random two-color gradient to a chart series. If you turn on the macro recorder while you apply a two-color gradient fill to a series in a column chart, you'll generate code something like this:

```
Sub Macro1()
    ActiveSheet.ChartObjects("Chart 1").Activate
    ActiveChart.SeriesCollection(1).Select
    Selection.Fill.TwoColorGradient _
      Style:=msoGradientVertical, Variant:=3
    With Selection
        .Fill.Visible = True
        .Fill.ForeColor.SchemeColor = 10
        .Fill.BackColor.SchemeColor = 8
    End With
End Sub
```

Although this macro contains some irrelevant code, it does reveal some interesting things. In particular, there is a TwoColorGradient method, and it takes two arguments (Style and Variant). Also the SchemeColor property is used to specify the two colors. I consulted the VBA Help system to find out more about these objects and properties.

The macro that follows generates random numbers within the appropriate range for the TwoColorGradient arguments and the SchemeColor property. It's a bit complicated because the Style argument of 6 is invalid. In addition, the Variant argument can be either 1 or 2 when the Style argument is 7. The macro uses If statements to handle these exceptions.

```
Sub ApplyRandomGradient
    Dim GrStyle As Long, GrVariant As Long
    Dim FColor As Long, BColor As Long
    'Get the random values
    GrStyle = Int(Rnd * 7) + 1
    If GrStyle = 6 Then GrStyle = 1
    If GrStyle = 7 Then
        GrVariant = Int(Rnd * 2) + 1
    Else
        GrVariant = Int(Rnd * 4) + 1
    End If
    FColor = Int(Rnd * 57) + 1
    BColor = Int(Rnd * 57) + 1
    'Apply the colors
    With ActiveSheet.ChartObjects(1).Chart.SeriesCollection(1)
        .Fill.TwoColorGradient Style:=GrStyle, Variant:=GrVariant
        .Fill.ForeColor.SchemeColor = FColor
        .Fill.BackColor.SchemeColor = BColor
    End With
End Sub
```

This macro generates some interesting color combinations — some good, some bad, and some downright ugly!

This macro uses VBA's Rnd function, which generates a random number between 0 and 1. To generate random integers between 1 and n, combine the Rnd function with the Int function:

Int(Rnd * n) +1

Conditional color formatting

In Chapter 8 I describe a technique to apply different colors to columns in a column chart, based on the value of the data point. The example in this section uses a macro to accomplish the same effect.

Figure 16-5 shows a chart that displays 30 columns. In addition, the cells in column D contain bins that determine which colors to use (the colors are displayed in the cells in column E). Each value in column D represents the lower value range. For example, a value greater than or equal to 0 (cell D2) but less than 10 (cell D3) is assigned the color in cell E2.

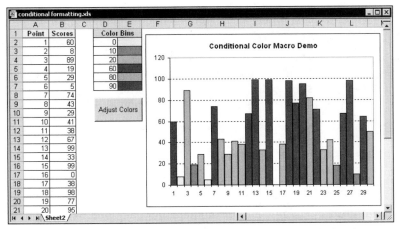

Figure 16-5: Using a macro to apply colors to columns based on their value

The macro to change the column colors follows:

```
Sub AdjustChartColors()
    Dim Ser As Series
    Dim Pt As Point
    Dim ColorBins As Range, cell As Range
    Dim i As Long
    Set Ser = ActiveSheet.ChartObjects(1).Chart.SeriesCollection(1)
    For i = 1 To Ser.Points.Count
        Ser.Points(i).Interior.ColorIndex = xlNone
        For Each cell In Range("D2:D7")
            If Ser.Values(i) >= cell Then
                Ser.Points(i).Interior.ColorIndex = _
                    cell.Offset(0, 1).Interior.ColorIndex
            End If
        Next cell
    Next i
End Sub
```

The AdjustChartColors procedure uses two loops. The outer For-Next loop cycles through each Point object. The inner For Each-Next structure loops through each cell in the bins range in column D. If the data point is greater than or equal to the cell value, the ColorIndex property of the Interior object of the Point object is set to the corresponding color.

Setting axis values

Figure 16-6 shows a worksheet with a line chart that uses the data in column A. In addition, the sheet has three named cells: AxisMin (D2), AxisMax (D3), and MajorUnit (D4). The button executes the following macro, which retrieves the data in the named cells and uses the values as property settings for the Axis object:

```
Sub SetAxisValues()
    With ActiveSheet.ChartObjects(1).Chart.Axes(xlValue)
        .MinimumScale = Range("AxisMin")
        .MaximumScale = Range("AxisMax")
        .MajorUnit = Range("MajorUnit")
    End With
End Sub
```

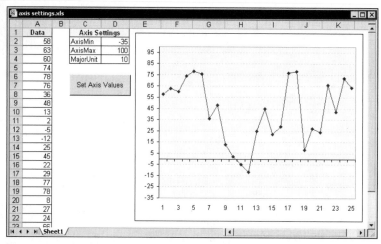

Figure 16-6: Using a macro to modify axis settings using values stored in cells

This macro accesses the Axes collection of the Chart object. Using the xlValue argument causes it to use the value axis. As you know, a chart can have additional axes. The following table shows how to access each of the possible Axis objects in a chart. Note that specifying xlPrimary as the second argument is optional (if omitted, xlPrimary is assumed).

Axis Type	How to Reference It
Primary Category (X) Axis	`Axes(xlCategory, xlPrimary)`
Primary Value (Y)(Axis	`Axes(xlValue, xlPrimary)`
Secondary Category (X) Axis	`Axes(xlCategory, xlSecondary)`
Secondary Value (Y) Axis	`Axes(xlValue, xlSecondary)`
Series Axis	`Axes(xlSeriesAxis)`

Keep in mind that the properties for an `Axis` object vary, depending on the type. For example, a category axis does not have the properties used in the preceding macro — unless its specified as a time-scale category axis. To make a category axis a time-scale axis, use a statement like this:

```
ActiveChart.Axes(xlCategory).CategoryType = xlTimeScale
```

Other `CategoryType` settings are `xlCategoryScale` and `xlAutomatic`. These correspond to the options available in the Axes tab of the Chart Options dialog box.

Freezing the text size of chart elements

You've probably noticed that the chart elements that display text are set to "auto scale" by default. When you change the size of the chart, the text size adjusts accordingly. In some cases, this is a good thing. But sometimes this automatic behavior can be very annoying and force you to do unnecessary editing after resizing a chart.

To turn off auto font scaling for all chart elements manually, access the Font tab of the Format Chart Area dialog box and remove the checkmark from the Auto Scale check box. However, doing this has an undesirable side effect: All text elements in the chart will have the same font formatting as the chart area!

Oddly, if you use VBA to set the `AutoScaleFont` property of the `ChartArea` object to False, this undesirable side effect does not occur. All the chart elements that contain text will also have their `AutoScaleFont` property set to False, but their current font settings will not change.

The `FreezeTextSize` macro that follows takes advantage of this quirk. It sets the `AutoScaleFont` property of the `ChartArea` object to False, and essentially freezes the font size of all chart elements that contain text.

```
Sub FreezeTextSize()
    If ActiveChart Is Nothing Then
        MsgBox "Select a chart."
        Exit Sub
    End If
    ActiveChart.ChartArea.AutoScaleFont = False
End Sub
```

The JWalk Chart Tools add-in, available on the companion CD-ROM, includes a utility to freeze the text size in charts.

Pasting a semitransparent shape to a series

In Chapter 6, I describe a technique to make chart bars or columns semitransparent by copying and pasting a shape object. The technique works well but requires several steps: Create a shape; format it to make it semitransparent; copy it; paste it to a chart series; delete the shape. The following macro automates this process.

```
Sub MakeSeriesTransparent()
    Dim TempShape As Shape
    Dim TheColor as Double
    Dim Ser As Series
    Dim BorderLineStyle As Integer
    Dim BorderColorIndex As Integer
    Dim BorderWeight As Integer
    If ActiveChart Is Nothing Then Exit Sub
    Application.ScreenUpdating = False
    For Each Ser In ActiveChart.SeriesCollection
        If (Ser.ChartType = xlColumnClustered Or _
         Ser.ChartType = xlColumnStacked Or _
         Ser.ChartType = xlColumnStacked100 Or _
         Ser.ChartType = xlBarClustered Or _
         Ser.ChartType = xlBarStacked Or _
         Ser.ChartType = xlBarStacked100) Then
            'Save the color and border settings
            TheColor = Ser.Interior.Color
            BorderLineStyle = Ser.Border.LineStyle
            BorderColorIndex = Ser.Border.ColorIndex
            BorderWeight = Ser.Border.Weight
            ' Create a Shape
            Set TempShape = ActiveSheet.Shapes.AddShape _
              (msoShapeRectangle, 1, 1, 100, 100)
            With TempShape
```

```
                .Fill.ForeColor.RGB = TheColor
                .Fill.Transparency = 0.4
                .Line.Visible = msoFalse
            End With
            ' Copy and paste the Shape
            TempShape.CopyPicture Appearance:=xlScreen, Format:=xlPicture
            With Ser
                .Paste
                'Apply saved border settings
                .Border.Weight = BorderWeight
                .Border.LineStyle = BorderLineStyle
                .Border.ColorIndex = BorderColorIndex
            End With
            TempShape.Delete
        End If
    Next Ser
End Sub
```

The `MakeSeriesTransparent` macro works with the active chart and loops through each series. If the series is a bar or column series, it assigns its fill color to a variable and uses additional variables to remember the border settings for the series. It then creates a temporary shape object, sets the transparency to 40% and removes the border, copies the shape, pastes it to the series, applies the stored border settings, and deletes the shape. This all happens instantly.

Figure 16-7 shows a chart before and after the series were made transparent. Note that in the bottom chart, the gridlines are visible through the columns.

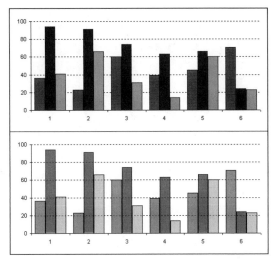

Figure 16-7: A chart, before and after using the
`MakeSeriesTransparent` **macro**

Assigning a Macro to a ChartObject

It's possible to assign a macro to an embedded chart. To do so, Ctrl+click the chart (to select the Chart object's container — a `ChartObject` object); then, right-click and choose Assign Macro from the shortcut menu. This displays the Assign Macro dialog box, in which you can select the macro to be executed.

After assigning the macro, clicking the embedded chart will execute the macro. If you assign the macro that follows, for example, clicking the chart will display a message box that contains the chart's name (the `Caller` property returns the name of the object that called the procedure).

```
Sub Chart_Click()
    Dim ChtName As String
    ChtName = Application.Caller
    MsgBox "You clicked " & ChtName
End Sub
```

Also, be aware that this macro makes it difficult to edit the chart because the chart isn't activated when it is clicked. To edit the chart, right-click and choose Edit Chart Object from the shortcut menu.

 This macro does not preserve gradients or patterns applied to a series, and it will overwrite any existing pictures pasted to the series.

Creating Charts with VBA

This section presents methods to create charts using VBA, and also discusses some of the potential problems that may result when you use recorded macros. VBA provides two methods to create a chart:

◆ **The Add method of the `Charts` collection.** This is used to add a new `Chart` object (that is, a Chart sheet).

◆ **The Add method of the `ChartObjects` collection.** This is used to add a new `ChartObject` (embedded chart).

Recording a macro

Figure 16-8 shows a simple column chart created from the data in A1:C7. The macro recorder was turned on when this chart was created, moved, and resized. The following macro is the result:

```
Sub Macro1()
    Charts.Add
    ActiveChart.ChartType = xlColumnClustered
    ActiveChart.SetSourceData Source:=Sheets("Sheet1").Range("A1:C7"), _
        PlotBy:=xlColumns
    ActiveChart.Location Where:=xlLocationAsObject, Name:="Sheet1"
    With ActiveChart
        .HasTitle = True
        .ChartTitle.Characters.Text = "Chart Title"
        .Axes(xlCategory, xlPrimary).HasTitle = False
        .Axes(xlValue, xlPrimary).HasTitle = False
    End With
    ActiveChart.HasLegend = False
    ActiveSheet.Shapes("Chart 1").IncrementLeft -146.25
    ActiveSheet.Shapes("Chart 1").IncrementTop -58.5
    ActiveSheet.Shapes("Chart 1").ScaleWidth 0.65, msoFalse, msoScaleFromTopLeft
    ActiveSheet.Shapes("Chart 1").ScaleHeight 0.75, msoFalse,
msoScaleFromTopLeft
End Sub
```

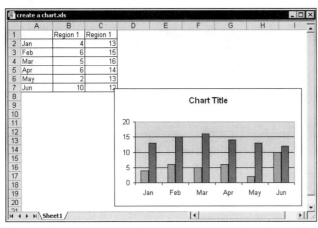

Figure 16-8: The macro recorder was turned on when this chart was created and modified.

Executing the recorded macro

You might expect that executing this recorded macro would create an exact copy of the original chart. In fact, it will create the chart, but you'll get an error message when the code attempts to move and resize the chart. The recorded macro accesses the `ChartObject` as a shape – and it uses its actual name (Chart 1). When you execute the macro, the chart object that's created will not be named Chart 1, and the macro will end with an error.

Macros that create charts can be useful, but (usually) executing a recorded macro isn't good enough. For example, you might prefer the chart to use the data that's currently selected. The recorded macro "hard codes" the original data range address.

Writing a macro to create a chart

The goal of this exercise is to write a general-purpose macro that creates a column chart from the selected data. Furthermore, this macro will delete the legend, add a title, size the chart to be 300 x 200, and position the chart at the lower-right corner of the selected range.

The macro that meets these requirements (named `CreateChart`) follows.

```
Sub CreateChart()
    Dim DataRange As Range
    Dim ChtObj As ChartObject
    Dim ChtTop As Long, ChtLeft As Long
    If TypeName(Selection) <> "Range" Then Exit Sub
    Set DataRange = Selection
    ChtTop = DataRange.Top + DataRange.Height
    ChtLeft = DataRange.Left + DataRange.Width
    Set ChtObj = ActiveSheet.ChartObjects.Add(ChtLeft, ChtTop, 300, 200)
    With ChtObj.Chart
        .ChartType = xlColumnClustered
        .SetSourceData Source:=DataRange, PlotBy:=xlColumns
        .HasLegend = False
        .HasTitle = True
        .ChartTitle.Text = "Chart Title"
        .Parent.Select
    End With
End Sub
```

The macro starts by declaring five variables that will be used. It then checks to ensure that a range is selected. If not, the macro ends. The `DataRange` variable is set to represent the selected range. Two other variables (`ChtTop` and `ChtLeft`) store the top and left coordinates of the new chart. These variables are calculated using the metrics of the selected range.

Next, a `ChartObject` object is added, using the `Add` method of the `ChartObjects` collection. Note that the recorded macro used the `Add` method of the `Charts` collection. This added a new Chart sheet, which was eventually relocated to the worksheet. Adding a new `ChartObject` is a more efficient approach because you can specify the size and position (as arguments) when it's created.

The remainder of the code sets various properties of the `Chart` object contained in the `ChartObject` object. The final statement (`Parent.Select`) selects the created `ChartObject`.

This basic macro can be modified in a number of ways. For example, you can specify a different chart type, set colors, add or remove gridlines, and so on.

Creating a chart from data on different worksheets

The example in this section uses a workbook that contains five worksheets. The `CreateFiveCharts` macro creates an embedded chart from the data on each sheet. One slight hitch is that the data in each sheet is not consistent – the sheets vary in the number of data rows, and each chart needs to use the data in the last row. Figure 16-9 shows one of the worksheets (the others are similar but have a different number of rows).

	A	B	C	D	E	F
1	**Region 2**					
2						
3	Sales Rep	Jan Sales	Feb Sales	Mar Sales	Q1 Total	
4	Johnson	$9,282	$3,486	$9,483	$22,251	
5	Wilson	$11,493	$10,696	$8,497	$30,686	
6	Hernandez	$10,172	$8,139	$9,704	$28,015	
7	Cavalier	$10,356	$3,251	$6,955	$20,562	
8	Wesner	$12,630	$3,763	$5,364	$21,757	
9	Pittman	$4,649	$8,484	$11,237	$24,370	
10	Total	$58,582	$37,819	$51,240	$147,641	
11						

Figure 16-9: One of five worksheets that will be used to create a chart

Although the following macro may seem complicated, it's really very straightforward. It loops through the sheets, creates a chart, and applies several types of customizations to the chart. The appropriate objects and properties were determined by using the macro recorder, and then the recorded code was incorporated into the macro. In other words, this macro was created in a number of small steps.

```
Sub CreateFiveCharts()
    Dim ChtObj As ChartObject
    Dim ChtTop As Long, ChtLeft As Long
    Dim ChtHeight As Long, ChtWidth As Long
    Dim Sht As Worksheet
    Dim LastRow As Long

    ChtTop = 1
```

```
        ChtLeft = 1
        ChtHeight = 180
        ChtWidth = 300
        Application.ScreenUpdating = False
        For Each Sht In ActiveWorkbook.Worksheets
            If Sht.Name <> ActiveSheet.Name Then
                LastRow = Sht.Range("B65536").End(xlUp).Row
                Set ChtObj = ActiveSheet.ChartObjects.Add _
                  (ChtLeft, ChtTop, ChtWidth, ChtHeight)
                'Add a series
                ChtObj.Chart.SeriesCollection.NewSeries
                With ChtObj.Chart.SeriesCollection(1)
                    .Values = Sht.Range(Sht.Cells(LastRow, 2), Sht.Cells(LastRow, 4))
                    .XValues = Sht.Range("B3:D3")
                    .Interior.ColorIndex = 3
                End With
                With ChtObj.Chart
                    'Specify chart type
                    .ChartType = xlColumnClustered
                    'Adjust the gap width
                    .ChartGroups(1).GapWidth = 20
                    'Remove color from Plot Area
                    .PlotArea.Interior.ColorIndex = xlNone
                    'Set font size
                    .ChartArea.Font.Size = 9
                    'Remove legend
                    .HasLegend = False
                    'Add title
                    .HasTitle = True
                    .ChartTitle.Text = Sht.Range("A1")
                    'Adjust scale
                    .Axes(xlValue).MinimumScale = 0
                    .Axes(xlValue).MaximumScale = 120000
                    'Modify gridlines
                    .Axes(xlValue).MajorGridlines.Border.LineStyle = xlDot
                End With
                ChtTop = ChtTop + ChtHeight
            End If
        Next Sht
        Application.ScreenUpdating = True
    End Sub
```

The macro starts by declaring the variables that are used. The `ChtTop` variable is used to position the charts (they are stacked vertically). The code then loops through each worksheet, but skips the active worksheet (the one that will contain the charts).

The charts plot the data in the last row. Because the number of rows varies, the last row must be determined dynamically. The last row of the worksheet is determined by using the End method. This is similar to activating the last cell in a column and then pressing End, followed by Up Arrow.

Next, a ChartObject is inserted and a new series is created by using the NewSeries method. Subsequent statements assign the data range (the Values property) and the category labels range (the Xvalues property). Note that the category labels range is in the same range on each sheet, so this range does not have to be determined by the code. The next statement changes the color of the columns.

The next series of statements applies various types of adjustments on the chart. Finally, the ChtTop variable is updated, ready to be used for the next chart's positioning. Notice that screen updating is turned off at the beginning of the macro. On slower systems, having this off may speed up the macro a bit.

Sizing and Aligning Charts

When you work with several embedded charts, you may prefer that the charts are all the same size and aligned. The following macro does the job.

```
Sub SizeAndAlignCharts()
    Dim ChtWidth As Long, ChtHeight As Long
    Dim TopPosition As Long, LeftPosition As Long
    Dim ChtObj As ChartObject
    If ActiveChart Is Nothing Then Exit Sub
    'Get size of active chart
    ChtWidth = ActiveChart.Parent.Width
    ChtHeight = ActiveChart.Parent.Height
    TopPosition = ActiveChart.Parent.Top
    LeftPosition = ActiveChart.Parent.Left
    'Loop through all Chart Objects
    For Each ChtObj In ActiveSheet.ChartObjects
        ChtObj.Width = ChtWidth
        ChtObj.Height = ChtHeight
        ChtObj.Top = TopPosition
        ChtObj.Left = LeftPosition
        TopPosition = TopPosition + ChtObj.Height
    Next ChtObj
End Sub
```

The SizeAndAlignCharts macro requires that a chart is active, and uses this chart as a "base." The procedure resizes all other charts on the sheet such that they are the same size as the active chart. In addition, the charts are repositioned so they are all aligned vertically.

The `TopPosition` variable stores the vertical position of the chart and is modified each time through the loop. The new vertical position is the previous vertical position plus the height of the `ChartObject` object. The result is a stack of charts, neatly aligned with no space in between each.

The JWalk Chart Tools add-in, available on the companion CD-ROM, includes a utility to resize all charts on the active sheet so that they match the active chart (see Figure 16-10).

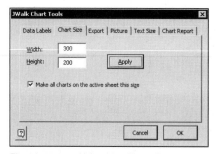

Figure 16-10: Using the Chart Size utility from the JWalk Chart Tools add-in

Applying Data Labels

As you may know, applying data labels to a chart series has a serious limitation: Excel does not enable you to specify an arbitrary range for the data label text. With a fairly simple macro, however, you can overcome this limitation and apply data labels from any range.

A basic data label macro

Figure 16-11 shows an XY chart. The goal is to label each point with the corresponding name in column A. The following macro accomplishes this goal.

```
Sub ApplyDataLabels()
    Dim Ser As Series, Pt As Point
    Dim Counter As Long
    Set Ser = ActiveSheet.ChartObjects(1).Chart.SeriesCollection(1)
    Ser.HasDataLabels = True
    Counter = 1
```

```
    For Each Pt In Ser.Points
        Pt.DataLabel.Text = Range("A1").Offset(Counter, 0)
        Counter = Counter + 1
    Next Pt
End Sub
```

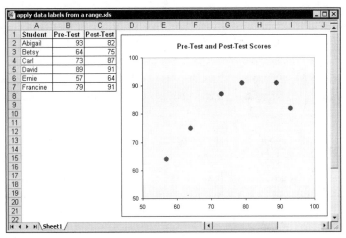

Figure 16-11: Excel does not provide a direct way to use the text in column A as data labels in the chart.

The `ApplyDataLabels` macro creates an object variable (`Ser`) that represents the chart's data series. It then sets the `HasDataLabels` property to True (without this statement, the macro would end with an error). The next statement initializes a variable (`Counter`) to 1. The next four statements comprise a `For Each-Next` loop, which loops through each `Point` object in the series. The code sets the `Text` property of the `Point` object's `DataLabel` object equal to a cell that is offset from cell A1. The offset row is specified by the `Counter` variable, which is incremented each time through the loop.

Applying linked data labels

A data label can contain a simple formula that refers to a cell. In such a case, the data label is linked to that cell — if the cell changes, so does the corresponding data label. It's a simple matter to modify this macro so that it creates links to the cells. Only one statement needs to be changed:

```
Pt.DataLabel.Text = "=" & Range("A1").Offset(Counter, 0) _
    .Address(True, True, xlR1C1, True)
```

This statement inserts an equal sign (to indicate a formula), followed by the Address property of the cell. The Address property takes four arguments. After executing the modified macro, the first data label in the series contains this formula:

```
=Sheet1!$A$2
```

The arguments for the Address property specify that the cell address be represented as an absolute reference (arguments 1 and 2), in R1C1 reference style (argument 3), and in "external" format (argument 4). Using the external format ensures that the sheet name is appended to the cell reference. The requirement to use an R1C1 reference style is an unusual quirk that's not documented.

Prompting for a range

The preceding macros hard-code the data label range, so they are not general-purpose macros. A better approach is to specify the range interactively. The following macro uses the InputBox method to display a simple dialog box in which the user can specify a range by clicking a cell (see Figure 16-12).

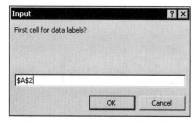

Figure 16-12: The InputBox method prompts the user for a range.

The DataLabelsWithPrompt macro, which follows, is similar to the preceding macros but contains additional code to display the dialog box. The cell specified by the user is assigned to a Range object variable (RngLabels). Notice that there's a statement that checks to see whether RngLabels is Nothing. That will be the case if the user clicks the Cancel button. If so, the macro ends with no action. The On Error Resume Next statement is present because clicking Cancel causes an error. That statement simply ignores the error. Also, notice the second Set statement that uses the RngLabels object. This statement ensures that if the user selects a multicell range, only the first cell in the selected range is assigned to RngLabels.

```
Sub DataLabelsWithPrompt()
    Dim RngLabels As Range
```

```
    Dim Ser As Series
    Dim i As Long
    On Error Resume Next
    Set RngLabels = Application.InputBox _
      (prompt:="First cell for data labels?", Type:=8)
    If RngLabels Is Nothing Then Exit Sub 'Canceled
    Set RngLabels = RngLabels(1)
    On Error GoTo 0
    Set Ser = ActiveSheet.ChartObjects(1).Chart.SeriesCollection(1)
    Ser.HasDataLabels = True
    Counter = 0
    For Each Pt In Ser.Points
        Pt.DataLabel.Text = RngLabels.Offset(Counter, 0)
        Counter = Counter + 1
    Next Pt
End Sub
```

 The JWalk Chart Tools add-in, available on the companion CD-ROM, includes a utility to apply data labels to the active chart.

Exporting Charts as GIF Files

Saving a chart as a GIF file is very easy: Just use the `Export` method of the `Chart` object. Here's a simple macro that saves the active chart as a GIF file named mychart.gif:

```
Sub ExportToGIF()
    If ActiveChart Is Nothing Then
        MsgBox "Select a chart."
    Else
        ActiveChart.Export "mychart.gif", "GIF"
    End If
End Sub
```

The macro first checks to ensure that a chart is active. If so, it saves the chart to the current directory.

If you prefer to be prompted for a filename and location, use the macro that follows. This macro uses the `GetSaveAsFilename` function to display a dialog box with a default filename (the chart's name) and directory. The user can then accept these defaults or select a different directory or filename. Figure 16-13 shows the dialog box that's displayed when this macro is executed. If the Cancel button is clicked, the function returns False. In such a case, the macro ends with no action.

```vba
Sub SaveAsGIF()
    Dim FileName As Variant
    If ActiveChart Is Nothing Then
        MsgBox "Select a chart."
        Exit Sub
    End If
'   Get the filename
    FileName = Application.GetSaveAsFilename( _
        InitialFileName:=ActiveChart.Name & ".gif", _
        FileFilter:="GIF Files (*.gif), *.gif", _
        Title:="Save chart as GIF file")
    If FileName <> False Then
        ActiveChart.Export FileName, "GIF"
    End If
End Sub
```

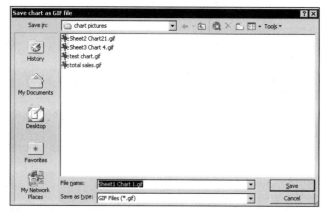

Figure 16-13: Using the `GetSaveAsFilename` function to prompt for a filename and directory

The JWalk Chart Tools add-in, available on the companion CD-ROM, includes a utility to export charts as GIF files.

VBA Speed Tips

VBA is fast, but it's often not fast enough. Following are a few tips to maximize the speed of your macros.

Turning off screen updating

You've probably noticed that when you execute a macro, you can watch everything that occurs in the macro. Sometimes this is instructive, but after you get the macro working properly, it can be annoying and slow things considerably. Fortunately, there's a way to disable the normal screen updating that occurs when you execute a macro. Insert the following statement to turn screen updating off:

```
Application.ScreenUpdating = False
```

If, at any point during the macro, you want the user to see the results of the macro, use the following statement to turn screen updating back on:

```
Application.ScreenUpdating = True
```

Preventing alert messages

One of the benefits of using a macro is that you can perform a series of actions automatically. You can start a macro and then get a cup of coffee while Excel does its thing. Some operations cause Excel to display messages that must be attended to, however. For example, if your macro deletes a sheet, you see a warning message. These types of messages mean that you can't execute your macro unattended.

To avoid these alert messages, insert the following VBA statement:

```
Application.DisplayAlerts = False
```

When the procedure ends, the `DisplayAlerts` property is automatically reset to True (its normal state).

Simplifying object references

As you probably have discovered, references to objects can get very lengthy — especially if your code refers to an object that's not on the active sheet or in the active workbook. For example, a fully qualified reference to a `Series` object may look like this:

```
Workbooks("MyBook").Worksheets("Sheet1").ChartObjects(1).Chart.SeriesCollection(1)
```

If your macro uses this range frequently, you may want to create an object variable by using the `Set` command. For example, to assign this `Series` object to an object variable named `ChtSer`, use the following statement:

```
Set ChtSer = Workbooks("MyBook").Worksheets("Sheet1"). _
   ChartObjects(1).Chart.SeriesCollection(1)
```

Continued

VBA Speed Tips *(Continued)*

After this variable is defined, you can use the variable `ChtSer` instead of the lengthy reference.

Declaring variable types

Usually, you don't have to worry about the type of data that's assigned to a variable. Excel handles all these details behind the scenes. For example, if you have a variable named `MyVar`, you can assign a number or any type to it. You can even assign a text string to it later in the procedure.

But if you want your procedures to execute as fast as possible, you should tell Excel in advance what type of data is going be assigned to each of your variables. This is known as declaring a variable's type. Chapter 14 contains additional information about data types.

Determining the Ranges Used in a Chart

You might need a VBA macro that must determine the ranges used by each series in chart. For example, you may want to increase the size of each series by adding a new cell. Following is a description of three properties that seem relevant to this task:

◆ **Formula property:** Returns or sets the SERIES formula for the Series. When you select a series in a chart, its SERIES formula is displayed in the formula bar. The `Formula` property returns this formula as a string.

◆ **Values property:** Returns or sets a collection of all the values in the series. This can be a range on a worksheet or an array of constant values, but not a combination of both.

◆ **XValues property:** Returns or sets an array of x values for a chart series. The `XValues` property can be set to a range on a worksheet or to an array of values — but it can't be a combination of both. The `Xvalues` property can also be empty.

If you create a VBA macro that needs to determine the data range used by a particular chart series, you may think that the `Values` property of the `Series` object is just the ticket. Similarly, the `XValues` property seems to be the way to get the range that contains the x values (or category labels). In theory, that certainly *seems* correct. But in practice, it doesn't work. When you set the `Values` property for a `Series` object, you can specify a `Range` object or an array. But when you read this property, it is always an array. Unfortunately, the object model provides no way to get a `Range` object used by a `Series` object.

One possible solution is to write code to parse the SERIES formula and extract the range addresses. This sounds simple, but it's actually a difficult task because a SERIES formula can be very complex. Following are a few examples of valid SERIES formulas.

```
=SERIES(Sheet1!$B$1,Sheet1!$A$2:$A$4,Sheet1!$B$2:$B$4,1)
=SERIES(,,Sheet1!$B$2:$B$4,1)
=SERIES(,Sheet1!$A$2:$A$4,Sheet1!$B$2:$B$4,1)
=SERIES("Sales Summary",,Sheet1!$B$2:$B$4,1)
=SERIES(,{"Jan","Feb","Mar"},Sheet1!$B$2:$B$4,1)
=SERIES(,(Sheet1!$A$2,Sheet1!$A$4),(Sheet1!$B$2,Sheet1!$B$4),1)
=SERIES(Sheet1!$B$1,Sheet1!$A$2:$A$4,Sheet1!$B$2:$B$4,1,Sheet1!$C$2:$C$4)
```

As you can see, a SERIES formula can have missing arguments, use arrays, and even use noncontiguous range addresses. And to confuse the issue even more, a bubble chart has an additional argument (for example, the last SERIES formula in the preceding list). Attempting to parse out the arguments is certainly not a trivial programming task.

I worked on this problem for several years, and I eventually arrived at a solution. The trick involves evaluating the SERIES formula by using a dummy function. This function accepts the arguments in a SERIES formula and returns a 2 x 5 element array that contains all the information in the SERIES formula.

I simplified the solution by creating four custom VBA functions, each of which accepts one argument (a reference to a Series object) and returns a two-element array. These functions are the following:

◆ **SERIESNAME_FROM_SERIES:** The first array element contains a string that describes the data type of the first SERIES argument (*Range, Empty,* or *String*). The second array element contains a range address, an empty string, or a string.

◆ **XVALUES_FROM_SERIES:** The first array element contains a string that describes the data type of the second SERIES argument (*Range, Array, Empty,* or *String*). The second array element contains a range address, an array, an empty string, or a string.

◆ **VALUES_FROM_SERIES:** The first array element contains a string that describes the data type of the third SERIES argument (*Range* or *Array*). The second array element contains a range address or an array.

◆ **BUBBLESIZE_FROM_SERIES:** The first array element contains a string that describes the data type of the fifth SERIES argument (*Range, Array,* or *Empty*). The second array element contains a range address, an array, or an empty string. This function is relevant only for bubble charts.

Note that there is not a function to get the fourth SERIES argument (plot order). This argument can be obtained directly by using the PlotOrder property of the Series object.

The following example demonstrates. It displays the address of the values range for the first series in the active chart.

```
Sub ShowValueRange()
    Dim Ser As Series
    Dim x As Variant
    Set Ser = ActiveChart.SeriesCollection(1)
    x = VALUES_FROM_SERIES(Ser)
    If x(1) = "Range" Then
        MsgBox Range(x(2)).Address
    End If
End Sub
```

The variable x is defined as a variant and will hold the two-element array that's returned by the VALUES_FROM_SERIES function. The first element of the x array contains a string that describes the data type. It the string is *Range*, then the message box displays the address of the range contained in the second element of the x array.

The VBA code for these functions is too complex to be presented here, but it's available on the companion CD-ROM. It's documented such that it can be easily adapted to other situations.

Protecting Charts

You're probably familiar with the ability to protect a worksheet using the Tools→Protection→Protect Sheet command. When a worksheet is protected, "locked" cells cannot be changed. By default, all cells are locked. They can be unlocked by using the Protection tab of the Format Cells dialog box. Protecting a sheet also disables modification of any embedded charts on the worksheet.

You may have also discovered that you can protect a Chart sheet — also by using the Tools→Protection→Protect Sheet command. When a Chart sheet is protected, the chart cannot be modified.

Beginning with Excel 2002, sheet protection has become more versatile. When you protect a sheet, you are presented with a list of options that can be performed when the sheet is protected. Among those options is Edit Objects. When this option is enabled, charts can still be edited when the sheet is protected.

Are Protected Sheets Secure?

Contrary to popular belief, protecting a worksheet with a password is not a security feature — it's a convenience feature. Sheet protection is intended primarily to prevent accidental erasure of cells. In a typical scenario, formula cells are locked and data input cells are not locked. Then, when the sheet is protected, the formula cells cannot be deleted or overwritten by values. It is a fairly simple matter to "crack" the password for a protected sheet.

Chart protection properties

Excel offers some other types of chart protection that most people don't know about. Specifically, a Chart object has the following protection-related properties (all these have a value of False, by default):

◆ **ProtectData:** If True, the SERIES formula cannot be modified.

◆ **ProtectFormatting:** If True, the chart's formatting cannot be modified.

◆ **ProtectSelection:** If True, chart elements cannot be selected.

◆ **ProtectGoalSeek:** If True, the user cannot modify the chart's data by dragging a data point.

It's important to understand that these properties are not persistent. In other words, they are not saved with the workbook. For example, if you execute a macro that sets a chart's ProtectData property to True, that property will be False when the workbook is closed and re-opened. You'll need to rerun the macro to set the property to True.

Protecting all charts when the workbook is opened

Excel provides a way to execute a macro automatically when the workbook is opened. This is done by using a procedure named Workbook_Open, which must be located in the code module for the ThisWorkbook object.

The following procedure is executed when the workbook opens. It loops though all worksheets and through all charts on each worksheet. It sets the ProtectFormatting property to True. In other words, after this procedure executes, no embedded charts can be formatted.

```
Private Sub Workbook_Open()
    Dim Wks As Worksheet
    Dim ChtObj As ChartObject
    For Each Wks In ThisWorkbook.Worksheets
        For Each ChtObj In Wks.ChartObjects
            ChtObj.Chart.ProtectFormatting = True
        Next ChtObj
    Next Wks
End Sub
```

Modifying Chart sheet protection properties directly

The preceding macros in this section were written for embedded charts. If you're working with a chart on a Chart sheet, the four chart protection properties listed previously can be set directly. Here's how to do it:

1. Activate a Chart sheet.

2. Right-click any toolbar and choose Control Toolbox to display the Control Toolbox toolbar.

3. Click the Properties button on the Control Toolbox toolbar. This displays the Properties box.

4. Make the changes to the appropriate properties (see Figure 16-14).

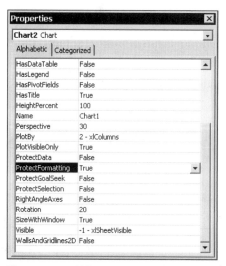

Figure 16-14: Using the Properties box to set the protection properties of a chart on a Chart sheet

Creating a Scrolling Chart

Figure 16-15 shows a stock market chart that uses named formulas for the series data. Cell I1 (named *StartRow*) specifies the starting row of the data, and cell I2 (named *NumDays*) controls how many days are plotted. Changing either or both of these cells causes the chart to display the appropriate data. The data consists of 747 days of data, spanning three years.

Refer to Chapter 6 for more information regarding the use of named formulas for chart series.

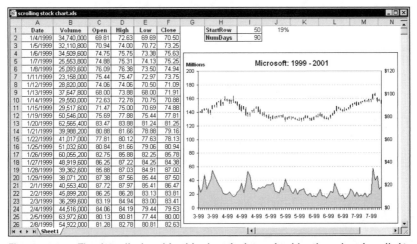

Figure 16-15: The data displayed in this chart is determined by the values in cells I1 and I2.

This workbook also contains a simple macro that increments the *StartRow* cell within a loop. The result is an animated chart that scrolls to reveal more data. The AnimateChart macro, which is attached to the button in the worksheet, follows:

```
Public AnimationInProgress As Boolean

Sub AnimateChart()
    Dim StartVal As Long, r As Long
    If AnimationInProgress Then
        AnimationInProgress = False
        End
    End If
```

```
    AnimationInProgress = True
    StartVal = Range("StartRow")
    For r = StartVal To 748 - Range("NumDays")
        Range("StartRow") = Range("StartRow") + 1
        DoEvents
    Next r
    AnimationInProgress = False
End Sub
```

This macro uses a Public variable, `AnimationInProgress`, to keep track of whether the chart is being animated. If so, running the macro sets the variable to False, and the procedure ends. This allows a single button to both start and stop the animation.

Event Procedure Examples

It's possible to write macros that respond to certain events. For example, opening a workbook is an event, and you can write a macro (called an *event procedure*) that is executed when that event occurs. For an example of a `Workbook_Open` event procedure, see "Protecting all charts when the workbook is opened," earlier in this chapter.

Worksheet_Change event procedures

The examples in this section deal with the `Worksheet_Change` event, which is one of many events available at the worksheet level. This event is triggered whenever a cell is changed in a worksheet. As you'll see, these types of macros can be very useful to update charts automatically.

The event macros in this section must be located in the code module for the worksheet (for example, the module named Sheet1). They will not work if they are contained in a standard VBA module.

When you activate a code module for a chart, sheet, or workbook, you can use the drop-down lists at the top to select an object and event. Figure 16-16 shows a code module for a worksheet. The object (Worksheet) is selected in the left drop-down list, and the right drop-down list displays all the events that can be monitored for the object. When you choose an item from the list, the procedure "shell" (consisting of the first and last statements) is inserted for you.

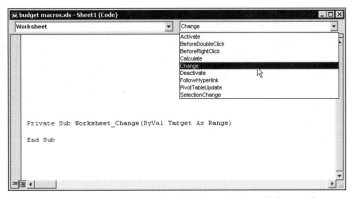

Figure 16-16: Using the drop-down lists in a code module to select an event

HIDING AND DISPLAYING CHARTS

The worksheet shown in Figure 16-17 contains five embedded charts, four of which are hidden. Cell B2 controls which of the five charts is visible. This cell uses Data Validation to display a list of values from 1 through 5, plus an additional entry: *(none)*.

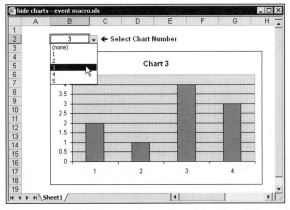

Figure 16-17: Cell B1 contains a drop-down list of chart numbers.
The selected chart number is visible and the others are hidden.

The worksheet uses a Worksheet_Change event procedure, which follows. The macro is executed whenever a cell is changed on the sheet. Notice that this procedure has an argument: Target. This argument is a variable that represents the cell or range that is changed. If the address of Target is $B$2, the macro performs two operations: It hides all members of the ChartObjects collection and then unhides the chart that corresponds to the value in cell B2. The On Error statement ignores the error that occurs if an invalid ChartObject number is referenced.

```
Private Sub Worksheet_Change(ByVal Target As Range)
    If Target.Address = "$B$2" Then
        ActiveSheet.ChartObjects.Visible = False
        On Error Resume Next
        ChartObjects(Target.Value).Visible = True
    End If
End Sub
```

The five embedded charts are stacked on top of each other, so they all appear in the same position on-screen.

ADJUSTING AXIS SCALING

Earlier in this chapter, I present a macro that changes the value axis scaling for a chart (see "Setting axis values"). That macro, when executed, adjusts the chart's value axis properties: MinimumScale, MaximumScale, and MajorUnit.

The macro in this section further automates the task by using an event macro. Figure 16-18 shows the worksheet. The Axis property values are entered in the cells in column D (named *AxisMin*, *AxisMax*, and *MajorUnit*).

```
Private Sub Worksheet_Change(ByVal Target As Range)
    If Target.Column = 4 Then
        With ActiveSheet.ChartObjects(1).Chart.Axes(xlValue)
            .MinimumScale = Range("AxisMin")
            .MaximumScale = Range("AxisMax")
            .MajorUnit = Range("MajorUnit")
        End With
    End If
End Sub
```

This procedure is executed whenever any cell in the sheet is changed. The first statement of the macro checks the Column property of the Target variable, which represents the cell that was changed. If the changed cell is in column 4, the property values are retrieved from the sheet and applied to the chart. Otherwise, nothing happens.

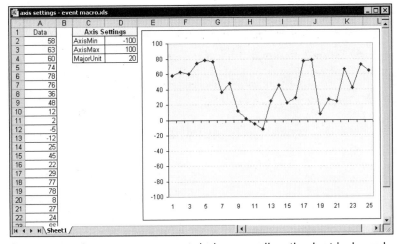

Figure 16-18: An event macro, executed when any cell on the sheet is changed, modifies properties for the chart's Value axis.

Chart event procedures

The preceding examples use an event associated with a worksheet. Chart sheets also have events, and these are listed in Table 16-1.

TABLE 16-1 EVENTS RECOGNIZED BY THE CHART OBJECT

Event	Action that triggers the event
Activate	The chart is activated.
BeforeDoubleClick	An element in the chart is double-clicked. This event occurs before the default double-click action (displaying the Format dialog box).
BeforeRightClick	An element in the chart is right-clicked. The event occurs before the default right-click action (displaying a shortcut menu).
Calculate	The chart receives new or changed data.
Deactivate	The chart is deactivated.

Continued

TABLE 16-1 EVENTS RECOGNIZED BY THE CHART OBJECT *(Continued)*

Event	Action that triggers the event
DragOver	A range of cells is dragged over the chart.
DragPlot	A range of cells is dragged and dropped onto the chart.
MouseDown	A mouse button is pressed while the mouse pointer is over the chart.
MouseMove	The position of the mouse pointer changes over the chart.
MouseUp	A mouse button is released while the pointer is over the chart.
Resize	The chart is resized. For a Chart sheet, this event is triggered only when the Sized with Window option is in effect.
Select	A chart element is selected.
SeriesChange	The value of a chart data point is changed by dragging the point.

Chart event procedures must reside in the code module for the Chart sheet (for example, Chart1). To use Chart event procedures with embedded charts, see the sidebar," Enabling events for an embedded chart."

USING THE MOUSEDOWN EVENT

The MouseDown event occurs when a chart element is clicked. There's also a MouseUp event, which occurs when the user releases the mouse button. Therefore, a single mouse click generates two events. This example focuses on the MouseDown event.

Figure 16-19 shows a chart with three data points in a single series. The goal is to make the chart serve as a clickable menu: Click a column and the corresponding worksheet is activated. For example, when the user clicks the South column in the chart, the worksheet named South will be activated.

Enabling Events for an Embedded Chart

Events are automatically enabled for Chart sheets, but not for charts embedded in a worksheet. To use event procedures with an embedded chart, you need to perform the following steps:

1. **Create a class module.** In the VB Editor window, select your project in the Project window and select Insert→Class Module. This will add a new (empty) class module to your project.

2. **Declare a public Chart object.** The variable should be of type Chart, and it must be declared in the class module using the `WithEvents` keyword. Following is an example of such a declaration:

   ```
   Public WithEvents EmbChart As Chart
   ```

3. **Connect the declared object with your chart.** Do this by declaring an object of type Class1 (or whatever your class module is named). This should be a module-level object variable, declared in a regular VBA module (not in the class module). Here's an example:

   ```
   Dim MyChart As New Class1
   ```

4. **Execute a statement to instantiate the object.** Example:

   ```
   Set MyChart.EmbChart = ActiveSheet.ChartObjects(1).Chart
   ```

   After the preceding statement is executed, the `MyChart` object in the class module points to the first embedded chart on the active sheet. Consequently, the event-handler procedures in the class module will execute when the events occur.

5. **Write event procedures for the chart class.** These procedures go in the class module. Here's a simple example:

   ```
   Private Sub EmbChart_Activate()
       MsgBox EmbChart.Parent.Name & " was activated."
   End Sub
   ```

6. **Execute a statement to destroy the object and stop monitoring events.** Example:

   ```
   Set MyChart.EmbChart = Nothing
   ```

All the examples that use Chart events are available in two versions on the CD-ROM: one that uses a Chart sheet and one that uses an embedded chart.

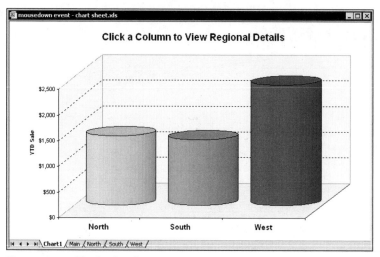

Figure 16-19: Monitoring the `MouseDown` event makes this chart function as a clickable menu.

The `Chart_MouseDown` event procedure follows. This macro is executed whenever a mouse button is clicked on the chart.

```
Private Sub Chart_MouseDown(ByVal Button As Long, _
  ByVal Shift As Long, ByVal X As Long, ByVal Y As Long)
    Dim ElementID As Long
    Dim arg1 As Long, arg2 As Long
    GetChartElement X, Y, ElementID, arg1, arg2
    If ElementID = xlSeries Then
        Select Case arg2
            Case 1
                Sheets("North").Activate
            Case 2
                Sheets("South").Activate
            Case 3
                Sheets("West").Activate
        End Select
    End If
End Sub
```

Notice that the procedure takes several arguments, which are used to determine what was clicked. The arguments important to this procedure are the X and Y variables. These represent the horizontal and vertical coordinates of the mouse pointer when the mouse was clicked. The `GetChartElement` statement uses these coordinates and returns three pieces of information, stored in variables:

◆ **ElementID:** A number that corresponds to the chart element at coordinates X and Y — for example, the value 3 corresponds to a Series. VBA also recognizes the built-in constant, xlSeries, which has a value of 3.

◆ **arg1:** Additional information about the element at coordinates X and Y. If ElementID is the code for a Series, then arg1 returns a number that corresponds to the specific series number.

◆ **arg2:** Still more information about the element at coordinates X and Y. If ElementID is the code for a Series, then arg2 returns the specific data point within the series.

Depending on the value of ElementID, the arg1 and arg2 arguments may not be used. For example, if the Chart Area is clicked, ElementID returns 2 (xlChartArea), and arg1 and arg2 are not relevant.

The chart in this example has only one series, so the Chart_MouseDown procedure focuses on arg2, which will have a value of 1, 2, or 3. A Select Case structure activates the appropriate sheet, based on the value of arg2.

USING THE MOUSEOVER EVENT

A common charting question deals with modifying chart tips. A chart tip is the small message that appears next to the mouse pointer when you move the mouse over a chart. The chart tip displays the chart element name and (for series) the value of the data point. The Chart object model does not expose these chart tips, so there is no way to modify them.

To turn chart tips on or off, choose Tools→Options. Click the Chart tab and select or unselect the two check boxes in the Chart tips section.

This section describes an alternative to chart tips. Figure 16-20 shows a column chart that uses the MouseOver event. When the mouse pointer is positioned over a column, the text box (a shape object) in the upper left displays information about the data point. The information is stored in a range and can consist of anything you like.

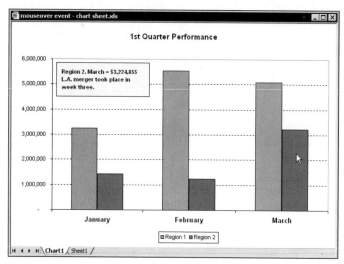

Figure 16-20: A text box displays information about the data point under the mouse pointer.

The event procedure that follows is located in the code module for the Chart sheet that contains the chart.

```
Private Sub Chart_MouseMove(ByVal Button As Long, ByVal Shift As Long, _
   ByVal X As Long, ByVal Y As Long)
    Dim ElementID As Long
    Dim arg1 As Long, arg2 As Long
    Dim NewText As String
    On Error Resume Next
    ActiveChart.GetChartElement X, Y, ElementID, arg1, arg2
    If ElementId = xlSeries Then
        NewText = Sheets("Sheet1").Range("Comments").Offset(arg2, arg1)
    Else
        NewText = ""
        ActiveChart.Shapes(1).Visible = False
    End If
    If NewText <> ActiveChart.Shapes(1).TextFrame.Text Then
        ActiveChart.Shapes(1).TextFrame.Text = NewText
        ActiveChart.Shapes(1).Visible = True
    End If
End Sub
```

This procedure monitors all mouse movements on the Chart sheet. The mouse coordinates are contained in the X and Y variables, which are passed to the procedure. The Button and Shift arguments are not used in this procedure.

As in the previous example, the key component in this procedure is the `GetChartElement` method. If `ElementId` is `xlSeries`, then the mouse pointer is over a series. The `NewText` variable then is assigned the text in a particular cell. This text contains descriptive information about the data point (see Figure 16-21). If the mouse pointer is not over a series, then the text box is hidden. Otherwise, it displays the contents of `NewText`.

	A	B	C
		Region 1	**Region 2**
1			
2	January	3,245,151	1,434,343
3	February	5,546,523	1,238,709
4	March	5,083,204	3,224,855
5			
6	Comments		
7		Region 1, January = $3,245,151	Region 2, January = $1,434,343
8		Region 1, February = $5,546,523 Two-week sales promotion in effect.	Region 2, February = $1,238,709
9		Region 1, March = $5,083,204	Region 2, March = $3,224,855 L.A. merger took place in week three.
10			

Figure 16-21: Range B7:C9 contains data point information that's displayed in the text box on the chart.

Appendix: What's on the CD-ROM

THIS APPENDIX PROVIDES YOU WITH information on the contents of the CD that accompanies this book. For last-minute updates, refer to the ReadMe file located at the root of the CD.

 Most of the Excel workbook files on the CD work with Excel 97 or later.

What's on the CD

The CD-ROM is organized using the following top-level directories:

- ◆ Book PDF
- ◆ Reader
- ◆ Chart Gallery
- ◆ Bonus Material
- ◆ Add-Ins
- ◆ Chapter Examples

The following sections further describe these directories.

The Book PDF directory

The complete text of this book is on the CD in Adobe's Portable Document Format (PDF). You can read the text and search through the file with the Adobe Acrobat Reader (also included on the CD).

The Reader directory

This directory contains a copy of the freeware version Adobe Acrobat Reader. Chances are, this software is already installed on your system. If not, installing the version on the CD will eliminate the need to download it.

The Chart Gallery directory

This directory contains about 250 image files that depict a variety of Excel charts. Most (but not all) of these charts are described in the book. These are GIF (Graphic Interchange Format) files, which can be opened by most graphics software. Chances are, your system already has a file association for viewing GIF files, so you can just double-click a file to view it. If you prefer, you can view the files sequentially using:

- ◆ **An Excel macro.** The Chart Gallery directory contains an Excel workbook named chart viewer.xls. This file contains macros that enable you to view the chart gallery files from within Excel.

- ◆ **Your Web browser.** The Chart Gallery directory contains an HTML file named viewer.htm. Double-click this file to launch your Web browser; use the buttons to view the files. Scripting must be enabled in your browser.

The Bonus Material directory

This directory contains supplementary material for the book. This material is presented in HTML files, so it can be read with any Web browser. Specifically, the files are:

- ◆ **index.htm** – This is the "master" file, which contains hyperlinks to the other files.

- ◆ **excel color system.htm** – This document contains detailed information about how Excel uses color.

- ◆ **chart faq.htm** – This document contains answers to common charting-related questions.

- ◆ **other resources.htm** – This document contains information about additional charting-related resources that you may find useful. It also contains links to related Web sites.

The Add-Ins directory

This directory contains four Excel add-ins (described in the list that follows) that were created by the author. Each add-in is in a separate directory.

Each directory contains a readme.htm file that contains additional information about the add-in, including installation instructions.

- ◆ **Power Utility Pak** – This general purpose add-in adds dozens of features new to Excel. The version on the CD is a 30-day trial version and requires Excel 2000 or later. You can use the coupon in the back of the book to purchase the product at a discounted price.

- ◆ **JWalk Chart Tools** – This add-in consists of six useful chart-related utilities. When the add-in is installed, the Chart menu will display a new menu item: JWalk Chart Tools. In addition, right-clicking an element in a chart will also display this command on the shortcut menu.

- ◆ **Gradient Contour** – This add-in creates a color gradient contour chart, using a 2-D data range (an alternative to Excel's contour chart type). The chart appearance is highly customizable, but it does not update dynamically.

- ◆ **XY Area Fill** – This add-in creates a shape object that fills the area in an XY chart series.

The Chapter Examples directory

This directory contains the Excel workbooks that are used as examples in the book. The directory contains a subdirectory for each chapter. For example, the example files for Chapter 8 are contained in the \Chapter08 directory. Some chapters do not use any example files.

Following is a description of the chapter example files on the CD.

CHAPTER 1 EXAMPLES

- ◆ **chart parts.xls** – Displays various parts of a chart

- ◆ **chart sheet vs embedded.xls** – Contains the same chart as a Chart sheet and as an embedded chart

- ◆ **hands-on example.xls** – Demonstrates the use of the Chart Wizard

CHAPTER 2 EXAMPLES

- ◆ **3-d charts.xls** – Contains examples of 3-D charts

- ◆ **area charts.xls** – Contains examples of area charts

- ◆ **bar charts.xls** – Contains examples of bar charts

- ◆ **bubble charts.xls** – Contains examples of bubble charts

- ◆ **column charts.xls** – Contains examples of column charts

- ◆ **cylinder cone pyramid charts.xls** – Contains examples of cylinder, cone, and pyramid charts

- ◆ **doughnut chart.xls** – Contains examples of doughnut charts

- ◆ **line charts.xls** – Contains examples of line charts

- ◆ **pie charts.xls** – Contains examples of pie charts

- ◆ **radar chart.xls** – Contains examples of radar charts

- ◆ **six chart types.xls** – Shows the same data plotted with six different chart types

- ◆ **stock charts.xls** – Contains examples of 3-D charts

- ◆ **surface chart.xls** – Contains examples of 3-D charts

- ◆ **user-defined type.xls** – Contains the data used to create a custom chart type

- ◆ **xy charts.xls** – Contains examples of 3-D charts

CHAPTER 3 EXAMPLES

- ◆ **add new series.xls** – Used to demonstrate adding a new series to a chart

- ◆ **combination chart.xls** – Contains a chart that combines five chart types

- ◆ **data orientation.xls** – Shows the effect of row vs. column orientation in a column chart

- ◆ **missing data.xls** – Demonstrates various ways to handle missing data

- ◆ **monthly sales.xls** – Demonstrates how to change or extend a series by dragging the range highlighting

- ◆ **named ranges.xls** – Demonstrates the use of named ranges in a SERIES formula

- ◆ **noncontiguous series.xls** – Contains a chart that plots a noncontiguous range

- ◆ **secondary axes.xls** – Contains charts that use secondary axes

- ◆ **series in different sheets.xls** – Contains a chart that uses data contained on other worksheets

- ◆ **series name.xls** – Used to demonstrate how to change a series name

- ◆ **series order.xls** – Demonstrates the effect of changing the series plot order

- ◆ **unlink charts.xls** – Demonstrates two ways to unlink a chart from its data ranges

CHAPTER 4 EXAMPLES

◆ **3-d charts.xls** – – Demonstrates 3-D chart formatting

◆ **axes.xls** – – Demonstrates axis formatting

◆ **borders.xls** – Demonstrates border formatting

◆ **chart area.xls** – Demonstrates chart area formatting

◆ **data labels.xls** – Demonstrates data labels

◆ **data table.xls** – Demonstrates a data table

◆ **gridlines.xls** – Demonstrates gridline formatting

◆ **legend.xls** – Demonstrates legend formatting

◆ **plot area.xls** – Demonstrates plot area formatting

◆ **series.xls** – Demonstrates series formatting

◆ **titles.xls** – Demonstrates chart title formatting

CHAPTER 5 EXAMPLES

◆ **appropriate data.xls** – Demonstrates data that is appropriate (and inappropriate) for a trendline

◆ **error bars.xls** – Demonstrates error bars

◆ **income and expense trendlines.xls** – Contains trendlines for income and expense examples

◆ **linear sales forecast.xls** – Demonstrates linear forecasting of sales data

◆ **linear trend - ht and weight.xls** – Displays a linear trendline for height and weight data

◆ **moving average.xls** – Demonstrates moving averages

◆ **other series enhancements.xls** – Demonstrates a variety of series enhancements

◆ **slope calculation.xls** – Contains formulas to calculate the slope, y-intercept, and r-squared values

◆ **trendline equations.xls** – Demonstrates how to calculate the coefficients for trendlines

CHAPTER 6 EXAMPLES

- ◆ **annotate charts.xls** – Contains examples of charts that have been annotated in various ways

- ◆ **call attention to cell.xls** – Contains an example of using AutoShapes to call attention to a particular cell

- ◆ **copy cells as pictures.xls** – An example of a chart that contains a range of cells, pasted as a picture

- ◆ **diagrams.xls** – Contains examples of the Excel 2002 diagram tools

- ◆ **flow diagram.xls** – Contains a simple flow chart

- ◆ **grouped shape and chart.xls** – Contains examples of charts that have been grouped with AutoShapes

- ◆ **overlay chart.xls** – Contains two charts, one overlaid on the other

- ◆ **picture in plot area of chart.xls** – Contains examples of charts that use a picture in the plot area

- ◆ **shapes in a chart series.xls** – Contains examples of charts that use AutoShapes in their data series

- ◆ **transparent column.xls** – Contains a chart in which the columns have been made transparent

- ◆ **word art.xls** – Contains examples of WordArt

CHAPTER 7 EXAMPLES

- ◆ **chart with scrollbar.xls** – Demonstrates using a scrollbar to determine the number of data points to plot

- ◆ **climate data.xls** – Contains an interactive chart that compares monthly climate data for two cities

- ◆ **daily.xls** – The hands-on example of creating a self-expanding chart

- ◆ **define series based on active cell - F9.xls** – Demonstrates a technique to define a chart series based on the active cell

- ◆ **define series based on active cell - macro.xls** – Demonstrates a technique to define a chart series based on the active cell (macro-driven version)

- ◆ **first and last point in series.xls** – Demonstrates how to use cells to determine the beginning and end points for a chart series

◆ **first point and number of points.xls** – Demonstrates how to use cells to determine the beginning and end point and the number of data points for a chart series

◆ **plot data in active row - F9.xls** – Demonstrates a technique to plot the data contained in the row that contains the cell pointer

◆ **plot data in active row - macro.xls** – Demonstrates a technique to plot the data contained in the row that contains the cell pointer (macro-driven version)

◆ **plot every nth value.xls** – Demonstrates how to plot every nth data point

◆ **plot last n data points.xls** – Demonstrates how to plot the last n data points

◆ **select series with checkboxes.xls** – Demonstrates how to use checkboxes to select series to display

CHAPTER 8 EXAMPLES

◆ **3d scatter plot - rotate.xls** – Contains a simulation of a 3-D scatter chart, with animation

◆ **area under a curve.xls** – Demonstrates how to calculate the area under a curve

◆ **bands in XY chart.xls** – Demonstrates how to display horizontal or vertical bands in an XY chart

◆ **bar and XY combination.xls** – Demonstrates how to display a line on a bar chart

◆ **box plot.xls** – Demonstrates how to create box plots

◆ **broken axis.xls** – Demonstrates two way to simulate a "broken" axis

◆ **conditional formatting.xls** – Demonstrates how to vary the colors in a column chart, based on values

◆ **data labels as markers.xls** – Demonstrates how to use data labels as markers in an XY chart

◆ **dummy axis.xls** – Demonstrates how to create a dummy axis

◆ **frequency distributions.xls** – Contains examples of frequency distributions and histograms

◆ **function plot 2D.xls** – A general purpose application to plot functions with one variable

- **function plot 3D.xls** – A general purpose application to plot functions with two variables

- **function plots.xls** – Contains simple examples of one- and two-variable function plots

- **gantt chart.xls** – Demonstrates how to create a simple Gantt chart

- **gradient contour demo.xls** – Compares Excel's contour chart with a gradient contour chart created with an add-in.

- **horizontal reference line.xls** – Demonstrates how to display a horizontal line on a column chart

- **identify max and min data points.xls** – Demonstrates how to identify the largest and smallest data point in a line chart

- **non-chart charts.xls** – Demonstrates a few ways to plot data without using a chart

- **normal distribution.xls** – Demonstrates how to plot a normal distribution (bell curve)

- **overlay charts.xls** – Contains examples of charts that are made up of two or more charts overlaid

- **population pyramid.xls** – Demonstrates how to create a population pyramid chart (comparative histogram)

- **shade between lines.xls** – Demonstrates how to apply shading between two line series

- **single data point charts.xls** – Contains several examples of charts that plot a single data point

- **stacked and grouped.xls** – Contains examples of charts that are stacked on top of each other, and then grouped together

- **stacked column chart variations.xls** – Contains several examples of stack column charts

- **step chart.xls** – Demonstrates how to create a step chart

- **text time line.xls** – Demonstrates how to create a simple time line that displays text

- **vary column width.xls** – Demonstrates how to create a column chart in which the width of the columns vary

- **vertical and horizontal bands.xls** – Demonstrates how to display vertical or horizontal bands in a chart

♦ **vertical line in column chart.xls** – Demonstrates how to display a vertical divider line in a column chart

♦ **xy chart circles.xls** – Demonstrates how to create circles (or squares) in an XY chart

♦ **xy chart variations.xls** – Contains several examples of XY charts with various enhancements

♦ **xy chart with colored quadrants.xls** – Demonstrates how to create an XY chart with four colored quadrants

♦ **xy charts as maps.xls** – Demonstrates how to create a map with an XY chart

♦ **z-score plot.xls** – Contains an example of a chart that displays z-scores

CHAPTER 9 EXAMPLES

♦ **bank data.xls** – Contains the bank database

♦ **employee list.xls** – Contains a database that demonstrates how to tabulate non-numeric data

♦ **frequency distribution chart.xls** – Demonstrates how to create a frequency distribution (histogram) from a pivot table

♦ **mileage records.xls** – Demonstrates item grouping, by date, in a pivot table

♦ **pivot chart from multiple sheets.xls** – Demonstrates how to create a pivot table using data on multiple worksheets

♦ **select row to plot.xls** – Contains a simple interactive pivot chart

CHAPTER 10 EXAMPLES

♦ **paste picture formats.xls** – Contains a chart copied and pasted in each of Excel's paste formats

♦ **save charts as GIF files.xls** – Contains a simple macro to save all embedded charts as GIF files

CHAPTER 12 EXAMPLES

♦ **analog clock chart.xls** – Displays a clock in an XY chart

♦ **animated charts.xls** – Contains several animated charts

♦ **animated shapes.xls** – Contains several animated AutoShapes

- **bubble chart mouse.xls** – Contains a mouse face in a bubble chart
- **contour chart patterns.xls** – Displays patterns using a contour chart
- **debbie gewand.xls** – Contains examples of custom clip art created from AutoShapes
- **dice roller.xls** – Simulates rolling two dice
- **doughnut chart spinner.xls** – A wheel of fortune in a doughnut chart
- **hypocycloid – animated.xls** – Displays an infinite number of colorful, animated curves
- **hypocycloid.xls** – Displays an infinite number of interesting curves
- **mountain ranges.xls** – A mountain range in an area chart
- **plot sin and cosine.xls** – Demonstrates how to plot trigonometric functions
- **radar chart designs.xls** – Displays interesting designs in a radar chart
- **xy sketch.xls** – Create simple designs in an XY chart

CHAPTER 15 EXAMPLES

- **hands-on macro recording.xls** – Contains the example recorded macro, plus the cleaned up version.

CHAPTER 16 EXAMPLES

- **apply data labels from a range.xls** – Macros that apply data labels stored in a range
- **axis settings - event macro.xls** – Demonstrates setting axis scaling using the `Worksheet_Change` event
- **axis settings.xls** – Contains a macro to change axis scaling using values stored in cells
- **axis scaling - calculate event** – Demonstrates axis scaling using the `Worksheet_Calculate` event
- **change chart location.xls** – Contains macros that change embedded charts to chart sheets, and vice versa
- **change series colors.xls** – Contains macros that change the colors used in column chart series
- **chart events - chart sheet.xls** – Demonstrates various events for a chart sheet

- ◆ **chart events - embedded chart.xls** – Demonstrates various events for an embedded chart

- ◆ **chart protection.xls** – Contains macros to protect and unprotect various aspects of a chart

- ◆ **conditional formatting.xls** – Contains a macro to change column colors based on values

- ◆ **create a chart.xls** – Contains a macro to create a chart using the selected data range

- ◆ **create five charts.xls** – Contains a macro to create a chart for the data in five worksheets

- ◆ **data label macro.xls** – Contains a macro that uses an Input Box to prompt for a range that contains data labels

- ◆ **freeze text size.xls** – Contains a macro to free the font size of chart text items

- ◆ **get series ranges.xls** – Contains functions that determine the data type and values of data used in a chart series

- ◆ **hide charts - event macro.xls** – Demonstrates the use of a `Worksheet_Change` event procedure to hide and unhide charts

- ◆ **looping through charts.xls** – Contains macros that use loops to perform operations on all charts

- ◆ **mousedown event - chart sheet.xls** – Demonstrates the `MouseDown` event for a chart sheet

- ◆ **mousedown event - embedded chart.xls** – Demonstrates the `MouseDown` event for an embedded chart

- ◆ **mouseover event - chart sheet.xls** – Demonstrates the `MouseOver` event for a chart sheet

- ◆ **mouseover event - embedded chart.xls** – Demonstrates the `MouseOver` event for an embedded chart

- ◆ **print all charts.xls** – Contains a macro to print all embedded charts on a separate page

- ◆ **random gradient.xls** – Contains a macro to apply a random two-color gradient to a chart series

- ◆ **save as gif.xls** – Contains a macro to save a chart as a GIF file

- ◆ **scrolling stock chart.xls** – Contains a macro to scroll a chart horizontally

- ◆ **size and align charts.xls** – Contains a macro to size and align all embedded charts

◆ **transparent series.xls** – Contains a macro to make chart series colors transparent

◆ **what object is selected.xls** – Contains a macro that displays the type of chart element that is selected

Troubleshooting

If you have difficulty installing or using any of the materials on the companion CD, try the following solutions:

◆ **Turn off any anti-virus software that you may have running.** Installers sometimes mimic virus activity and can make your computer incorrectly believe that it is being infected by a virus. (Be sure to turn the anti-virus software back on later.)

◆ **Close all running programs.** The more programs you're running, the less memory is available to other programs. Installers also typically update files and programs; if you keep other programs running, installation may not work properly.

◆ **Reference the ReadMe.** Please refer to the ReadMe file located at the root of the CD-ROM for the latest product information at the time of publication.

◆ **CD-ROM files are read-only.** Keep in mind that files on a CD-ROM are read-only files. Therefore, if you open a workbook file from the CD-ROM and make changes to it, you cannot save it back to the CD. You'll need to save the modified file to your hard drive.

If you still have trouble with the CD, please call the Wiley Customer Care phone number: (800) 762-2974. Outside the United States, call 1 (317) 572-3994. You can also contact Wiley Customer Service by e-mail at techsupdum@wiley.com. Wiley Publishing, Inc. will provide technical support only for installation and other general quality control items; for technical support on the applications themselves, consult the program's vendor or author.

Index

Symbols and Numerics

continued

continued

continued

Wiley Publishing, Inc.
End-User License Agreement

4. <u>Restrictions on Use of Individual Programs</u>. You must follow the individual requirements and restrictions detailed for each individual program in the About the CD-ROM appendix of this Book. These limitations are also contained in the individual license agreements recorded on the Software Media. These limitations may include a requirement that after using the program for a specified period of time, the user must pay a registration fee or discontinue use. By opening the Software packet(s), you will be agreeing to abide by the licenses and restrictions for these individual programs that are detailed in the About the CD-ROM appendix and on the Software Media. None of the material on this Software Media or listed in this Book may ever be redistributed, in original or modified form, for commercial purposes.

5. <u>Limited Warranty</u>.

(a) WPI warrants that the Software and Software Media are free from defects in materials and workmanship under normal use for a period of sixty (60) days from the date of purchase of this Book. If WPI receives notification within the warranty period of defects in materials or workmanship, WPI will replace the defective Software Media.

(b) WPI AND THE AUTHOR OF THE BOOK DISCLAIM ALL OTHER WARRANTIES, EXPRESS OR IMPLIED, INCLUDING WITHOUT LIMITATION IMPLIED WARRANTIES OF MERCHANTABILITY AND FITNESS FOR A PARTICULAR PURPOSE, WITH RESPECT TO THE SOFTWARE, THE PROGRAMS, THE SOURCE CODE CONTAINED THEREIN, AND/OR THE TECHNIQUES DESCRIBED IN THIS BOOK. WPI DOES NOT WARRANT THAT THE FUNCTIONS CONTAINED IN THE SOFTWARE WILL MEET YOUR REQUIREMENTS OR THAT THE OPERATION OF THE SOFTWARE WILL BE ERROR FREE.

(c) This limited warranty gives you specific legal rights, and you may have other rights that vary from jurisdiction to jurisdiction.

6. <u>Remedies</u>.

(a) WPI's entire liability and your exclusive remedy for defects in materials and workmanship shall be limited to replacement of the Software Media, which may be returned to WPI with a copy of your receipt at the following address: Software Media Fulfillment Department, Attn.: *Excel Charts*, Wiley Publishing, Inc., 10475 Crosspoint Blvd., Indianapolis, IN 46256, or call 1-800-762-2974. Please allow four to six weeks for delivery. This Limited Warranty is void if failure of the Software Media has resulted from accident, abuse, or misapplication. Any replacement Software Media will be warranted for the remainder of the original warranty period or thirty (30) days, whichever is longer.

(b) In no event shall WPI or the author be liable for any damages whatsoever (including without limitation damages for loss of business profits, business interruption, loss of business information, or any other pecuniary loss) arising from the use of or inability to use the Book or the Software, even if WPI has been advised of the possibility of such damages.

(c) Because some jurisdictions do not allow the exclusion or limitation of liability for consequential or incidental damages, the above limitation or exclusion may not apply to you.

7. <u>U.S. Government Restricted Rights</u>. Use, duplication, or disclosure of the Software for or on behalf of the United States of America, its agencies and/or instrumentalities "U.S. Government" is subject to restrictions as stated in paragraph (c)(1)(ii) of the Rights in Technical Data and Computer Software clause of DFARS 252.227-7013, or subparagraphs (c) (1) and (2) of the Commercial Computer Software - Restricted Rights clause at FAR 52.227-19, and in similar clauses in the NASA FAR supplement, as applicable.

8. <u>General</u>. This Agreement constitutes the entire understanding of the parties and revokes and supersedes all prior agreements, oral or written, between them and may not be modified or amended except in a writing signed by both parties hereto that specifically refers to this Agreement. This Agreement shall take precedence over any other documents that may be in conflict herewith. If any one or more provisions contained in this Agreement are held by any court or tribunal to be invalid, illegal, or otherwise unenforceable, each and every other provision shall remain in full force and effect.